Elbert Hubbard

Little Journeys to the Homes of English Authors

Elbert Hubbard

Little Journeys to the Homes of English Authors

ISBN/EAN: 9783743316584

Manufactured in Europe, USA, Canada, Australia, Japa

Cover: Foto ©ninafisch / pixelio.de

Manufactured and distributed by brebook publishing software (www.brebook.com)

Elbert Hubbard

Little Journeys to the Homes of English Authors

ROBERT CHARLES STUART
MORRISON-SCOTT.

From a photograph by Miss Alice Hughes] *[Frontispiece.*

Ella C. Sykes.

Through Persia

on a

Side-Saddle

BY

ELLA C. SYKES

WITH ILLUSTRATIONS FROM PHOTOGRAPHS AND A MAP

LONDON
A. D. INNES & COMPANY, Ltd.
1898

THIS BOOK

IS DEDICATED TO THE MANY FRIENDS

WHOSE GREAT KINDNESS

MADE MY TRAVELS IN PERSIA SO PLEASANT

PREFACE

THIS book has no pretensions to be either historical, scientific, or political, being merely the record of a very happy period of my existence, which I have, in a way, re-lived by writing about it.

My information, however, may claim to be correct as far as it goes, my brother, Captain Sykes, who has travelled for some years in Persia on Government service, having revised my manuscript.

As I believe that I am the first European woman who has visited Kerman and Persian Baluchistan, my experiences may perhaps interest other women who feel the "Wanderlust" but are unable to gratify their longing for adventure.

My thanks are due to Haji Khan, a member of his Highness the Farman Farma's suite, and to the Armenian photographer at Tehran for several of the illustrations in this book, while the rest were taken by my brother and myself.

CONTENTS

CHAP.		PAGE
I.	THE JOURNEY TO THE CAPITAL OF PERSIA	1
II.	TEHRAN	15
III.	FROM THE CAPITAL TO FATIMA'S SHRINE AT KOOM	31
IV.	AS FAR AS KASHAN	44
V.	ON THE MARCH TO YEZD	54
VI.	THE GOAL OF OUR JOURNEY	68
VII.	HOUSEKEEPING AT KERMAN	82
VIII.	KERMAN AND ITS ENVIRONS	100
IX.	OLLA PODRIDA	117
X.	FOUR VISITORS AND A MAID	134
XI.	OUR STAY IN THE HILLS	144
XII.	IN THE FOOTPRINTS OF MARCO POLO	154
XIII.	OUR SOCIAL CIRCLE AT KERMAN	166
XIV.	ARABABAD AND SAGOTCH, PERSIAN LADIES AND SOME PERSIAN CUSTOMS	180
XV.	A PICNIC AT KERMAN	198
XVI.	LAST MONTHS AT KERMAN	212
XVII.	GOODBYE TO KERMAN	226
XVIII.	THROUGH THE DESERT TO BAMPUR AND PAHRA	240
XIX.	TO KUHAK AND THE FRONTIER COMMISSION	256
XX.	WITH THE PERSO-BALUCH BOUNDARY COMMISSION	270
XXI.	TO QUETTA WITH THE ENGLISH COMMISSION	285
XXII.	UP THE PERSIAN GULF TO BUSREH	300
XXIII.	THE KARUN RIVER AND AHWAZ	315
XXIV.	FROM BUSREH TO TEHRAN AGAIN	332
XXV.	TEHRAN REVISITED, AND THE JOURNEY HOME TO ENGLAND	341

LIST OF ILLUSTRATIONS

	Facing page
THE BAZAAR AT RESHT	5
A GATEWAY AT TEHRAN	15
MY INVITATION TO THE PARTY IN THE SHAH'S ANDEROON	17
PERSIAN LADY IN INDOOR COSTUME	18
PERSIAN WOMEN IN OUTDOOR DRESS	40
THE GARDEN OF FIN AT KASHAN	50
A DERVISH	64
THE FAÇADE OF THE CONSULATE AT KERMAN	81
GROUP OF SERVANTS AT THE CONSULATE	92
DAKMÉ, OR PARSEE TOWER, WHERE THE DEAD ARE EXPOSED	108
NASRULLAH KHAN AND HIS FRIENDS	126
BARGI	139
NOMAD WOMEN	155
MOSQUE AT MAHUN	164
H. H. THE FARMAN FARMA AND HIS SUITE	167
COURTYARD OF THE MOSQUE AT MAHUN	174
PERSIAN WOMEN IN INDOOR DRESS	186
A PERSIAN GUITAR-PLAYER	206
KALAH-I-DUKTAR	213
BREAD-TICKET ISSUED BY THE FARMAN FARMA	216
THE LUNCHEON CAMEL	234
A BALUCHI WELL	241
BALUCHIS	252
THE PERSIAN FRONTIER COMMISSION	255
A BALUCHI BAND	261
KUHAK	265
KAIANIAN MALIK TOMB	278
DERVISH WHO ACCOMPANIED THE FRONTIER COMMISSION	290
MIRZA RIZA, ASSASSIN OF THE LATE SHAH	298
THE CHILDREN OF H. H. THE FARMAN FARMA	343
A PERSIAN GARDEN	349

THROUGH PERSIA ON A SIDE-SADDLE

CHAPTER I

THE JOURNEY TO THE CAPITAL OF PERSIA

THE "gorgeous East" has always possessed a strong fascination for me, and after reading "Eöthen," that most delightful book of travels, the indescribable attraction of the Orient became, if possible, stronger than before.

However, I never had any idea that my longings to leave the beaten track would be realised, and always regarded them merely as "Châteaux-en-Espagne" with which to while away idle hours.

But Fate was kinder to me than I deserved. In June, 1894, my brother, Captain Molesworth Sykes, returned from his second journey in Persia, and in the following October he was asked by the Foreign Office to found a Consulate in the districts of Kerman and Baluchistan, those parts of Persia having been hitherto without a representative of her Majesty.

He suggested that I should accompany him, and although I felt somewhat uncertain as to how I should adapt myself to an uncivilised existence, never having quitted Europe before, I was delighted at the prospect opening out in front of me.

We could only allow ten days for our manifold preparations, as it was all important to cross the Elburz Range before the winter snows began, and I am sure that no member of my family will ever forget the rush and hurry of that time. It was necessary to take sufficient clothing to last for over a year, to buy a complete camp equipment, and to lay in furniture, linen, glass, and crockery for the new establishment at Kerman, and, what was perhaps more important than anything else, to engage a maid.

However, all was accomplished in good time, and on November 2nd we left London for Marseilles, travelling to Constantinople on a "Messageries Maritimes" boat, and crossing the Black Sea to Batoum on an "Austrian Lloyd." From this point the Trans-Caucasus railway conveyed us to Baku, and one of the flat-bottomed Russian boats took us across the Caspian, and at the beginning of December we reached Enzeli, the harbour of Persia.

As the sea was somewhat rough, there was much anxiety among the passengers as to whether the tiny launch would be able to cross the breakers of the sandbar at the mouth of the harbour, and come out to convey us and our luggage from the steamer to the shore.

If it had not done so we should have had to return in our steamer to Baku, and make the journey afresh, as friends of ours had done a fortnight previously.

However, our luck did not desert us, and we were all landed safely on Persian soil, having Mr. Preece, H.B.M.'s Consul of Isfahan, and Mrs. Stainton, whom he was escorting to Tehran, as our fellow-travellers.

I can never forget my feelings of joy and exultation when I realised that I was at last in Persia, on the threshold of a new life, which I ardently trusted might have its quantum of adventure. I had been civilised all my days, and now I had a sense of freedom and expansion which quickened the blood and made the pulse beat high. The glamour of the East penetrated me from the first moment of landing on its enchanted shores, and although many a time I encountered hard facts, quite sufficient to destroy the romantic illusions of most folk, yet they struck against mine powerlessly.

I was under a spell throughout my stay in Persia—a spell that endowed me with rose-coloured spectacles, and which even as I write, fills me with a strange yearning for the country which became a much-loved home to me, and where I spent the happiest years of my existence. Yes, I was on Persian soil at last! "Lalla Rookh," with its rose gardens in which the "bulbul" eternally sings, and its maids of peerless beauty, loved by heroes of surpassing valour, with its brave fire-worshippers and awful Veiled Prophet, came into my mind, mingled with a dozen books of travel, in which the romance is stripped away remorselessly, and Persia, bare and barren as she is in reality, is exposed to the view.

I was, in a way, prepared for much that might come by the perusal of Mr. Curzon's comprehensive work on Persia. Visions of many a fatigue and hardship rose up in my mind's eye, long days on horseback, short nights in desolate caravanserai or airy tent, the glory of the dawn, and the crimson flush of the sunset. And with this return to Nature, as it were, with this free open-air life, mingled the thought of studying a new race, of doing my best to see with their eyes, to enter as far as I could into their unfamiliar lives. For we were bound to the real East, where we should have none but Orientals for our daily society, and our home would be in a city, by contrast with which Tehran would seem almost Western.

But I fear I may have already wearied my reader with this digression on my private emotions, and so will begin some account of my journey up to the capital of Persia.

It was the beginning of December, and Enzeli lay flooded in the glorious sunshine which hardly ever fails in the "Land of the Lion and the Sun." It looked very pretty under a turquoise sky, the squalid village backed by the snowy Elburz Range, while the harbour made quite a picture with vessels lying at anchor, and the Shah's smart yacht in readiness by the pavilion—a sort of glorified pagoda—to take off a Persian grandee, who was going to Baku in the steamer we had quitted to pay his respects to the new Tsar and lay a wreath on the grave of the late one.

A large detachment of servants met our party on landing, and my brother's little Indian syce, Fakir Mahomet, seemed to be one gleam of white teeth in his joy at seeing his master again, and worked as hard as half a dozen ordinary Persians in his zeal to serve him. We made our way to the hotel, a bare, scarlet building with a long balcony, dirty, and most scantily furnished, and as soon as our boxes were brought up from the steamer we removed the dubious bedding, replacing it with our own, and then took a walk along the sand-dunes by the sea, where pelicans, vultures, cormorants, and elegant grey cranes were disporting themselves. Young Mr. Churchill, brother of H.B.M.'s Consul at Resht, joined us that afternoon, and his good spirits cheered us through a sort of Barmecide dinner, with long waits between each meagre course. However, I was told that this so-called hotel was palatial luxury compared to what we should encounter further on, so I felt I must not be critical. Here I tasted the Persian bread, or *nàn*, for the first time—flabby, unleavened cakes made of coarse, brown flour. It is much more palatable when toasted crisp instead of being in the damp state in which it was offered to us, and certainly some of the varieties I ate later on were better than this my first attempt; but throughout my stay in the country I never got quite accustomed to it.

Next morning we started off early in two fair-sized boats across the great Enzeli Lagoon for Pir-i-Bazaar. We six Europeans sat in one under an awning, and our six rowers, miserable-looking ragged fellows, worked very hard, using their long, spoon-like oars by raising themselves almost upright with each stroke, at the same time emitting a sharp hissing noise. It took two good hours' hard rowing, aided by a tattered sail, to get across the Lagoon to the mouth of the river, up which they towed us for another two hours, while we ate lunch, relieved of their strong odour of garlic. The Lagoon was full of life. Flocks of pelicans and gulls were feeding; cormorants fishing, their long, snake-like necks alone visible; while cranes, ospreys, eagles, teal, and snipe flew, swam, or dived, all seemingly as tame as possible. Fish were leaping out of the transparent water, and we passed fishermen drawing in their nets, the spoils of which would go to supply the "Russian Fisheries"—a line of buildings on our left where much of the "*caviare*" of commerce is prepared. The scenery

THE BAZAAR AT RESHT.

became quite homelike as we left the Lagoon and its islets of reeds and rushes, and turned into the muddy river, the banks of which were bordered with rowans, hollies, willows, and trails of briony; but whatever the flora might be like there was nothing to recall England in the landing-place at Pir-i-Bazaar. To my dismay I found that we had to step into a veritable sea of liquid mud, and struggle as best we might along a plank sunk in mire, up a bank on to what was comparatively solid ground. A false step would have landed us in most unpleasant plight; and it was with great relief that we saw our baggage carried up, as we had heard that a bride coming out to Tehran, had her entire trousseau ruined by her boxes falling into the water at this crisis of her journey. And, to multiply instances, the piano of another Tehran acquaintance could not be hoisted up that fatal bank, and lay for months at its foot, serving as a most convenient landing-stage for passengers. However, we were fortunate enough to escape all such mischances, and were soon packed into small and rickety carriages to drive the six miles to Resht. My experiences in Constantinople had only prepared me in a very small degree for the inexpressible badness of this road, streaming with mud and water as it was. We bumped in and out of holes, were nearly overturned at exceptionally bad bits of the road, and my companion and I had to cling tightly to one another to save ourselves from being thrown out. Every moment I felt that our dilapidated vehicle must perforce come to pieces, or that the insecurely fastened wheels must succumb to the repeated shocks as we jolted painfully along, and it was a relief to reach the pretty town of Resht embowered in autumnal-tinted trees, the red-tiled roofs of its houses giving it at a distance much the look of an English country village.

We drove through street after street of bazaar, the long eaves of the houses nearly meeting overhead, and put up at a romantic-looking hotel, seemingly composed of stained glass and stucco work and standing in a garden of oranges.

The best room had a series of plaster medallions of the Madonna all round its walls, a somewhat incongruous adornment in a Mohammedan country, and mirror-work in plaques upon the ceiling, while its windows gave on to a large blue-tiled tank full of goldfish.

The English Consul and his wife showed us much hospitality during our two days' visit here, and we were specially glad of their company on the second day, when it poured incessantly, for this real Resht weather made the pretty hotel feel very damp and chilly, many of the little stained-glass window-panes being broken. When we dined at the Consulate on the wet night we arrived disgracefully early, as our carriages came to the hotel long before the time, the drivers insisting on our coming at once, saying they would not wait in the rain, and would return to their homes unless we did so!

Our hostess amused us by displaying an account-book kept by one of her Persian cooks, in which, as the man could not write, he had drawn everything in the funniest manner. For example, a special kind of oval meant eggs to the initiated, and specks piled up on a dish meant rice, while a *jujeh*, or chicken, posed as a quaint heraldic creature, totally unlike the ducks or pheasants delineated next to it. Mr. Preece, to cap this, told a story of how *his* cook constantly entered "bottle of English Powder" in his accounts. Being asked what this was, he said it was a particularly good baking-powder, and he produced several empty bottles of Eno's Fruit Salts to explain his statement!

The next morning we were all ready to start at ten o'clock, but no carriages appeared till 12.30, the drivers merely remarking that they had felt sure we should not require them till that hour.

Mr. Churchill and his brother rode part of the way with us, as is the friendly custom in Persia, along a charming road bordered with rowans, birches, beeches, oaks, acacias, and pollarded willows, and having high hedges overgrown with ivy and maidenhair fern. Handsome little cattle wandered about among the trees, their humps being considered a delicacy when cured, and the one we got at Resht was our great standby on our way up to Tehran. The bridges here were peculiar, going up into a sharp point in the middle, the steep cobbled inclines being very slippery for the horses, which, however, galloped up and down them at a great rate. We passed "wattle and dab" houses with thatched roofs, strings of camels and donkeys, veiled women riding astride, and men in long coats, pleated at the waist, and wearing high astrachan caps.

Our destination that night was a great bare building opening on to a courtyard at the back, round which were the stables for the horses. We mounted a dirty staircase, with steps of abnormal steepness, and reached the *balakhana*, or upper story (our word balcony comes from this), where we were agreeably surprised to find a couple of clean rooms with matting on the floor, and actually tables and chairs. And now our servants showed to advantage. They unpacked our belongings, covering the floors with carpets, hanging up curtains before the draughty doors and windows, setting up our folding wrought-iron bedsteads, removing the leather covers from the enamelled basins which contained all our washing apparatus, and mounting the aforesaid basins on wooden tripods. All our bedding was carried in "Sykes' Tent Valises," an invention of my brother's, patented by the advice of the Manager of the Army and Navy Stores. This valise is very handy, as, when unrolled on the camp bedstead, the bed is ready for use, the stout canvas of which it is made forming the mattress, and a bag at the head containing night things, dressing-gown, brush and comb, &c., which, if stuffed with clothes, acts as a bolster. In the morning the whole thing is merely rolled up and strapped—an operation taking about a couple of minutes. The "tent" part is a mackintosh sheet drawn up over the head from the feet, and kept off the face by iron supports which fit into the head of the bedstead. This is only necessary when sleeping in the open, but, on cold nights, I was glad to use the sheet as a quilt. By the time we had washed in our folding indiarubber baths, the servants had prepared us an excellent dinner of soup, *pillau*, woodcocks, stewed fruit and custard, everything done so briskly and willingly that it was a pleasure to be served by such men. The meal was laid on our "Paragon" camp tables, ingenious arrangements of laths, string, and oilcloth, large, light, and strong, yet folding into an absurdly small compass. They had the advantage of being able to be repaired easily, and even if considerably damaged to be quite fit for use. Our chairs were the "Bavystock," which can be made into a lounge armchair at will, or fold up flat, and are the best all-round article for camp work that we ever came across.

As the nights were very cold we had big wood fires, or iron basins of burning charcoal in our rooms, and my particular bedding consisted of a *lahaf*, or wadded cotton quilt, over my small mattress, three woollen sheets, and three thick blankets all doubled, with an ulster, dressing-gown, and thick cape added thereto.

On the second day's march all the baggage was started off on the mules by half-past seven, and we ourselves mounted the sorry post-horses about ten o'clock, and slowly wound up among the hills.

They were thickly wooded with birches, beeches, chestnuts, and acacias, all gorgeous in their autumn golds and scarlets and pinks; masses of maidenhair fern and harts'-tongue clustered about pretty waterfalls, and here and there long grass "rides" stretched away among the trees, reminding us much of the New Forest.

Very soon the steep parts of the road began. At times we had to climb veritable precipices, the horses finding foothold up these stony staircases with marvellous skill. For my part I did not attempt to guide my steed, but gave him his head, clung on to his mane, and fervently trusted that he would not slip back. I should have much preferred to scramble up on foot, but this was impossible, as the whole place was a sea of liquid mud. Coming downhill it was far worse, however, as the horses had to pick their way over and among great boulders greasy with mire. Fortunately they knew every step of the road, and were very clever at finding out the best places, frequently refusing to go where I wished, and if I persisted unwisely in forcing them against their will we invariably floundered into a series of big holes, so filled in with mud as to look all right to the uninitiated eye. They splashed along very slowly, probing each step before they trusted their weight to it, and being particularly cautious when we crossed the half-rotten plank bridges, and at intervals we got peeps through the forest of a long line of hills, flaming with rich colouring, the river flowing along below us in its broad bed. Just at the worst parts of the road we came upon ghastly mementoes of its difficulties. In one place lay a dead mule covered with mud, and I had to lash my startled horse vigorously to get him past it. A few paces further on we nearly stumbled over a defunct donkey lying across the track, and had hardly passed this when we came upon great camels mangled by the vultures and crows, horrible and pitiable sights.

Half-way through the day we descended into the river-bed, where we halted and lunched to stimulate us to brave the further dangers of the road, which soon wound up again among the hills. We kept meeting trains of heavily laden pack-animals, and on these occasions I rode close behind my brother, who flicked them to one side of the path with his long hunting lash, their loads being carefully avoided by the seasoned traveller, as they could easily knock him out of his saddle. Mr. Preece told a tale of being met close to a river by two mules laden with packing-cases. One came on either side of his horse, and he was lifted bodily out of his saddle and flung right into the water! That day we forded the Rud Safèd (White River), and other rivers no less than five times, the water being occasionally unpleasantly deep, owing to the late rains. It was an odd sensation for me, as my horse never seemed to make any progress, looking, to my inexperienced eye, as if it were being carried down stream, and I invariably had a curious feeling of dizziness. We got to fairly level ground before we reached our destination, Rustemabad, where we left the rainy zone of Resht behind us for good, and now saw real Persian scenery—bare hills rising up from sandy valleys scantily sprinkled with scrub and tamarisk, and snow-clad peaks in the distance.

All the *chapar khanas*, or post-houses, as far as Tehran had been wonderfully smartened up, as the British Minister and his party had preceded us by some three weeks, and in some of them the rough plaster walls were entirely covered with scarlet Turkey twill, which looked cosy and cheerful. For the most part the beams and thatch forming the roof were left unplastered, and I always suspected that it was from there that unpleasant nocturnal visitors dropped down upon us, consisting of three species, each one worse than the last! The unwelcome presence of so many bedfellows, however minute, was not conducive to slumber, and I could often have echoed the words of the Frenchman tormented in a like manner, who exclaimed : " *Ce n'est pas la piqûre dont je me plains, c'est la promenade !* "

Our third day's march was disagreeable, the high wind blowing clouds of dust into our faces, and the road very steep in parts, quite dry, however, except through the little villages, which were a sea of slush between their booths.

The heat of the sun forced us to wear double *Terai* hats and blue goggles, and it was a pleasant change when about half-way we reached the olive-groves of Rudbar, the only ones in Persia, and lay under the trees for lunch, the servants squatting down, opening their cooking boxes, and producing omelets, potato-cakes, and *fasanjan* in a wonderfully short time. This favourite Persian dish is composed of bits of meat steeped in a black compound of liquid fat, pomegranate juice and many other condiment, and is eaten with *chilau*, or plain boiled rice, but is by no means to the liking of every one.

The remarkable celerity displayed by the servants was partly due to the fact that there were three cooks among them, who took it in turns to prepare our meals, and were keen rivals.

Shortly after remounting we reached a precipitous descent, with a stream running down among the boulders which formed the pathway, and were met by a string of laden mules, escorted by a couple of men on horseback. One man's steed got alarmed, kicked out wildly, and would have rolled with its owner over the precipice if the latter had not sprung off promptly and then held on firmly to its bridle.

The experiences of the day before had quite hardened me by this time, and I was positively surprised at finding that I was able to ride down places never imagined even in my wildest dreams, with scarcely a tremor, which was something to one who had always been a timid horsewoman.

We crossed various streams, traversed some stony ground, saw a few skeletons of pack-animals by the roadside, went over the great Menjil bridge, notorious for the high wind always encountered upon it, reminding us in this respect of a famous bridge near Tarascon, and reached our halting-place, which we were warned was a nest of thieves.

Here Mrs. Stainton was surprised to see her favourite servant putting a large parcel under her pillow as he arranged her bed, and on her inquiring what this might be, he said it was a purchase of clothing for himself, which he had placed there in safety for fear of robbery! Next day the hills were very fine, composed of a sort of *detritus*, rising up in wild shapes, perfectly barren, save for a little tamarisk scrub, but tinted in all shades of brown and yellow and crimson, and the river Chinar ran at their feet.

As usual the weather was superb; brilliant sunshine, cloudless blue skies, and a purity of atmosphere that enabled us to see the smallest details at a great distance. After cloudy England, this clearness was most deceptive, as objects several miles off seemed quite close, merely a five minutes' walk or so. In this country a panorama of over a hundred miles in extent may be enjoyed from the top of a mountain, as, for example, the Caspian Sea may be seen from Mount Demavend. Often at the commencement of a day's march, if over level country, the halting-place for the night, some thirty odd miles away, can be clearly discerned, and as mile after mile is traversed, the traveller does not seem appreciably nearer to his goal than when he started to reach it.

We found the post-horses worthy little animals, carrying us over places that an English horse would not dream of attempting. As a rule, we went at the rate of about three miles an hour, slowly plodding over stony ground, my brother and I walking as fast as the horses when we dismounted at intervals to have a change of motion; and indeed our steeds were so covered up that it was difficult to urge them on, as they were impervious to ordinary gentle reminders.

Our fifth day's march was the critical one, as there is always a fear of a snowstorm blocking the Kharzān Pass, in the Elburz Range, which we were about to cross. We got up at five o'clock that morning, and everything was packed and ourselves mounted by half-past seven, winding up and down the hills in the cold grey dawn, getting higher and higher, until we reached the snow-line. Fortunately there was not much snow on the track, but what there was had become a mass of frozen ice, over which our horses floundered nervously, and it took us some hours to struggle to the summit of the pass, where a great circle of snow-covered mountains stood up round us, somewhat resembling the majestic panorama seen from the Gornergrat.

The day was bright, but a bitter wind was blowing; so we did not enjoy the fine sight as much as we should otherwise have done, especially as the wind pierced our wraps as if they had been made of paper.

Low hill after low hill was crossed, and at last we got free of the snow and reached Mazrah, our lunching-place, about half-past one, all feeling very ready for a meal after the early breakfast. From here we made our way to Agha Baba, a picturesque village with castellated mud walls and round towers; and, as we approached, the flocks and herds were entering its gates. From one side the buff, brown, or black sheep, with intelligent faces, long ears, and enormous tails, were streaming in, accompanied by shaggy goats, resembling miniature bears, and followed by the prettiest of donkeys; while from the left little dark brown and black cattle approached, much like those in the Highlands.

The setting sun was flooding the whole scene in a rosy light, glorifying the mud walls of the village, beautifying its dirty though picturesque inhabitants, and casting a glamour and enchantment over the most sordid detail of the picture before us.

We were now on the great Iranian Plateau, stretching from here right down south of Kerman, keeping a height of 4,000 to 6,000 feet, thus ensuring the traveller one of the most superb climates in the world, bracing, exhilarating, and free from great extremes of heat and cold.

Two dilapidated, prehistoric broughams were in readiness to convey us to Kasvin. One having no glass in its windows, a piece of tin, painted scarlet, was nailed on to one side to supply the deficiency. The much-worn velvet cushions smelt extremely musty, and both ramshackle vehicles jolted us terribly, springs being left out of their construction.

It was nine o'clock when we reached Kasvin, which has the remains of past grandeur in its green-tiled mosque and elegant minarets, having been the royal city until Shah Abbas built Isfahan for his capital; and driving up to our hotel along an avenue of fine trees, we found an imposing building with a pillared verandah and tiled façade. Inside, the large rooms had curtained windows, beds and washing apparatus, and the table was covered with dishes of apples, pears, pomegranates, and innumerable plates of small macaroons stuck on to sheets of paper. We hoped to have started off early the next morning, but our faithless muleteer never turned up with his mules till past eleven o'clock; so we selected in haste what baggage we should take with us to Tehran, and it was carefully weighed, then packed along with our servants into a big *fourgeon*, while we ourselves got into the rickety carriages again for our ninety-mile drive.

The jolting on the so-called road was excessive, therefore my brother and I walked on whenever a halt was made to change horses, four of which dragged each vehicle. As darkness approached we passed several caravans of camels reposing for the night, some being the handsome, short-legged, cold weather ones, with great bunches of wool on their forelegs, and others the tall, long-legged, long-necked, ordinary kind. It was weird to come upon these encampments in the clear moonlight, the animals folded up, as it were, into heaps, two or three usually erect, deliberating whether to lie down or not. My brother and I, striding on ahead of the carriages, aroused the guardian dogs, who rushed out barking furiously at us, and we should probably have felt their teeth if we had not hurled stones at them liberally.

In the rest-house that night we were amused to observe that a felt skull-cap, to serve as a nightcap, lay on the pillow of each bed ; and the hair-comb and tooth-brushes provided for travellers all bore signs of constant use!

We left for Tehran early the next morning, so as to reach the city before the gates closed at sunset, and the sun rose over the snowy Elburz Range as we drove across the great plain, the road improving as we neared the capital, and got our first glimpse of the cone of stately Demavend.

In the distance Tehran seemed a patch of greenery set in the midst of a desert, but we could distinguish walls and buildings as we got closer, and about three o'clock reached one of the gateways, where we were met by a *gholam* (mounted servant) from the Legation, who galloped in front of the carriages, and soon after old friends of my brother's rode up to accompany us to our destination, the British Legation, where we were received by Sir Mortimer and Lady Durand with a hospitality and kindness never to be forgotten.

A GATEWAY AT TEHRAN.

CHAPTER II

TEHRAN

I CONFESS that I was a good deal disappointed with Tehran, regarded as the capital of Persia, when we entered the city by the Kasvin Gate, one of the twelve entrances covered with tiles, which depict the heroic deeds of Rustem and other national heroes, or portray the modern Persian soldier of to-day in his uniform. The gateways look imposing at a distance, from their size and colouring, but are crude and ill-executed when seen near at hand. Then we drove through a scantily populated district, squalid booths alternating with waste places or new mud buildings in course of erection, showing that the city had not, as yet, spread out to the full extent of its walls. The roads were a mass of loose stones on a foundation of mud, which became liquid after a fall of rain or snow, and every here and there were large holes into which some one had thrown two or three stones, all carriages zig-zagging across the street to avoid these places, the cause of which was obvious when we saw men digging up mud from the public highway to mix with chopped straw for the manufacture of sunburnt bricks!

High mud walls on either side hid the gardens for which Tehran is famous, and although these barricades were pierced here and there by handsome doorways, the latter seemed to accentuate the dirt and general tumble-down appearance of the streets, about which the pariah dogs prowled. The European quarter lies to the north of the town, in a region of roads bordered with trees, and boasts a tram-line, shops with European goods in their windows, and lamp-posts on which small oil-lamps are burnt, which, however, when lit at night only serve to make the winter darkness visible.

Most of the houses belonging to the different Ministers are here, and among them the British Legation is conspicuous, being a large building in an Anglo-Indian style of architecture, with a clock tower, and surrounded by a beautiful garden containing avenues of trees and an abundance of running water.

Four square English-looking houses standing at a little distance from the main building, accommodate the secretaries, military attaché, doctor, and vice-consul, and I was puzzled at first to account for the presence of a stone roller on each of the flat roofs. It was, however, explained to me that after a fall of rain or snow it was imperatively necessary to roll the mud roofs, as if this were not done they would leak badly, and in all probability fall in.

Not far from the British Legation are the headquarters of the Indo-European Telegraph Line, which deserves mention, as it is one way by which India is connected with Europe. The line runs from Karachi along the Persian Gulf to Bushire and then traverses the whole of Persia, being a wonderful achievement of English energy over Oriental obstructiveness. As in many places the wire crosses high passes, it naturally often gets broken down during the winter snows, and the telegraph clerks, whose duty is to test it so many times daily, are frequently forced to sally forth to repair it, however inclement the weather may be.

It is on record that these men, who are often many miles from any other Europeans in their solitary stations, have sometimes died in the performance of their hard task, and on one occasion a clerk was robbed and stripped by brigands, but nevertheless accomplished his work all the same.

In *Longmans' Magazine* (June, 1897) there is a thrilling account of an attack on one of these telegraph stations, written by Mr. Basil Williams, who was travelling through Persia shortly after the events occurred that he has narrated so graphically.

* * * * *

در روز چهارشنبه هشتم مهر ماه در نهار خوار کهی آقا است

به تکرردات ملوکه تمغادرات مبارک معتبر میدوار

امری عالی تر از اردوان همراه بر رسم معمولی علی وضیع مخصوص خواهد

باد مخوار قرص هر رست خواهد بود و در روز هموار معدل بعد از ناهار پشیمی

در عمارت اندرون حضور بعد از ناهار صرف تزیک

MY INVITATION TO THE PARTY IN THE SHAH'S ANDEROON.

I took to Persia and things Persian at once, and never felt better in my life than at Tehran. The climate seemed to exhilarate me in the most delightful way, and to one accustomed to English winters it was a treat that never palled, to wake up morning after morning to a world bathed in brilliant sunshine, with perhaps a covering of crisp white snow on the ground.

The intense dryness of the air was very trying to the nerves and general health of many of the European ladies, and most of them complained of it; but for my part I revelled in an atmosphere in which cakes and biscuits retained their freshness for long periods when uncovered, and in which all ivory articles cracked, and wooden ones became badly warped, as I found to my cost at Kerman.

* * * * *

During my stay at Tehran the entertainment that interested me most was that given by one of the Shah's wives, the mother of the Naib-es-Sultaneh, Commander-in-Chief of the Persian army. Crowds of carriages were waiting at the gate of her palace as we drove up, and a long carpet-covered palisade had been erected inside the entrance, so that no curious eye might penetrate the recesses of the *anderoon* garden. A eunuch escorted us past this, and up an avenue of trees to a large building, in front of which women dressed in all the colours of the rainbow were squatting on the ground or strolling about. We ascended some stone steps, and passing through a hall crammed with women, made our way up a staircase into a fine room covered with paintings by Persian artists. This was thronged with yet more women, who looked at us curiously as we were shown into an inner room with a long range of windows giving views of the pretty garden below and the grand Elburz Range beyond, white with snow.

Here were assembled the Shah's many wives, who received us very graciously, and most of the female aristocracy, European and Persian, of Tehran were present.

All the Persian ladies wore loose-sleeved jackets of the richest brocades and velvets, and had short, much-stiffened-out trousers, which did not reach to the knees, and gave them somewhat the look of a European ballet-dancer, the costume completed with coarse white stockings or socks. Before the Shah went to Europe the Persian ladies all kept to the old national costume of long, loose, embroidered trousers, but on the return of the monarch, this present ungraceful costume became the fashion in the royal *anderoon*, and has spread throughout the whole country, it being, I believe, a fact that the dress of the Parisian ballet-girls so greatly fascinated the Oriental potentate that he commanded it to be adopted at once by his wives.

Over this, which is the usual indoor dress, was a long, shapeless piece of brocade, covering the back and all the lower part of the body, and sticking out in a comical manner from the waist, for all the world as if its owner were wearing a crinoline.

A square of stiff white muslin was bound round the head and hung down behind, concealing the hair, which was worn loose or in plaits.

The portly mother of the "Naib," was clad in pale green brocade and velvet, and her stout son in a dark blue uniform and *kolah* (high black lambswool hat) sat beside her on a gilt chair, as did all the rest of the company.

The favourite wife was brilliant in a vivid blue silk, and the majority of the ladies wore fine jewels, big rubies, diamonds, and emeralds galore, buttons of precious stones, bracelets and necklaces of pearls, and sometimes the entire front of the jacket a mass of diamonds, sewn on in patterns. We sat and sipped tea or sherbet, partook of sweetmeats and biscuits, handed round by slaves as gaudily attired as their mistresses, and watched these latter smoke *kalians*.

This pipe is composed of a bowl for the water, above which is an elaborately adorned holder for the burning charcoal and tobacco, the whole thing corresponding to the Turkish *hubble bubble*. I never thought that it was a very satisfactory invention, as it is troublesome to light, and when ready, the smoker only enjoys half a dozen puffs or so, a servant sucking at it for some seconds, first of all, to get rid of the fumes of char-

PERSIAN LADY IN INDOOR COSTUME.

coal, and then bringing it to his master or mistress at the right moment.

All Persian ladies delight in the *kalian*, and when they visited me later on they used to beg me to follow their example, but although a Persian proverb says, "If you are in a room be of the same colour as the people in it," I always declined, as it was not pleasant to put my lips to the same tube at which a servant had been vigorously puffing; although such trifles do not weigh with Orientals. Some of the Europeans who mix much with Persians are in the habit of carrying their own mouthpieces with them, and it is a good plan, as the *mollahs*, and the especially strict followers of the Prophet, consider a European touch a defilement.

On the occasion of this royal party, I wished very much that I could have talked Persian, as one lady in a magnificent cashmere shawl examined my bangles without ceremony, laughing pleasantly as she thrust her hands into my muff, which was handed on to others to examine, and looking quite disappointed when her efforts to draw me into conversation were in vain. I did not see a really good-looking woman among the crowds present, although most of the ladies had quite fair complexions, regular features, and fine eyes. The wives were all very stout, and to European ideas the lengthening of their eyebrows with streaks of *kohl* so as to make them meet, and also to be double their natural breadth, was not becoming; neither did I appreciate the occasional little *kohl* moustaches, nor the thickly rouged and powdered cheeks and the henna-tinted nails.

There was a sad lack of intelligence on most of the faces, which, however, all at once brightened up, and there was quite a commotion among the throngs of women as the Shah entered the room. His wives pressed forward smirking and smiling, only to be waved aside by their royal master, a European lady doing the honours of his court, and presenting us in turn to him. Lady Durand then sat beside his Majesty on a gilded couch, and they chatted in French, while I observed the splendid rubies and diamonds decorating the front of the Shah's uniform, the well-known diamond aigrette, and his trick of pushing up his spectacles on to the front of his *kolah* at intervals. He was accompanied by Sultan Aziz, the youth who is always with him, and whom he regards as a sort of fetish, believing that his royal life depends in some way on that of his favourite, who looked about twelve, but was, in reality, aged eighteen.

After awhile the monarch rose, and calling out "*Étrennes! étrennes!*" presented each European lady with a small gold coin, as a memento of her visit, and then he, the Naib, and the "fetish" retired, and dancing commenced.

Half a dozen women sang (to my ears the performance was a series of howls and yells!) thumping on a sort of tambourine and a tom-tom. One scraped a bow across a melon-shaped stringed instrument, while another emitted doleful sounds from a species of zither struck with two small wooden spoons.

The first dancer was a little girl about ten years old, dressed in crimson velvet, with a short, stiff skirt, and long expanse of white-stockinged leg. Her hair hung down in multitudinous plaits, a coin at the end of each, and she postured and came forward with her legs bent, progressing by pushing her feet from side to side, a peculiarly ungraceful movement which elicited much applause from the spectators. Then she knelt and screamed a weird song, clacking metal castanets as an accompaniment to her voice.

A second small damsel, clad in purple velvet, now appeared, and went through the same shuffling performance, which she accentuated by raising her eyebrows alternately, and smiling so impertinently at the assembled ladies, that I fancy it would have relieved the feelings of some of the Europeans present to have boxed her ears! Two scarlet-clad sisters succeeded these performers, and their great feat was to bend their bodies right back until their heads touched the ground, and then to raise themselves very slowly, crimson in the face from their exertions.

After awhile the head-wife clapped her hands, and the entertainment was adjourned to the garden, where we sat in a circle, and the eunuchs, stout, ungainly fellows, pushed their mistresses about unceremoniously, bursting into their conversation on every occasion, and seemingly on the best of terms with them.

The little sons and grandsons of the Shah stood round about, and a dwarf was pointed out to me, said to be sixty or seventy years old, but in appearance a boy of ten. A renegade Armenian woman, in a shabby European blouse and skirt, performed a dance, which, to the uninitiated, appeared a series of ungraceful jerks, the idea being that she was trying to make a salaam but did not know how to do it.

When we came away we passed many ladies waiting for their carriages, completely shrouded, in great black *chaddars*, which only permitted a glimpse of full, green trousers, their faces being entirely concealed with a white covering fastened with a jewel at the back of the head, and having a strip of lace-work in front of the eyes.

I was told that many of the fine ladies we had met that afternoon would give large sums in the European shops at Tehran for any brocade or silk which struck their fancy, and would wear it at the next party to which they invited their friends, flaunting the new toilette ostentatiously before them to fire their jealousy. Usually, however, one of the guests would pay her hostess out by buying some more of the same material and having it made up for one of her slave-women. She then would invite a large company to tea, and the cups would be handed round by a negress adorned in the rich silk with which the quondam hostess is probably arrayed, and later on, the same slave would dance before the assembled guests, to the intense mortification of one and the equally keen amusement of the others.

In passing it may be well to make mention of the *karsi* that I noticed in one of the rooms of the palace, and which is an ingenious arrangement for having a most economical fire during the winter months. A circular hole in the floor is filled with burning charcoal, and standing over it is a sort of wooden table covered with *lahafs*, under which the women creep for warmth, hardly leaving the spot either by day or by night.

The "At Home" that I have just described was a great contrast to another at which I was present a few days later.

On this occasion we were ushered into a grand European drawing-room, where the cut-glass chandeliers and silk-shaded lamps, the handsomely upholstered chairs and couches, and the statuary and flowering plants gave me a feeling of surprise that the hostess had not adopted European dress likewise. She was a well-mannered, elderly woman, speaking only Persian, but her daughter-in-law was very different, being a girl of about three- or four-and-twenty, clad in a gorgeous pink brocade, loaded with lace, and made in an ugly European style, her hair fastened back with a ribbon, and diamonds in her ears. She had been educated in Constantinople, spoke French fluently, played the piano passably, and was, I fear, miserable in Tehran, telling me frankly that it was all very well to receive visitors in her own home, but that as she was never permitted to return their visits she found life somewhat dreary. The eunuch brought in a real English tea-tray, and the daughter-in-law poured out tea, handing round milk and sugar quite *à l'Anglaise*, and afterwards we had a stroll in the fine gardens with their fountains and long avenues. I bade goodbye to this Europeanised Persian with regret, feeling that her lot was by no means a happy one, and being reminded of the caged starling in the Bastille that all day long kept crying "Let me out! let me out!"

On one occasion we made an expedition to the bazaars, passing on our way through the Tupkhana Meidan, Artillery Square, grandiose and crude like the twelve gateways, which are indeed the most characteristic features of Tehran, a city so singularly deficient in mosques and their attendant minarets. This is owing to the fact that it is practically a modern town, being taken by Agha Mohammed Khan for his capital not much more than a hundred years ago, as being more in touch with the Turki tribe from which the Kajar dynasty sprung, than was Isfahan, the old royal city. At one end of the square is the Persian Bank with a brilliantly coloured stucco façade, and on two sides are the low artillery barracks, ornamented with a long series of bas-reliefs of the "Lion and the Sun" on a red ground, both the animal and the luminary having queer, semi-human faces. There is always plenty of life and colour in the Meidan. Soldiers in shabby blue uniforms with red facings, and old-fashioned red-tufted shakoes, lounge about, escorting the Naib as he drives to the palace in his brougham, or bestride camels, sitting aloft on their bedding with their cooking utensils hanging about them; or perform the strange military music which Mr. Curzon has described so feelingly.

Passing through this square and under an ornate gateway, we had a glimpse of the Ark or palace of the Shah, a beautiful feature of which are two towers close together, forming one pavilion and entirely covered with brilliant tiles. No windows are to be seen on the sides towards the street; but there are charming balconies, adorned with pilasters and encrusted with mirror work which flashes and gleams in the sunshine.

The Bazaars themselves are a network of vaulted passages, lighted from above, and leading into courts and spacious halls at intervals, some of these latter having beautifully tiled stucco roofs in the honeycomb pattern. European goods of the shoddy order vastly preponderate over the Eastern products, Tehran clothing itself from the West, while Austria supplies every kind of inferior crockery and cutlery, with masses of the cut-glass candelabra and lustres, so dear to the Persian soul.

Laden camels, mules, and donkeys struggle along the passages, while horsemen push their way among the pedestrians, who never trouble to give any one room to pass, the veiled women gazing intently at small cases of jewellery being the chief offenders, as they bargain furiously for a pair of earrings or a tawdry-looking brooch.

It was interesting to watch the making of brass jugs and basins for rose-water, the fashioning of *kolahs*, the turning of *Kalian*-tops, and the adorning of travelling trunks. These latter are very roughly made of strips of deal, and then covered with leather, dyed red, which is painted with black patterns according to the fancy of the artist. The boxes are then strengthened with long strips of tin nailed at intervals all round the sides, and the cumbrous articles are complete.

The sweetmeat stalls were quite a sight, displaying large sugar-candy bowls with stalagmites of candy branching up from the bottom, almond paste, toffee and macaroons of every description; while some of the confectioners seemed to be engaged in a tug-of-war, pulling boiled masses of sugar, until the stuff sprang apart into the finest threads.

The clothes stalls had a few green and blue silk undercoats for the men, and gauze veils and embroidered velvet jackets for the women; but these were entirely swamped by the dingy browns and blacks and greys of the great majority of the garments.

It was forcibly borne upon me that here was by no means a place to shop for the traveller in search of carpets and curios. The trade in such things seemed to be entirely in the hands of the *dellals*, or merchants, men in turbans and flowing robes, who came frequently to the Legation, carrying big bundles, from which they produced all manner of treasures, coins, silks, brass-work, embroideries, handsome old velvets, brocades and what not. They would leave their goods for days in our possession, coming at intervals to haggle about the price if we wished to purchase some particular article, and asking double or treble its value at first, as a matter of course.

Having heard of the celebrated turquoise mines in Nishapur in Khorassan (the place where Omar Khayyam lived and died), I thought I should like to purchase some of these stones, but found the prices very high. As a matter of fact, we obtained some later on at Kerman from a merchant of our acquaintance. This man had quantities of turquoises of all sizes and with every kind of flaw, set for the most part in rough silver rings to sell to the Baluchis. He only possessed three stones of any value, telling us that, fond as Persians are of jewellery, no one in Kerman was rich enough to purchase them. We quite believed him, for the gentry of that place seemed very poor, living on the produce of their lands, and without any ready money.

During my walks and rides about Tehran I often wished that the Persians had kept to the brilliant clothes worn by their ancestors. The European trousers, always out of shape from their owner's habit of squatting on his heels, the drab frock-coat, much pleated at the waist, and the black lamb's wool *kolah* affected by the townsmen, making prince and servant look precisely alike to the uninitiated eye, give but little idea of what one has always been led to expect in the East.

I was assured by Persians that this costume was a copy of the old French Court costume, and they appeared hurt when I inquired what had become of the lace cravats and ruffles, the handsome buttons, and the lappets; while they were quite incredulous when it was represented to them that silk stockings and buckled shoes were necessary to complete the toilette! Turbans are discarded by all save the *mollahs* (priests), the merchants, the *hajis* (those who have made the pilgrimage to Mecca), and the *seyids* (descendants of the Prophet).

The peasants have loose blue cotton blouses and trousers, a cloth swathed round the waist, holding bread, tobacco, and money, and a yellow felt skull-cap on the head; while during the winter the soldiers are huddled into old brown overcoats, and the shapeless black-shrouded women are a dreary sight, especially in wet or snowy weather, when they flip-flap through mud and slush in the thinnest of heelless slippers.

The townsfolk were quite as fair-complexioned as Italians, and, as a rule, were tall, well-built men, with handsome features and large dark eyes, although often the upper classes were delicate and undersized, owing to their unhealthy mode of life.

From highest to lowest their manners were most courtly, and the nation prides itself on a knowledge of etiquette and a profuse use of elegant phrase and compliment. For example, the British Minister told me that the words "Telegram received" were expanded, on reaching him, into "The message of the most exalted threshold has become a place of pilgrimage!" "Your place is empty;" "May your shadow never grow less," are usual forms of greeting; although it must be confessed that, with all their love of politeness, the Persians are by no means behindhand in vituperation, should occasion require it.

"*Pider-i-sucht*," "son of a burnt father," is a common expression, referring to the supposed abode of the relative in question, and our servants used frequently to reduce one another to tears by their ingenuity in casting aspersions upon the belongings of those whom they wished to insult.

During our visit to Tehran the Shah had a big review of all his troops on a gravelly plain below his palace of Doshan Tepe, which is a group of white buildings on a hill, some two or three miles outside the city, and reached by a road bordered with poplars. His Majesty was mounted on a bay horse, and his *kolah* and as much of the breast of his uniform as his fur overcoat revealed, positively sparkled with precious stones. The large plain was scattered with troops, and we had a good view of the march-past, the shabby infantry approaching the saluting point in waving lines, hopping every now and then to get into step, while the outside men gave little runs at intervals to keep up with the rest. The cavalry, however, was a decided improvement on the infantry, the so-called Cossacks in full white linen coats to their heels, and white sheepskin caps, having some dash about them, though it was odd to see the long tails of their horses knotted up to keep them out of the dust, while the finest men were the Shah's *gholams*, or bodyguards, who rode past in detachments on horses with silver collars and trappings. There were about six bands of music altogether, the conductors dancing along in front of their men and giving great leaps from sheer excitement, as they waved their batons frantically. One band was composed of boys of all ages, wearing a sort of caricature of a hussar uniform; and most of the others were clad in almost as many different uniforms as there were men.

We were at Tehran altogether for seven weeks, instead of the three we had intended to spend in the capital, as, on the day of our would-be departure, my maid was pronounced unfit to travel, and we were obliged to prolong our stay.

Feeling that I should have to start housekeeping very soon, I asked all my lady friends for hints on this momentous subject, and it was not very encouraging to hear on all sides accounts of the thievish propensities, uncleanly habits, and numberless other delinquencies of the Persian servant. One lady assured me that a head-waiter, whom she had dismissed, had tried his hardest to injure her ever since. Articles of clothing sent home from the wash were torn in an unaccountable way, and inquiry elicited that Akbar Mirza had been seen in close conversation with the washerman. Far worse than that, one of my friend's carriage horses was killed by means of a nail driven into its foot, and, strange to say, Akbar Mirza had been at the forge that day during the operation of shoeing the poor animal. All sorts of movable property began to disappear from the house, until it was discovered that the dismissed servant was in collusion with the lady's *bargi*, or maid, and he had to turn his talents in another direction. His great ingenuity prevented any of these misdeeds being brought home to him, and he tried yet another malicious trick, when waiting at table at the house where my friends were dining. Ice pudding was handed round by Akbar Mirza, and, as is customary in Persia, the waiter puts the cream ready into the big serving spoon, so as to save the guests the bother of cutting it for themselves. My friend put her spoonful on her plate, and at the first mouthful found she had all but swallowed a pin, that lay concealed in her portion of the pudding. She felt Akbar's intense gaze of expectation, and was convinced that he alone was the culprit; but it was useless to make a fuss about the matter, as the whole blame would inevitably have been thrown upon the cook.

Another lady gave me an account of what happened to her, when her husband left her at their house in the country and took a short tour round Demavend. After a couple of days the entire body of servants deserted her and spent their time in the Bazaars at Tehran, leaving her and the children without any food in the house.

As it is practically impossible for a European to buy anything for his or herself, and as meat is always got in daily during the summer heats, my friend spent an unpleasant twelve hours, until the return at nightfall of her semi-intoxicated men. She then summoned one of the secretaries of the British Legation to her aid, and his prompt action greatly improved matters, all the Persian servants having a great respect for the Feringhee Sahib, and very little for the *khanum* (mistress), unless she has a man to back up her authority.

I was particularly warned to keep a watchful eye on any jewellery or small silver trifles that I might happen to possess, the servants being in the habit of carrying such objects off to the Bazaar for sale. The coveted article is removed, and if its owner notices its loss at once, and makes inquiries in all directions, it will probably be replaced; but if any length of time elapses before the discovery of the theft, it will already have been sold. A gentleman told me that on more than one occasion he had seen valuable objects, which he recognised as belonging to some of his friends, exposed for sale in the Bazaars, the rightful owners never realising their loss until informed of it by him.

The Christmas gaieties were beginning at the time of our visit, and every one was goodness itself to us, so that we had our fill of amusement, which was the more enjoyable to me, as I had the opportunity of conversing with half a dozen different nationalities at each party—a novelty which I much appreciated.

My brother had bought several horses for our prospective journey, which we named as a rule, after their former owners. I did not know at the time that this would be taken greatly amiss by the Persians, to whom they had belonged, as these Orientals believe that in such a case their health and even life will in future depend on that of the horse.

On my return to Tehran some two years later it was quite pathetic to observe the almost frenzied eagerness with which a Persian gentleman inquired about the welfare of a horse that he had sold us, and that I laughingly told him was called by his name as a compliment. Until then we had not the faintest idea that such "compliments" are not appreciated in Persia!

As horses are supposed to be peculiarly liable to the evil eye, every well-regulated stable has a wild boar within its precincts, which animal is considered to possess the power of warding off the malign influence, and usually goes out exercising with its equine *protégés*.

During the first part of our stay at Tehran, the English got up paper-chases on horseback, and several *Gymkhanas*, where tent-pegging and lemon-cutting were practised, and the ladies tried their skill at "tilting at the ring." The snow began just after Christmas, making the streets almost impassable on foot, so that it was a decided improvement when the real cold commenced a few days after the New Year. On New Year's Day Lady Durand received nearly every European in Tehran at the Legation. It was most amusing to me to see English, French, Germans, Austrians, Russians, Belgians, Dutch, Turks, and Persians pouring in, in an unending stream, each man sipping a cup of tea, making a few conventional remarks, and then hurrying off on his weary round of visits. Very few ladies assisted at this function, but I was interested in one funny little couple, he a Frenchman, she an Englishwoman, and neither speaking the language of the other. They explained that they had conducted their love-making in Persian, which was the language they had in common!

Two pathetic "Sœurs de Charité" with enormous flapping white caps arrived from their hospital at the Kasvin Gate. I feared Persia did not suit them as well as it did me; for one Sister, who had been fourteen years at Tehran, was merely an animated skeleton, and both ladies confessed to suffering constantly from fever.

As the winter was an unusually cold one there was excellent skating, the lakes of Yusufabad and Kasr-i-kajar, some three miles from the city being frozen hard, and on this latter lake, in one of the Shah's gardens, we spent several most delightful afternoons. The palace of the Shah, which is built above it, has been compared by travelled Persians to Windsor Castle ; but considering that it is merely a huge, white, barrack-looking building, standing on the summit of several terraces, its claims to architectural beauty are hardly worth the mention.

The long Elburz Range, used to look magnificent as we returned to Tehran at sunset, its freshly fallen snow being flooded with a soft rose-light, which gradually became deeper and deeper, and seemed to throb and flush, as it reached its climax. Then, as the sun sank, chilly green-grey shadows crept up, chasing away the glory from peak after peak. But Demavend was always the last to yield, and when all the rest of the landscape looked cold it kept a rosy light on its cone, a sort of crown, which gradually diminished until it, too, was enveloped in gloom.

No other peak is comparable to this semi-extinct volcano. It is the great feature of the landscape, and every traveller to Tehran comes to feel a personal affection for it, as he sees its clear-cut pyramid defined, day after day, against a brilliant sky. Or perhaps it may be illumined with sunlight, while the rest of the mountains are covered with black clouds, the storm as it breaks seeming to respect mighty Demavend, around which half the legends of Persia take their rise.

On January 31st we made our second attempt to leave Tehran, and this time it was successful. I felt the parting far more than if we had left when we first intended, and no words of mine can adequately describe the exceeding kindness we had met with on all sides. As I said goodbye to the Durands and our Legation friends it was almost as if I were leaving home again.

We were escorted for a stage out of the city, through interminable squalid streets, past the little railway which runs to the shrine of Shah Abdul Azim, and into the country, along a tree-bordered road. Then we stopped and said last farewells, and thus were speeded on the long journey which lay before us.

CHAPTER III

FROM THE CAPITAL TO FATIMA'S SHRINE AT KOOM

IT was midwinter when we left Tehran at the end of January, and the bare, deserted-looking country lay white and cold around us, an icy wind blowing from the ranges of snow-covered hills. The "great cold" was supposed to be past by this time, but I fancy that this year it had encroached upon the season sacred to the "little cold," as the dirty, draughty rooms of the Karizek *Mehman Khana* were below freezing-point, and somewhat depressing after the comforts of the Legation. This guest-house was one of several constructed by the English Company, when they made their excellent road from Tehran to Koom, and though, like all things in Persia, it had partly fallen into disrepair, yet we looked back upon it, and upon all the other rest-houses along this route as palaces in comparison with the *chapar khanas* and *serais*, the unpleasant acquaintance of which we were to make later on.

There are only two carriage-roads in Persia—one from Kasvin to Tehran, and the other from the capital to Koom. This latter might pass muster even in England, and is very different to the rough track from Kasvin, with the frequent broken places, which make it almost impassable after heavy snow or rain. However, as we were riding, the quality of the road was not of great importance to us.

At Karisek we were joined by Nasrullah Khan, a Persian gentleman of good family, who was to act as secretary to my brother, and who proved a most pleasant addition to our party, being more or less anglicised in his ideas, the result of an education in England, and it was owing to his kindness that I gained a good deal of information about Persian manners and customs, as he was always ready to enlighten me on these points.

Until we got to Koom the nights were bitterly cold, as no curtains could keep the wind from blowing in at the holes which often did duty for windows, or whistling under the doors, which were too much warped to shut properly. We made ourselves as comfortable as we could, spreading carpets on the mud floors and lighting big wood-fires, in spite of which our water and sponges would be frozen every morning when we reluctantly turned out of bed before sunrise.

I remember in particular one night at Hassanabad, when the cold was intense. Try as we would, we could not manage to get the room in which we dined above 34°, though a big wood-fire was blazing, and five people were in it, not to speak of carpets on the floor, and curtains nailed against the rickety doors. We drank hot brandy and water, shivered under our wraps; and for my part I felt a great sympathy for the Esquimaux when it was time to wash and dress the next morning. Every traveller blames them roundly for their want of cleanliness, but, after my experience at Hassanabad, I shall ever have a fellow-feeling for them! Our bill for firewood up to Koom was tremendous, as we were obliged to supply it liberally to the stable, and our various hosts sold it at famine rates.

As soon as we were dressed in the mornings the servants would rush into our rooms, packing up bedding, carpets, and washing apparatus, while we ate our breakfast in haste. That finished, everything was cleared away to the last chair, and we were left in an utterly bare room, with nowhere to sit, save on the mud floor of dubious cleanliness. Here we must stay until the mules were all loaded up and well started off by nine o'clock. If we rode on ahead we should only reach our next halting-place hours before they did, and must wait, minus servants, food and fire, until their arrival; for absolutely nothing can be bought in these places as a rule, although occasionally some *soi-disant* landlord, more enterprising than his fellows, may provide firewood, a cup of tea, and a bit of coarse bread.

Sometimes, when tired of standing by the embers of the wood-fire, we would brave the piercing wind, and go out on to the raised mud terrace in front of the building to watch the mules start. They were fifty in number, fine animals with high pack-saddles, hung with bells, and the head muleteer's white horse, decked with masses of brilliantly coloured, big woollen tassels, always led the procession, and was an imposing animal to look at. Some of the mules carried enormous bells, one on each side, which emitted full, deep tones, and must have been most uncomfortable, as, besides being very heavy, they knocked against their ribs at each step.

We were now travelling in an uncivilised country, and needed stores of every description, as our route lay practically through a desert region. Therefore we had packed supplies of rice, tea, coffee, sugar, flour, wine, jam, dried fruit, &c., enough to last us for a fortnight, in two stout wooden boxes, and replenished them, as required, from the big cases full of stores which we were carrying along with us. The servants all fed themselves, as is customary in Persia, getting a *kran* (4½d.) extra for each day that they were on the march, and a good outfitting allowance at Tehran in addition to their ordinary wages.

Our personal staff consisted of nine servants. First on the list came Sultan Sukru, an Indian cavalry N.C.O., who was to assist in mapping and surveying. My brother thought so highly of this man, who had accompanied him throughout his second journey in Persia, that he had taken him home to England, where he had greatly enjoyed a four months' stay in London, and was a most conspicuous figure in the streets that summer. He spoke English fairly well, was quite a gentleman in his way, and would have scorned to do anything mean. He once remarked to me that if he "ate the bread" of any one, he felt he must do his utmost to serve that man, and indeed he carried out his principles into practice with us, being most loyal to our interests.

The Indian *syce* (or groom), Fakir Mahomet, came next, a

little man to whom I became quite attached. He was devoted to his horses, and a jack-of-all-trades, being cook, saddle-maker, cobbler, carpenter, and tailor as required. He had also been with my brother before, and had awaited him during the summer at Tehran. So curiously fond was he of his *Sahib* that if the latter were displeased with him he would be unable to eat or sleep, so he affirmed, until restored to favour.

The rest of our servants were Persians, chief of whom was Hashim, the good-looking young *pishkidmet*, or waiter. He took a great interest in us and our belongings, and was ever anxious to join in our conversation, as he had picked up a little French and less English at Tehran. The cook, Seyid Abu, a descendant of the Prophet, who wore a green waistcoat to signify his illustrious ancestry, was clever, dishonest, and thoroughly unscrupulous as to his method of "doing" us by hook or by crook. On the march he was entrusted with the buying of supplies; but as he always made out his bills with an average of fifty eggs a day, and meat and fowls in proportion, his office was transferred to Sultan Sukru shortly after we reached Kerman, by which time I had sufficiently mastered Persian to be able to housekeep on my own account.

All the servants looked most picturesque on the road. Hashim, for example, tied a gorgeous red, yellow, and purple drapery over his astrachan *kolah*, wrapping it round his ears and under his chin; and was, moreover, huddled in a shapeless, cinnamon-coloured garment, lined with vivid green silk; completing his costume with big top-boots and two pairs of purple woollen gloves, drawn one over the other. All of them had similar vagaries in the way of clothing, the *syce* favouring a white drill suit, which only lasted clean the day of the start, and another a European ulster, which contrasted oddly with his felt skull-cap, swathed in a magenta silk handkerchief, the long fringe of which was for ever hanging into his eyes.

Each servant saw that his mule was loaded with his bedding and personal property, then mounted on to the pile with some difficulty, seized the rope attached to the animal's head, and started off, steering his steed with this, and kicking his legs against its sides to hasten its movements. The cook was our boldest rider, and frequently came to grief, as he insisted on galloping, and as often as not was seen flying over the head of his mount, which he would then capture and remount good-humouredly, in spite of the chaffing of the other servants who looked upon his mishaps as a sign that he had not attended to his religious duties that day!

All Persians muffle up their heads in winter, tying them in so many wraps that it is useless to address a question to any of them on the march. They do not seem to feel the cold in other parts of their bodies, and I have often seen cotton-clad peasants riding barefoot on donkeys, yet with their heads and faces so covered up that only the eyes were visible.

Besides our personal attendants there were some twelve to fifteen muleteers, who loaded up their animals every morning, walked alongside them all day, and, on getting into camp, were most energetic in unloading, giving a helping hand to the servants, and later on currycombing their charges with an iron instrument that rattled curiously. They were fine, handsome, wiry fellows, who could walk many hours without fatigue. Their usual dress was a loose jacket of a sort of glorified sacking, *gheleem* by name, woven in stripes of red, blue, and brown, below which peeped out the ends of two or three long shirts made of gay-coloured cottons, and they wore short, blue cotton trousers, and bound their sinewy legs with *puttis*, while their *givas*, or rag-shoes, were very long, with the toe part curling over the foot. (These *givas* are incomparable for mountaineering, the soles being made of compressed rags, which never slip over the boulders and stones, and the "uppers" of a coarse, cotton crochet-work). In bad weather they donned huge felt cloaks, which also formed part of their bedding at night, rendering them almost impervious to cold, but being by no means ideal garments in heavy rain.

Their felt skull-caps were swathed with scarlet handkerchiefs, and across their shoulders and round the waist a leather strap was fastened, which served as a belt and carried everything, the treasured pipe being slipped into it at the back. A bag of yarn to do up sacking, a leather case of packing-needles, a curious steel instrument to protect the palm of the hand when using these latter, a bit of steel-chain with a thong for a whip, and little bags for money and tobacco all hung from this strap, while a packing-needle stuck behind the ear completed the costume. These men were most kind to their mules, in which they took great pride, and I never saw them chastise their charges with the long, thick staves they carried. They were, moreover, very abstemious, eating nothing but a bit of bread during the day, and if thirsty, lying flat down on their chests to drink at any stream they passed, seemingly quite indifferent as to the quality of the water. At night, however, they were all given a feed of rice and *rogan*, or lard, as part of their wages.

My maid and Diana (the dog given me by Colonel Wells, at Tehran), travelled in the *tachteravan*, or litter, which we had bought at Tehran in case of illness, the conveyance used by Persian ladies of position; while those of the lower rank must content themselves with the *kajaveh*, or panier, hung on the side of a mule.

Our *tacht* was a kind of large, blue-painted box, long enough to lie down in, with a door on each side and round windows. It was furnished with scarlet, cloth-covered mattress and cushions, and had an outer chintz cover in case of heat, or more probably for greater elegance. At each end were two long shafts, to which were harnessed mules, that plodded steadily along, their burden swaying with each step, in a manner uncomfortably suggestive to me of being at sea, but which Marie, being a good sailor, quite enjoyed.

On the third day we reached Aliabad, meeting the Jellal-i-Dowleh, son of the Zil-i-Sultan, on his way to Tehran to visit his grandfather, the Shah. My brother had a chat with him and found him pleasant, but was sorry to see such a young man so terribly stout. The *mehman khana* here was an imposing mud building with castellated towers built round a square, in which was a big tank of water with ducks swimming on it, and streams running among the beds of oleanders and wallflowers. The stone-floored vaulted rooms were cold as cellars, however, and we were careful not to enter them without a wrap, after sitting in the hot sunshine, as we did not wish for a bout of fever. They were all painted blue, and the warped, ill-fitting doors were, as usual, fastened with a bit of chain, which hooked on to a staple on the lintel above.

Everything in this way was very primitive, and of ventilation there was seldom any lack, for as glass was not then made in Persia, it was an expensive luxury, used by no means lavishly, and, when broken, seldom replaced. Frequently the windows were mere holes in the walls, often without even a rough wooden shutter to keep out the draught.

Hashim had not yet grasped that we objected to see him touch everything with his fingers at meals, handing us pieces of bread with these useful members, taking up spoons and forks by their wrong ends, and so on. He was much hurt when we told him to use a spoon for helping us to lumps of sugar, and proudly displayed a pair of purple gloves, dirty and travel-stained, which he felt must completely alter the case!

This reminds me of an old Persian servant who invariably insisted on putting the sugar into the teacups with his fingers, completely ignoring the tongs, which he always put ready by the basin. His master remonstrated with him, but to little purpose, as on the next occasion he laboriously picked up the sugar with his fingers, crooking them like pincers, and saying triumphantly, "You want me to use tongs for the sugar and so I do!"

We were thankful that the weather was now warm, comparatively speaking, as the withered tufts of a little shrub was all the firewood we could procure, there being no vegetation among the low, barren hills through which we had come. Just outside our "hotel" a striking-looking hill from which Tehran and Koom could be seen, rose abruptly, and from it we got a good view of the Salt Lake and the beginning of the *kavir*, or Salt Desert, the lake with its salt-encrusted shore putting us in mind of pictures of the Dead Sea, with its bright blue waters, pink shores, and the desert all round it. Some twenty years ago there was no water here at all, but the road to Koom passed across what is now its bed, and a large caravanserai gave refuge to travellers. This did not suit the Sadr Azem, or Prime Minister, who was interested in the present route, so, by destroying the dam of a river, he flooded the caravanserai and a large portion of the plain, thus compelling all travellers to use the road he wished them to take. Out of evil, however, often comes good, and the lake is said to have much improved the climate of the district by inducing a greater rainfall.

Next day we had to skirt it, and, having left the low hills from which the snow was rapidly disappearing, emerged on to a broad plain with grassy tussocks, passing near a nomad encampment. A low stone and mud wall, built in a semi-circle, surrounded four or five huts, covered with a sort of sacking made of black goat's-hair, and near at hand were stacks of pampas grass, with which the framework of these dwellings is formed. The women did not cover their faces, and wore short, blue cotton petticoats and jackets with mufflings round the head and neck, all having bare legs and feet. One old woman flaunted a marvellous mass of bright red hair, in striking contrast to the jet locks of all the others. Steadily riding on, we left the plain after awhile, and wound up among the hills to the top of a pass, from whence we could see Koom, nineteen miles off, with its beautiful background of snowy peaks. Its golden mosque glittered in the sunlight, and some travelling Persians halting near us made profound genuflections towards the spot where Fatima lies buried, visited every Friday, so our servants assured us, by the holy saint, her father, the eighth *Imam* Reza, whose bones repose at Meshed.

From here it was quite a short march to the sacred city, along a broad road with part of the Salt Desert stretching away on either side, and then low sandy hills, and always before us the curious double hill near which Koom lies.

In this desert dwells the wild ass, the animal once chased

by the Sassanian monarch, Bahram, who lost his life in a quicksand while pursuing his favourite quarry, and is immortalised in the following lines from Omar Khayyam:—

> "And Bahrâm that great Hunter—the Wild Ass
> Stamps o'er his Head, but cannot break his Sleep."

About two o'clock we climbed the last hill, which is strewn on either side with fantastic little piles of stones, set up by the faithful as a sort of shrine, and descended into the plain, Nasrullah Khan being surprised that we had passed no caravans of corpses on the road, as all the devout who can possibly manage it take their dead to be interred within the precincts of the sacred city.

Our rooms at Koom opened on to a broad expanse of roof, where I sat most of the day and sketched the wonderful mosque. The small cupola, overlaid with plates of gilded copper, has two graceful, gold-tipped minarets, and the effect of the whole building, covered as it is with brilliantly coloured tiles, would be charming, were it not for the presence of two huge tiled minarets, which completely dwarf the original design. These were erected by the present Sadr Azem to the memory of his father, and it seems a pity that there was nothing to prevent the perpetration of such an eyesore. Moreover, besides the mosque proper, there are countless ugly mud buildings clustered round it, and a vast expanse of graves, so that in reality Fatima's resting-place is most imposing from a distance, when only the glitter of dome and minarets catch the eye. A soft-toned clock chimed the hours *à la Perse* from a gateway, and at noon and sunset the melodious voices of the *muezzins* calling to prayer resounded throughout the whole city.

Nasrullah Khan visited the mosque, which is a sort of Westminster Abbey, sharing with Meshed and Kerbelah the honour of being the last resting-place of the Shahs of Persia, and saw marvellous old carpets, embroideries and jewellery which I would have given a good deal to have been able to inspect. However, merely to attempt such a thing would have been almost certain death in one of the most fanatical cities of Persia, where the wife of the telegraph clerk was accustomed to go about clad as a Persian woman, that being the only way to secure her from insult. Mrs. Bishop, in her book on Persia, gives an amusing account of how she borrowed the aforesaid dress, and her adventures as she shuffled about the city in it.

Our way out of Koom led through a mile of crowded bazaar, narrow, vaulted passages with booths on either side, and thronged with men and animals. A string of loaded camels blocked the road in one place, and separated me from my brother, whose old cavalry charger threaded his way in and out with wonderful agility; and when we freed ourselves from these, my steed and I got mixed up in a crowd of little donkeys carrying panniers full of firewood. As donkeys in the East never make way for any one, we had to bide their pleasure, and my disgusted horse revenged himself by backing into the stalls containing dried fruits, vegetables, and odd drinks in curiously shaped bottles. However, we got free at last, and I was able to watch men working at bits of leather or stamping sheets of brass, though none seemed to have any press of business, our caravan coming as a welcome distraction to the hundreds of felt, skull-capped heads.

Outside the bazaar we were obliged to wade through narrow lanes, fetlock deep in mire, with high mud walls rising on each side. These roads had originally been paved, but, as nothing in Persia is ever kept in repair, many of the stones were displaced, and the horses floundered about in the mud holes thus left. We were therefore glad to reach the shabby arch, which forms one of the entrances to the town, with four tumble-down shrines near at hand, on the blue-tiled, extinguisher roofs of which the storks had built their nests.

Our first camp was at Langrun on a stony plain, and it was interesting to watch the long procession of mules being unloaded, and to see them roll, pack-saddles and all, directly the boxes were taken off. In fact, their desire to have a

PERSIAN WOMEN IN OUTDOOR DRESS.

dust-bath was so strong that the muleteers had to be very prompt in unloading them, as, if not, our portmanteaux and other belongings ran a considerable chance of being crushed. Our first thought always was to release the two pairs of turkeys bought at Koom; and Rustem and Zohrab, with their mates Fatima and Fanny, became a great addition to our party. They would surround the afternoon tea-table, snatching bits of bread from our fingers, and Rustem was particularly good at high jumps after tempting morsels held up in the air, though frequently his sharp beak did not sufficiently discriminate between the food and our hands, and he would leap with astonishing agility to intercept a morsel on its way to our mouths. Fatima and Fanny did their duty in laying eggs during the whole journey to Kerman, which eggs were carefully kept, the result being a little family later on.

We usually got into camp about 4 p.m. every afternoon, and so could have our baths before the sun went down, after which it became cold, and we needed our thickest wraps. The evenings, however, were most beautiful when the moon was at the full, flooding mountains and plain with a wonderful light, as it rode across the deep purple sky.

The only part of camp-life that I did not appreciate was the getting up in the mornings. We were always dressed by seven o'clock, and at that hour a tent seemed an uncomfortably airy apartment, especially when a keen wind was blowing—a frequent occurrence at that time of year. While the tents were being struck we would eat our breakfast at a table in the open, huddled up in capes, and finding the whole landscape exceedingly grey and chilly-looking, and then were obliged to wait about an hour, until the loading up of the mules was finished. We usually walked for another hour, leading our horses, until by nine o'clock the sun was well up in the heavens, and we could discard our wraps, mount, and proceed slowly, often across stony deserts with the scantiest sprinkling of thorny scrub, and our destination, some fifteen miles off, well in view.

About noon we would make a halt for lunch, near water if possible, but often in the open desert, sitting on a carpet, to partake of *pillau*, or *kabob-i-sikh*. The former dish is usually a mound of chopped-up meat, rice, liquid butter, and peas, saffron, &c., while the latter is composed of pieces of meat with alternate layers of fat and onions stuck on skewers, and roasted over a charcoal fire, the skewers being constantly turned.

There is a great art in preparing the rice, which should be washed in five or six different waters before cooking, and each grain, when boiled, should be distinct from the others and yet full of moisture.

Puddings were a difficulty, as milk and eggs were seldom to be got; but we had dried fruits of all sorts as a stand-by, apricots, figs, and dates, together with pistachios, almonds, and a bright yellow pea, these latter having been fried in salt.

It used to amuse me to see Hashim lay the cloth on a windy day, as he would spread it carefully, and then go off to get a stone to prevent it being blown away. On his return it was usually flying across the desert, and he had a chase to capture it, then would unfold it again with the stone at one corner, and leave it to hunt for further stones. Probably it would be off once more on its travels before he got back; but he never seemed to tire of the game of pursuing it. When it was finally secured in its place it was a trial to one's patience to see him lay plates and dishes upon it, altering their positions again and again to suit his fastidious taste. One evening he spent at least ten minutes in settling the places of four bottles, arranging them in a dozen different ways, and at last giving them perilous standing-room on the extreme edge of our somewhat rickety camp-table.

He never could resist taking an unasked part in our conversation, and whenever he did anything specially stupid, such as upsetting the coffee-pot, or overturning the contents of a dish on to the tablecloth, he always regarded such a mishap as a capital joke, and it was hard not to smile when he looked round for applause.

Moreover, he always insisted on being given the title of *khan* (mister) by the other servants, and reminded them so frequently that he was superior to them from the fact of his father having been secretary to a nomad chieftain, that Nasrullah Khan was obliged to rebuke him with the time-honoured Persian snub for such cases, viz.: "A fool once said, 'My father was Vizier to the Sultan,' and I replied to him, 'What is that to you?'"

While eating our lunch the procession of mules would pass us, slowly jogging along to the night's resting-place, and we usually waited two hours, so as to give them a good start, amusing ourselves by studying Persian, and practising with my small rook-rifle.

There were plenty of skulls scattered about the plains to use as targets, and after awhile I became a fair shot at a hundred and fifty yards, though I could never vie with my brother in severing the bit of twine, by which sometimes our mark was suspended, or in hitting some minute twig on a tree. About two o'clock we would proceed on our way, and generally had a good canter into camp, as all the horses were exceedingly fit, and up to anything, despite the marching day after day of a distance, on an average, about fifteen miles.

The second waiter, Shah Sowar, had tea ready for us, and while the tents were being pitched we often strolled off to look for game, and if we were in the region of *kanat* holes, I would fling stones into their depths, and my brother would hold his gun in readiness to fire at the pigeons as they flashed out of these roosting-places.

We were thankful beyond words that it was not too cold to sleep in tents, for the caravanserais were most uninviting-looking places. They are put up as an act of charity by various Persian benefactors, and are open to all, man, horse, and mule alike. No one is expected to pay a penny for the accommodation thus provided, and I believe that Persians never do so, although Europeans usually give a couple of *krans* (ninepence) to the man in charge, who makes his livelihood by selling forage and occasionally firewood. He does not consider it incumbent upon him to keep the place clean, and, as it is no one's duty to repair it, it slowly falls into ruins, the mud walls crumbling away as the years pass by.

CHAPTER IV

AS FAR AS KASHAN

IT appears to me that the East either powerfully attracts or as powerfully repels those who have left the West for the first time. Most real travellers, however, succumb to a charm which is somewhat difficult to describe, as it is the mixture of many things that makes up the undoubted fascination of the whole. Probably there is a spice of the nomad in every one, and, if so, Persia is the very land to call it forth. There is a great sense of freedom in travelling day after day across vast plains, where often the only sign of life is the withered scrub, which at night will do duty for firewood, the traveller ever pressing forwards to some range of superbly coloured hills, which must be surmounted in the future.

Day after day the sun's rays shine down from a deep-blue heaven, in which there is seldom a cloud, and pierce through an atmosphere so pure that every seam and fissure in peaks, several miles off, may be clearly distinguished. The air blows free and untainted across the deserts, an air so fresh and exhilarating that it feels almost like champagne in the blood, warding off fatigue, and endowing the wayfarer with such vigour that he is enabled to enjoy everything thoroughly, taking the bad along with the good. The shackles of civilisation are left behind. There are no trains or steamboats to be caught, no crowded hotels to put up at. The traveller leaves one guest-house after another without regret; camp after camp is pitched and then struck, inducing a constant eagerness to press on and reach the next stage of the march. And yet there is no hurry about it all. The caravan halts at the pleasure of its master, and stops as long as he chooses, the tent-life making the journey one delightful picnic. And the charm of the life is increased tenfold to those who love horses, and who travel, as we did, with their own animals. In the East the horse becomes a friend. It will often follow its master like a dog, will wander about camp unpicketed, strolling up to beg for a bit of bread or sugar, and is, in short, such a comrade that the traveller gets into the habit of spending all odds and ends of time in the congenial occupation of "looking at the horses." Usually his last thought at night is to see if they are all comfortably wrapped up in their thick felts, and his step is the signal for a low neighing from his equine friends, those lying down not attempting to get up, so confident are they of his good intentions.

Then again the great solitude of Persia strikes the imagination. Days may pass without coming across a village or meeting an inhabitant. Man seems indeed a small thing, as the caravan slowly crawls over some vast plain always encircled by peaks, flushed with many a shade of madder or mauve, standing up, sharply silhouetted against the intense blue of the great cloudless vault above them. Such a contrast to the bustle and hurry of the West—a contrast between lands, in one of which time is money, and in the other of no account at all—forces the mind to view everything from a new standpoint. Civilisation appears to fall away here, and man is brought back to the simple facts of humanity, and has an uneasy sense that up to now his life has been sadly unreal and artificial. He feels that he has been vouchsafed a broader, truer glimpse of existence, and as he mingles with a people whose standpoint of morals and manners is an entirely different one to his, he learns not to judge at sight, and the precept of "live and let live" becomes deeply engraved on his soul.

And through it all, with each fresh experience, the sense of a glad freedom is interwoven. The traveller knows that joy in living—a joy which our civilisation has done its best to improve away. Pessimism is unknown here, morbid thoughts cannot exist, and life is better, because so much happier.

Perhaps, however, I have not really hit upon what constitutes the glamour of the East. My love of it may be partly owing to the novelty of my experiences, partly to a longing for travel and adventure never satisfied hitherto, and, it is possible, chiefly to the fact that I had never been so well in all my life before.

I awoke morning after morning feeling at my very best both mentally and physically, almost inclined to do homage to the lavish floods of golden sunshine, and with, I believe, the uncommon experience of being perfectly happy and knowing it all the time.

Between Koom and Kashan there was very little traffic, as we made our way across great plains, several narrow paths running parallel to one another forming our road. The only sign of vegetation on the stony wastes was a withered thorny plant, the inadequate firewood of these districts; but, notwithstanding the apparent lack of food, the crested larks chirped briskly, rising up in front of our horses' feet, too tame to flit off far, and several species of lizards fled with lightning speed. Usually these were the small, long-tailed kind; but fat, unwieldy monsters with orange stomachs were often seen near water, and I once picked up a small saurian, looking somewhat like a miniature chameleon, which uttered a curious cry, and did its best to bite my fingers with its toothless mouth. The Persians have a dread of all these creatures, imagining that they are poisonous. We seldom came across snakes. Nasrullah Khan killed a couple one afternoon sunning themselves on the side of a *kanat* hole— long, greenish creatures with black markings and white speckled stomachs. The *syce* insisted on carrying them back to camp to show the *Sahib* who was shooting in the hills near, and it was amusing to see his terror when they slipped at intervals off the stick over which he hung them, as he could not bring himself to believe that they were really dead. Occasionally my brother killed others with the lash of his whip, cutting at them from horseback as they wriggled along across the road, but, as far as we could judge, there seemed to be very few in this part of Persia.

Crows, and an occasional vulture or hawk, completed the life to be found in this district, unless one looked carefully enough to perceive the slowly moving woodlice, half their bodies black and the other half rust-colour, so perfectly harmonising with the soil that, unless in motion, they could hardly be distinguished. Their holes, however, were easier to see than themselves, as all round the entrances lay a quantity of minute particles of gravel, quite different in appearance to the soil above. Then there were the tiny greenish-grey grasshoppers, most active inhabitants of the deserts. Speaking of these reminds me how one day, sitting on a barren hillside, I idly picked up what I thought was a fragment of withered thorn, bleached a yellowish-white by the sun. To my surprise it moved in my hand, and turned into a sort of mantis, which imitated the plants on which it fed so exactly that it seemed to be all limbs without a body, and its movements were exactly the aimless, slow driftings of a scrap of thorn blown hither and thither by the lightest of breezes.

Patches of salt lay on the plains, and little columns of dust whirled over them as the wind blew from the pink and brown ranges on either side of us, while the great silence was hardly broken by an occasional Persian passing with his mules or donkeys or a string of camels moving majestically along; although when we met a caravan of mules there was noise and shouting in plenty, the animals going here and there across the track at their pleasure, necessitating some care to avoid an unpleasant collision with their loads.

On the fourth day after leaving Koom we reached Kashan, near which were many villages and much cultivation. It was an oppressively hot morning, and a burning wind blew the dust up in great clouds, obscuring the outlines of the mountains, and making us thankful for the halt for lunch at a *abambar*, or tank, half-way. This was a mud-domed building with a long covered flight of stone steps leading down to the water beneath, which dripped pleasantly from a huge brass tap, the latter object being a most unusual sight in this country. These tanks are built all over Persia as acts of charity, and I can hardly imagine a more acceptable benefaction in a land where water is so scantily distributed, and where one can so fully understand the force of the Prophet's expression the "shadow of a great rock in a weary land."

Kashan itself seemed even more in want of repair than Koom, and its ugly, bare mud buildings stood in a confused mass on the plain, the telegraph office outside the town and one lofty minaret being the only structures that caught the eye among the hundreds of low-domed, squalid-looking houses. We took up our quarters at the former, being hospitably received by the official in charge, and spent three days in the unprepossessing ruined city. As far as Kashan we could see Demavend, which rose up in greater grandeur daily, the rest of the snowy Elburz range dwindling away, so that we could appreciate the true proportions of the majestic volcano. When we finally lost sight of its beautiful outline, we felt as if some familiar friend had left us for good. Our last glimpse of it was at Kurrom Dasht, some twelve miles beyond Kashan. We climbed to the top of the highest hill in a barren range we were crossing, and, while my brother "plane-tabled," I gazed at the white cone, showing faintly against the vivid blue of the sky, at a distance of some two hundred miles, its attendant peaks having quite disappeared.

Kashan was once famous for its brass-work and silk, and the Persian name for a tile, *kashi*, is derived from this town, which supplies these beautiful decorations for mosques and palaces.

It has an unenviable reputation for scorpions, which has passed into the saying, "May you be stung by a Kashan scorpion," when a Persian wishes to call down a specially unpleasant curse on his enemy's head, and its inhabitants share with Koom the following agreeable proverb: "A dog of Kashan is better than a nobleman of Koom, yet a dog is superior to an inhabitant of Kashan"; and even among Persians they are notorious cowards.

However, here was the centre of the Persian silk trade, and we spent several enjoyable hours in selecting purchases from the big bundles of textile treasures of all kinds that the *dellals* brought for our inspection.

There were silk cloths and sashes striped with all the colours of the rainbow, lovely scraps of old embroidery, softly shaded velvets, and white veils worked with gold thread. These latter were once used by the ladies to drape round their heads, but now, being considered old-fashioned, they make original coverings for European tea-tables. Many of the modern productions were staring combinations of emerald-green and magenta, or vivid purple and yellow; and the velvet curtains, of which I had heard so much, were crude to a degree, the aniline dyes looking doubly garish when displayed next the exquisite colouring of the old materials.

The *dellals* came daily, bringing fresh things for us to see, and lowering the prices they demanded for the pile of goods we had picked out and set apart, until both sides arrived at a mutual understanding. They would squat on the floor, a party of six or seven, each man with his private bundle beside him, the *rôle* of salesman being entrusted to one of their number, who was gifted with a remarkably glib tongue, and was moreover an excellent hand at a bargain.

Besides silks, we bought quaint, incised metal boxes and old brass bowls, one of these latter being once the stock-in-trade of a native doctor. The signs of the zodiac are inscribed all round the outside of such bowls, and inside are engraved descriptions of the different diseases that afflict man, combined with prayers to Allah. The doctor possesses a small key for each prayer, and his mode of curing a patient is thus: he fills the basin with water, drops the key against the prayer suitable for the complaint with which he is dealing, and, if the invalid swallows the water in a believing spirit, his recovery from illness will be effected. Women, wishing to gain the love of their husbands, use these bowls, repeating an invocation to the Prophet as they pour the water over their heads.

We had left the cold weather behind us since Koom, and the delicate green of the young crops was springing up all over the plain, which was intersected everywhere with channels of water. As so little rain falls in Persia, the irrigation is artificial, and is performed by letting water over the fields for so many hours at a time. The ground being of different levels, low banks of earth cut up the whole country under cultivation into irregularly shaped small pieces, and act as dams to prevent any of the precious liquid from escaping, and to allow of one portion being flooded while its next-door neighbour remains dry.

Throughout Persia the water supply is provided by means of *kanats*. These are underground aqueducts made to conduct the water from the hills to the towns and villages. The soil, thrown up in digging these channels, form mounds at the mouths of the deep shafts, which penetrate to the water at intervals of some twenty yards, looking, as Mr. Curzon remarks, like chains of "portentous molehills" thrown up across all the cultivated plains. The *kanat* makers are a special craft, and are supposed to guard the secrets of their trade very jealously.

Several of the holes have an entrance dug down to the water, and here the women wash themselves and their clothes all day long, usually polluting the stream just before it flows into the town; but Persians think little of this, as they have a proverb which informs them that nothing can be amiss with running water. Moreover, each house has a tank, which is filled from the stream after dark, when the washing has ceased, though this method is by no means an ideal one, as the tanks are so seldom cleaned out.

The *kanat* holes are somewhat dangerous to riders galloping across country, as many of them are flush with the ground, and therefore impossible to see until close upon them. What is perhaps worse is that if a stream dries up, or if its course be diverted, the shafts are left to fall in, and the earth between them breaks away under the feet of a horse crossing it. Once I was riding among a number of disused *kanats*, and the ground between them had become so rotten that, in going up an apparently substantial bank, the whole of it gave way, and I and my horse came rolling down together.

One afternoon we all rode to the garden made by Fath Ali

THE GARDEN OF FIN AT KASHAN.

Shah, in the little village of Fin, about four miles to the west of Kashan. We took a long time in getting out of the cobble-paved city lanes between their high mud walls, and scarcely were we free of them when the stony paths of the rambling village began, winding in and out interminably, until we reached the imposing entrance of our destination, a gateway on which Persian soldiers were depicted in stucco-work. The garden was laid out in avenues of big cypresses, these, and poplars, being the favourite trees of Persia; and at their feet channels of warm water ran over blue and green tiles. The large tanks which fed these ducts swarmed with small fish, and here and there were fine archways frescoed with the exploits of Fath Ali Shah. There were also portraits of his many sons, who looked like young ladies, with smooth faces, "wasp" waists, long garments reaching to their feet, and pretty little crowns on their abundant hair.

We were shown the tiled bath-room, now in ruins, where Mirza Taki Khan, the great Persian Minister, was put to death by order of the present Shah. He was anxious to civilise and reform Persia, but became suspected of conspiracy against the throne, and fell a victim to intrigue.

It is said that his wife, a daughter of the Shah, was passionately attached to him, and, knowing the designs against his life, watched over him night and day. However, all human endurance must have its limits, and on the day her vigilance was relaxed the emissaries seized their opportunity and despatched their victim.

During our stay at Kashan we increased our poultry by the addition of a cock and three hens, of a breed only to be found in that town, and said to have been originally brought from Burmah. They had large tufts on their heads, and such short legs that they looked as if sitting when really standing, the hens were jet-black, and the cock a speckled brown.

As we were leaving Kashan Nasrullah Khan told me of one of the superstitions of the country, to wit, that if any one setting off on a journey hears a sneeze it is a warning to him to postpone the start to another day, as, even if he repeats a certain invocation to Allah, harm is sure to follow. Oddly enough, a beggar chanced to sneeze as our *mirza* prepared to mount his steed, and I was amused at the ill-concealed expression of anxiety which clouded his face, and, as he always attributed a serious fall from horseback some years ago to the effects of a sneeze which he had boldly disregarded, I could partly sympathise with his feelings!

On the other hand, Persians believe that if they much want anything, and are wishing for it at the moment when any one sneezes, they are certain to obtain their heart's desire.

A gentleman told me that as a boy he had a great longing to visit England, and one day while thinking on the delights of Feringhistan he heard a sneeze, and was firmly convinced that destiny would send him thither. Although he had to wait some six or eight years before his wish was fulfilled, yet his faith in that sneeze of good omen never wavered.

The same acquaintance had also another curious superstition, which was, that a day would be lucky or unlucky, according to whose face he saw as he awoke. He was in the habit of gazing at his favourite servant Haji the first thing in the morning, so as to ensure a fortunate day for himself; but occasionally, by some evil chance, he would happen to see another visage, and in that case things had invariably gone wrong with him.

He classified all our servants into "good" or "bad" faces, but admitted that only experience could decide to which category an untried face belonged!

It was also imperative to look at some one immediately after seeing the new moon, and he amused me by remarking that as Haji was not near him on one such occasion, he had gazed at my brother instead!

Before we left Tehran Dr. Odling gave me the excellent piece of advice to secure the horse that walked the best for my mount, as a good walker would be indispensable to my comfort on the march; and day after day I proved the wisdom of this counsel.

At first I preferred to ride my Arab "Nawab," with his perfect manners and beautiful mouth; but, being a young horse, he soon got tired, and my great stand-by was "Charters," a sturdy little grey. His faults were a hard mouth and a tendency to put his head down and bolt off with me at every opportunity; but his springy, tireless walk would have made ample amends for much greater failings. During the longest march he was always keen and on the alert, ever ready for a canter; and in going up hills and steep places he was unsurpassed. He would pause to consider the obstacle before him, brace every muscle, and then rush to the attack. When I add that he was remarkably sure-footed, a capital jumper, and that his pluck never failed him, the reader will understand that I had almost an ideal horse for my needs.

Our stud was certainly a quarrelsome one, and every now and then one or another would break loose, and a battle royal ensued, which, however, the grooms generally managed to stop before any real harm was done. With us they were invariably on the best of terms, and much appreciated being fed with scraps of bread and melon-rinds from our *al fresco* lunches.

The Indian *syce* was devoted to the whole seven, but "Cotmore," my brother's *waler* (Australian charger), was his special pride, and he would let the old horse take lumps of sugar from between his lips. "Cotmore" always gave a peculiar confidential whinny when he saw his friend approaching, and after awhile some of the other horses copied it, with more or less success, when they perceived that it resulted in food. There was the utmost confidence between the grooms and their charges, although the former would not have hesitated for a moment to rob the animals they petted so constantly of their forage, could they have done so unperceived.

CHAPTER V

ON THE MARCH TO YEZD

WE were not at all sorry to leave the mud walls and dilapidated houses of ruinous Kashan behind us, and emerge into the open country again.

As my brother had travelled to Yezd on a previous journey by the ordinary caravan route, he was anxious to reach that city by another road, and accordingly we followed a new track further east, which ensured us tolerable water, and gave my brother a chance of ibex and moufflon shooting, besides the opportunity of mapping in a hitherto little known part of the country.

At first our way led through a most sterile district, and our surprise was great when, late in the afternoon of the second day, we cantered to the brow of a hill and looked straight down upon a tiny village spread at our feet at the bottom of a deep and narrow valley the whole place a mass of verdure and springing crops.

There were fields green with barley; mud dwellings; the blue-tiled dome of a mosque; and many trees beside a torrent which dashed through the secluded spot. Everything was in miniature, and as pretty a sight as I ever saw in Persia, our white tents and cavalcade of mules adding considerably to the picture. Enormous masses of conglomerate rose up in fantastic shapes, towering far above the toy-houses, and on the summit of one of them was perched a castellated caravanserai, looking for all the world like an old baronial residence. The whole place reminded me somehow of Grimm's Fairy Tales, the little hamlet hidden away so securely from the outer world by these weird rocks, which in old romance would certainly have been giants bewitched, or fair princesses turned by enchantment into stone, and I cannot tell what besides.

The feeling of adventure was increased by finding that the descent to the doll's village below was seemingly over a sheer precipice. We were accordingly forced to dismount, and lead our horses to the camp down a steep and almost invisible track, along which they stumbled and slid in perilous fashion in the dim twilight.

Our way next morning, towards the large and populous village of Natunz, led us along narrow paths, stony with the *débris* of the high mountain ranges among which we were passing, and the sky was dark and fierce gusts of wind blew from the mountains as we rode through the lanes of the village planted with trees beside running water. Business seemed to be at a standstill in the long vaulted alley of the bazaar, and the fine old mosque with its minarets was almost entirely denuded of the tiles that once covered it, some of the beautiful *reflet métallique* of its interior being now in South Kensington Museum. The inhabitants came out in crowds to our stony camping ground, making picturesque groups in their blue, purple, or pale green cotton blouses and trousers, and brown sheepskin *pushteens*, and we noticed that the country women seldom veiled their faces, and were for the most part sturdy creatures, though prematurely aged. The long cotton shawl which they wore over their heads changed in pattern and colour with the district, being here a check material, while further on navy blue was the fashion, and at Kerman white was *de rigueur*. We found the villagers invariably most polite, looking upon us and our camp as a sort of theatrical representation. They never tired of gazing at the "elephant-birds," as they called our turkeys, and were always greatly excited at witnessing the descent of Marie from the *tacht*, judging that she must be a princess at least, to be carried in such a conveyance. The servants would employ them freely in putting up the tents and in fetching water, evidently considering that the novel sight of three

Europeans and their belongings was an ample reward for their labours.

Natunz is celebrated for its gardens, in which grow huge pears, and is often a summer residence of Persian royalty who shoot in the mountains, which are close to the town, on the summit of one peak being an old hunting-lodge, built by Shah Abbas some three hundred years ago.

From Natunz we moved our camp to Pabokh, and then on to Murg, one of the villagers speeding us on our journey by opening a small pocket mirror, although he omitted the orthodox accompaniments of a flower and some leaves (orange for choice) in a glass of water. We were pestered for alms by two well-fed and well-dressed *dervishes*, clothed in white woollen garments, like nightgowns, with bare heads and flowing hair. They were young and strong, and carried handsomely inlaid battle-axes over their shoulders, and curiously shaped bronze boxes in their hands, in which to collect alms. These men live entirely by the proceeds of begging, and it has been hinted that they often attack and rob people in lonely places unless their demands are complied with.

The hills in this district were of the most vivid shades of crimson, amber, and pink, giving the name to a lovely shimmering silk made at Meshed and Kashan, and were castellated in appearance, and at times shot up abruptly in quaint shapes from the stony plains over which we passed, one sandstone mass strikingly resembling an English cottage, thatched roof, chimneys and all. Between Robat and Vartun we came to a break in the gorgeous-hued ranges, and in the distance saw the once royal city of Isfahan, with the hill near Julfa towering over the town. With our field-glasses we could clearly distinguish the great mosque built by Shah Abbas, who was a contemporary of our own Elizabeth, and Nasrullah Khan pointed out various objects of interest to us.

From Natunz onwards the water was slightly brackish, but at Vartun the taste was especially disagreeable, quite spoiling our tea, even though we squeezed an extra amount of lemon juice into it to correct the taste. However, curiously enough, the horses and mules preferred it to a more flavourless liquid.

It seems strange that a large village should be solely dependent on such water, yet the women came in crowds to draw it at sunset, draped in dark blue and white *chaddars*, and carrying tall classic jars, narrow at the neck, and running to a sharp point at the base. These were most inconvenient *kuzehs*, despite their graceful appearance, for they toppled over unless tilted up against something. As the women gossiped by the salt stream, great flocks of goats and sheep came to have their evening drink, their patter-patter sounding like a heavy shower of rain. They stood in long lines, and when satisfied, politely gave place to the eager rows behind them, all quite orderly and well-behaved. Then they made their way to the village, followed by the women carrying their pitchers on the nape of the neck, keeping them steady with one hand, or, if they bore two, getting a friend to hoist one on each shoulder.

The usual stony waste had to be traversed before we reached the town of Kuhpah, which is almost in the middle of a plain, though its name means "at the foot of the mountain." It was quite a large place with a fair bazaar, and through it passed the rickety poles of the Persian telegraph line, which joined Isfahan to Yezd.

Our camp lay near the cemetery, which was, as usual, unenclosed, and the last resting-places of the deceased only to be recognised by bits of brick or stone stuck into the ground. Sometimes there are elaborately carved white slabs in the graveyards, but everything is, as a rule, falling into decay, even to the domed erections put up to the memory of the rich dead. As the Persians take gravestones without ceremony to bridge over bad places, to mend their mud walls and so on, it is a wonder that any one cares to go to the expense of putting up a monument, knowing what, in all probability, its ultimate destination will be.

There were many small fish in the brackish *kanat* near which we halted, so the drag-net was produced, two servants held it at a suitable place, and we thrashed the water for some distance up stream to force the "finny fry" into it. The excitement among our men was great when the net was hauled in full of struggling captives, which we ate later on for dinner, finding them somewhat tasteless and exceedingly bony, but a welcome change from mutton and fowl.

Not far from us half a dozen men were playing a game called *toupé*, something like "tip and run" with the run left out. A man hit a ball with a stick high into the air, and if it were caught by one of those standing at a short distance from him, he was out, and the catcher took his place.

It was a holiday for every one, as the great *Mushtehed* at Kerbelah, the Archbishop of the *Shiahs* was dead, and the bazaar was closed for some days. Nasrullah Khan told us how he had begun life as a simple *moonshi*, or clerk, at Shiraz, but gave up his position there to study law and philosophy at the feet of the then *Mushtehed* at Kerbelah, and in course of time succeeded to his master's office, being accounted by all as the most talented of his pupils. If a man is a *seyid*, or descendant of the Prophet, it is a great help towards becoming a *mollah* (or priest); but unless the candidate be able to master all the intricacies of Arabic law, and to parry or answer all the hard questions which the established *mollahs* will put to him, he will never rise high in his profession.

The whole of the next day we had a gale, and violent dust-storms, life in camp being anything but pleasant under such circumstances. The sand drifted into the tents, covering our clothes and faces, getting into our hair and eyes, and invading our food in appreciable quantities, while the *ferashes* (tent-pitchers) were employed every ten minutes in hammering down the tent pegs as the gusts of wind pulled them out, and in arranging boxes and packing-cases on the felt edging of the tents to prevent these latter from being blown away bodily. The whole landscape was hidden by a murky, yellow cloud of sand, and it was a relief when heavy floods of rain came down and somewhat abated the hurricane.

Although it was a cold and dreary morning when we left Kuhpah, yet we could see that spring had come even to these desolate regions. Clumps of mauve crocuses were blossoming among the thorns, many of which were bursting into bud and leaf; a most unpromising-looking shrub was now a mass of pink flowers resembling "London pride"; while a species of mimosa was covered with tender green leaves, though still retaining the dried-up blossoms of last year. As my brother quoted to me from the "Gulistan" of Sadi: "Not only the nightingale in the rose-bushes sings his hymn of praise, but every thorn is itself a voice of adoration to the Deity."

We crossed the stony plain, and after winding among low hills, halted for the night at the village of Guchkun, a curious place, perhaps never before visited by Europeans. The mud domes of the old village were built on the crest of a high hill, so as to secure the inhabitants from the raiding parties so frequent half a century ago. However, during the peaceful reign of the present Shah (now the late one), most of the villagers have descended from their eyrie and constructed new dwellings at the foot of the hill, many of the old houses being in ruins. It was one of the most picturesque spots imaginable, the rocky spur rising up boldly, distinct from all the neighbouring hills, although so well hidden by them, that the traveller comes almost by chance on the village.

The ruined domes and arches seemed a part of the rock itself, so closely did they resemble it in colour, and from a short distance it was hard to believe that the fantastic outline of the hill before us was due to art and not to nature. It was a mystery how the people made their way in safety along the narrowest of paths into their special rabbit-warrens, the entrances to which in many cases were hewn out from the side of the precipice; and we were convinced that there must have been a great mortality among the children when the old village was inhabited.

The great fast of *Ramazan* had begun, coinciding this year with our Lent, Ash Wednesday being next day, and the villagers had worked as usual, eating nothing from sunrise to sunset. It is a religious observance which presses cruelly on the poor, as they are forced to toil on empty stomachs, while the rich sleep and visit the mosques during the day and at night feast with parties of their friends.

Our servants came in a body to ask whether they ought to fast or no; but Nasrullah Khan absolved them from this duty as they were travelling; and, as a matter of fact, many Persians take a journey at this time, so as to escape it. The Europeans at Tehran told me that they all suffered indirectly from *Ramazan*, their domestics being too languid to perform more than the most perfunctory service, in the intervals of which they lay down and dozed. Persian boys begin to fast at the age of fifteen, when they are legally men, and the girls are considered to reach womanhood when only twelve years old.

The old and pious frequently extend their fast to three months' duration, and it is considered an act of peculiar sanctity to commence it two or three days earlier, thus " meeting Mahomet " as they say.

Next day we lunched at a tiny hamlet nestling below the ruins of an old fortress on a hill, and found that all the villagers were fasting, and looking very hungry as they grouped themselves near to observe us. We gave them a dish of rice, and could see how they longed to pounce upon it; but an aged man, evidently one in authority among them, packed it away inside his coat, explaining that no food must pass their lips until after sundown. So we had to content ourselves with feeding the children who were exempted for the present from a rule which must be terrible in the heat, as thirst as well as hunger must then be endured, and is certainly hard enough in cold weather. It is a wonderful example of the compelling power of Islam that these poor folk without mosque or *mollah* of any kind, should so strictly follow the observances of their religion year after year. They showed us their small crops of young barley, saying that they were all they had to depend on in the way of food, and that probably the locusts would devour them about *Noruz*, the Persian New Year's Day, falling on March 21st. The peasant class in Persia lay in barley for the whole year, taking it to be ground as they require.

I was informed that the rate of wages at Kerman for an under-gardener was a *kran* (4½d.) monthly in cash, and in kind about 200 lbs. each, yearly, of corn, barley, and millet—a very insufficient provision one would think for a man and his family.

We found the nights among these hills bitterly cold, and the horses, picketed out, and wrapped up in their great felts, used to sneeze and cough at intervals. Breakfast eaten in the open, with the thermometer at 30° was not a particularly cheerful meal, as an icy wind was usually blowing at that time of day; but we always walked some two or three miles to get warm before mounting. Sometimes on the road we would inquire of a peasant how far it was to our night's halting-place, but we discovered that he invariably halved the distance, following the Persian custom of encouraging the traveller by a series of kindly fictions. The idea is that it is an act of true charity to persuade him that his journey is nearly at an end; to tell him that he is close to the caravanserai, has only to ride round the hill before him and he will be upon it, and so on, whereas in reality he may be six or eight miles off.

We halted at Uskh and then Mazra, and at this latter place toiled up the Kuh-i-Chiras, a mountain 7,400 feet high, at the end of a short range. At the summit we had a view of many miles in all directions. The Zender Rud, the famous river of Isfahan, ending abruptly in a broad lake on the plain below, and the snowy ranges of Shiraz and Yezd rising dazzlingly white against the intense blue of a Persian sky, while nearer lay low hills seemingly scattered at haphazard about the plain and looking very insignificant from our elevated perch.

In descending, the peasant who carried the mapping apparatus, let several loose stones drop near my brother and Sultan Sukru, who were in front. The latter, imperturbable as ever, merely called out to the man that however many hens he might have up above, neither he nor the *Sahib* wished for any more of their eggs!

On our way to Serv we crossed a plain where herds of

camels from Isfahan were feeding on the spring scrub. The young ones were queer, woolly creatures, with enormously long legs; and some of them followed us, so terrifying the horses with their uncanny appearance that when we halted for lunch and the friendly little monsters gambolled around us, there was a general tearing up of picket-ropes, and only prompt measures averted a regular stampede. As this part of the country is often visited by parties of raiding Baktiari, we rode well armed, and were amused at finding that the men in charge of the camels took us for these bandits, being greatly alarmed and snatching up their guns, when some of us galloped towards them to inquire the way. I should not have imagined, as evidently they did, that *Terai* hats and European costumes were affected by Baktiaris!

Nodoshan, our next halt, three marches away from Yezd, was quite an important place, backed by a fine mountain range, on one of the spurs of which stood an old mud fort. We rode through an imposing brick gateway into the town, which is surrounded by castellated mud walls, and was apparently quite empty. However we found a man who piloted us back across a dry river-bed to a broad plateau of rock opposite the town, which is built on a like plateau, and here we found our camp pitched. Here also the entire population of Nodoshan was assembled to see the spectacle, and over the fields, women, like ghouls in their long white coverings, were flitting towards us. Our tents were on a shingly platform of conglomerate, backed by a semicircle of rocks of the same formation, and it was owing to this shelter that we were not blown bodily away by the hurricane that raged during that night.

For the last ten days high winds had invariably commenced after sunset; but here the climax was reached, and it says much for our tents and their stout pegs, that we were not suffocated as we lay, trying in vain to get a little sleep. The poor servants scarcely rested at all, and spent their time in piling barricades of boxes round the tents, and in hammering in the pegs as they were torn up. The hours went by very slowly, the jackals howling round us in small packs, their yells at a little distance sounding exactly as if children were crying; then the owls gave their melancholy hooting, and the musical entertainment was varied by the hideous shrieking of the hyæna, half a scream, and half a bloodcurdling laugh.

Persians much appreciate these spring gales, as they say that they "awaken the leaves"; but Nodoshan did not appear to require much rousing, as its masses of fruit trees, which supply the Yezd markets, were all in full blossom. Here I saw the lofty *badgir*, or wind-towers, such a characteristic feature of Yezd. They somewhat resemble Italian campaniles, and are built of brick with a shaft which continually sends a current of cold air down to an underground chamber where the owners sit during the hot weather.

From here we had a long march of twenty-five miles to Nasirabad in bitterly cold and windy weather, and though we passed a magnificent amphitheatre of mountains and were privileged to see a wonderful sunset glow upon their snowy peaks, yet after nine hours in the saddle, and no dinner till half-past ten o'clock, I was too tired to enjoy anything, and my one idea was to go to bed. However, it is marvellous what a restorative a good night is, and we were off by eight o'clock on the morrow, quite forgetful of our late fatigue.

Taft was our last day among the hills, and we rode through a grand pass to reach it. On the one side the limestone mountains were exactly like the bastions of a great fortification extending for miles, and the nearer we got to this enormous scarped mass, the more closely it resembled fortified outworks, shutting in the valley entirely, save at one end, where an abrupt fissure revealed Yezd, enveloped in a soft mauve haze. The pretty village of Taft, the summer resort of the Yezdis, was a mass of gardens, and we wound in and out among its narrow lanes beside running streams and fine trees, until we reached our camp, which was pitched in what Persians call a garden, *anglicé*, an orchard with a crop of lucerne covering the ground.

The next morning as we left the village, riding along the

stony bed of a dry watercourse which acts as the highway to Yezd, a stalwart dervish, in long brown cloak and white turban, stopped us and sang an ode in our honour, trolling out the words in a fine, rich voice, the best I ever heard in Persia. Here, for the first time, I saw that persecuted people, the Parsees, who still keep their ancient faith, and are a handsome and manly-looking race. They are chiefly to be found at Yezd and Kerman, intermarry among themselves, wear a distinctive dress, and their good-looking women do not cover their faces.

Yezd looked an extremely dreary city as we approached it on March 6th, having accomplished two-thirds of our long journey to Kerman.

It is set in a desert and surrounded by high mud walls which are obviously needed to resist the encroachments of the sand piled up in heaps against them—the desert being a far more insidious enemy to the town than those against whom the defences were erected in the first instance, and making the old prophecy that Yezd will one day be destroyed by sand seem not at all improbable. Not a tree nor a scrap of greenery was to be seen, crops having but a precarious existence in such a light soil, and all the gardens being hidden from view by high walls. A great expanse of squalid mud dwellings met the eye, relieved here and there by lofty minarets and a liberal sprinkling of the *badgirs*, which are striking objects, and are much needed in a place where the heat in summer is little short of suffocation for Europeans.

As we reached the environs of the city the road became worse, with yawning holes at frequent intervals not pleasant for riders after dark, and we got enveloped in a maze of winding tracks, here and there coming across caravans of groaning, grunting camels, sometimes laden with pomegranates which left a rosy trail behind them. Occasionally we had to wait as the great creatures blocked up some crossroad, lying down and declining to budge until the vigorous remonstrances of their owners cleared us a passage, our horses at first being considerably alarmed at these encounters.

A DERVISH.

So, by degrees, we made our way towards the house of the Fergusons (Mr. Ferguson being British Vice-Consul, and manager of the Imperial Bank of Persia at Yezd), who, with true hospitality, had insisted on putting us all up, though we were ashamed to quarter ourselves upon them, being such a large party. They met us with the warmest of welcomes; and it was a treat after our hot and dusty ride to drink afternoon-tea in a beautiful room, the whole of one side of which was a series of big stained-glass windows, and which looked out upon their garden, cool with plenty of trees and big tanks of water in which goldfish were swimming about.

The week we spent at Yezd was a delightful change from tent life. To live in comfortable rooms where a huge budget of letters and papers awaited us, to play tennis with the European contingent, and take long rides over the rolling sands outside the city, more than made up for the hot, airless nights which prevented us from sleeping at first, especially as the contrast between an airy tent and a furnished room is considerable.

However, to judge from the youthful European of the place, the Fergusons' baby boy, a perfect picture of health, Yezd must possess an uncommonly good climate in spite of its trying heat.

One day the Fergusons got up a picnic to the Parsee *dakmé*, or place of exposure of the dead, some six miles off. The party consisted of all the Europeans in the place, about ten, including ourselves. One gentleman was terribly nervous on horseback, and rode his pony at a walk, a servant holding it by the head the whole way there and back. Much as I regretted that Persian eyes should be regaled with such a spectacle, yet it was a matter of thankfulness that the European in question was not a compatriot.

The two towers in which the dead are exposed are erected on the summits of hills near together. We climbed a rocky spur to get a view of the old *dakmé*, which was merely a large, square, low-walled enclosure, full of bleached bones and skulls; but the new one was more carefully built, so that not even the most curious eye could get a glimpse of the relics of mortality within its high walls, and it had one small door through which the bodies are carried to be eaten by the ever-expectant vultures and crows.

The Parsees, or *Gabres* (infidels), as they are called in Persia, believe that if the birds pluck out the right eye of the corpse first it is a sign that the man's soul is in bliss, but if it unfortunately happens that the left eye is given a prior claim, then the survivors are forced to hold gloomy views regarding the future residence of the deceased.

The men who carry the dead to these Towers of Silence are unclean; and so afraid are Parsees of incurring contamination by coming in contact with a corpse, that they often leave the dying untended towards the last, lest these latter may expire while their friends are in the act of touching them; and they hold that they are defiled if they so much as brush against the wall of the *dakmé*. A dog is usually called in to decide whether a Parsee is dead or not. A piece of bread is placed on the breast of the supposed corpse, and if the canine arbitrator devours this, it is a sure sign that life is extinct.

A dust storm came on as we rode home, blotting out the entire landscape, and rendering the minarets and *badgir* of Yezd invisible, the sun looking like a little white blotch through the dun-coloured haze of sand which enveloped us, and which only allowed us to see a small portion of the track just in front.

Next day a Parsee deputation waited on my brother. Eight venerable leaders of that race arrived; fine old men, but attired in coats and turbans of a hideous shade of mustard brown. Their Mahommedan oppressors will not permit them to wear the flowing *abba*, or Persian cloak, and restrict them to dingy yellows and browns. However, no one seems to have interfered with the dress of the women, who have long, loose jackets of parti-coloured chintzes, and wonderful baggy trousers, a mass of embroidery worked on stripes of different colours; so that with many checked handkerchiefs wrapping up their heads, they present a very gay appearance.

A Hungarian traveller, M. de Rakovszky, was stopping at Yezd *en route* to Kerman. He had been *chargé d'affaires* at the Austrian Legation at Tehran, so that we had many mutual friends, and trusted that his search for old carpets and antiques would keep him longer at Kerman than he anticipated. As moreover, Mr. Carless, one of the Isfahan missionaries, intended to arrive at our new home some five weeks after our installation, we felt that we were by no means going into the exile that some of our friends prophesied for us, and it was with light hearts and high hopes that we left our kind friends at Yezd and set off again "on the march."

CHAPTER VI

THE GOAL OF OUR JOURNEY

SPRING was coming on fast as we left Yezd; and, indeed, it seems almost absurd to talk of winter in Persia, where it only lasts for a few weeks at the most. Even during the cold of January the barley may be seen springing up in the fields, and cauliflowers, lettuces, and many other vegetables were never lacking in the Legation gardens at Tehran. It was nearly the middle of March when we began the first stage of our two-hundred-mile journey to Kerman, leaving our "next-door neighbours," the Fergusons, behind us.

We were fortunate enough to have a guest on the second night of our journey, for M. de Rakovszky *chaparing* down to Kerman turned up about six o'clock, and we passed a most enjoyable evening in his company. He was engaged in writing a book describing the different types of horses to be found in Central Asia, and intended to illustrate it with many photographs. Besides his fondness for horses he had much artistic taste, and it was specially interesting to hear him talk about Persian handiwork, and I remember the description of one of his carpets, which had taken five years to weave, and must have been a perfect "marvel of the loom," the design worked out in many-coloured silks on a ground of bright gold filigree thread. He was one of the examples of the profound attraction which the East possesses for travellers, bringing them back to it again and again almost against their will. Persia was his loadstone; and when he spoke of the freedom of its limitless deserts; of the magnificent panorama of its barren ranges, and of the joy of life engendered by its perpetual sunshine, I felt all the charm which had held me from the beginning increase and intensify.

For the next few weeks we had high spring winds and frequent heavy showers of rain, and were obliged to take refuge for the night in *chapar khanas* (post houses) whenever we could, as often it would have been impossible to pitch the tents, so violent were the gales. Unpleasant though the weather was, yet the landscape effects were so fine as in great part to compensate for it. We could see the black storm-clouds rushing up and covering one part of the vast expanse of sky, while the sun would be shining brightly in a turquoise heaven in another quarter, and half the mountain ranges would be obscured in mists, while the other peaks would be gleaming with the most brilliant tints. At Shims, where we spent our fifth night after leaving Yezd, the best room was allotted to me, a small apartment with a rickety door, the frame of which was partly broken away from the mud walls, and so warped that it could not be induced to shut closely, the window being a mere round hole minus glass or a shutter. Towards evening the wind became so violent that it burst open the door, and it needed all my force to hold it while my brother brought box after box to pile against it. Before this happened, however, I amused myself by watching from the roof a big caravan of camels partaking of their evening meal. They are always divided into messes of ten or a dozen, and kneel down like a company of Persians round their sacking tablecloth, heaped with chopped straw. There is no quarrelling whatever, each animal munching solemnly away, thrusting his long neck forward to take a mouthful, and conducting himself with the utmost propriety.

We were now in Kerman territory, and guards persisted in escorting us during each march, while at Anar, our first halt where there was any considerable population, a guard of honour came out to greet the Consul. This consisted of ten men armed with guns, and wearing for uniform short blue cotton coats with red cotton shoulder-straps, which had a comical effect, as their long Persian coats, worn underneath, hung far below them. Their leader carried a stick and had the distinction of sporting brass buttons on his coat. They drew up as we rode towards them, attempting a salute—not a brilliant success, as they persisted in bowing at the same time—and then they marched proudly in front of us towards the town, hopping at intervals to keep step with one another. All the inhabitants turned out to stare at us as we passed through the mud gateway, but our odd escort struck out at them vigorously until they disappeared, only to reappear in our wake. We were conducted to our quarters, an unfinished mud house in a so-called garden, with unplastered walls, no fastenings on the doors, and no glass in the windows. As a high wind was blowing up clouds of dust from the surrounding desert, this was by no means an ideal resting-place; yet a Yezd acquaintance, *chaparing* down to Kerman on business, was thankful to put up with us, instead of stopping at the caravanserai. His eyes were sore from the dust, and he was much fatigued with his rapid journey, as he usually left at one o'clock every morning, reaching his night's quarters late in the afternoon.

It may not be amiss here to explain the difference between this fast mode of travel by post-horses and our slow one by caravan. To go by the latter is a somewhat leisurely proceeding, but to my mind the most pleasant conceivable of making a journey when the weather is good, and the servants, horses, and supplies ditto. The other way is to *chapar*, or post, from stage to stage, and this system comprises the maximum of speed with the minimum of comfort. The European, usually accompanied by one servant only, invariably tries to break the record as to the number of *farsakhs* (three miles) he can ride in a day, changing his wretched steed at the end of every twelve to twenty miles, according to the stage, and snatching a hasty meal or half-hour's repose while fresh animals are being got ready for him to proceed upon his journey. He can, of course, carry scarcely anything with him in the way of bedding or food, and when he arrives, worn out, at his resting-place for the night, he is lucky if he can get a room fairly free from draughts, and such luxuries as eggs and fowls for supper.

It may be easily understood that *chaparing* necessitates the traveller keeping to the main roads where there are post-houses, instead of being able to choose his own route, as we did with our caravan. The horses being few in number, he will often find that they have already been monopolised to carry the mails or some traveller just ahead of him. In that case he has the choice of remounting the tired animal which has brought him thus far on his way, or of spending several hours in the dirty, unfurnished rooms of a Persian *chapar khana*. It needs a strong constitution to withstand the fatigues and privations of a long *chapar* ride, and a bad attack of fever is no uncommon sequel to such an exploit.

The high winds still blew continuously as we proceeded on our way, across plain after plain clothed with the scantiest of scrub, and encircled with the barrenest of hills, and we found our luncheons in the open air somewhat trying in a country where there was never a tree or even a rock to protect us from the fury of the blast.

These spring gales apparently did not allow any rain to descend on the low ground, although we had an experience one day, which showed us how heavily it had been raining in the mountains.

After passing Kush Kuh we came upon our whole caravan at a dead halt, and found the country was flooded for some miles, looking like a great lake. The muleteers wanted to return to the village we had left, and wait for the morrow, hoping that the floods would subside by that time; but as the afternoon was still early, and the water did not seem to be at all deep, they were ordered to cross at once. The first mule was unlucky, falling right over on its side, and the united efforts of six men could not lift it on its legs until they had unloaded it; and even then they were obliged to half carry it to a shallower part. The muleteers bared their legs and probed the water in every direction with their long staves, coming across nasty holes here and there; but with all their efforts the small hoofs of the mules had less chance in the liquid mud than the larger ones of the horses. We watched for some time, and as animal after animal fell and had to be pulled up again, we felt we had better cross ourselves and press on with the "tea mule" to our halting-place. We were careful to keep to the road, though the ground often looked better at some distance from it, my brother saying that the track from constant traffic must be far harder and safer, and that if we left it we should inevitably get stuck in bad places. The first three streams were the worst. It was a horrible sensation to feel my horse slipping and floundering under me, and I got ready to spring off if he came to grief. However, though he nearly "sat down" three or four times, and I got quite dizzy with the water swirling round me, and the curious feeling that my steed was making no way at all, yet we both stumbled through our six miles of flood in safety, and reached Dafa some time after sunset, our horses taking three hours to do this short distance, and the mules seven. It was past ten o'clock that night before we got any dinner, but we were thankful to be safely over that piece of our road; for if it had rained again we should probably have been obliged to wait some two or three days until the flood had subsided. The only box whose contents were seriously damaged was the one containing my brother's uniform, part of which, unluckily, was quite ruined, but we could not complain, as we felt that we had really been most fortunate in getting the greater part of our baggage safe and sound.

Our next march was to Bahramabad, and as we could not find a good place at which to halt for breakfast, my brother decided to go to Mehdiabad, a small village at some distance from the road, where he had spent a night with the Farman Farma (a Persian prince, formerly Governor of Kerman), two years ago at the house of its owner, Mahomet Khan. The villagers, however, said that the garden was no longer in good order, and took us into a dirty courtyard, full of women and young children, which they declared was the identical place of which we were in search. As we were remounting our horses in disgust, my brother's old friend suddenly appeared, gesticulating furiously and calling out hearty welcomes. He insisted that we should lunch with him, and, leaving a servant to conduct us to his house, disappeared on hospitable thoughts intent. The entrance to his mansion was, as is customary in Persia, of the shabbiest, and we waited for him in an untidy courtyard, with dilapidated rooms built round it, his *biroon*, or outside dwelling-place, where he would receive all visits of ceremony or business. After awhile he reappeared, and seizing my brother's arm with effusion (he obviously disapproved of poor me!) led us along passages into a prettily laid-out garden, with a tank in the centre, round which were the living-rooms, or *anderoon*. Pulling aside a curtain, we found ourselves in his drawing-room, white-plastered and alcoved, with a row of windows along one side, opening on to the garden, their glassless panes being filled in with fine white linen. The furniture consisted of two sets of big cushions on either side the windows, where we were invited to seat ourselves, while the floor was laid with felts, covered with lengths of a gaudy cotton material. At one end was a fireplace, above which was a row of the commonest of brass lamps, and there was quite a collection of art treasures arranged in the alcove.

Several badly coloured prints in stamped cardboard mounts, gilt-framed mirrors of inferior quality, and Bohemian glass ornaments of a kind I have often seen in my visits to English cottages, gave an undesirable European *cachet* to the sunny room. It was curious to notice what a passion these Persians had for duplicates of their pictures, half a dozen copies of several of these works of art being stuck up on the walls, all close to one another, as if their owners desired to compare the excellence of their printing.

Our stout, toothless, rosy-cheeked host, clad in European trousers, full-skirted, blue frock-coat, and brown felt skull-cap, talked incessantly in a high key, while the women of the house peeped at me eagerly through the windows. Seeing this, Mahomet Khan darted out of the room and brought his wife and daughter-in-law up to the window to be presented to me. They bowed and smiled as I leant out to them, obligingly drawing aside the scarlet sheets in which they were shrouded to show me rich brocaded jackets, short, stiffly-standing-out skirts and long, white trousers, while their necks and arms were hung with strings of beads. I should have much liked to have talked to them, but as my knowledge of their language was of the most elementary order, I judged it better to confine myself to salutations and smiles. The son of the house, a languid young man, appeared before long, and I felt sorry for him and his father, as they sat uncomfortably, European fashion, on a high plaster platform, their dangling white-stockinged feet tacitly reproaching us for being in boots. The whole household had been asleep, as the month of *Ramazan* was not yet over, but our visit had roused them up, and women rushed frantically hither and thither to prepare our lunch, while my brother's conversation was enjoyed, not only by our hosts, but by two young men-servants, who stood outside leaning in at the open window, interposing their remarks and comments at intervals.

Hashim, who brought in our table and chairs, at once burst into a flood of eloquence, and was listened to with the respectful attention that Persian gentlemen invariably accord to the utterances of servants. The preparations for lunch seemed interminable, and although it made its appearance about two o'clock, yet after my seven o'clock breakfast and ride, I felt half-famished, and was glad of the invitation to set to on the somewhat unsubstantial feast of sweetmeats, cream cheese, and bowls of *mast*, or curds, with which the table was spread as a sort of *zakoushka*.

At last some excellent chicken-rissoles, an omelet and *kabobs* arrived, our glasses being filled up with lumps of ice before clear water was poured into them, and I found the curds went very well with one of the sweetmeats, which consisted of boiled sugar spun to the fineness of thread. I could not help feeling sorry as I perceived our hosts and the servants watching us hungrily, reflecting that it must certainly double the severity of their fast to see others enjoying what they must perforce abstain from till sunset. The conversation, however, never languished. The old gentleman entered with the keenest interest into all the details of my brother's journey through

Baluchistan during the past year, examined our rifles minutely, and told us how his son was a great traveller, having visited Mecca, Kerbelah, and even Tiflis and Constantinople. Upon this the pallid young man roused himself to ask if we should like to see a collection of photos he had of his travels, and despatched one of his servants for a large leather-covered box. This he opened with great ceremony, by means of a key hanging round his neck, and produced a small scarlet book priced at a franc, containing common lithographs of all the chief cities of Europe; being a French production, London naturally coming near the end. Seeing the reverence with which he regarded this memento of his adventurous journeys, we had perforce to feign an intense interest in it; but it was a welcome diversion when a dwarf, with a jolly, shrewd face and grey beard appeared, who, in his blue cotton blouse and old felt cap, looked the very image of the German gnomes with which the illustrated fairy tales of my childhood had familiarised me. He was no bigger than a child of six or eight years old, but they told us he was some fifty years of age, and joked with him in great style, evidently looking upon him as the buffoon of the establishment.

The women peeped in upon us at intervals, and the old man, perceiving that my eyes were fixed on a baby that one of them carried, sprang out of the window and brought his tiny granddaughter in to display her to us. The dear little thing was rosy and laughing merrily, but its lot as a Persian infant was not an enviable one, as its whole body was tightly bandaged in scarlet chintz, the arms bound to its sides, though its hands were free. A richly embroidered velvet cap on its head and a big muslin frill round the neck completed one of the quaintest costumes I had ever seen on a mother's darling. The grandfather was immensely proud of it, but the languid father took not the slightest notice of his child beyond saying, when my brother spoke against the practice of bandaging, that he himself thought it very foolish, but that the women would have it so. When we said goodbye to our kind entertainers the whole village was assembled to see us off; a *tomtom* was beaten, and hospitable old Mahomet Khan escorted us a mile or two on our way, promising to ride over the next day to see us again.

There was a slightly undulating country between us and Bahramabad, barren and treeless, as is usual in Persia where there is so little water; but we perceived a good deal of cultivation as we neared the town, which lies low down on the plain. Somewhat to our dismay we found that we had not yet done with floods, as about a mile of water was stretching in all directions, encircling Bahramabad with a gleaming girdle, and covering the fields of young barley, which we trusted would not be irretrievably damaged by such a long-continued submersion.

Some soldiers rode out to guide us in—a necessary precaution, as the ground was intersected with irrigation channels, now of considerable depth, and every here and there were large holes filled up with water and having a most deceptive appearance. As we splashed along to the gateway of the town, where a great crowd was assembled to welcome the consul, I confess I felt somewhat nervous lest my floundering horse should finally roll over and deposit me in the mire, which would be a by no means dignified entrance.

However, no such catastrophe occurred, and when we reached dry land we could spare our sympathy for the miserable condition of the town, half the houses having collapsed during the recent rains, mud being but an indifferent building material for wet weather, and the whole place apparently standing in a morass. The inhabitants, poor things, seemed to forget their troubles for the time in their interest at our appearance, and looked a most picturesque throng in all the colours of the rainbow, the snowy turbans crowning the greens, blues and scarlets of their tunics, while sheepskin coats here and there added to the general effect.

A loud *salaam* resounded from hundreds of throats, and hundreds of eyes fixed themselves in one concentrated stare upon us (on these occasions I always used to wonder what sort of an impression we made upon the aborigines!); while a huge grey monkey, led with a chain, made obeisances in fine style; and the usual squalid guard presented arms and fell into rank, marching before us to our quarters—some rooms open on all sides to the air in a swampy garden. We put up our tents *inside* the rooms, and when we had settled in, our Yezd acquaintance arrived to dinner, as the floods had delayed him on his journey to Kerman. He told us that from the roof of the Bahramabad caravanserai he had seen houses collapsing one after another around him, and the drainage channel was turned into a roaring torrent some thirty yards wide, sweeping away everything in its course.

Next morning deputations of Parsees and Hindoos came to call on my brother, and the Governor arrived later to pay his respects, all bringing offerings of lambs, sweetmeats, and loaves of sugar, gifts which are somewhat of the nature of white elephants to their recipients, who are obliged to give about double their value in money to the men who bring them, and are, moreover, expected to hand over the lion's share to their voracious servants. We were just sitting down to lunch when cheery old Mahomet Khan and a youthful relative of his came in. I was so sorry that they must again fast while we were eating, but they took great interest in our illustrated papers, and turned to Hashim for explanations, who gave them volubly, while Shah Sowar (our second waiter) more honestly confessed his inability to comprehend what the Feringhee pictures were about. Hashim much enjoyed that meal, as for once in a way he understood the conversation, joining frequently in it, to help it along. He must often have been dull when waiting on us, owing to his lack of comprehension of our language, for which we were truly thankful; but his ears were ever on the alert, as if by any chance he heard an English word resembling some Persian one he would immediately rush into speech, and expatiate at cross-purposes on what he imagined we were talking about. That evening he and Abu, our cook, had one of their periodical quarrels, and when later on the former came to us with his arm streaming with blood, I at once jumped to the conclusion that knives had been in requisition instead of their usual weapon, the tongue. However, it appeared that Hashim was in the habit of inflicting a weekly bleeding upon himself, judging it to be good for his health, and this time having cut deeper than he intended, he was seized with mortal alarm and needed much bandaging before he could be induced to believe that his life was not in danger. I was considerably pestered here by the women, who swarmed into the flooded garden to survey me. They were dressed in full white trousers and were covered in white or blue sheets, and unveiling their faces, which were wreathed in smiles, they said they really *must* look at me, for such a sight as a European lady had never before delighted their eyes, and I had not the heart to drive them away.

The road out of Bahramabad was by a labyrinth of tiny paths, along the side of streams. We passed house after house gutted by the floods; and our horses had to pick their way gingerly for fear of the numerous mud-holes. The inhabitants followed us in crowds, and every here and there we came upon fresh detachments, looking as gay as flower-beds in their brilliant garments. I heard afterwards that I was the great attraction, as it passed their comprehension how I could sit on a horse sideways and not come off when I cantered. It was a cold, dull day, and as soon as we had left the town a wind began to rise, and got worse as we rode on; great clouds of dust arose and blotted out the landscape, half blinding us and cutting our faces, driven against us with such force as almost to hurl us from our saddles. The swirling sand completely covered the track in places, so that we must have lost our way if the blasts of wind had not swept it clear at intervals, and we were thankful to arrive at Kabutarkhan with nothing worse than sore eyes.

A few inhabitants, shivering in their cotton garments, had struggled to the entrance of the village to receive the Consul, whom they would have honoured by slaughtering a sheep in front of our horses if my brother had not stopped the sacrifice just in time.

The house assigned to us was one belonging to the Sahib Diwan (Governor of Kerman), two of its few rooms being carpeted, and one boasting a divan. My room had no less than ten doors, the majority serving as windows, their top halves divided off into panes, filled in with torn white paper.

Although by no means a dust-proof abode, here we had to stay two days until the fury of the gale was abated, and heavy floods of rain fell, clearing the atmosphere. We were not sorry for the halt, as all of us, including the horses, were suffering more or less from the effects of the storm and, curiously enough, all the watches of the party were temporarily deranged.

We made our way to Robat through an undulating country seemingly composed of a series of hillocks having deep fissures cut into their sides by the winter torrents, and found our tents pitched on a sandy plain. An old friend of my brother's—I forget his name—rode from his eyrie in the hills to greet the Consul. He was a gaunt figure in long top-boots, with a blue smock showing beneath his short brown jacket, his costume completed by a huge, flapping, felt hat. These men resemble mediæval barons, sole lords of villages at long distances apart, their society consisting of their families and retainers. They ride forth after game with hawk and hound, followed by a horde of attendants, sons of the house, poor relatives and servants, all mixed up together and treated much alike, without any fine distinctions of person.

On March 30th my brother made his entrance into Kerman as Consul. The servants could hardly attend to any of our wants the day before, so busy were they getting his uniform into order and smartening themselves up in preparation for the *istakbal*, or procession, in which most of them were to take part. From lowest to highest Persians have a passion for any kind of show, and their own proverb, "Fill the eyes of a Persian," serves to illustrate this love of display.

On *Noruz*, or New Year's Day, it is customary in Persia to give every servant either a suit of clothes or a month's wages. My brother had fitted up our following at Tehran with dark blue cloth liveries, and these they now donned for the first time in order to make an impression on the Kermanis.

We halted some eight miles from Kerman on the evening preceding the great day, and my brother and most of the servants went off about half-past seven the next morning, leaving me with two or three men to come on in the afternoon.

It seemed an interminably long time to all who were left behind. The servants slept and smoked, coming to me every half-hour or so to ask if it were time for my lunch, and finally getting it ready at half-past nine.

For my part I read and wrote; but my thoughts were full of the goal of our long journey. Now that the travelling was at an end, I longed to settle down and begin housekeeping in the home which Nasrullah Khan had gone on ahead some days ago to engage for us. About three in the afternoon the *syce* turned up leading my horse, his face one broad grin of joy. He did not say a word good or bad to any one until he had mounted me and we were off. Then his tongue was loosened, and he burst into a flood of information about our new house, having no words adequate to describe its beauties, and therefore gave himself free rein on the subject of the *istakbal*. He told me that the *Sahib* had met the procession a couple of miles from Kerman, where a tent was pitched, in which the leading men of the town were assembled, and where they made his acquaintance over tea and sherbets. He was then invited to mount a minute steed with a Persian saddle, gorgeous in velvet and gold trappings, but declined to part from his faithful "Cotmore."

My little groom then waxed eloquent about the soldiers in uniform; the *ferashes* bearing silver maces; the led horses; the civic worthies; and the army who saluted the procession at the city gates with kettledrums, repeating the performance at intervals until the Consul had reached his own residence. He told me with many a chuckle how the Governor, the old Sahib Diwan, saw all unobserved, as he imagined, from his citadel near the town gate, but was as a matter of fact seen by everybody in turn. As we neared Kerman, which appeared like a mud-walled enclosure, crowded with domed mud houses and a sprinkling of mosques and shrines, we were met by my brother, and made a long round outside the walls to our new residence. No words can describe my intense eagerness to

FAÇADE OF THE CONSULATE AT KERMAN.

see the home where we expected to spend the next year of our lives. At last I espied a white façade gleaming among the trees, and we had reached the Consulate. We passed through an archway, guarded by soldiers, into a paved courtyard, with the usual tank of goldfish and beds of marigolds and irises, round which were built rooms with prettily moulded white walls; then up a steep flight of high steps to the *balakhana*, or upper storey, where much of my life would be passed. This consisted of four rooms, with windows on each side opening on to broad terraces, and giving views of the large garden cool with big trees and running water on the one side, and of the two picturesque ruined fortresses of old Kerman on the other. I examined my pretty sitting-room, with its many stained-glass windows set in six large arches, its artistic plaster mouldings on the walls and lofty ceiling; and as I watched the sunset behind the western hills, and we rested, enjoying the soft air, and lulled by the liquid music of frogs and tree-crickets, I was filled with a great content, for my new home far surpassed anything that I had hoped or even wished for.

CHAPTER VII

HOUSEKEEPING AT KERMAN

IT was the end of March when we began our new life at Kerman, which we entered upon at the most charming season of the year in Persia, before the heat of summer had commenced to scorch up all the flowers and vegetables.

During the previous October we had sent off our stores and luggage from London *viâ* Karachi to Bunder Abbas, on the Persian Gulf, and as this port is only a fifteen days' journey from Kerman, it was a disappointment, on our arrival at the latter town, to find that only about half our baggage had reached its destination.

Our glass and china, piano, camera and pictures, with many other treasures, were still at the coast, nor could repeated letters to the Custom House officials and Persian agents there bring our belongings to Kerman before the end of September, while the piano only turned up half-way through January of the following year, just three days before we left our home for good!

I had started life in Persia, however, with a firm determination not to worry more than was strictly needful, and so was not greatly overcome when I discovered that some of my dresses were ruined by bilge-water getting into the packing-cases, our consignment of wax matches being two-thirds spoilt from the same cause, while our packets of compressed tea and coffee had become mysteriously soaked with kerosene.

Our life was so novel that we could well afford to see the comic side of such little *contretemps*, and, as most of our small supply of furniture was waiting transport at Bunder

Abbas, I set to work to arrange our drawing-room somewhat after the manner of the couple in "Our Flat," improvising tables, seats, stands for nicknacks and so on, out of packing-cases draped with Como rugs and Persian embroideries, which really gave the room quite a home-like look, when I brought out my photos and nailed up a few fans and pictures on the small spaces of white plastered wall between the ranges of stained-glass windows. The servants seconded me manfully, taking the deepest interest in our "Lares and Penates," and plying hammer and nails with much zeal but indifferent skill. Hashim, who from the very first had assumed a sort of partnership in our belongings, was, however, greatly upset at the non-arrival of our glass and crockery, saying sadly to me in the intervals of house decoration, " Ah, *Khanum* " (mistress), "we (!) shall not be able to give really good parties with only our camp-things."

We were both so fully occupied at first that we did not go beyond the garden for two or three days. This was some six acres in extent, enclosed with high mud walls, and planted with long avenues of poplars and fruit trees ; while most of the ground was taken up with crops of barley and lucerne, the vegetables proper, such as spinach, beans, onions, and so on, growing all together in one plot. Four great trees grew in the middle, shading a couple of mud *takts*, or platforms, where Persians love to sit, drink tea, and sleep in hot weather, while running water, trailing vines, and bursting rosebuds added charm to a spot whose wildness and luxuriance reminded me of a deserted Italian garden.

On the third day after our arrival M. de Rakovszky appeared, and at once agreed to stay with us, we being only too delighted to welcome such an interesting guest, more especially as he was the only European besides ourselves in the place. He was in treaty for the ancient carpet in the famous shrine of Shah Niamatullah at Mahun, some twenty miles from Kerman ; but so intricate are the ways of Oriental bargaining that it was over a month before he got it into his possession. This carpet, which I saw later on, had been presented to the shrine by Shah Abbas in the sixteenth century, was much worn and cut up into as many as thirty pieces, which the Persians had re-joined with no regard to the pattern. But in spite of being nearly threadbare, so that the original colours were difficult to discern, one could not but admire the design of grand medallions on a dark crimson ground, filled in with leaves and branches, and bordered with verses in Persian characters on a series of oblongs. Cruelly as it had been treated, yet the lovely yellows, rich reds, and indigos were still undimmed in places, and now it must be the pride of the museum to which its possessor presented it.

On our arrival at Kerman the weather was very unsettled for some time, and nearly every afternoon we had the by no means agreeable experience of a sand storm.

The sky would become quite dark, and the beautiful blue of the heavens would be obscured with a thick yellow cloud, which would advance towards us, blotting out the entire landscape, even to the trees in the garden below. The servants would rush to shut all the windows and doors, but the puttyless panes of the former and the ill-fitting fastenings of the latter were but a poor protection against fine sand. Another moment, and we could hear the cloud break against our barriers with an odd gritty swish, leaving floors, books, and ornaments covered with a thick layer of reddish dust; and then the wind would carry the sand on its way, and usually a heavy shower of rain would descend and clear the atmosphere, making everything deliciously cool and fresh.

We settled into a routine as time went on; my brother went off to the stables and then on to his office after breakfast, and I began my housekeeping—a novel experience into which I entered with all the enthusiasm of a beginner. My kitchen was an unplastered, large, mud room, opening out into the courtyard, and contained a big oven which had to be heated by burning logs of wood in it, and then raking out the embers, and a long charcoal range, consisting of a series of square tiled holes, above which the saucepans rested. We had taken the trouble to bring out an English oven of a new description, *i.e.*, a couple of big, iron boxes with shelves, and a place for the fire between them; but our cooks invariably excused themselves from using this apparently most convenient arrangement.

Mud *takts*, or niches to hold pots or pans, and a deep hole in the mud floor down which to pour all dirty water, vegetable peelings, &c. (a plan which ensured the maximum of smell, and the minimum of cleanliness, as it was a big operation to have it emptied), completed the furnishing of my kitchen. No dresser, no shining crockery, no table or chairs, and a noticeable absence of knives, forks, and such small articles. The saucepans were of copper, tinned inside, with the exception of those we brought with us from England, and were a perpetual anxiety to me, as, although I had them re-tinned every fortnight, yet certain favourite ones were always in use, and were unfit to cook food in after a week. My first act every morning was to inspect each cooking vessel, and it took a considerable amount of energy to get the remains of one meal emptied out of the saucepans before a fresh dish was commenced in them, and I soon found that I must explore the recesses of the large cooking-boxes, as my cook had an unpleasant habit of hiding vegetables cooked a day or two before, so as to save himself the trouble of preparing a fresh lot for each meal. To fine Abu ten *shahis* ($2\frac{1}{4}$d.) for each dirty vessel was the only way of appealing to his feelings, although it was an unpleasant method to resort to, as it made him sulky, and covertly insolent to boot. He would tell me lie after lie, with such admirable self-possession, looking me straight in the face with such guileless eyes the while, that he often fairly staggered me. However, his perversions of the truth were not consistent, and this betrayed him. Thereupon I would say, "That is not true," and when he perceived that he was found out, he would answer cheerfully and without a trace of shame, "Yes, *Khanum*, it was a lie!"

From the kitchen I went to the store-room, cook and kitchen-boy carrying a regiment of pots and pans behind me, and here fresh trials of patience awaited the housekeeper. All Persian servants enter service to get as much out of their master as they possibly can by fair means or foul. They look upon it as a sort of sport, do not think it wrong, and set more store on the chance of perquisites than on the rate of their wages.

In Persian houses the servants are fed, finishing up the *pillau* when their masters have eaten their fill, and are paid little, if anything, in coin; but Europeans give good wages, and expect their dependents to cater for themselves.

Abu was a thorough thief, rapacious to a degree, and I confess I was by no means a match for him at first. As I was determined not to worry overmuch about trifles, I got into the habit of considering that I was playing a game with my cook and the other servants. At first they won all round, but after awhile I began to score myself, and felt considerably elated when Sultan Sukru informed me one day that all the servants were blaming him, and saying that he had told the *Khanum* so much that they could hardly cheat at all now! I also learnt by experience that a margin must be allowed for housekeeping in the East, as, if not, the friction becomes incessant, although I must confess that the margin was considerable when a dinner-party was in prospect, as every house-servant, on such an occasion, expected to share in the meal which I had to provide for the servants of our guests.

On the whole, I had a harassing six months with Seyid Abu, and was only too thankful when I was at last quit of this descendant of the Prophet.

It happened in this wise. He took to himself a wife in Kerman, and, in the enjoyment of her society, forsook us almost entirely, turning up about 9 a.m. in the morning to get his orders from me for the day, and to assist at the giving out of supplies. Then he would take all he could lay his hands on and return to the town till the same time the next morning. Meanwhile the kitchen-boy cooked everything as well, if not better, than his master; so one morning Abu was told that his merely nominal services were no longer required, and I entered upon a reign of peace with two small *shagirds* (kitchen boys), who developed shortly into really excellent cooks, and who, when their master fell from power, brought me stores of stolen butter which he had hidden away in the kitchen.

In Persia, and I believe throughout the East, it is not possible for the upper classes, be they European or Oriental, to do their own shopping in the Bazaars. If a Persian gentleman ventured to buy something at a stall in riding through the long, covered alleys, he would be considered to have laid a deadly insult on the servant accompanying him, and would at once get a "bad name" in the place, a thing much dreaded in the East.

The custom of the country is to entrust all purchases to a *nazir*, or steward, who goes every day to make them, handing in his account periodically. An honest *nazir* takes about 10 per cent. on all commissions, and this custom cuts both ways, because, although your servant makes his profit, yet he gets the articles far cheaper than you could possibly do, bargain as you might.

Seyid Abu, my cook, used to do the shopping at first, but as his ideas of percentage were seldom lower than fifty, and as we had, in consequence, unpleasant scenes over his accounts, which I insisted on checking and settling daily, the *syce*, Fakir Mahomet, was entrusted with the coveted position, and I had the satisfaction of feeling that however much *he* might be imposed upon, he would invariably deal fairly with his mistress, as his honesty was his strong point. Nasrullah Khan used occasionally to wax sarcastic when we dined off stringy roosters, aged sheep, or inferior rice, and used to quote a Persian proverb to the effect that when the Lurs (a nomad tribe) came into the bazaar, every one produced articles that they could not pass off on their ordinary customers; and he would apply this to the *syce*, who, however, gained experience in time. His great mania was to save our money for us, and occasionally this parsimony on our account was a little trying, as when I grumbled about the quality of his purchases he would triumphantly cite their extraordinary *cheapness!*

Certainly living in Kerman was by no means expensive, as meat and bread were under a penny a pound, eggs ten a penny, chickens twopence, a minute lamb fourpence halfpenny, and all the ordinary articles of food in the same proportion. Our bill of fare, however, had a sameness about it; the "eternal mutton and everlasting fowl," being only occasionally varied by pigeons, quails, partridges, and a rare *ahu*, or gazelle, while we never tasted beef until December, when the weather was cool enough to keep meat for a considerable time; no Persians at Kerman, or indeed elsewhere, indulging in that food, which they look upon as low class.

We paid a penny daily for our vegetables to the old gardener who rented the garden from our landlord, advancing to twopence in the fruit season, when we consumed any quantity of mulberries, apricots, peaches, melons, figs, and grapes. The same man also supplied us with milk, hiring out to us a cow which was tethered in the garden, with its calf, and carefully fed. We had been advised to bring a churn out with us from England, but we never had sufficient milk to make use of it, the calf always taking a large portion at each milking-time, and occasionally breaking loose, and depriving us of the whole day's supply. It is an Oriental article of faith (I believe it to be a fiction), that no cow will give her milk unless she sees her calf; and if this latter die its skin is stuffed with straw, and laid near its mother to appease her.

So our butter was made every morning, in most primitive fashion, the *syce* prowling round the courtyard and shaking some milk in a bottle, the soldiers on guard taking turns to help him.

Nearly all the vegetables came at the same time in the spring, and were soon scorched up by the fierce summer sun. The beans and lettuces only lasted some three weeks, and towards the end of May there was not even spinach to be got. As the marrow and cucumber season had not commenced, we had rice for our only vegetable, all our potatoes being used up, and none forthcoming until the autumnal crop was ripe. The homely cabbage is, in Persia, entirely a winter vegetable; but during the spring we had *kangra*, a sort of white thistle, much like the *chardon* I have eaten in France, which was excellent when boiled in milk; *gatch*, a big yellow, edible fungus, which we always stewed, and rhubarb. This latter, white and flavourless, was very unlike the English plant. It grew wild on the hills round about Kerman, and its stalks were banked up with earth by any one who discovered it, the Persians liking to eat it raw with salt as a relish.

The fruit, like the vegetables, came in a rush, and was quickly over. In April the sickly tasting, small, white mulberries were ripe, all the villages near Kerman being planted with these trees, which bore abundant crops, and were too common to be sold as fruit.

Then came the cherries, apricots, and peaches, of which I made jam, and the *aluche*, a sort of greengage, after which a long gap ensued before the melons, black mulberries, figs, and grapes were ready. I scarcely ever saw an apple in Kerman, the few pears were hard and flavourless, but the quinces and pomegranates were beyond reproach. I made a great deal of jam, and found that cherries and apricots did the best, although my first batch was spoilt, owing to Abu purloining most of the sugar. Oranges, lemons, and limes complete my list, the juice of the latter being bottled and sold all over Persia, the best *abi limu* coming from Shiraz.

Sherbets are the great Persian drinks. I used to imagine that they were composed of the white fizzing powder that goes by that name in England, but found in reality that they were fruit syrups. The best, to my mind, was a mixture of quince and limes, most of the others being far too sweet. *Scangebee* is the universal summer beverage, a compound of vinegar, *mast* (curdled milk), mint, and sugar, which, after repeated straining, turns out a pale golden liquid. The *mast* is much like Devonshire junket, and the Persians love to chop up cucumbers in it, making a curiously indigestible dish.

The Persian table decoration I never admired. It consisted in nipping off the heads of countless flowers and laying them in patterns on the cloth; sticking melons all over with hollyhock blossoms, or making up a sort of maypole of flower-heads a foot high, which faded before it was put on the table.

After a time we got to like Persian food better than our European cooking as interpreted by Persian cooks. *Chilau kabob* was one of the best dishes. Soft pieces of meat, flavoured with onions, were disposed on a big mound of boiled rice, and raw eggs and butter, on separate plates, were its accompaniments. *Pillaus* of boiled rice with fragments of meat, were of many kinds. There was the pea *pillau*, the cabbage, bean, and, best of all, the vegetable *pillau*, saffron, cinnamon, and other spices being invariably mixed with the rice and meat. (The great point with all these dishes was the perfect boiling of the rice, a peculiarly Persian art). *Kabob-i-sikh*, lamb cutlets, cooked in vine leaves, and small lambs, not much larger than an English hare, roasted whole with a stuffing of onions and walnuts, all varied our somewhat limited menu, while, as thirteen pounds of ice were to be had for a penny, we indulged frequently in ice creams, and our drinks were kept cool in the hottest weather.

When I had disposed of the food question for the day I used to ascend the steep steps to the *balakhana*, and make a survey of the rooms there. We numbered two *ferashes*, or sweepers, among our servants, and yet our apartments would have been left untouched from one week to another unless I called for these men every morning and set them to work. They always informed me with unblushing effrontery that they had done their sweeping while I was breakfasting, and I was obliged to resort to the device of leaving bits of paper and such-like trifles lying about in order to convict them of mendacity. The floors of the rooms were made of beaten mud, like the whole house, and although they were covered with felts, over which striped cotton floor-cloths were spread, yet we were never free from dust; and a careful attention to the clearing out of corners was imperative, if we did not wish to be overrun with tarantulas or scorpions.

I included a survey of the dining-room among my morning duties, as our two waiters were far too lazy to clean silver and knives, to refill salt, mustard, and pepper pots, and to keep cake and biscuits in the proper receptacles unless looked after sharply. Tablecloths and serviettes disappeared in an unaccountable manner, and I have reason to believe they were used as dishcloths, while all my neat English dusters vanished very speedily, the servants using them for their own purposes and seldom for *my* work.

Hashim was in charge of our weekly supply of coffee, tea, and sugar, and he and I had many a discussion over the quantities required of these two latter articles, as our opinions on this point were widely divergent. I must, however, do him the justice to say that he invariably gave in with a good grace when he perceived that I was inexorable.

Although he was our best servant, yet he perpetually played a comedy to mulct me of small articles of food. At first, however much sugar I gave out, the supply was never sufficient; but when I forcibly remonstrated with him, he would produce some, telling me, with touching pathos, that he had bought it for us out of his own money.

On one occasion we were using some tins of English machine-cut sugar, and the usual scene was enacted, but on this occasion our waiter did not come off well, as my brother at once remarked that he was not aware that this particular sugar was to be found in the bazaar at Kerman, as only *loaves* of sugar were sold there. Hashim saw that he had made a mistake, and burst into a fit of laughter, much enjoying what he considered a good joke, even though it was at his own expense! He was also entrusted to purchase our daily supply of bread, as the *syce*, being a Hindustani, was ignorant of the different kinds. We paid the highest price for bread, *i.e.*, $4\frac{1}{2}$d. for $6\frac{1}{2}$ lbs., of the thin brown cakes which go by that name in Persia, and always disliked the sort with which Hashim provided us, but never suspected that Kerman could produce anything better.

One day one of our visitors remarked to Nasrullah Khan, that he wondered at the Consul liking to eat the common bread given out as rations to the soldiers, and which cost about half what we were paying! A storm broke forthwith on our waiter's head, and henceforth our "staff of life" was of a very different quality.

We found our Persian servants, from highest to lowest, afflicted with an incurable laziness, and although we had over a dozen men to minister to our various wants, yet three or four good English servants would have done all the work they did and a great deal more besides. They were quick-witted and pleasant-mannered; but after awhile the ready answer of "*Bally, bally, Khanum,*" or "*Chash, chash, Khanum*" (Yes, yes, mistress!) when I gave an order, became a weariness to the soul, as I got by degrees to understand that nothing would be accomplished unless I saw to it personally, or at least reiterated my commands several times.

As our establishment, in common with all houses in Kerman, was unprovided with bells, the servants had to be called by sound of voice from the masterly inactivity of sleeping and smoking, in which they indulged during the greater part of the day, varying these occupations with incessant chattering which would have put a parrot or a monkey to shame, so greatly do Persians excel in this art of *gufti gu*, or gossip. In passing, it is curious to note that one summons an Oriental by bending the hand *down* instead of upwards, as in Europe.

It is no exaggeration to say that to keep things up to even a very low European standard is an exceedingly exhausting task.

Every lady in Persia with whom I discussed the "servant question," confessed to an intense irritation of the nerves, engendered by struggling with these lazy Orientals; and one went so far as to say that she sometimes felt as if she could have killed her cook, a particularly insolent fellow, and then "laughed to see his corpse!"

It is disagreeable to feel that there is seldom much personal attachment between master and servant, such as is the rule in India; and certainly the Persian domestic's idea of service, which is to purloin as much as he possibly can, is hardly calculated to produce such a feeling. Once I called Hashim, who was an adept in such practices, a thief. He was deeply

GROUP OF SERVANTS AT THE CONSULATE.

hurt, and explained to me at considerable length that it is not accounted stealing to take food, as the more of his master's food a servant eats, so much the stronger is he to serve him—a novel idea!

All our servants had a perfect passion for soap and matches, expecting me to supply them with these articles whenever they asked for them, which was every two or three days. As we both felt that cleanliness ought to be encouraged, my brother advised me to humour them in moderation; but I always had certain suspicions which were confirmed when M. de Rakovszky mentioned to me one morning, as a most remarkable circumstance, that his servant had bought him a piece of English household soap in the bazaar, at a shop where they had several chunks of the same commodity. He said he knew Russian or even Indian soap could be purchased at Kerman, but never English. To set my mind at rest I asked to see this piece of soap, and at once identified it by its lettering, as having been cut off one of my long bars, so next day when Abu and Hashim began their parrot-cry for soap I remarked, with sarcastic intonation, that doubtless they could buy some of the same brand in the bazaar, whereat they giggled nervously.

Later on I discovered that ten wax matches fetched a penny in Kerman; and this cleared up the mystery that why, when so many matches were supplied, no servant could ever produce a single one if they were ordered to light lamps or candles, and why the matchboxes in sitting and bedrooms were invariably rifled unless carefully hidden away.

As soon as our servants were settled down at Kerman each man started a "slavey" who, as far as I could see, did the entire work, for which he got no money, but was fed with our food as payment. The cook had picked up a grimy kitchen-boy at Bahramabad; Hashim and Shah Sowar had a youth in common, as had the *ferashes;* while every groom seemed to have his personal hanger-on, so our staff became considerably increased. Shah Sowar had a genius for starching and ironing—a gift so rare in Persia that he felt raised on a pedestal far above the other servants, and at first used to pursue me all day long with specimens of his skill. Much as I appreciated well-got-up linen, yet it was a decided strain on my powers of admiration to have each collar, cuff, and shirt brought up in turn for approval! He also arranged for our washing, charging, as I found out later, exactly double the proper price for each article, and then naively complaining to Nasrullah Khan that he did not make nearly as much on our wash as he had done at Tehran!

The proper price at Kerman was a penny for five articles, no difference being made for size, a handkerchief and a sheet being washed for the same money. This did not include soap, starching, or ironing, and, although cheap, I do not think Kerman washing deserved higher pay, as our woollen garments shrank to half their original size, and all linen articles acquired a brownish tint, besides developing an unaccountable amount of holes. I was quite in despair over my new table-linen, which, in less than a month, was completely spoilt by the energetic, green-trousered lady who came every Monday to wash for us in the stream running past our doors; for no European in Persia ever allows his "wash" to be taken into a Persian dwelling to be done.

Unfortunately Shah Sowar was a drunkard, and soon got into the habit of absenting himself after every ironing day, only returning some five days later to see about the next wash. Threats and remonstrances were tried in vain, and on one occasion we returned from a picnic to find him helpless in the courtyard. Sultan Sukru was deputed to chastise him, and amused me next day by telling me that when our ironer abused him roundly, he merely answered him with, "*Sahib* ordered me to beat you, and I did; if *Sahib* ordered me to kill you, I would do it." Which remark silenced the complainant, who relapsed into wordless astonishment. However, nothing had any effect on him, and he got worse and worse, varying his orgies with fits of abject penitence, in which he begged my brother to cut his tongue out if he offended again. Unluckily, he felt that whatever he did, he was secure, as we could not get on without him, and after about six months of misconduct he left us one day without warning, telling the servants that he was going to start a flourishing laundry business in Kerman, and would certainly not return if his wages were not doubled or trebled. I thought of trying my prentice hand at the ironing, but discovered to my relief that Nasrullah Khan's servant, Haji, had been in the habit of assisting Shah Sowar, and now filled his vacant place with great credit; and when his instructor returned to us in poverty, and begged to be taken on again, he found that he was no longer needed.

All our servants were much in the habit of getting ill. Fever was the staple complaint, but the slightest cold, the smallest scratch or cut would bring them to me at once for medical assistance; while their eyes were in a perpetual state of inflammation from exposure to the sun, keeping my lotion-dropper well employed. I never met such a set of cowards. They would moan and lament over a tiny bruise, or an imperceptible burn, and at a touch of real illness they invariably gave up all hope and had visions of shrouds and the graveyard. Their constitutions seemed to be fashioned in cast-iron, and a dose suited to a horse had no power over them; but it was extraordinary what an appetite they had for physic, swallowing the nastiest potions with a keen relish, and ever eager to be dosed on the smallest occasions; they were singularly indifferent to kindness, and never took the trouble to say "thank you" for medicine or tendance, in marked contrast to the Indian *syce* who was almost overpowering in his gratitude.

From first to last the ruling passion of our domestics was a fondness for display. This was good for us in some ways, as they looked on themselves as part of the Consulate, and spent most of their money in buying clothes to enable themselves to live up to what they imagined was an exalted position. Persians have a proverb to the effect that no one knows what a man eats, but that his clothes are apparent to every eye, and another saying as to the advisability of being well dressed is, "New sleeves get a good dinner." The origin of this is, that a certain *mollah* went in shabby attire to the house of a rich man, who was dispensing hospitality with a free hand during the month of Moharrum, but the servants, imagining that he was a beggar, would not admit him, and he had to go away hungry. However, he managed to beg or buy a new garment, and the next night craved for admittance again, was ushered in with great honour and was placed at the head of the table. He could not get over his surprise at this treatment, and kept on saying that he was the same man who was turned away the night before, but that evidently his new sleeves had procured this excellent repast for him, and his remark has passed into a proverb.

Our servants were also very good in cleaning up the whole establishment if a visitor were expected, and would perform prodigies in the way of cooking and waiting on such occasions, as they said it would never do to let people think that our retainers were slacker or less skilful than other domestics; and they had a curious horror of the Consulate getting a bad name in the bazaars.

However, this *tashakhus*, or love of show, had its evil side. Not content with hiring underlings to do most of their work, our men one and all sported murderous-looking knives, and ruffled it among the Kermanis, as their aim was to show that they were greater swells than the retainers of the Governor.

Naturally their habit of forcing every one to give way to them when they took their walks abroad, led to altercations, and on one occasion a disgraceful row ensued, which had to be taken notice of, as four of them drew their daggers on the populace when in a state of intoxication. In Persia, to be tipsy in public, is looked upon as a great offence, as drinking is strictly prohibited by the Mahommedan religion. Our servants were accordingly offered the choice of being beaten at the Consulate or at the Governor's Palace, and having chosen the former alternative, punishment was meted out to them by Nasrullah Khan, who took a keen interest in the proceedings, and gave me an account of the whole affair afterwards. He arranged that any servant who had a grudge against any other, was to be given the rod to be used on his enemy! For example, Akbar was the son of the public executioner of Kerman, and, as such, was said by every one to possess a "black heart." His father had been forced, in the course of his duty, to despatch our second sweeper's brother, and Nasrullah Khan, therefore, told off this servant to beat Akbar, the poor boy calling out that the man was thus avenging his brother's death! The little *syce*, who was not implicated in the business, wept the whole time, and sobbed violently when Nasrullah Khan offered him the stick as a treat, in case he had any insult to avenge; while Hashim, also innocent, acted the part of intercessor, urging me to get my brother to let the sinners off their deserts.

The cook, who was the ringleader, got off the best, as he called out that he was a *seyid*, or descendant of the Prophet, and so worked upon the feelings of all, that he was beaten very lightly. In Persia it is the custom to give servants a *khelat*, or present, after a beating. A new coat or a few *krans* is generally the reward of misconduct, completely destroying the moral effect of the punishment; but our servants knew my brother too well, to dare to ask for the customary gift.

Next to the Indian *syce*, the soldiers ranked highest in my estimation. Our guard of six men, with turkey-twill trousers, navy blue coats with scarlet shoulder-straps, and queer shaped helmets with a flap in front, were the cheeriest and most willing fellows it has been my lot to meet.

They had a ration of bread, and we gave them the usual pay of $1\frac{1}{4}$d. daily, and heard that because they got this meagre pittance they were forced to square their officer with a considerable *douceur* for the privilege of guarding the Consulate, as otherwise he would have changed them at once for what they considered a lucrative post!

The Persian soldier is a soldier for life, but his lot is by no means as hard as one might think. Each village is forced to give its quota of men to serve in the ranks, but the soldier's leave is of long duration, and he gets plenty of time to go home, cultivate his land, if he has any, and help in with the crops. Moreover, by virtue of being in the army, he has a high position, and in all towns has the office of money-lender and exchanger, sitting by a table of copper money, and calling out his wares with the well-known cry of *poul-i-sir* (black money). Persian soldiers on the march are a curious sight, as each man has a minute donkey which he loads with his bedding and food, strapping his rifle on somehow. These little steeds trot along at a surprising pace, even carrying their owners at intervals, and when halting at villages *en route* they are let loose to graze in the standing crops of barley.

As a rule the soldiers are fine, well-made men—a great contrast to their officers, who, in common with the great majority of the upper classes, are of poor physique. If such a thing as patriotism were known in Persia they would probably form a splendid army, but as it is the officers seem merely to be interested in getting what money they can out of their men, often leaving them to be officered by a set of *ferashes*, or common servants.

It was surprising to see the interest that the Persian gentry took in our servants. If a visitor called, and accompanied us on a ride, he would invariably drop behind us after awhile to have a talk with the grooms, and if he stayed to a meal with us, he would ask after Hashim's health with effusion, and always exchange a few words with him. This kindly concern as to our domestics was constantly shown if any of them were dismissed. The culprit would at once betake himself to the guest he thought we liked the best, and beseech him to intercede for him. His request was always promptly granted, and soon a caller would come to the Consulate to know whether we would not take back so-and-so. As no Persian ever seemed to have the least idea of what we understand by justice, they could not comprehend that we would not re-engage a thief or a drunkard because they asked us to do so; and they used to inquire of Nasrullah Khan as to whether it was the *Sahib*, or the *Khanum*, or he himself who had "taken a dislike" to the servant in question!

The *tashakhus*, inherent in the whole nation, urged them to these efforts on behalf of our domestics, for, if their intercession were successful, the reinstalled servant would treat them with especial deference and consideration when they came to the Consulate, and would also, doubtless, be able to satisfy the insatiable curiosity which they had regarding us and our doings.

They all imagined, I fancy, that the particularly simple life we led was merely a blind to cover deep designs or extraordinary doings on our part, and therefore assiduously cultivated our servants so as to get glimpses of light thrown on our inexplicable European characters.

CHAPTER VIII

KERMAN AND ITS ENVIRONS

WHEN the traveller looks back on the past history of Persia, and remembers what a mighty kingdom it was, and how many powerful rulers it counted among its tributaries, he is surprised not to come across more frequent relics of its departed grandeur. Tehran, the capital, is, to all intents and purposes, quite modern; there is but little to admire in Kasvin, the old royal city, while I am told that even in Isfahan it is difficult to conjure up from the buildings that remain a clear picture of its magnificence and splendour in the days when Shah Abbas held his court there. Shiraz, according to most travellers, is a decided disappointment, save perchance to ardent students of Hafiz and Sadi, and is probably more visited on account of its proximity to the beautiful ruins of Persepolis than for its own merits. So Persia is by no means a country to recommend itself to the ordinary globe-trotter, who is insatiable in the matter of "sights," and who would hardly consider the ruinous cities of Koom and Kashan worth a visit, when he could only glance at mosques from a safe distance, and would never be allowed to enter them and gaze at their treasures of old carpets and embroideries.

The contrast between Persia and India in this way is very marked. Throughout the latter country every town of any note has fine temples, palaces, and shrines, many erected by Persian architects, or under the influence of Persian taste, notably the Wazir-i-Khan Mosque at Lahore. In India Persian art is copied, Persian literature studied, and Persian at the present day is spoken in polite circles, as many nations speak French. And yet, how comes it that the disciple has accomplished so much more than the master? A plausible answer to the question is in the successive floods of invaders who have swept over the country, pillaging and destroying. But, on the other hand, has not India been the battle-ground of Asia for centuries? And was not Nadir Shah one of the most notorious of her invaders, enriching the Persian treasury with untold wealth after his famous sack of Delhi in the eighteenth century?

Perhaps the real reason may be that Persia was always an essentially poor country, with but few internal sources of wealth. Also the national predilection for mud as a building material is not conducive to a fine or enduring architecture, however beautiful may be the tiles with which it is covered.

Whether I am right or wrong in these conjectures, it is certain there are few traces left of a civilisation once world-renowned.

I cannot refrain from giving a short outline of the history of Persia, as this kingdom has such a grand past, and even now, nearly 2,500 years since the accession of Cyrus, it is still existing, while so many great monarchies have arisen and fallen into ruins.

Leaving its rich legendary history, which is the subject of Firdusi's fine epic poem the "*Shah Nameh*," I will commence with Cyrus the Great, who descended with his hardy Persians upon the civilised Medes, and became the founder of the great Achæmenian line.

Under Darius I. the empire reached to the Indus, and included Syria, Egypt, Mesopotamia, and the whole of Asia Minor; and yet the armies of this great king and those of his successor hurled themselves in vain against the insignificant kingdom of Greece.

The last of this line, a Darius, was conquered by Alexander the Great, upon whose death Persia lapsed into anarchy under the rule of his generals, until the warlike Parthians, a kindred race to the Persians, possessed themselves of the land.

This new monarchy, which lasted for four hundred years, successfully checked the advance of the Romans eastward, defeating their armies under Crassus and Mark Antony, and later on repulsing the legions of Trajan and Macrinus.

On the decline of the Parthian power, Ardeshir, one of the old Persian line, founded the powerful Sassanian dynasty in 227. He defeated the Roman Emperor Alexander Severus, his immediate successor forcing Valentinian's army to surrender, and keeping the hapless emperor a prisoner until his death; while Sapor II. crushed the legions of Constantine, conquered Julian in a battle in which the emperor lost his life, and dictated ignominious terms to Jovian.

The great Belisarius was sent in vain against Persia, and his royal master Justinian was forced to pay tribute to Chosröes I., the second monarch of that name ousting the Romans from Asia and Africa, and only being restrained from seizing Constantinople by the despairing efforts of the Emperor Heraclius.

When the Arabs invaded Persia, the conquered nation, after awhile, became *Shiahs*, and turned against their *Sunni* masters, forming a national dynasty, the greatest ruler being Shah Abbas.

Upon his death the kingdom fell more or less into anarchy, until Agha Muhammed Khan succeeded in crushing the Zend dynasty and in 1794 founded the Kajar line, which is on the throne of Persia at the present day.

Kerman, the capital of the ancient province of Caramania, was second only in importance to Isfahan, as once the trade of Europe flowed through it on its way to the Persian Gulf. The first mention we have of it is in Herodotus, who speaks of Caramania as one of the Satrapies; and Alexander and his army marched through the province on their way home from India. In time it became part of the Parthian empire, until Ardeshir, well known in local legend, captured Kerman and founded the Sassanian dynasty, and it was to Kerman that Yezdigird III., the last of the Sassanian monarchs, is supposed to have fled, when the Arabs, under Omar, conquered Persia. Kerman, in the Middle Ages, was actually a Nestorian See, part of that great missionary Church which had schools of divinity and philosophy throughout Asia during the fourteenth century, and of which the so-called Syrian Church is the last remnant. Perhaps, however, one of the most interesting facts about it is its connection with the great Venetian traveller, Marco Polo, who visited the city twice at the end of the thirteenth century.

Few places have suffered more at the hands of invaders. Kerman has been sacked by Omar, Jenghiz Khan, Timur, the Afghans, and Nadir Shah in turn, while in 1794 the savage Agha Muhammed Khan, founder of the present Kajar dynasty, almost entirely demolished the city. Lutf Ali Khan, the last of the Zend dynasty, held out here against the fierce besieger with great gallantry, and sustained a severe siege, two-thirds of his troops dying of privation, until the city was betrayed by treachery into the hands of the enemy, and its brave prince had perforce to make his escape to Bam. Agha Muhammed Khan then gave over Kerman to his soldiery, who worked their will on its hapless inhabitants; nor, it is said, would he withdraw his troops until he had received a gift of 20,000 pairs of human eyes! It is not surprising to hear that the city never recovered from this crushing blow, and among Persian towns it is a byword at the present day for its poverty and the number of its beggars.

Kerman, as we knew it, was rebuilt on a small scale in the reign of Fath Ali Shah, and is about a quarter the size of the old town. It is enclosed by a high mud wall, and is surrounded by a deep moat, at one end being the castellated citadel, the residence of the governor for the time being.

I am unable to give any personal account of the interior of the city, as, during the whole of my stay close to it, I did not go inside its walls, my brother fearing I might be mobbed by the populace who had never seen an Englishwoman before. However, he and every one else assured me that there was absolutely nothing to be seen, save tumble-down mud houses, dirty bazaars, and a profusion of beggars, so that I do not think I missed much.

The one really old building left in the town is the *Gumbaz-i-Subs*, or Green Mosque, built before the time of Marco Polo's two visits to the city, the date of 1242 being visible in an inscription in the interior, and its blue-tiled cupola, of which half was in ruins, could be seen for several miles across the plain. It was built in honour of Torkhun Khatun, a strong-minded princess, who married two governors of Kerman, and, when her brother succeeded them, killed him; but in her turn she was murdered by her sister-in-law.

Its partial destruction is owing to a governor who imagined that buried treasure was concealed beneath its walls, and pulled down half the mosque in the vain attempt to find it.

Perhaps the oldest buildings in or near Kerman are the two ruined fortresses, standing on steep limestone spurs about half a mile to the south-east of the new city. They are attributed to Ardeshir, and are built of sun-dried mud bricks, so exactly the colour of the rocks that, at a little distance, it is difficult to tell which is natural and which artificial. We explored them over and over again, trying to find out for what purpose the masses of ruined buildings which crowded the two hills were originally intended—a difficult task in which we were by no means successful. Nor could we hit upon the subterranean passage which tradition affirmed connected the larger citadel with the town.

One of the rocky pinnacles had been made into a small platform, approached by a flight of steps cut in the limestone, and was probably the *nuggelkhana*, or spot from which bugle or drum would summon the garrison to arms or prayer.

The Persians, however, insisted that it was the Tarpeian rock of the ancient city, and that from it all criminals were hurled, although a fall off it would have been no serious matter, and there were other spurs far better adapted for such a purpose.

The ruins of old Kerman lie between these two fortresses, and from the mud walls, now fast crumbling into their original dust, we obtained may fine *reflet métallique* tiles, which indicate the scale on which the town was built when in its prime.

Firdusi in the "*Shah Nameh*" expatiates on a tradition

concerning a princess who founded Kerman and gave it its name, from the fact of her finding a *kirm*, or worm, in the apple that she was eating on the site of the future town.

Mr. Stack, in his "Six Months in Persia," tells a legend of another princess, the daughter of Ardishir, who, rather than marry an objectionable suitor, shut herself up in the larger fortress, and was vainly besieged by her irate father for twelve years. At last a dervish passing through Kerman counselled the king to cut off the *kanat* supplying water to the fort, and this action brought about the immediate surrender of the rebellious princess.

From our sitting-room windows we could see these two old fortresses, and the older and larger was called the *Kalah-i-Duktar*, or Maiden Fort, a name which, perhaps, has some connection with Ardeshir's daughter, or with the local legend I am about to narrate. When the tide of Moslem invasion flooded Persia, the prosperous city of Kerman was not exempt from the common fate, although it seemed at one time as if it would repel the enemy from its walls, as its defenders withdrew themselves into their impregnable citadel. The chief and his followers had provisioned the place for a long siege, and there was, moreover, a a deep well within its walls and a secret subterranean passage by which its defenders could leave it at will. All would probably have gone well if the *Gabre* chieftain had not had a most beautiful daughter, who was to him as the very apple of his eye. He had ever loaded her with silks and jewels, and, in the days before invasion had been dreamt of, had laid out for her a lovely rose-garden on a sunny plain below the fortress. She was so beloved and trusted by one and all, that she could come and go as she would, and had plenty of opportunities of watching the movements of the besiegers. Again and again she had noted the bravery of the young Arab general, who led his men persistently to the attack, and exposed his own person recklessly to the shower of arrows and missiles launched incessantly from the castle walls. Day after day she gazed upon him, falling ever deeper and deeper in love with the violent *abandon* of an Eastern woman, and after awhile she managed to communicate with him. By a trusty messenger she let him understand that she would give up everything for him, would act the traitress and let the enemies of her land into the castle through the secret entrance if he would promise to marry her.

He consented readily enough, and one dark, moonless night the maiden opened that hidden door, and an awful massacre ensued, in which the fire-worshippers were ruthlessly exterminated, and the standard of the Prophet was planted on the topmost summit of the pile. The general had given careful orders to his soldiery to see that no harm came to the girl, and when the assault was over she was brought into his presence. He was fairly astounded at her loveliness, but not being able to find a reason for her treachery, he asked her whether her father had been very cruel to her, that she had thus betrayed him. She replied that, on the contrary, he had cherished her with a never-failing tenderness and that her slightest wish had been as a law to him. At this glimpse of her hard heart the young chieftain's love was turned into loathing. He gave orders for her to be tied to a wild horse, which his cavalry pursued with savage shouts across the plain, and thus the Tarpeia of Kerman perished miserably.

Kerman lies on the great oblong plain of Rafsinjan, some eighty miles in length, and stretching northwards beyond Bahramabad. Near the town different tracts are brought into cultivation in alternate years, and oxen plough up the hard soil for crops of barley, opium, castor-oil, melons, and cotton, donkeys bringing panniers full of the crumbled mud-walls of the old city to be spread on the ground as manure.

Beyond this lie many miles of *put*, or solidified mud, and it was here that we usually went for our long gallops across country. For the most part the only vegetation is a sort of vetch, but a little grass grows near the few streams, and it was in these favoured spots that we came across the flocks of sheep and goats, from whose marvellously fine fleeces the famous carpets and shawls of Kerman are made. It is said that there is no wool in the world to equal it, and although

Fath Ali Shah tried to introduce Kerman sheep into other parts of Persia, the experiment resulted in failure, owing, Persians say, to lack of some special quality in the water.

And it is the extremely scanty supply of this water that makes Kerman almost a desert. Old chronicles speak of the hundreds of wells that once contributed to make the surrounding country one of the most fertile in Persia, but now, alas, they are all choked up and have completely disappeared, while a long chain of *kanats* brings a stream of water from the hills to the city, a stream frequented by all the washerwomen of the place before it enters the gates.

We ourselves obtained our water from the Sar-i-Assia rivulet, some two miles from our house, sending a man on a mule daily to fill up one of our wooden water-barrels, a mode of conveyance preferable to the Persian *mushk*, or skin bag, which frequently discolours the liquid, and usually lends it a faint, disagreeable smell and taste.

Much nearer home was another spring, celebrated in local tradition as having been made to burst out of the hard rock at a blow from the hand of Ali. Upon the steep side of a black mountain the words *Ya Ali* were painted in huge, white Persian characters, and below them the merest trickle of water exuded, making one feel that the saint, while about it, might have done the thing more handsomely. All day long women climb up to this spot to collect the slowly dripping water from the sacred stream, and to hang tallow-dips from the branches of the one small tree growing by it, which votive offerings will ensure to them the joys of motherhood, and must be a small food-supply for the jackals during their nightly prowls. Sick women, on the other hand, make their pilgrimage to a spur of the hills on which stand the old fortresses, and deposit bread, meat, sugar, and fruit in a small mud room. If on their return their offerings are eaten, they believe that the Queen of the Fairies has taken pity on them, and will cure them of their complaints.

As is usual in Persian cities, Kerman is built upon a plain, and has many ranges of hills in its near vicinity. To the south towers the splendid mass of Jupa, the great feature of the landscape, its picturesque peaks nearly always tipped with snow, and beyond it rise the higher Lalazar Range and Kuh-i-Hazar's remarkable pyramidal-shaped peak, while the lofty pink plateau of Kupayeh forms a bulwark to the north-east against the rolling sands of the great desert on the edge of which Kerman stands.

The district towards the Kupayeh Range was one of the most desolate in the neighbourhood. Not a sign of any vegetation, never a trace of habitation, only dunes of shifting sand and frowning mountains. It was here that I saw one of the few wolves that I came across in Persia, louping along, apparently in quite a leisurely manner, although when we urged our horses and galloped after it, we found it was impossible to get up with it, try as we might. This waste was also enlivened by the jerboa, called by the Persians the "two-pawed mouse," which hops about on its hind-legs, like a tiny kangaroo, and appears such a lively little creature that we always wanted to have one for a pet to brighten the house with its agile movements.

Here in this dreary district are the towers on which the Parsees expose their dead, built invariably on abruptly rising hills. One was of oblong shape, a buttressed wall with a small door at one end, entirely surrounding the summit of the hill, thus rendering any observation of what lay inside quite impossible. The newer one was built on a rocky spur, facing the one I have described, and was merely a large round tower with an iron door half-way up its side; and not far from these two *dakmés* lay a third "Tower of Silence," now falling into ruins. Near the boulder-paved causeway, along which the corpses were carried out from the city, was a two-storied mud building, where banquets for the spirits of the departed were deposited. The survivors were wont to lay the food out elegantly in the *balakhana*, and return later to see whether it were devoured or not, as, just after death, the disembodied spirit is supposed to be much in need of nourishment.

To the east of our house lay a small, hill-encircled plain, thickly covered with ruined dwellings, many still containing great portions of their original mosaic flooring, and having

DAKMÉ, OR PARSEE TOWER, WHERE DEAD ARE EXPOSED.

elaborate friezes of *gutch*, or plaster-work, ornamenting their mud walls. Amidst this suburb rose a small domed building, called *Jubal-i-Sang* (Mount of Stone), composed of big, irregularly shaped stones set in mortar, its walls being of great thickness. It reminded me somewhat of the Pantheon, as it had a large aperture in its domed roof, which was covered with beautiful tiles some years ago; but these, however, had all been removed by the Mayor of Kerman to decorate his own house. This building, with its Arab arches, was always somewhat of an architectural puzzle to our friend M. de Rakovszky, and the inscription upon it, "I was built between two Paradises" (Persian for gardens), gave no clue to the date of its construction, beyond that it must have been in the palmy days of the city, when Kerman was celebrated for its gardens, which supplied attar of roses to half the civilised world.

Some ten days after our arrival at Kerman we were strolling about with M. de Rakovszky at the foot of the old fortresses, and were examining some of the mud ruins which are supposed by the Persians to be haunted by *jinns*, *afreets*, and *deeves* (the latter being cat-headed, white-skinned men with horns, having claws on their hands and feet), when our guest picked up a pretty piece of tile, and said that it was *reflet métallique*. At Tehran I had been shown a tiny cup and saucer of this ancient ware, but so ugly were they in form and colouring that I felt no desire to possess any specimens myself. However, this was very different—a brown design shot with gold on a pure white ground, a thing pleasing to the eye even of the Philistine.

The making of this *reflet*, with its peculiar glaze, is a lost art, and it is over six hundred years since any of the ware has been manufactured. Blue, brown, red, and purple were the colours principally employed in these tiles, which have a wonderful metallic iridescence when turned to the light.

Our imaginations were greatly fired at the sight of countless fragments of this beautiful ware lying around us, and when the Kermanis understood that we wished to buy tiles, plenty of them, although usually, alas, in a broken condition, were brought to the Consulate.

We obtained some pieces of a kind of frieze with a design in golden brown, relieved by bands of turquoise blue. Some of the tiles had raised Kufic characters on them, and one was inscribed with the words "Hail, Omar!" in curious contrast to the way in which this *Khalif* is now hated by all orthodox Persians. Bits of lattice-work made of pottery, and dainty turquoise blue tiles, with birds or rabbits traced on them in gold, might once have formed part of the palace *anderoon*, while some very handsome, much broken, pieces, with the word "Allah," evidently once belonged to the mosque. In these latter the letters were of a deep purple, and were raised from the white, brown traced ground, as were also the large rich blue leaves, and Mr. Reade, of the British Museum, considers that these fragments are perhaps some of the best *reflet métallique* ever brought to England.

Besides the tiles we got quantities of broken porcelain and pottery, the former evidently of Chinese origin, and the latter, as a rule, a vivid green or yellow. Moreover, bits of a curious sage-green pottery were scattered about, very fine, and with a beautiful glaze on both sides. This, I have been told, is a sure sign of Arab occupation, and is met with wherever Arabs have been. Some of the ware had classic designs, notably the Greek "key" pattern upon it in black or indigo.

So keen were we at this time on the subject of these tiles, that when my brother bought a new horse, the very lightest chestnut I have ever seen, we called him "Reflet," because in the sunlight his silky coat had a wonderful gold and red lustre. The servants soon caught the name, changing it, however, to "Leflef," a word applied to boys who eat greedily and in a hurry. As "Reflet" was invariably half-mad with eagerness just before feeding-time, and "set to" with tremendous gusto directly he was served, both names were singularly appropriate.

Mosaic was found everywhere, often in beautiful patterns, in which blue, black, white, and soft fawn colours figured. It reminded us of the description of Ahasuerus's palace at

Shushan, where the people feasted in the courtyard "upon a pavement of red and blue and white and black marble" (Esther i. 6).

There was also a great deal of plaster-work, with bold designs of white flowers and leaves let into a buff groundwork, which had a very pleasing effect.

One night we walked up to the summit of the big fortress in the moonlight, and wandered among the crumbling mud walls, the old brick archways, and ruined chambers, wondering what treasures of mosaic, of tiles, and of bronzes might not be hidden beneath the unpromising mounds of earth, strewn with many a human bone, gleaming white in the moon's rays. Kerman lay mapped out below us in the soft light which glorified its squalid mud houses, its ruined blue domes, and general air of decay, and the silence was intense, broken only by the curious groaning in the distance of a Persian water-wheel, worked by a buffalo. All at once we noticed two or three jackals, stealing away down the hillside more like phantoms than creatures of flesh and blood, and in another second the first gave tongue, followed by another and another, till the garden beneath us rang with heartrending yells, causing M. de Rakovszky to say that their cries reminded him of a soul in the grasp of a despair so deep, so hopeless, that it could only murmur in the absence of all stay, all support, "*C'est fini!*"

This nocturnal visit of ours to the fortress caused much remark in the town, and we were told that our guest had the unusual power, by means of his camera, of being able to see thirty feet deep down into the earth, thus anticipating the Röntgen Rays, darkness being specially favourable to the operation. On this particular night it was affirmed that he had seen a golden vessel, buried far below his feet, and having dug it up, it was found to be filled with valuable coins! After this the whole of Kerman made up its mind that we were after treasure, and I was informed that the interest we excited was great.

Very little was found in the fortresses beyond mosaic floors, a curious corroded pipe as big as a drain-pipe, some coins, tiny agate and cornelian beads, and bits of cotton manuscript paper, one recording a complaint of looting in the Jabal Bariz district, dated some six hundred years ago. After awhile somewhat curious things were brought for sale, among which a small Queen Victoria medal and a torn sheet of one of my brother's *Pioneer* newspapers were offered, both, according to their would-be salesman, having been dug out of the fortress at a great depth below the earth; while we were frequently offered commonplace modern tiles, evidently fetched from the mosques in the town.

One day we came across the Necropolis of old Kerman. The graves reminded us a little of the Catacombs, with a difference, as long, square niches were dug out of a mud mass, just the length of the corpse, which was slipped in feet foremost, the entrance being sealed up with a tile. The vaulted roofs were of tiles, set at an acute angle, and the niches were in rows, one above the other, in the thick sand walls, which seem to have been originally built round a square.

Our *ferash* pulled away some of the tiles, and in one grave there was a skeleton, its skull covered with thick, short, brown hair. My brother wanted to keep this, as it might have thrown light upon these early inhabitants of Kerman, but the relic fell to bits when touched. Curious low chambers roofed with rough plaster-work opened out on to the square, and may once have been inhabited by those whose duty it was to bury the dead.

One day we lunched early and rode out to see the ruins of Dugiyanus, of which we had heard a great report as being extensive and full of relics of bygone splendour. They lay across the desert to the south-west of Kerman, and we had to pass round the city on our way to them, and found a crowd assembled at the big gate of the town, listening to a professional story-teller, who was reciting poems to his audience, with violent gesticulations. My horse shied violently at him, and nearly precipitated himself and his mistress into the deep, empty moat surrounding the city; and when we had recovered ourselves Nasrullah Khan drew a moral by telling me that most Persians, especially ladies, make a point of giving alms to the first beggar they meet when riding out. This pious deed ensures them against accident, and even if they nearly come to grief they feel that their almsgiving has enabled them to escape all evil consequences. We had much trouble in finding the ruined city of which we were in quest, as all that remained of it was a bit of mud wall and the ruins of a house with the long, narrow Arabic arch, dating probably from the first century of the *Hejreh*. It seemed a queer site for a town, among all these sand-heaps, ribbed and furrowed with the wind and perpetually shifting their position; but amid the desolation a chain of villages was dotted across the plain, and we rested in the garden of one of them, a sort of fruit-orchard with a stream running through it, and drank tea with the fine Jupa Range rising in front of us. Then we rode home through part of the ruins of old Kerman, wandering along the narrow, deserted streets and admiring the pretty honey-comb patterned arches of doors and window-frames, while long rays of the setting sun gilded the ruins of Ardeshir's fortress, lighting up fragments of masonry and giving them the weird effect seen in pictures of those great granite figures which eternally gaze across the Egyptian desert.

Here and there in the mountain range east of us were several caves, and we explored these in due course. The most interesting was a very large one, half-way up the side of the hill, which we visited, furnished with candles, and ferreted about in its recesses.

M. de Rakovszky was convinced that prehistoric *Troglodytes* had inhabited it, and pointed out the traces of prehistoric smoke on its roof. In one part was a large mass of boulders, and among these we hunted for the prehistoric bones and arrow-heads which we made no doubt were lying hidden there. Our guest was anxious that we should set men to work to dig up the floor, hard as concrete, but we so infinitely preferred *reflet* to relics of cave-dwellers that we never followed his suggestion.

During our stay at Kerman curios were brought to us for sale from time to time, and we purchased several great pottery jars, also various low, square pottery spice-boxes divided into partitions for different condiments and having lids, and a queer hollowed stone used by the *Gabres* for pouring water over the feet of the deceased. It is somewhat difficult to buy in Persia, as the seller invariably puts an extortionate price on his wares, and will never conclude a bargain outright, but wastes much time, which certainly is of no value to him, by coming daily to reduce his demands, until he finally descends to the sum offered by the purchaser at the commencement.

This account of Kerman would be incomplete without mentioning its carpets, felts, and shawls, which are famous throughout Asia.

The felts, or *numads*, are made of wool with pretty coloured designs on buff or brown grounds, and the shawls, resembling those of Cashmere, are in great request for *khelats*, or robes of honour, which are given by the Shah or by men of high rank to those to whom they wish to show signal favour. They are also made into inner coats, and worn by most Persians of position.

The Kerman carpets are of wonderfully fine texture, having the pattern clearly indicated on the reverse side, and are coloured with exquisite vegetable dyes. Like most Oriental carpets, they become handsomer after years of use, their colours blending into a mellow richness and subdued brightness. As a rule they are only made in small sizes, unless specially ordered, and are by no means cheap. We paid £8 for several of our carpets, not much larger than rugs, that being the cost price in Kerman. Birds, beasts, and even human figures are introduced into these carpets, and as this is entirely contrary to the tenets of Mohammedanism, it shows that the Kerman patterns are of great antiquity, and are prior to the Arab invasion of Persia.

A quantity of carpets are made by the *Ilyats*, or nomad tribes in the province of Kerman. These are all of coarse texture, and usually the pattern is the favourite *shawl* one on a dark indigo ground.

Unfortunately, the modern Persian affects designs which to the European eye are utterly devoid of taste. One Kerman acquaintance showed me with much pride his choicest carpet, which reminded me of a nursery wall-paper. It was many feet in extent, and was adorned with a series of designs, such as an English dairymaid milking a cow, a soldier embracing his ladylove, a group of Indians in front of their wigwam, and so on, each picture repeated three times, the colours being of the crudest.

Naturally I could not live in a Mohammedan country without becoming interested in its religion, and as previous to my stay in Persia my ideas of Mohammed had been of the haziest, perhaps some of my readers are in the same condition, and may welcome a few facts about the rise of Islamism.

Mohammed was born at Mecca A.D. 570, of noble but impoverished Arab parents, and when he grew up became camel-driver to the rich widow Khadija, whom he afterwards married. At this time his country was steeped in the grossest idolatry, infanticide, and many corrupt practices being rife. It was not until his fortieth year that the Prophet began to preach his mission, and for twelve long years, amid persecution and insult, he never faltered in proclaiming that there was but one God, and that the countless idols worshipped by his fellow-countrymen were but senseless blocks of wood or stone. Mecca, his native city, persisted in rejecting him, and in A.D. 622 he and his adherents fled to Medina, where he was received with unbounded enthusiasm. This flight of the Prophet, known as the *Hejreh* (from which the Mohammedan world counts its years, as we do from Christ's birth) marked the turning-point in his career. Eight years later he returned as a conqueror to Mecca, and henceforth war became a religious act, the followers of Mohammed feeling that their mission was to convert the world by means of the sword; the fruits of this doctrine being that at the present day one-sixth of the whole human race is Mussulman.

"Islamism" means "submission to the will of God," and rules to guide the Faithful were laid down in the Koran (the book), which consists of a series of revelations supposed to be made to the Prophet, chiefly by the Angel Gabriel. The four principal rules are—prayer five times daily, almsgiving, fasting, and the going on pilgrimages. With all his faults, Mohammed was one of the greatest of religious, moral, and political reformers, and although Islamism cannot be mentioned in the same breath with Christianity, yet it is eminently suited to the East. As a writer has observed, "It is the religion of the shepherd and the nomad, of the burning desert and the boundless steppe," and it appears to be able to lay hold of and elevate savage races which Christianity seems powerless to touch.

In Persia, however, it has grafted itself upon a light-hearted, irreligious race, which sets at nought many of the observances enjoined by the Koran, and are moreover *Shiahs*.

The Mohammedan world is divided into the two great sects of the *Sunnis* and the *Shiahs*. The former are the orthodox, and consider that the first four *Khalifs*, who succeeded the Prophet, were not greatly inferior to him. The latter, on the other hand, hold that Abu Bakr, Omar and Othmar, the first three *Khalifs*, were all usurpers, and that only Ali and the eleven *Imams* succeeding him were the true rulers of Islam after the Prophet. The *Shiahs*, who are confined to Persia, consider Ali as almost divine, execrate Omar, the conqueror of Persia, and often ignore the pilgrimage to Mecca, turning their steps instead to Ali's shrine at Kufa or to that of his son Hussein at Kerbelah; and the Persian Passion Play, performed yearly to commemorate Hussein's martyrdom, further widens the gulf between *Shiah* and *Sunni*.

CHAPTER IX

OLLA PODRIDA

AS I have mentioned in a previous chapter, we reached Kerman ten days after *Noruz*, the Persian New Year, which falls on March 21st. This day is always kept as a great festival, with much feasting, presents being exchanged and tables spread with lighted candles, springing barley, and every kind of fruit, cake, or sweetmeat, as the sun passes into the sign of the Ram; and the servants are not left out of the general rejoicing, every man receiving either a month's wages or a suit of new clothes. This is the day for calls of ceremony on the Prince or Governor of the town, and at Tehran the Shah sits in state on the famous peacock throne, and holds a reception for the diplomatic corps and his loyal subjects, thus copying Cyrus the Great and the Achæmenian kings, while the horse-races, so fruitful in excitement, take place.

Nasrullah Khan was most anxious to arrive at our destination before the New Year, as Persians believe that if they are on a journey on this particular day they will be obliged to travel throughout the following twelve months; but he was unable to do so.

The first thirteen days of the year are kept by the people more or less as a holiday, and on the thirteenth day every one must keep out of doors, as some trouble or accident will surely befall them if they stay in the house. By spending the whole day in the open air the evil influence will be kept entirely away from their homes, and Persians employ the time between sunrise and sunset in swinging, beating drums, and singing their peculiarly monotonous songs.

It was quite a sight to see the hundreds of white-shrouded women sitting in great crowds near the old fortresses, entirely separate from the men in their gaily coloured garments; our usually deserted part of the town, the *Baghistan*, or Garden District, assuming a most festive appearance.

From inquiry I found that the holidays during the year were legion, and they soon became impressed on my mind, because on every *Eed* the bazaars were all closed, and I invariably needed something that Fakir Mahomet should have remembered to have purchased on the previous day.

About this time my brother and I began to make a collection of insects. A friend, an entomologist, had set me up with a net and lethal bottle, and our daily walks in the garden became full of interest. There were many different species of butterflies, most however, being similar to the ordinary English sorts: great, black, burnished carpenter bees boomed about, and grasshoppers of all kinds fell an easy prey, together with many varieties of wasps.

During the month of May the vetch, which grew in patches on the Kerman plain, was thickly covered with handsome scarlet and black and orange and black capricorn beetles, and great, flat-bodied black beetles, resembling those living in the mud walls of the houses. Rust-coloured and black lice, and the curious little ant-eaters were in thousands on the sandy soil, these latter burrowing holes, at the bottom of which they lurked concealed to devour the ants that slid down the pit and into their jaws.

Bright yellow locusts made short, swift flights, but had appeared too late to damage the crops, which were nearly all ripe. They afforded us some fine chases on horseback, my brother wielding the net, and the servants and I doing our best to head the whirring creatures, which were by no means easy to capture. Another kind were coloured a delicate green, resembling the young crops, had filigree-like wings and huge mouths out of all proportion to their size.

My greatest find was a large tarantula. I was beetle-hunting in the desert, when a big yellow and scarlet object appeared from under a patch of vetch. For an instant I thought it was a frog; but a glance at its hairy legs, big eyes, and beak-like mouth undeceived me, and I began my hunt with considerable trepidation, Nasrullah Khan helping me to get the loudly hissing spider into my net. Then came the unnerving operation of securing it safely in the lethal bottle, the mouth of which was sadly small for such big game, and the triumphant moment when I corked down the fiercest and most active insect I had ever come across. Once inside it speedily collapsed from the fumes of the naphthaline, and when I examined it at leisure I found that its head and body measured three inches. The Governor's doctor calling next day said that he did not think its bite was so venomous as the Persians say, because a cat belonging to him had once been bitten by a very large tarantula and had recovered after suffering from a sort of paralysis for twenty days, during which she was perpetually shivering. He affirmed that they could leap considerable distances if disturbed, and had been known to attack men in this way. However, this assertion did not prevent me from applying the proverbial grain of salt to Nasrullah Khan's Munchausen-like story of how one of his acquaintances, when out riding, had been pursued so closely by a tarantula that he had been forced to gallop hard to escape from it!

Very large hornets with cinnamon and yellow banded bodies abounded during the spring, but appeared to be remarkably good-natured insects. It was rather alarming at first when they came booming into the room, blundering all round, and coming with quite a bang against one's head or cheek; but although they flew about in numbers, I never heard of any one being hurt by their formidable stings.

There were wasps of all sorts and species, the prettiest being a beautiful lemon-colour, and which, when flying, had a long pair of back legs hanging gracefully behind it. They were indefatigable in building their mud nests all over the house and verandah, and it was a great amusement to watch these miniature plasterers at work. We were fortunate enough to discover various insects unknown to science, and one small wasp which now bears the name of *Odynerus Chawneri*, in honour of my friend, the entomologist, has the proud distinction of having a special illustration all to itself in a new book on entomology.

I was anxious to get insects that only venture out by night, but all my attempts to do so ended in conspicuous failure.

Under M. de Rakovszky's guidance I prepared a board which I smeared with honey and placed under a tree in the garden one evening with a lighted lantern beside it, but the jackals frustrated my plan by licking up all the honey and breaking the lantern into the bargain. Pieces of wood bedaubed with a kind of glue met with similar treatment, and the only time we caught anything worth having was by putting a lamp against the white façade of the house, and being on the alert with the net to capture the moths that flew against it.

We could have had quite a menagerie of pets that spring if we had taken only a tenth of all the birds and beasts brought to us for sale. I was greatly tempted to purchase the dearest baby gazelle, but refrained, as it was unfortunately afflicted with mange and a bad cough, I found no difficulty, however, in resisting another denizen of the plain in the shape of a great porcupine, which a couple of men led by a rope, and which rattled its quills in its ungainly movements. Of course all kinds of young birds were pressed upon me. Tiny swallows which had fallen from their nests in our courtyard, which I returned at once to their homes; beautiful little nightjars, and one very small orange-eyed owl, which attracted me more than all the rest. I had, however, to decline it, as Nasrullah Khan assured me that the whole household would be in a state of panic if I kept it, considering that I should be bringing an evil thing into the place, and that ill-luck would take up a permanent abode at the Consulate if I granted it admittance.

We were quite besieged with swallows that spring. I could not keep them out of the sitting-rooms, where they perched upon the beams supporting the ceilings, and twittered away so prettily all day long, building their nests in the dining-room and office, while two or three invariably insisted in passing the night with me. The Persians consider that they bring good luck, and put up little perches for them, to induce them to frequent their houses. The water-wagtail, the *sparrow water-carrier* as Persians call it, flirted round our tank, doing nothing with a great air of industry, while the occasional call of the cuckoo took us back to the green fields and hedgerows of old England; and out on the wide Kerman plain we came across the plover, or *kaka Yusuf* (brother of Joseph), so named from its wild cry.

Our garden seemed filled with handsome young magpies, which spent the greater part of the day in squabbling. Akbar caught a delightfully bold and friendly bird, which hopped about all over the house. He gave the poor thing a dose of opium one day, telling Nasrullah Khan, who noticed it staggering about, mortally sick and dizzy, that if once it took to opium it would never want to leave the place. This pleasing fiction was, however, disproved, as before very long the magpie deserted us and rejoined its mates.

Bats flitted about in the evenings, reminding us of the Persian legend that once a lump of clay in the form of a mouse was brought to Christ, Who was asked whether He could endow it with life and the power of flight, and a bat was the result. The small owls had a peculiarly plaintive cry, but a huge one, that haunted our terraces, indulged in a most lugubrious shrieking, so exactly like a dog in pain that it was some time before I could grasp the fact that it was a bird, not an animal, that produced those weird yells and moans.

It was curious to hear the dogs in the town answer the howling of the jackals, night after night, with furious barking.

The Persians have a story that once the dogs were the outsiders, while the jackals enjoyed life in the towns. The former animals, however, cunningly pretended illness, and persuaded the guileless jackals to exchange places with them until they recovered. This was agreed to, on condition that the change should only be of three days' duration, and at the end of that time the jackals returned, and inquired whether their canine friends were convalescent; but they received for answer a vigorous "No, no!" the dishonest dogs never having had the slightest intention of quitting the comfortable town life for the cold and slow starvation of the country. Hence it comes that the dishoused jackals vainly ask the same question every evening at dusk, coming round the city walls, to get the same answer from their deceivers!

And at night as we sat on the terraces in the moonlight, we could almost give credence to this tale, as we heard the doleful howls of the packs of jackals, calling one another to the meeting-place agreed upon. One used to sing a sort of scale at irregular intervals, rising higher and higher until he reached a note beyond which his voice would not go. Again and again he would try to manage this note, invariably "breaking" on it in the most comical way, until answered by the yelps of his friends, and off the whole pack would go in a great hurry, their cries, as they receded, sounding exactly like weeping children, and in the distance the notes becoming wails of despair.

I had many nocturnal visits from jackals, owing to the carelessness of our guard, who seldom could manage to close all three of the approaches to our terraces. The first time I was certainly startled, when I was awakened by something prowling round my room, making a loud breathing noise, and in the moonlight saw the rough coat and bushy tail of a jackal. However, I soon got used to such harmless visitors, which disappeared like phantoms at the least sound, and never returned during that night at least.

The Persians have various proverbs about these animals, one of which is: "The jackal dipped himself in blue dye and thought he was the peacock;" and another says, "Only a Mazanderan dog can catch a Mazanderan jackal," the equivalent of our "Set a thief," &c.

The sandflies were a great pest, causing me an intense irritation on arms, wrists, and ankles. These tiny insects are almost invisible, consisting of a pair of minute shadowy wings, and no body to speak of, while, alas, no ordinary mosquito-curtain can keep them out. I used to resort to much stratagem to secure a comparatively quiet night, undressing hurriedly, placing the light at the corner of the room furthest from my bed, and doing my best to slay a few of the dancing, phantom-like sprites, that speedily surrounded my candle. I would then proceed to make an examination of my curtains, and was usually filled with despair, as my enemies were invariably there before me, waiting in readiness on the linen ceiling, and so light were they that it was a matter of the utmost difficulty to kill them.

When the candle was extinguished I would steal furtively to my couch, slip under the curtains, and hope for a good night; but usually I was doomed to disappointment, for hardly had I settled myself to my slumbers when a prick, sharp as a needle, would effectually rouse me, and the torture continued until my foes were sated. The only thing that dispersed these active insects was a through draught, which was impossible of achievement during the hot season. These sandfly bites seemed to be peculiarly poisonous, for evening after evening the old ones swelled up, and caused me fresh irritation that only a paste of carbonate of soda could soothe.

Besides the nightly concert given us by the jackals, the tank in our courtyard supplied us with a "frog symphony,' which I always enjoyed, as it reminded me of the gurglings of those artificial nightingales produced by means of a pipe and a glass of water. This aforesaid tank was a constant worry, as, having no exit, the water had all to be baled out and the receptacle cleaned frequently, as we did not want it to become coated with "frog's clothing," as the Persians call duckweed. The servants were only restrained by forcible measures from washing their persons and all the dirty dishes of the establishment in it, and during April it was swarming with tadpoles, most of these luckily perishing, as their music would probably have become too vociferous to be pleasant.

When we first settled in at Kerman, we were never free from cats. At any time of day we were sure of finding one or another sitting on our beds and cushions, and at night they were especially troublesome, bringing food into the house, where they would devour it with a great crunching, and when "shooed" out would return again after the shortest of intervals. What was even worse, they were in the habit of settling their disputes in our rooms at night, with much spitting and caterwauling, even jumping on our recumbent forms in the heat of argument; and the celebrated remark of the middy might with justice be applied to them, as "manners they had none, and their customs were beastly."

I asked Sultan Sukru one day, to whom all these intruders belonged, and was somewhat taken aback when he solemnly replied, "To God, *Khanum*." My brother waged incessant war upon them with his shot-gun, and after awhile despatched most of them, although one black cat eluded his utmost vigilance for a long time. One of the servants rushed upstairs one evening, and pointed out to my brother a dusky form sitting on the edge of the tank in the courtyard. He had his gun ready in a trice, and fired from the window at his enemy, which, to our great amusement, turned out to be a hot-water can, which was completely riddled by the shot! The Persians got quite alarmed at the many lives apparently possessed by this cat, affirming that it was a spirit, and that, if we did not take care, it would turn into some monstrous shape and annihilate us; and when it too met its fate, they inspected its corpse with a great awe.

Our garden had masses of tumbled-looking pink roses, and it was one of the occupations of the women to nip the heads off to make rose-water, and great fun they had during this operation. One day I came across a group of laughing girls, their ghostly white sheets thrown back, who were surrounding one of their number lying flat on the *takt*, or mud platform, in the garden, and gleefully burying her in the fragrant pink blossoms.

The famous attar of roses is no longer manufactured in Kerman, the reason being that the roses grown in the few gardens round the town are not nearly sufficient to render the distillation of the renowned perfume worth while, if indeed the Kermanis have not lost the secret of the art.

Plenty of rose-water, however, is made, being used by the rich for their ablutions, and by all classes to flavour their sherbets. The process of making it was a very simple one, masses of rose-heads being put into a great iron pot of water, and the vessel heaped round with burning charcoal. A jar filled with cold water was then placed on the flowers, and the perfumed fluid slowly dripped from a tube passed through the cold water into a bottle placed to receive it. Whoever was making this *gulabi* always insisted on drenching our handkerchiefs with the warm liquid, which had a most sickly odour.

In some gardens certain rose-trees grew to a great height, forming a sort of arbour, a mass of pure waxy white or yellow or vivid orange blossoms—a wonderful sight to behold ; and in their mazes the sweet-voiced little *bulbuls* sang at intervals all day long ; while about this time the pistachio-trees were most beautiful, their nuts hanging in pale green bunches, flushed with a brilliant crimson.

Besides roses, we had many of the common flowers one finds in English gardens, such as jessamine, petunias, marigolds, asters, hollyhocks, dahlias, and so on, which fact surprised me, until I learnt from a botanist that most of our garden flowers come from Persia. There were also spikes of a curious white, pink, or purple flower, which is called "the tongue at the back of the neck," Persians saying that this shameless flower put out its tongue at its mother, and was punished in perpetuity by that member being made to grow out behind instead of in front.

One of the nice traits about the Persian upper classes is their intense love of a garden. They have no desire to work in it, to see that it is well weeded or kept in proper order, or to trouble overmuch about what flowers and vegetables, or even crops, their gardener may grow in it. It may be as wild and neglected as it pleases, but it must contain running water, shady trees, and a few mud platforms ; all these are essential. A Persian gentleman is quite content to gather his friends round him in such a place, during the hot summer days, where the grateful shade of the trees, and the plash of the water gliding by are conducive to those long philosophic or religious discussions so beloved of Orientals, while tea and *kalians*, slumber and hours of prayer all play their part in helping the time to slip pleasantly away.

And while I am on the subject of gardens, it may not be amiss to say a few words about the system by which they are watered. As water is perhaps the most valuable property in Persia it is guarded with jealous care, and it is said that it is a more fruitful and fatal cause of bloodshed than anything else. Our house, situated in the midst of several gardens, was supplied by an underground stream from the hills, and this was allowed to be used by the gardens in turn for so many hours at a time. Our landlord had only paid for twelve hours' water once in every ten days, and this was a sadly insufficient supply, as our vegetable and flower-seeds from Sutton testified by withering up as soon as they had appeared above the ground. We had our compensations, however, as the stream, which supplied the quarter, was obliged to pass through our garden on its way to all the others, so that we were never without running water, which, nevertheless, it would have been little short of a crime to use for our plants, although it was allowable to take what we wished for purposes of washing and drinking.

The Persian rainfall is certainly a very scanty one. During our nine months' stay at Kerman I do not think it rained for even a week; but if a system of storing the water which rushes down the hills when the snow melts, were adopted the sterility prevailing in many parts of the country, which is in reality most fertile, would be greatly lessened.

By the middle of May the opium crop, one of the principal products of Kerman, was quite ready. The white petals having fallen off, the big calyx heads were scored four times with a kind of steel comb, the juice that oozed out being collected, dried, and kneaded into small lumps for exportation. During this operation the whole vicinity of the town became so impregnated with the smell of the drug as to make one feel quite sleepy when passing near the fields of poppies; and we were told that the innocent-looking flowers were a curse to the place, many of the women having become confirmed opium-smokers,

NASRULLAH KHAN AND HIS FRIENDS.

and cases among our own servants showing us the fatal power of the drug when abused.

One of our grooms was wasted nearly to a skeleton from this practice, his eyes had a glassy stare, and he was in a dreamy state all day long, quite unfit for his work. Later on he much wanted to accompany us into Baluchistan, but when he heard that no opium was to be purchased in that uncivilised region, he gave up the idea; this resignation on his part, however, being quite unnecessary, as my brother would never have thought of taking such a man on a long, toilsome journey.

The amount of electricity in the air that summer was curious. As I drew the blankets off my bed at night, the profusion of sparks was quite startling, making me wonder whether it were possible for my mosquito curtains to catch fire.

On our tea-table was a silk cloth which was covered with a damask one at tea-time. When the servant cleared away the white cloth we used sometimes by chance to lay our hands on the silk beneath it, and received quite violent electric shocks, the cloth retaining its unpleasant power for some moments; while words fail to describe the crackling of my hair and the long sparks that flew from it when it was brushed and combed.

Towards the end of April Mr. Carless, one of the missionaries from Isfahan, came for a couple of months to Kerman, as he wished to see whether the latter town would prove a good field for missionary enterprise. We felt quite in the world again, being a party of four Europeans, until M. de Rakovszky left, to our regret, at the beginning of May. It was a great thing to have an Englishman with us on the occasion of the Queen's Birthday, and I took unusual pains with our dinner that evening, in order to do as much honour to the event as was possible in Kerman. We gave the servants a big feed of *pillau*, over the distribution of which Nasrullah Khan presided, to see that no unfairness took place. He quoted a Persian proverb to show me the strong feeling that this meal might have power to arouse: "All pains can be forgotten in forty days, but the pain of having been defrauded of food lasts for forty years!"

Mr. Carless had brought a native apothecary with him, and

the garden of his house in the town was always crowded with applicants for medical assistance. He was kind enough to allow two or three of our servants to be treated for an eye complaint, common enough in Persia, and brought on by exposure to the sun; but after going once to be operated upon, they actually preferred bad eyes to the trouble of walking a mile to Mr. Carless's residence; and from remarks they made, we could see that they considered they were doing the apothecary a favour by visiting him.

The Indian *syce*, an absurd coward, who used to sob like a child in anticipation of the pain, was the only one who went regularly, and one day had the impertinence to ask us to praise him for this astounding piece of virtue on his part! My Parsee maid, not to be behindhand, developed a complaint, alarming me greatly, as she took to groaning and moaning all day long, doing no work and sleeping in and out of season. We were informed, however, that her ailment was insignificant and of many years' standing; but despite the intense anguish that to all appearance she was suffering, she could, with difficulty, be induced to take her medicine. She always insisted that either my brother or I should examine it first, and then she required us to look on while she brought water and drank it off in our presence.

Mr. Carless told me of several ways in which Persian doctors prescribe for their patients. On one occasion a poor child was brought to him with an abnormally big head, the parents telling him that it was possessed by a demon, but that the cure recommended by the native doctor had unfortunately failed in its effect. The prescription had been to leave the child for some hours in an open grave, during which time the malignant spirit would either kill or quit its little victim. The parents fed the child well, and it soon fell asleep in its novel cradle, in which condition it was found at the appointed hour, but, strange to say, not a whit the better or the worse for the experiment!

Another child, which had been terribly burnt, was submitted to his inspection, its wounds being smeared all over with soot from the bottom of cooking vessels—a treatment somewhat analagous to that of "the hair of the dog that bit you." A pearl ground up is considered to be a powerful restorative, when the patient is apparently at the point of death, and powdered emeralds and rubies are supposed to give strength; while a Persian afflicted with an epileptic fit is said to be undergoing a beating at the hands of devils. All diseases are classed as hot or cold, moist or dry, the doctors still following Galen and Hippocrates, although Western ideas are gaining ground in all the towns.

Some families possess an infallible remedy for the stings and bites of scorpions and tarantulas, in the shape of certain small stones, which are kept as heirlooms, and handed down from generation to generation as most cherished possessions.

These are believed to be a secretion from the eyes of an unfortunate prince, turned by enchantment into an ibex, which lamented its cruel fate with floods of tears, that hardened as they fell on the barren Persian hills, among which it was condemned to wander.

These antidotes are used in the same way as the celebrated Indian "snake stones," being pressed on to the wounded place, from which they are believed to suck the poison.

The Arabs have a far less agreeable remedy for the sting of a scorpion. The sufferer is laid in a freshly dug grave, and upon him are heaped the garments of seven married and seven unmarried men. If he is unable to survive this suffocating treatment, he is buried forthwith in the grave so considerately prepared beforehand.

Those happy days at Kerman flowed by very uneventfully. Our mornings were spent in working and insect-collecting, while after lunch we took long rides, exploring the country in every direction. M. de Rakovszky was an enthusiastic horseman, and my brother improvised a riding-school in the desert, to which we would all adjourn and go through the manœuvres as practised in the British and Austrian cavalry.

Frequently when Persians came to call, they were swept off with us for a ride, and it was comic to see their wild endeavours to copy my brother's lead. The townsmen, however, were usually inferior horsemen; but the nomad chieftains were very different to these. I remember one day, how a certain Reza Khan, a wild leader among the dwellers in tents, called on my brother, and accompanied us to the tent-pegging course which had been laid out. This chieftain wore a sort of uniform, his blue, full-skirted coat being adorned with brass buttons, and boasting a small piece of gold braid on its collar. When riding, his trousers were for ever rucking up, and his white socks for ever coming down over his boots. I noticed this fact because he was the first Persian I had seen galloping; but, later on, I observed that it was the usual habit of Persians when riding, and gave them a most untidy appearance. His two sons were clad in green and purple silk jackets under their long coats, and his ten followers rode on a medley of wretched horses, mules, and donkeys. They were excessively dirty, ill-dressed fellows, with wild elf-locks flying in the wind, and always kept uncomfortably close behind us, all agog to listen to our conversation. At intervals they would gallop their steeds wildly over the worst bits of stony ground, dashing madly on in front, to show off their paces: one of them came down, horse and rider rolling over together, and both picked themselves up unconcernedly, as if it were a matter of daily occurrence. All were armed with guns, and had a bold, fierce expression, very different to that of the timid towns-folk.

The *Khan* could hardly keep his eyes off me, so impressed was he at the sight of a woman on horseback, as he could not comprehend how I kept on; but his surprise was yet greater when he was informed that our dog, trotting behind us, had a weekly bath! He invited my brother to try a Persian sport. An egg was placed on a tiny mound of sand, and the *Khan* unslung the rifle from his shoulder, and waving it round and round in the air put his spirited pony at full gallop, looping his reins over the high peak of the saddle. He made a feint of aiming at the egg before he reached it; but when he had passed it at full tilt, he stood upright in his stirrups, and turning round in the saddle, fired, and hit it. He was much piqued when my brother followed suit, and crashed an egg to smithereens with a shot-gun; and became very angry with his youngest son, whose horse bolted with him each time he let go the reins. It was a relief when this young gentleman desisted from this sport, as a loaded rifle is a dangerous plaything in inexperienced hands; and it was then proposed that they should try lemon-cutting with a sword. Their indifferent success in this sport somewhat depressed them; but they cheered up considerably during a performance which they gave of throwing the *taghala*. This is a stick heavily loaded at one end, which the rider flourishes in the air, high over his head; then breaks into full gallop, stands up in his stirrups, and bowls the missile in such a way that it leaps several times off the hard ground. Some Persians catch it during these leaps, but it is not part of the game to do so. I never saw much point in this performance, and it was a dangerous one to boot, as many have had their eyes gouged out by the flying missile, and on one occasion, a player, noticing that only one half of his stick lay on the ground, and reining up to see what had become of the other half, found it embedded in his horse's chest!

The amusement I enjoyed most at Kerman was to ride out to some garden to tea. Sometimes we would go to a mountain village, set in the midst of a stony desert, its fertilising stream making it an oasis in the dreary desolation all around. Tea would be spread on a carpet, perhaps in a garden of pomegranates, the scarlet blossoms glowing like flames out of the gloom of the surrounding trees, and the proprietor of the place would bring us a great tray of mulberries, apricots, and the much-esteemed short, fat cucumbers. The children peeping shyly at us, would be offered pieces of cake or biscuits, and the *pourboire* given as we rode off would sometimes draw down a shower of blessings on our heads from its simple recipients, who would prophesy for us every kind of good thing, not only in this, but in the next world. The heat would be over as we rode home in the fresh air, and a sunset which I have no words to describe would give a beautiful finish to the day. Sometimes returning in the dusk, we would come across an odd little company. Several young men would be marching along joyously to the shrill notes of a pipe and the quick rattle of a drum, followed by a crowd of the spectral-looking women in full white garments. Absurd as it may seem, such a sight always reminded me of a Greek procession, and the darkness, hiding possible dirt and ugliness, made the whole thing quite idyllic.

On Thursday evenings the whole population of Kerman would be wandering about the cemeteries, all the shops in the Bazaars being shut, in preparation for Friday, with its weekly bath and worship in the mosque. The beggars were always assembled in full force, demanding alms clamorously, and offering in exchange their prayers for the souls of the departed relatives of the donors; while white-turbaned *mollahs* repaired in a body to sit on the graves, reading chapters of the Koran, at a fixed rate of payment, for the benefit of the deceased. The children of the town were also given sweetmeats on this day for the same purpose.

Persian graveyards are, as a rule, the dreariest and most neglected of places, the monuments invariably falling into ruins. The one at Kerman, however, was better kept, a pretty shrine, with a blue and white tiled dome, rising from amid the flat grave-slabs, made of sun-dried bricks. We often came across a procession wending its way hither, the coffin being carried in a litter. On arrival at the grave the shrouded corpse was lifted out of the coffin and laid in the earth, tiles being placed over it before it was finally covered up and left to its long repose.

Thursday evening has been mentioned as being the time when Persians resort to the cemeteries, but, curiously enough, all evenings in Persia are antedated, the particular evening I have mentioned being always called *Friday* evening, the idea being that it is the eve or vigil of Friday. This habit naturally causes mistakes among Europeans new to the country and its ways; as if, for instance, a Persian be asked to dinner on *Monday* night, he will turn up on *Sunday* instead, to the probable embarrassment of his host.

Our life at Kerman, simple and uneventful as it was, was

one of the most enjoyable that I have ever led, and this was mainly owing to the superb climate of the country. We were on the great Iran Plateau, stretching from the north of Tehran to some marches south of Kerman, and were living at an altitude of 5,600 feet, in such a bracing, exhilarating air that it was a joy merely to be alive.

Morning after morning I woke up to see the golden sunshine pouring into my room and gilding the graceful columns on the terrace outside, and rose with a feeling of overflowing energy, far more than sufficient to cope with the small domestic worries I should in all probability have to encounter during the day. Throughout our entire stay at Kerman neither of us had a touch of illness of any kind, but were invariably in the best of health and spirits.

For my part I was never dull for a moment, throwing myself with the keenest zest into my housekeeping, and finding the Persians surrounding me intensely interesting, in that they afforded endless opportunities for studies in character. The weekly post and our picnics were our amusements, the former taking exactly five weeks to reach us from England. It used to make me laugh when I received letters from friends who pitied me being " in exile " as they imagined, and to whom the fact of my being two hundred miles from my nearest European neighbour seemed quite appalling! They little knew that I was passing through some of the happiest months of my whole existence, although I must confess there are not many women with whom the Persian climate agrees as it did with me. My Tehran friends told a very different tale. Most of the ladies lost both health and nerves; several were subject to constant attacks of fever, and one and all complained of the exceeding dryness of the atmosphere, and longed for the day to come when they could return to Europe; but I revelled in the perpetual sunshine, which I had never before enjoyed to the full, and was absolutely content, with scarcely even the proverbial crumpled rose-leaf to mar my fortunate lot!

CHAPTER X

FOUR VISITORS AND A MAID

WE had only been settled a few days in our new home when we had a visit from the old Sahib Diwan, Governor of the province and grandson of the notorious Ibrahim Khan, by whose instrumentality the Kajar rulers of to-day wrested Persia from the Zend dynasty a century ago.

Having expressed a wish to see me, the Sahib Diwan came dressed in plain clothes, as he was told that to appear in uniform would be to change his call into an official visit at which I could not be present.

He arrived about half-past three, but long before that hour the servants were in a state of much excitement over their preparations for afternoon tea, bustling about in a purposeless way, and flourishing the white cotton gloves of which they were inordinately proud, and which were only produced on great occasions such as the present. The white tea, to which Persians are so much addicted, was seething in the teapot above the burning charcoal of the *samovar*, the sherbet was ready with a large assortment of cakes, sweets, and biscuits, and Hashim was fingering everything to give the cakes a more appetising appearance, when a carriage drove to the entrance of the courtyard, and in a few moments the great man himself had panted up the steep steps leading to our sitting-room. He was nearly eighty years of age, with scanty beard and moustache, well-cut nose, and bright, intelligent eyes, and was clad in a long-sleeved tunic of pale blue silk, over which he wore a coat of fine cream cloth, and on top of all a big lemon-coloured mantle lined with scarlet. The orthodox *kolah* of black lamb's-wool completed his costume, and he entered leaning on a stick, the handle of which was thickly studded with turquoises.

After we had shaken hands, I thanked him in my best Persian for a present of sherbets which he had sent me that morning, and he chatted volubly as he tasted our European delicacies, took snuff, and smoked several *kalians*, one of his own being quite a work of art in ebony and gold. He announced his intention of giving me some specimens of the rare Jiruft partridges, which accordingly arrived some days later, but were so wild that they resisted all my efforts to tame them, and finally were sent to our Zoological Gardens, undergoing the long voyage remarkably well, and rearing a flourishing little family before they reached their destination.

The Sahib Diwan did not stay long at Kerman, for an intrigue at Tehran ousted him from his Governorship towards the end of April. When my brother paid him a farewell visit, just before his departure, there was a sad change in his establishment, as in place of the busy throng of servants and parasites, who were wont to surround him, only two or three of his personal domestics were now to be seen.

The system of government in Persia is that the Shah farms out the different parts of his kingdom for so many thousand *tomans* (about 4s.) a year to the highest bidder. This arrangement always takes place at *Noruz*. The Governor then proceeds to his province, and recoups himself doubly or trebly for his outlay, collecting the money as fast as he can, for next *Noruz* will not be long in coming, and he may then be turned out, or at all events have to give the Shah a much larger sum to enable him to continue in office.

Sorry as we were for the Sahib Diwan, who had been hardly a month in power, yet we could not but be glad at his departure, for we heard that the Farman Farma, my brother's old friend, had been appointed Governor in his place, and as this prince was a man of enlightened views, with a civilised

French-speaking suite, we looked forward to having quite a pleasant society at Kerman.

Not many days after this my first lady visitor arrived, attended by a hideous old Abyssinian negress. Both women were completely hidden from view by large black silk *chaddars* edged with gold gimp, long pieces of white silk hanging over their faces, with small oblongs of lacework in front of their eyes, the whole arrangements kept in place by being fastened at the back of their heads by clasps. When her outer wrap was slipped off the mistress disclosed an emerald-green velvet jacket trimmed with bands of vivid purple, sky-blue silk gloves embroidered with red roses completing a curious discord in colours, while her head-dress was a piece of stiff book-muslin, fastened under the chin and flowing behind, giving a nun-like look strangely at variance with the rest of the toilette. It was a warm afternoon, and the *balakhana* windows were open while we drank our tea, which was poured out by Marie, as of course no man-servant might enter the room while my visitor was present. Every now and again the lady would espy one of the labourers in the garden, or some one would come across the courtyard below, and in a second she would envelop herself in her wrap and veil, until the danger, purely imaginary to my eyes, was past. The old negress was far coyer than her mistress, and giggled like the most bashful of schoolgirls, when she disclosed her dusky charms to my feminine gaze.

During her first visit my guest and I exchanged little more than a series of compliments, but later on in our acquaintance she confided her wrongs to me. Her husband had taken a second wife, and, entirely contrary to Persian etiquette, both ladies inhabited the same house, had the same servants, and lived in common. Such a state of things was unbearable, as my friend bitterly complained to me. She, the chief wife and mother of his children, was put second to a woman, her inferior in social position, and whose son by another husband was made much of.

She was always eager to hear about my life in England, but I fear that my accounts only made her lot the gloomier and she said frequently that she could never understand why I came to Persia, when I could live in such a well-regulated country as the one I had described to her.

She amused me by invariably taking with her at the close of each visit specimens of all the biscuits, dried fruits, and sweets that were laid out on the tea-table, as she wished to display them to the second wife, her object being, I believe, to awaken jealousy in the breast of that lady with highly coloured accounts of the "party" she had been to, which accounts the European food would bear out in some degree.

One of our most constant visitors was old Haji Muhammed Khan, son of the famous Vakil-i-Mulk, once Governor of Kerman. Before the Crimean War he had spent several years in Paris, and always looked back with regret to that halcyon period of his life. He was most pompous in manner, insisting in calling my brother "*Votre Excellence*," in spite of our remonstrances, and once asked me where the fleet lay of which my brother was the admiral, as he knew already that he was a general in the army, and evidently had an idea that these high appointments went in pairs!

In a certain book on Persia, the writer of which visited Kerman, a paragraph was devoted to our friend, in which he was stigmatised as an intolerable bore, officious, inquisitive, impertinent, and what not besides. One day I could not resist the temptation of asking Haji Khan if he remembered the author of the book in question. "Remember him!" he cried enthusiastically; "he is one of my dearest friends. He writes to me constantly, and has sent me his photo just lately!" I did not give the credence to this that I might perhaps have done if Haji Khan had not already regaled us with anecdotes of his long-gone-by visit to London, and of the affable way in which he had been received by the Prince of Wales. He affirmed that his Royal Highness pressed the Order of the Garter upon him, which the Persian, from no ostensible reason, politely but firmly declined, and later on in our acquaintance with him he would relate that it was the Queen herself who was so anxious to enrol him as a member of that distinguished order.

Our old friend used generally to bring an orange with him, which he would present to me as if offering a bouquet, with much ceremony, and he invariably inquired as to the age of the Queen, and the progress of the war between China and Japan, putting the latter question regularly long after we had assured him that the whole thing was over.

In spite of all refusals, he was most anxious to press the society of his wife and daughters upon me, offering frequently to send them on a three or four days' visit to the Consulate, and apparently quite callous as to the risks they would run in a house where there was no *anderoon*, or women's apartments.

Another of our visitors told us his family history one afternoon, no uncommon one some half a century ago in Persia.

His grandfather, a rich man, left at his death a large sum of money to the father of our friend. News of this was brought to the predecessor of the reigning Shah, who promptly sent a body of soldiers to extort it from the heir, who was from home at the time. The men ransacked the house, turning the women out of doors, two of whom died from the cold and starvation consequent on their exposure during the winter, and carried off everything, even to the doors of the rooms. The unfortunate heir was imprisoned for two years, and on his release the Shah graciously gave him back his dismantled dwelling, saying, "We are not savages, that we should take everything from you."

The man returned to his home a beggar, no one dared greet or speak to him, and in his despair he was on the verge of committing suicide when his eye was caught by an old wooden chest, the single piece of furniture left in the pillaged house. He remembered having hidden ten thousand gold pieces in this same chest, which contained the shrouds of his family kept there in readiness for their obsequies; but he could hardly summon up courage to lift the lid, so fearful was he lest this last gleam of hope should be extinguished. Marvellous to relate, however, the money was there, the piety of the captain of the soldiers having prevented the

BARGI.

shrouds from being disturbed. But the troubles of this sorely tried man were by no means ended. He had wealth, but it would have remained with him for barely a day if he had dared to display it. Therefore he was obliged to resort to the stratagem of battering one of his coins till the inscription was obliterated, and then selling it for less than half its value to a Jew, telling him that he had dug it up by chance. And so for years he was forced to live like a beggar, keeping no servant, and disposing of his coins one by one to buy the commonest food. His dead father had left him many villages; but the soldiers had taken the title-deeds of these properties and had sold them. In Persia, however, it is considered a sin to usurp land in this way, so little by little the heir was enabled to get back his lost papers, paying for them and conducting the transactions with the utmost secrecy, until the happy day arrived when his friends were able to intercede for him with the Shah, and by means of their efforts he was once more free to enjoy his own again.

As Marie, the Swiss maid I had brought out with me, proved entirely unsuited to a life of travel, we took the opportunity of sending her to Karachi under the escort of Sultan Sukru, who was anxious to visit his relatives in India after his long absence, and I engaged one of the despised *Gabres*, or Fire-worshippers, to wait upon me in her place. *Bargi*, as I called her (a Turkish word meaning sister, and always used by Europeans when addressing their maids), was a pretty little woman, and toddled about in baggy white trousers, a gay chintz jacket, and a long white cotton veil draping the back of her head and hanging gracefully behind; while several checked cotton handkerchiefs were tied round her face. She kept herself and my rooms spotlessly clean, and was most anxious to be instructed in all the mysterious ways of the Feringhees; but was very nervous at first, brushing my hair with little trembling pats, and using the comb with a ferocious energy, which forced me to remind her that she was not operating on a mule. By degrees her rudimentary sewing became quite a work of art, although she always stitched backwards;

and she was abel to make up my summer cottons, which Marie's departure had left "in the piece"; but she never had the patience to master the art of darning, and would patch the stockings in a most remarkable manner if left to herself. *Bargi* was a widow with two children, and these facts made her consider herself entitled to indulge in a peculiarly whining tone of voice. She informed me that throughout her life she had "eaten sorrow," but when she mentioned that her late husband had ill-treated her, and then demanded sympathy from me on account of his death, I told her plainly that her apparent desolation was a cause for rejoicing. Persians consider a lachrymose address a great attraction in a woman, it being "genteel"; but we, however, did not appreciate it, and when we used to hear her grumbling about everything, complaining that the food we gave her was *khaili karab* (very bad) and so on, we used to send a servant to request her to remove at least a mile off if she wished to persist in her lamentations, and this request very soon cured her and in a short time she settled down comfortably into her niche, and I could not have had a brighter and more willing handmaid. She became very fond of her mistress, and was of such a marvellous honesty that after awhile I trusted her entirely with my belongings, and never once had cause to regret the confidence I placed in her; and certainly she was an example of the Persian saying, "Man is a slave to his benefactor." Curiously enough she would never own to being over twenty years of age, though her son was aged twelve, and her daughter eight. At first I had more than enough of *Bargi's* children, as they and flocks of lady visitors used to come to see my handmaid in her new surroundings, and I objected strongly to their wandering on the terraces at all hours, gazing at me with the half-reverent wonder that they would have accorded to an idol in a shrine, and bringing me offerings of oranges, cucumbers, and roses. But I found when I put a stop to these visits that *Bargi* would descend to her friends in the garden and would have sat chatting with them all day long, if I had not sharply remonstrated with her. The great function of the week to her was her departure to her bath every Monday, this being her "day out," as her ablutions seemed unable to be completed under ten hours. However, it was some distance to the town, and a snail might almost have kept pace with her, so slowly did she progress in her quaint heelless slippers turned up at the toes.

Of religion she had none, as far as I could find out, except a respect for fire, extinguishing a candle or match with her fingers when I ordered her to put them out, as human breath would be a pollution to the sacred element.

After being with me for some time, however, she commenced to blow out candles boldly as I did, looking at me in a scared way at first as if afraid lest some awful retribution should overtake her!

She had some funny superstitions, such as refusing to wash anything on a Tuesday, as she affirmed that it would never get clean. Once or twice I made her wash my hair on this ill-fated day, and she always performed the task with much reluctance and remonstrance, though I fancy that she soon saw that the curse did not cling to Europeans. She used also to tie a little white shell to a pair of scissors I gave her, saying that she was always losing them, but that now she would never have trouble in finding them again. I amused myself occasionally by asking her for them, and then laughing at her when she failed to produce them in spite of that infallible shell.

In common with many Orientals she considered her skin to be of lily whiteness, and was much upset when I presented her with a photo of her brown little self, saying that I had made her black, and that her mother had wept over the insult to her daughter when shown it. For answer I placed one of my hands beside her dark one, but, not to be outdone, she said promptly, "Yes, *Khanum*, you are white because you use that beautiful Feringhee *sabûn*, and henceforth she always begged for scraps of my Pears' soap, which she took when she went to her bath. I wonder if she imagined that she became whiter in consequence, but of course I never dared to make inquiries on a subject which was evidently a tender one with her!

One day she observed that she supposed I was a Mohammedan, as she knew for certain that I was not a Parsee. I rather wondered at her making such a remark, as Mr. Carless during his stay at Kerman gave us a service every Sunday in our sitting-room, and it was *Bargi's* office to keep " Diana " away during the time it lasted, as her behaviour was too demonstrative on these occasions. I felt at the time how much an ardent missionary would blame me for not taking advantage of this opening to make a convert. But even if I had explained the rudiments of our religion to her, she was totally incapable of understanding them, as her brain-power was about equal, if not inferior, to that of Diana. It may be heresy to say it, but it seemed throughout my stay in the East that our religion was one far beyond a race which was really only sufficiently civilised to comprehend and be bound by the rigid fetters of Islamism. The *Gabres* believe in Hormuz, the God of Light, who is in eternal conflict with Ahriman, the power of Darkness. Once in prehistoric ages, the sun-god overcame the evil spirit for a time, but since then he has gained no decisive victory, and the result of the daily fight is still doubtful. His worshippers say themselves that they only worship the sun and fire as being symbols of the vital forces of the earth. The Mohammedans look down upon them because they affirm that they have no " book," subjecting them to various restrictions in the matter of dress and occupation, and not intermarrying with them, while they place Christians, from the fact of their possessing a Bible, on a much higher level.

The Parsee women are unveiled, but have an absurd number of coverings on their heads. First of all is a close-fitting, black silk skull-cap with a gold gimp edging, over which a square white handkerchief is knotted, and then a flowing white drapery, which falls over the back of the head and shoulders. Over this come two checked handkerchiefs, and the long outdoor wrap, six coverings in all—a contrast to the body, which is clad only in the parti-coloured tunic and trousers. A married woman is supposed to hide away her black locks very carefully, and on the rare occasions when I chanced upon Bargi divested of her headgear, she was much shocked that I should see her in such *déshabille*, as she considered it, and would cover her hair up in a terrible hurry. Even at night she would only divest herself of one or two of her many handkerchiefs; but the Parsee children wear half a dozen long plaits, which fall picturesquely below the little white coif that they affect.

Contrary to the Persians, they have no prejudice against dogs, and *Bargi* was quite devoted to "Diana," although on one occasion she was much upset when the latter stole some of her food. She rushed round the courtyard weeping and lamenting, and finding the servants unsympathetic, cried out that neither they nor the dog were her friends. This remark caused quite an uproar in our establishment, our whole staff rushing in a body to Nasrullah Khan to complain that *Bargi* had dared to put them on a level with the unclean animal.

The *Gabres* are careful not to pollute earth, air, fire, or water; hence their peculiar mode of burial. They never smoke, as such an act would profane the sacred fire that they worship, and their priests wear veils over their mouths while officiating, so as not to pollute the holy flame with their breath. This fire, burning brightly on a tripod, is never suffered to go out, and when a little colony of Parsees wish to start a temple of their own they procure the object of their worship from Yezd, where it has burnt unextinguished for centuries.

The men wear a belt tied in a peculiar knot, the three cords of which it is composed being symbolic of the good thoughts, good words, and good deeds which are the basis of their religion, and they refasten this girdle five times daily at their hours of prayer.

Centuries of oppression seem powerless to really degrade this race, and the very Persians who consider their touch a defilement give them the highest character for honesty. They say, with a refreshing candour, that a *Gabre* will never steal, because he has "lost heart" to do anything of a risky nature, putting down to fear the practice of a virtue almost unknown to themselves.

CHAPTER XI

OUR STAY IN THE HILLS

BY the end of May the heat and insects were sufficiently unpleasant, but both became quite intolerable during June, and a temperature of 90° in the house, hot, airless nights, and the worry of legions of flies made us begin to think seriously of seeking cooler quarters.

However, it was no light undertaking to leave our home as, owing to the total absence of locks on any of the doors, and a want of confidence in the honesty of the *ferashes*, who were left in charge of our premises, we were compelled to dismantle the entire house. There were boxes of stores to be packed, camp equipment to be examined, and the usual difficulty about transport presented itself, while the helplessness of our Persian servants made personal supervision of every detail indispensable. To add to my worries *Bargi* pestered me at frequent intervals for advice as to the toilettes she should take with her, and I do not know how we should have been able to make a start if it had not been for the unfailing energy and activity of my willing ally the *syce*.

We were awakened on the day of our departure at an early hour by our servants, who presented a somewhat curious appearance. The ordinary felt skull-caps and *givas* of every-day use were replaced by big flapping hats and top-boots, while one and all carried murderous-looking knives in their belts, and were provided with blue goggles and *aftabgurdans*, or shades for their eyes. They evidently regarded our departure with much approval, and were in high spirits, looking forward, no doubt, to the *jira* (journey-money) of a *kran* a day, which it is customary in Persia to allow servants when travelling. "Much travel is needed to ripen a man's rawness" is a well-known Persian proverb, which is further amplified by the saying, "The man who has seen most of the world is the greatest liar."

Bargi had apparently become a person of some importance among her co-religionists in Kerman, for shortly before the caravan started we descried a long line of Parsee women approaching her through the garden, looking curiously nun-like in their sombre *chaddars* as they shuffled silently in her direction with offerings of cucumbers. Gravely taking them, she presented one to me with the same solemnity of manner which had so impressed me when, on the occasion of entering my service, she had begged my acceptance of a wizened little orange.

The office of treasurer on this tour devolved on me, and, as neither gold nor notes were in circulation at Kerman, I was compelled to take all the money we needed in one or two-*kran* pieces. The *kran* is a silver coin worth fourpence halfpenny, rather larger than our sixpence, and considerably thicker, while the two-*kran* piece is somewhat smaller than an English florin.

Our caravan started for the village of Ismailabad at ten o'clock, and we followed in the afternoon, our road lying over a sterile desert, crossed at intervals by chains of high sand-dunes, which were constantly being shifted by the wind.

A fifteen-mile ride brought us to our destination, and trotting up an avenue of fine plane-trees, we were received by the village dignitaries, who escorted us to the large garden belonging to my brother's friend, the son of the Vakil-i-Mulk. We strolled among the vines and pomegranates till dinner, and mounting to the roof of a little pavilion, styled the *Kolah Feringhee* (English hat, from a fanciful resemblance to that article), we stood for some time admiring the beautiful effect produced by the sun setting on the Jupa Range, to which the long avenues of cypresses and plane-trees, with brightly coloured orioles and blue jays flitting among them, formed a charming foreground.

We left Ismailabad the following afternoon, and as we issued from the gateway we found a large crowd of Parsee women assembled to speed us on our way, and to avert the evil eye from our path. Their manner of compassing this latter was somewhat novel to me. On a large brass tray a mirror and some burning scented herb had been placed, and as we were about to mount, one of the women advanced and held the tray towards us, thus securing us from all danger on the road.

We were now over a thousand feet higher than Kerman, and felt our spirits rise at having left the heat behind us; but when we reached the small courtyard where we were to pass the night I was surprised not to see "Di," who had preceded us with the caravan, rushing out to greet me, and on hurrying inside to discover what could be the matter I found her lying strangely stiff and still in a corner, and the sad truth flashed upon me that she must be dead, all our efforts to revive her being in vain. The servants declared that she had been carried the whole way, and had been fed, but that directly on arrival she lay down, apparently very tired, and, to their surprise, died. I felt bitterly that if we had reached our destination even half an hour earlier my poor dog's life might have been saved, and I could not bear to think of her dying all alone without a friend near her. We fancied that she might have been stung by a snake, but whatever it was, I lost a most faithful and loving companion, and it took me many a long day to get over her death.

On going to bed that night I found on the wall of my room, which looked as if it had not been swept for years, a large yellow scorpion. My conscience reproved me for not capturing it, but as my net and lethal bottle were packed up, the fear that it might escape while I was getting them, and visit me during the night conquered my passion for collecting, and I hastily called my brother, who demolished it with a boot.

We had now left the fine Jupa Range behind us, and were making our way towards the snowy Lalazar Mountains, while to our left the pyramid-like peak of Kuh-i-Hazar was the great feature of the landscape, as it sprang up to the imposing height of 14,000 feet. We had exchanged the plains for the hill country, and the scenery was daily becoming more beautiful.

On one of our marches we passed through a deep gorge, on both sides of which shale cliffs rose magnificently, their base washed by a rippling stream bordered with tamarisk and sweetbriar, and we lay under the willows and drank glass after glass of the delicious water, watching the delicate, blue dragon-flies skim over the rivulet, before we climbed to the top of the gorge and crossed a pass in the hills vivid with most brilliant colours.

Travelling seemed to agree with the horses, who became livelier and stronger day by day. When "Cotmore," the *waler*, my brother's mount, and my Arab "Nawab" were not on duty they accompanied the caravan. On such occasions they were not led, but trotted in the rear, cropping the scanty herbage where it could be found, an imperative *beá* (come) from the grooms being sufficient to bring them up if they lagged behind. My brother used occasionally, when it was "Cotmore's" turn to be ridden, to dismount and walk, the sagacious horse following him, halting if told to do so, and standing quite still until called to come on. On approaching the camp my brother would often say, "Go to your *syce*," whereupon the intelligent creature would trot off slowly to find his friend, neighing to apprise him of his arrival. Sometimes when lunching on the march "Cotmore" and "Nawab" would stand over us as we sat on our carpet, and eat bits from our fingers, behaving with the utmost propriety, their hoofs never infringing on our domain, eager for food though they were.

On June 18th we reached the large village of Lalazar (place of tulips) entirely hidden from view by groves of tall poplars, and we camped outside on great mud platforms, specially erected for that purpose, close to a stream, by a former Governor of Kerman.

It was an ideal halting-place, as the village was situated in a long, grassy valley resplendent with flowers. The air was scented with the perfume of sweetbriar and peppermint, an odd combination; the *euphorbiaceæ* grew in sheets of vivid yellow, varied with pink patches of lousewort, while the lavender, sage, camomile, daisy, celandine, and a little convolvulus were in full bloom with many another flower. This charming spot was unfortunately too distant from the hills, where my brother hoped to have some sport, and he left at daybreak next morning in search of a good camping ground, sending the *syce* back about ten o'clock with a message to say that he had found a suitable place, and that I was to follow as soon as possible.

From the day on which we left Kerman there had been a certain amount of friction between our servants and the muleteers, which was caused by the indescribable laziness of the former, who, not content with declining to afford any assistance in the loading up of our personal baggage, invariably forced the muleteers to undertake the loading of the mules which had been provided for their use. The *katirchis*, not unnaturally, objected, but fearing to make my brother angry, hath hitherto refrained from open revolt. On this particular morning the storm burst, and servants and muleteers rushed at one another in a free fight, and for my part I felt extremely annoyed to think that they were profiting by my brother's absence to pay off old scores. They stopped, however, when I appeared and spoke to them; but the baggage had already been torn from the mules, and the muleteers, throwing themselves on the ground, refused to replace it.

I remonstrated with the head-man, who got up and began to reload; but just as matters were getting quiet Hashim nearly reopened the whole business by striking one of the muleteers, and was so beside himself with rage that it needed all my limited command of the language to restrain him.

As soon as order had been quite restored we set off for the new camp, and found that our road followed up the course of the Lalazar River, crossing and recrossing it, as the hills, running sheer down to the water's edge, rendered further progress impossible, now on the right bank and now on the left, and the river became, as we advanced, a brawling torrent, the mossy banks of which were bespangled with orchises, white clover, primulas, and other small flowers.

The vegetation became scantier and scantier, and we found our tents pitched on a broad slope at the foot of the mountains, which the huntsmen affirmed were well stocked with game. We were at a height of 11,000 feet, and our camp was the solitary dry spot in an extensive morass of boggy turf, our drinking-water being drawn from a tiny stream which trickled from the snow lying in large patches on the bare and mean-looking hills, and had the usual attributes of snow-water, being designated by the Persians as *zangín* (heavy). There was nothing pretty near the camp for me to sketch, and as the innumerable stones, which completely covered the ground, precluded all possibility of riding, the horses were sent back to the village of Lalazar.

My brother was in the habit of starting at daybreak, and often did not return for ten and sometimes twelve hours, and invariably came back completely tired out. I hoped to have accompanied him occasionally on his shooting trips; but I gasped so much and experienced such an odd feeling of suffocation whenever I attempted to go uphill, that I was forced to abandon the idea. The air was evidently too bracing and the height too great for me, and I felt drained of all energy, even the slight exertion of rising in the morning making me pant.

My brother bagged three or four moufflon after a week of hard work, and they made a most welcome addition to our larder, which his friend, Rustem Khan, of Rahbur, supplemented with gifts of cheese, cherries, unripe plums, sour grapes, lambs, and the most delicious honey.

It was a land of thorns, and I always returned from my strolls near the camp with my dress torn and my shoes pierced. They were most deceptive plants, often a mass of pink and mauve blossoms, while one species looked so mossy and comfortable that it seemed made expressly for sitting upon, and was called by the Persians " Turban of the head *mollah*." I can speak from experience of their sharpness, for on slipping once on the hillside I fell right on to one of these cushions, and its bristles remained in my flesh for some days.

Bargi gave some trouble on our arrival in camp. It appeared that she had represented to the head muleteer that she had received neither food nor wages since entering my service, and had so worked upon the man's feelings that he had fed her from the day we left Kerman. Hashim and Shah Sowar, who had discovered this, came in considerable excitement to tell me, saying that probably *Bargi's* behaviour would give the Consulate a bad name in the Bazaar, Persian servants having an intense dread of any adverse report being spread about them or their masters. News was brought meanwhile that the subject under discussion had taken French leave, and was already on her way to distant Kerman, and although I did not believe my informant at first, yet on emerging from my tent I saw *Bargi's* gaily dressed little figure at some distance down the valley. She turned a deaf ear to all shouting, refused to return with one of the muleteers sent after her, and I became seriously alarmed when finally she disappeared from sight. A couple of the servants, mounted on mules, succeeded, however, in restoring my errant handmaid to me, who, on being questioned as to the reason of her escapade, wept like a very Niobe, affirming with vehemence that she had only been taking a little evening stroll, a statement open to considerable doubt. After this she spent her days in washing clothes in the stream, and so much in love was she with this occupation that she paid no attention to the darning and mending I gave her to do, replying with a smile when I reproved her, "*Furdà inshallah*" (To-morrow, please Allah!), or remarking that she was too much busied with the garments of the servants to attend to my work. It needed the threat of fining her on each occasion that she left my tasks undone for theirs to convince her that her mistress had prior claims on her time. At Lalazar I missed my poor "Di" more than ever, as *Bargi* was a most unsatisfactory companion on my walks, her progress, partly owing to her heelless slippers, being of the slowest, so that I soon had to dispense with her services.

On the last night of our stay in camp the *shikarchis* (huntsmen) gave us a display of what they called *atish barzi*, or fireworks, setting light to the abundant scrub on the castellated crest of a hill close to our camp. The scene reminded me of descriptions I had read of the sack of some old baronial stronghold. The sheets of flame shooting up into the darkness, the rolling masses of smoke, and the crowd of silhouetted figures rushing wildly around the keep-like summit, all fostered the illusion, while the air was heavy with the aromatic scent of the burning sage and thyme.

It was with no regret that I left camp next day on a morning so raw and chilly that we sat huddled up in big capes while eating our breakfast, and, at the same time were forced to wear blue spectacles to save our eyes from the strong glare of the sun. Abu, our cook, sported a huge newspaper shade which, sticking out from under his felt skull-cap, gave him a very comic appearance. Like all Persian servants he was keenly sensitive about his looks, and scanned my face narrowly as he placed a dish of eggs on the table. Involuntarily my lips twitched slightly as the queer apparition met my gaze, and in a twinkling the shade was torn off, and Abu turned away so crestfallen that I did my utmost to soothe his ruffled feelings by remarking that such an excellent protection against the sun had better be replaced by another as soon as possible. He followed my advice without loss of time, and I had the satisfaction of seeing him set off on the march with a huger shade than ever flapping over his eyes.

It was during this tour in the hills that Seyid Abu took to doctoring on his own account. He treated one poor woman, who was afflicted with sore eyes, by rubbing some of our boot-blacking upon her inflamed lids, and she presented him with a kid by way of fee for his skilful tendance!

Our horses, which had had a week's holiday with no stint in the commissariat department, were beside themselves with excitement, and my little grey was as one possessed, squealing, trying to attack the strange horses of the *shikarchis*, leaping recklessly down all the bad places, bucking and kicking up. At last, however, his foes were left behind, and we turned up a long valley down which a broad stream dashed over and between great boulders. On the hills the lofty assafœtida was growing some four to six feet in height, its thick stems springing up from the cluster of serrated leaves at its base and terminating in big yellow flower-heads, which I have heard compared to cauliflowers in appearance; the tall spires of mullein were in full bloom, while large bronze dragon-flies darted over the water in myriads. Our new camp was pitched in a bend of the winding defile under clumps of willows, and was a charming spot, shut in on one side by the river and surrounded by picturesque peaks which I did my best to copy with pencil and brush. To reach the road up the valley we had to wade across the stream, which was somewhat of an undertaking as the current was rapid.

We were five hundred feet lower than at our last camp, and I found to my great satisfaction that I could clamber about the huge iron-grey boulders strewing the hills without much fatigue, collecting among them vivid green and yellow spiders, exactly matching the plants on which they lived, and curious leaping black spiders having an appendage much like whiskers. Although our camp was at an altitude of 10,500 feet, yet we were much bothered with flies in our tents, these pertinacious insects never ceasing to tease during the day, and commencing their work of torment at an unconscionably early hour in the morning, while in the evenings we were haunted by small buff tarantulas, which gave alarmingly long jumps when we tried to catch them.

During our stay in this valley we made an expedition to ascend Kuh-i-Shah, one of the highest peaks in Southern Persia, being 13,700 feet in altitude.

As we were able to ride part of the way, the climb was by no means arduous, although we made an early start from our camp, for the road was a difficult one, huge boulders blocking up the track at intervals, rendering it necessary to cross and recross the torrent to avoid them. At one place we were obliged to rush our horses up a veritable wall of rock, a feat that only animals accustomed to the hills could have performed successfully. Two broad snow bridges at the head of the valley had to be traversed, but at that early hour they were hard and firm, although on our return after the heat of the day they became perilously soft, and our horses' hoofs plunged so deeply into them that a speedy descent into the stream below, which flowed out from beneath them, seemed not improbable.

On the top of the snow-clad peak was a primitive shrine, consisting of a circle of rough boulders, a flat stone in the centre being covered with an odd collection of offerings: there were amber and agate beads, glass and copper bangles, various coins (among which lay a Queen Victoria token of 1837), and many scraps of iron and bits of clothing. This shrine was visited in honour of a certain saint called Haider, who was said to cause explosions here during the summer months, the name *Kuh-i-Shah*, meaning Mount of the Saint, the title Shah, in Persia, being applied to a holy man as well as to the sovereign. The view was magnificent, the Jupa and Jamal Bariz ranges, great Kuh-i-Hazar, and many another peak, standing up well defined against a pure, blue sky, the atmosphere being so clear that we enjoyed a mountain panorama some eighty miles in extent. On our return to camp at sunset a wonderful crimson glow shone over everything. The whole sky seemed to be a quivering mauve, fit background for the rosy mountains; while every tree and stone and plant had apparently undergone transformation into something strange and exquisite, the very foam on the swirling stream being dyed red as blood. It was a scene of enchantment such as I have never seen, even in Persia, where the sunsets are so grand, and was an appropriate finale to our stay in the pretty camp by the Lalazar River.

CHAPTER XII

IN THE FOOTPRINTS OF MARCO POLO

WE were now to leave the pleasant hills, with their running streams, twisted willows, and perfumed sweetbriar, and descend to Rahbur, the only village of any importance in this district, situated on a hot plain too stony for riding out of a foot's pace.

Our way lay along a narrow track on the side of a range of hills, an unpleasant road, as it overhung a precipice for the most part, and at specially bad bits we had to dismount and lead our horses. My grey, "Charters," an animal of much character, always picked the best path, and if I tried to force him along one not of his own choosing, he would resolutely refuse to follow me, planting his feet firmly and looking the picture of obstinacy until I gave in to him.

Yet, in spite of all his common sense, he and I nearly came to a bad end on this particular ride. My brother was some distance ahead of me when my horse, starting violently and snorting, declined to proceed, and at a touch from my whip twisted round on the narrow path, and all but slipped over the abyss. His struggles and the long ride had loosened my saddle-girths, and I had some difficulty in getting free of the pommels, which slipped down with my weight. Once dismounted, I dragged my horse back to *terra firma*, and, looking about to see what had alarmed him, espied a dead and malodorous partridge lying not far from us on the track. I managed to reach the bird with my whip and push it over the edge, but "Charters" would not be pacified, and did his best to break from me, trembling violently, and I alarmed

NOMAD WOMEN.

him still more by putting a handful of dust into his mouth, having read somewhere that this was an infallible remedy if a horse were frightened! By this time, however, my brother had come to my rescue, and by dint of much patting and coaxing we got him past the fatal spot, and soon reached our halting-place for the night in a wide valley with a group of black nomad tents at one end.

Meshtedi Medhi, one of the leading merchants of Kerman, who was on a business tour, here made his appearance, and accompanied us for a few days. He was a British subject, being of Indian extraction, and looked quite an imposing figure, his long black robes set off by a snowy beard and moustache, white turban and girdle, while he bestrode a jet-black steed, and held a white umbrella, lined with black, over his head. He conducted us next day to a grove of fine walnut-trees outside Rahbur, where we lunched, chiefly off several kinds of fruit, and inspected the carpet-making done by the nomad women. It was carried on in one of their curious tents, which had a large piece of black felt stretched over a pole to form the roof, three sides being enclosed with a fine twig matting, while the fourth, and a space between the sides and the roof, were left open to facilitate the escape of the smoke of the large fires usually burning in these shelters.

Several rather handsome women were in this tent, unveiled, as is customary among nomads, but covered from head to foot in bright cotton sheets, and wearing a profusion of glass and bead bangles, with strings of silver coins to set off their black hair. They were naturally much interested in the first European woman they had ever seen, and giggled a great deal as they stared at me, evidently picking me well to pieces in their whispered comments to one another. The carpets being woven were, alas, of a hideous European pattern, the familiar one of scarlet roses on a black ground, which may be seen in any cottage parlour in England, and as they were of very fine texture, their manufacture was exceedingly slow. Threads of twine were stretched tightly, close together and several deep, across a frame, and on to these the wool was worked with a steel-toothed comb, two women sitting at each carpet, weaving from the sides and meeting in the middle. They knew the pattern by heart, and every few moments a hank of wool of a fresh colour had to be used, as the design progressed imperceptibly, although the women worked with incredible speed.

The usual *istakbal*, a small body of horsemen in this case, was in readiness to escort us to the tree-embowered village of Rahbur. Mehdi pointed out one of these cavaliers as being deeply in his debt, and related how the man had been near death with fever three or four days ago, and his relatives, thinking that his last hour had come, had turned his feet towards Kerbelah in readiness for his departure. At this crisis Mehdi had arrived, and, seeing with horror that his debtor was apparently slipping from his clutches, he employed his smattering of European doctoring to such good effect that he restored him to life again!

Our quarters were in a tumble-down pavilion in a garden of apricot, cherry, and plum-trees, but I had my tent pitched, as I did not fancy the dark, unplastered rooms, the twig-stuffed ceilings of which appeared to me only too good harbourage for scorpions and tarantulas. I was installed, therefore, under a big walnut-tree, which we were told had been visited by bears the night before in search of the fruit, walnuts being, according to Persians, Bruin's favourite dainty. The fine walnut-trees in this part of the country grow huge excrescences, which are used in Europe for veneering, so beautiful is the grain of the wood; and shortly before our visit an Armenian merchant had penetrated to this remote district to purchase them from the inhabitants.

The wives of one of the principal *Khans* sent a message saying they would like to call upon me, and I was nothing loth to be "*tashrif dared*," or "at home," as I was always much interested in Eastern women and their restricted lives. Hashim did his best to lay out an elegant tea-table, although I had but little variety in the way of cakes and biscuits, and came to me later on to inform me that a great company of ladies and slaves was approaching, and that he was quite sure the room would be too small to hold them all. I confess to having felt a little nervous at this news, but ordered my *pishkidmet* to see that the coast was clear of our men-servants, and, when my guests arrived, was relieved to find that only three ladies appeared with a few children, five women slaves, and two youths—these latter to guard the door of the room and the slippers which their mistresses had left there on entering.

I received the ladies with many a "*khosh amadid*," (you are welcome) and other polite expressions culled from my phrase-book, accepted with effusion their gift of a sour green apple, and ushered them to their seats at the table, while the slaves squatted on the floor, holding the pallid, sickly-looking children in their arms. *Bargi* served out tea in tiny glasses, putting four or five lumps of sugar into each, and helped on the conversation by giving a short biography of her mistress, expatiating largely on my accomplishments of riding and letting off a gun. They drank glass after glass of steaming tea-syrup—all Persians liking to swallow the beverage when almost boiling—and they sampled my European delicacies with much relish.

I thanked them for a present of saddle-bags, made of the famous Rahbur carpet, and had to explain to them that unfortunately the gifts I hoped that they would accept in return were at Kerman, but that I would deliver them over to their husband when he made his next visit to the city to pay his respects to the Farman Farma, who was shortly expected as Governor.

They answered with much politeness that the poor trifles they had brought me were unworthy of further notice, and thereupon produced various engraved seals, which they had knotted up in corners of their handkerchiefs. These were made of agate or cornelian, and were inscribed with Kufic characters, animals, and, in a few cases, with figures, some of them being beautiful little works of art, and all dug up from the ruins of a certain buried city, mentioned by Marco Polo, near which the ladies dwelt during the winter months. My brother, who had visited this place on a previous journey through Persia, had told their husband, the Governor, how much he was interested in curios, and that he would be glad to have anything found among the *débris* of what was once apparently an important town.

So eager did the ladies become, when they saw how much I appreciated the seals, that they insisted on giving me some set as rings, which they were wearing, and even tore off others stitched on to the caps of their children in quite a frenzy of enthusiasm, until I felt ashamed of robbing them in such wholesale fashion, although as a matter of fact their gifts were of no intrinsic value.

The three wives were loaded with bangles, rings, and necklaces, and when they threw back their gaudy cotton sheets they disclosed handsome velvet jackets, and enormously stiffened-out trousers, which did not reach to the knee, well above which coarse white stockings were drawn. During the intervals of conversation they puffed at *kalians*, served to them by the youths at the door, and professed to be much concerned that I did not participate in what to them was evidently an intense pleasure.

The children, who cried a good deal, were given tea and cakes to pacify them, and their respective mothers took them every now and then from the slaves to show them off to me, but got tired very soon of holding their treasures.

As is customary, the slaves entered largely into the conversation, drank tea like their mistresses, but were obviously somewhat suspicious of my eatables, and when I produced a bundle of illustrated papers they crowded round to see the show. This exhibition was a somewhat embarrassing one for me, as whenever, in turning over the leaves, I chanced upon any female figure, they would regard it fixedly, and then stare at me, as if comparing me feature by feature with the picture, and would cover me with confusion by bursting out into a sort of chorus, " She is beautiful, but *you*, you are far lovelier!" As they did this without the least discrimination, it was impossible to feel greatly flattered; but I could not help wondering whether they expected me to pay them compliments in return!

By and by the chief wife began to sigh and groan a good

deal, and I was forced, in very politeness, to ask what was the matter with her. My inquiries having elicited that her ailment was a very simple one, I opened the medicine-chest with much ceremony, and delighted her with a gift of pills. Straightway the third wife started a most curious complaint, affirming that whenever she smelt a flower or a fruit terrible pains would run through her whole body. This remarkable malady was entirely beyond my small skill, and I firmly declined to cope with it, putting away the medicines somewhat hastily as the slaves showed signs of wishing to be doctored for that universal, but somewhat vague complaint entitled *dard-i-dil* (heartache).

I now began to wonder when my guests would take their departure, for the two hours of their visit had completely exhausted all the ideas that I could express in Persian. Conversation was flagging lamentably when *Bargi* appeared, and with her most engaging smile remarked to the assembled company that the *Sahib* was just coming.

This announcement caused a general stampede: the cotton sheets were hastily adjusted, slippers put on, children and *kalians* snatched up, and with warm handshakes and "*khoda hafiz-i-shumas*" (goodbyes), my visitors and their train went off in a great hurry. As soon as they were gone Hashim came in to clear away, and being surprised at not seeing my brother, who had been calling on the Governor of Rahbur, I asked my waiter where he was. Hashim giggled, and became much confused, but finally confessed that, thinking my guests had stayed quite long enough, he had hit upon this means of sending them away. I felt that I ought to reprove him for conduct, which in a European servant would have been most reprehensible, but could only feel grateful to him for having relieved me of the thirteen or fourteen persons who had crowded into my small room!

We were not sorry to leave the hot, stony plain on which Rahbur stands, and return to the hills, crossing one of the branches of the Halil Rud River, and leading our horses up and down some such steep places that on one occasion I remember that "Charters" slid right down upon me, knocking my feet slightly with his hoofs before he could recover himself. We had now reached the little-known region of Sardu (traversed by Marco Polo in the thirteenth century), and that night we halted on a grassy upland near a big nomad encampment, the women in blue cotton jackets and skirts pleated as fully as kilts, their heads bound up in white wraps, coming out to survey us, accompanied by children dressed in defiance of all hygienic principles, their only garments being a scanty jacket open in the front, and trousers fastened below the hips. This is the usual costume of juveniles in Persia, and as it is unchanged during the rigours of winter, must have a good deal to do with the great mortality among Persian children. The men were far better clad, as they supplemented their cotton clothes with home-woven woollen wraps in black and red and blue and red checks, which they draped over their shoulders in the manner of a Highland plaid.

A light breeze was blowing, which soon after our arrival wafted a small swarm of big cockchafers over our tents. The whiteness of the canvas evidently attracted them, for they descended promptly and invaded us, booming about with long, feathery feelers, and crawling over tables and chairs, even creeping into our bedding in a most unpleasant way. It took a good deal of trouble to get rid of them, and our experiences with insects were not over with this episode, for after dinner a yellow scorpion was discovered sitting confidingly on my brother's knee, in such a position that it was a wonder that he did not lay his hand upon it!

Late that evening the nomad men sat in a crowd outside their encampment, and kept us all awake by celebrating *Moharrum* (the month in which Hussein and his family were martyred on the plain of Kerbelah) with a religious song, to the accompaniment of beats on the ground, when they came to the frequent chorus of "Hussein! Hassan! Hussein!" The tune was weird and melancholy, with the monotony inseparable from Oriental music, and all joined in it with much fervour, thudding vehemently at the end of each verse. Directly it was over one of their number turned the whole thing into ridicule, and the crowd roared with laughter at the parody on the sufferings of the martyrs, whose fate they had just been lamenting with religious zeal. This episode reminded us of the Miracle Plays in the Middle Ages, when the spectators would weep one moment as the mysteries of their Faith were presented to them, and at the next would break into peals of merriment as the Devil, playing the part of a buffoon, was brought upon the stage.

On leaving this camp we had the first rain that we had experienced for months, coming down in a heavy deluge, soaking us all to the skin, and making our horses look but sorry objects. We were passing through a rich upland, gleaming with long stretches of ripe corn and barley, and with plenty of water and willows. Flocks and herds were grazing on the fresh grass, the cows being handsome humped creatures, while a river rushed along a deep gorge near a picturesque little domed shrine. This district was one of the breeding grounds for horses which supply Kerman, and we had some trouble in crossing a valley where many mares were feeding, as "Nawab," free as usual, joined them with head and tail erect, looking as handsome as I ever saw him. My brother turned back to assist in his capture, which was not an easy matter, as he was unhaltered, and they had to grasp him by his floating mane or forelock. It was a scene of wild confusion. Grooms, muleteers, servants and nomads all joined in the chase, shouting and yelling, while the kicking, stampeding, neighing, and squealing were so infectious that it was all I could do to keep "Charters" from joining in the fray otherwise than with loudly uplifted voice.

Partridges swarmed in these hills, their cheerful note in the early morning and late in the afternoon resounding about our camp, the peculiar clucking call when feeding changing into a shrill whistle if they were disturbed. Their soft, brown-grey plumage, with its black and white markings on the wings, makes them almost indistinguishable from the boulders among which they live, so that my brother, when out shooting, invariably lost three or four birds, which dropped down wounded among the scrub and stones, where the most diligent searching failed to discover them. The huntsman sometimes brought out a big, square screen made of many-coloured patches, holding it up before him to attract the partridges, which are excessively curious birds, and then shooting them as they approached his shelter to examine it.

We halted for a few days near the steep pass of Dilfa, which we inspected with much interest, as it was crossed by Marco Polo on his journey to Kerman; and it added to the interest on my part to feel that in all probability we were the first Europeans who had visited Sardu since the time of that illustrious traveller.

One day when here we had a visit from seven nomad women, the principal ladies of their tribe, who brought us offerings of cheese and *mast*. They refused to take money in return, saying that they intended to see the *Khanum*, and would sit near our camp until I had interviewed them, even if I kept them waiting for days. So they were all ushered into the tent where we were sitting, fine-looking women for the most part with fresh complexions and beautiful eyes and teeth. They left their shoes at the door, and an old lady in white cotton garments, wearing many bead and amber bracelets and several turquoise rings, entered first, and sat, or rather squatted, well to the front. This personage demanded medicine for her eyes, which were inflamed, and accordingly I gave her a lotion for them; but she was not at all content with this, and pulled my skirt as she begged in the most insinuating manner for any and every kind of remedy, until my brother, yielding to her passion for drugs, gave her a few drops of chlorodyne on a lump of sugar to assuage her *dard-i-dil*, the only complaint she could muster, being in remarkably robust health. She retired at last with some Elliman's Embrocation to rub into an imaginary stiff shoulder, grumbling bitterly, saying that we had given her nothing at all, and beseeching us, up to the end, to be more liberal with the contents of our medicine-chest. The younger women acknowledged, to our surprise, that they were in the enjoyment of the best of health, and chatted away to us without ceremony about the details of their migratory existence, until Shah Sowar came to lay the table and routed them mercilessly.

But it was now time to say goodbye to these delightful uplands, for the Farman Farma was on his way to take up his governorship at Kerman, and we did not wish to be absent from the city when he arrived. We made our way therefore to Rayin, passing along the route once traversed by the great Venetian, the track winding through narrow valleys, in which we came upon the ruins of long-deserted caravanserais, and finally emerging on to the great Rayin Plain, giving us a glimpse of the large fort which dominates the town. We saw here the Kerman Desert, which stretches six hundred miles from Tun and Tabbas in the north to Bampur in the south, its golden sands looking quite alluring in the sunshine, and came across a party of pilgrims from Bashagird, bound for the sacred shrine at Meshed—a picturesque group in many-coloured garments, busily engaged in one of their five times of daily prayer. Some were standing, others kneeling, others again bowing profoundly, yet one and all suspended operations to stare at us with much interest as we rode past them.

Soldiers, attired in pea-green smocks, led us to our camp in Rayin, keeping off the curious populace and a crowd of hale and sturdy beggars, clad in garments of dubious whiteness. The huge fort, which used to contain the entire population, was in good repair, a rare thing in Persia, and in marked contrast to the castellated fragments of a second fortress, from the picturesque ruins of which trees were springing up. The little town was evidently prosperous: every house was embowered in fruit trees, the crops appeared to be excellent, and the people carried on the arts of glass-blowing, cutlery, and such-like, being quite an independent community.

The beautiful mountains among which we had been travelling, the Sardu, Sarbizan, Kuh-i-Shah and Kuh-i-Hazar ranges, disappeared gradually as we left Rayin and struck the road to Abigarm, passing on our way a ruined serai, near which hot springs were oozing out of the ground, forming natural baths of which many people were availing themselves for skin complaints. At Abigarm we were assured that we were only four-and-twenty miles from Kerman, *viâ* Ismailabad, and the idea of being close to home so greatly excited our servants that the advance-guard set off at an unearthly hour next morning to get lunch ready for us at Ismailabad. My brother and I left before sunrise to make our way down into the great Kerman Plain, the three *farsakhs* supposed to lie between our camp and Ismailabad expanding into several as we proceeded on our way. At last, however, we thought we saw the blue dome of Jupa's shrine ahead of us, and rode over a ground thickly strewn with stones and small boulders towards it.

As we got nearer my brother remarked that the village reminded him strongly of Mahun, and suddenly the truth flashed upon him that we were indeed there, and passing by the Farman Farma's garden, where he had stayed the year before with the Prince.

We had a faint hope that our servants and muleteers might have had the sense to stop here, as, by going on to Ismailabad, we should be at least six miles away from the direct road to Kerman. Naturally, however, they had displayed no such intelligence, and we pressed on over the stoniest of deserts, feeling exceedingly hungry after our twenty-five-mile ride, and very thankful to reach the Ismailabad garden, although no food of any kind was ready, our advance-guard having arrived only just before us. After a good rest we rode off again about four o'clock, our horses in the highest spirits as soon as they realised that they were going home, racing up and down the sand-dunes on the road as if they had done no work for a week. We steered our course towards the solitary great plane-tree, beneath which the little Hindoo colony was wont to burn its dead, and soon the ruined fortresses of old Kerman, which we had seen from the commencement of our ride, rose up close before us, and in a few moments we were at the gate of the Consulate.

We had ridden thirty-nine miles, a long distance for me, as much of the going was very bad, but I forgot my fatigues in

THE MOSQUE OF MAHUN.

the pleasure of being at home once more, and although, just at first, the nights seemed hot and suffocating after the fresh hill air, yet the real heat was over, and we settled down again to our old life, well content.

CHAPTER XIII

OUR SOCIAL CIRCLE AT KERMAN

ON July 20th, the day after we came home from our tour among the hills, the cannon of the city announced at an early hour that his Highness the Farman Farma was about to make his official entry into Kerman. We were much pleased at his arrival, as he and my brother were friends of over two years' standing, and he was considered to be the most civilised and enlightened of Persian princes. His home and property were at Tabriz, and his wife was the daughter of the Vali Ahd,[1] the heir-apparent to the throne, while he himself was cousin of the Shah. He was not accompanied by his wife and family, and so lived as a bachelor at Kerman.

When the Prince came to return my brother's call our servants were greatly excited, and pursued me all the morning to ask endless and often irrelevant questions concerning the serving of the tea, *kalians*, and sherbet, and the ceremonial to be observed on the occasion. I impressed on Hashim, however, that any inquiries on these points were to be made beforehand, as he had a habit, to which I strongly objected, of whispering confidentially to me in the presence of visitors.

It was about five o'clock when his Highness arrived and came upstairs with his doctor, leaving his followers below. He was a short, slight man of about five-and-thirty, and wore

---

[1] Now the present Shah.

H.H. THE FARMAN FARMA AND SUITE.

spectacles, being very near-sighted. He could speak French fluently, the acquisition of that language being one of the chief accomplishments of the Military College at Tehran, where he had been educated ; and I found him most chatty and agreeable.

He was anxious that I should attend the dinner that he was giving to celebrate the Shah's birthday in a few days' time, but although I was assured that all the guests would be "most civilised," as he expressed it, my brother thought it better for me to decline the invitation, and I had to content myself with enjoying a distant view from my windows of the fireworks in the city square. I had many a dinner, however, with the Prince later on, and was surprised at finding that we had tables, chairs, linen, glass and crockery, all as in Europe, while the cookery was an excellent mixture of Feringhee and Persian dishes.

Of all European languages French is undoubtedly the most in vogue among educated Persians. Its study was first encouraged by Fath Ali Shah, who, on the great occasion of his receiving a letter from the first Napoleon, was mortified to find that he had not a subject in the whole of his kingdom capable of translating the Emperor's message. To prevent the recurrence of a like catastrophe he sent a band of chosen youths to be educated in France, and French has ever since been spoken by a cultivated minority, the Shah himself being able to speak it with tolerable proficiency.

Persians struck me often as much resembling Frenchmen in their love of compliments and courtly phrases, and by their mannerisms of talk and gesticulation ; and when they waxed eloquent about their feats of war and their prowess in the chase they would put the immortal Tartarin himself to the blush. I fancy that Parisians would, however, be considerably astonished were they to hear their language as spoken in the France of the Orient. French taught by Austrians to Persians must necessarily undergo remarkable changes as regards accent, and I met few Persians out of Tehran who had the slightest respect for gender. "Il" was the only personal pronoun used, and as they seemed to imagine all adjectives need only be used in the masculine, it was often most confusing to follow a conversation. I have had to listen to long family histories in which wives, sisters, brothers, and a variety of other relations were all mixed up indiscriminately, the effort to understand who was who leaving my brain in a perfect whirl.

While we were at Kerman the Prince began to learn English from a *Gabre* (Parsee) youth who had been to Bombay, and he and the doctor had daily lessons for some time; but, finding they did not make the progress they expected, they got discouraged, and I fancy such phrases as "The cat sat on the mat" marked the highest point of proficiency that they managed to reach, although his Highness used to bring his reading-book when he came to dine with us, bursting out at intervals into fragmentary sentences from it for my edification.

Fazl Ali Khan, an elderly gentleman in the Farman Farma's suite, was the great authority on English, as many years ago, at the age of nine, he had been sent for a short time to a school at Brighton. Another of his accomplishments was that of photography, and as his productions were almost professional in their excellence, I was very grateful for the hints he gave me freely when my camera arrived. With the exception of the Prince and his Deputy-Governor the Bejat, he was the only Persian I ever met who was really energetic. Like most of his compatriots who have been to Europe he was much discontented with his country and its institutions, and, amusing as his strictures on everything were, one always felt sorry that a man who could appreciate better things should be condemned to an existence for the most part so curiously aimless. When the "Photographer," as we called him, and the other members of the Prince's suite rode out with us, he alone could keep up on his knock-kneed old white horse, which came down with him frequently. Steed and rider would roll over together in the dust; but the latter would scramble to his feet in a moment, shake himself and remount, remarking smilingly that his horse's qualities required to be known to be appreciated.

The Prince's doctor, whom we saw frequently, had been some five years in Paris studying medicine, and was a quiet, gentlemanly man. He was very kind-hearted, doctoring the poor free of charge, and was one of the few Orientals I came in contact with who had a regard for animals, and could not bear to see them suffer in any way.

The Bejat-i-Mulk (Gaiety of the Empire), to whom I have referred before, was an enormously stout Persian, who acted as Deputy-Governor to the Prince, and was in some sort his *fidus Achates*, as he and his master had been bound together by interest and friendship for many years, and on more than one occasion the Prince owed much to the calm common sense of the Bejat, who had a truly British solidity about him. He greatly enjoyed tent-pegging, although it was almost a miracle how the small horse he rode did not succumb under his weight as he galloped it recklessly about. His great virtue in my eyes was that he could argue out any question intelligently, being able to concentrate his mind on the point at issue, and without making remarks at random as many of the others did.

Among the other French-speaking members of the suite were Suleiman Mizza, a cousin of the Prince's, and Beough Khan.

The first-named was the commander of the Prince's army, and was proud of being the only man in Persia who could "make a map," as he said. I was much impressed with this statement until I found that his productions were only tracings from English maps, the English names of the places being translated into Persian.

Beough Khan, a delicate youth of about nineteen, was colonel of the artillery, and had a great admiration for Europeans and their doings, offering frequently to spend all his spare time at the Consulate—a proposal which did not meet with the warm acceptance that was anticipated. All of them were pleasant, and treated me with much courtesy, seeming to enjoy coming to us, and appreciating our European cooking, the wines and sauces in particular winning their warm approbation. They always came to the picnics we gave at different points of interest in the neighbourhood, although they considered the long rides to reach the spots fixed upon for lunch as a species of martyrdom.

I must confess that after a time their company became somewhat wearisome. To find fresh subjects of discussion was my great difficulty. One could not (at least *I* could not) talk for ever about sport and horses, and it would have been contrary to all laws of Eastern etiquette to question them on their womankind, in whom I was deeply interested. Books were scarce at Kerman, and as they had not the vaguest idea of history, geography, or of the events that were even then passing in the world, I was often completely nonplussed in my attempts at conversation.

I should have managed much better if I could have realised that they were but children mentally, and must be talked to as such. What they needed were facts from the "Child's Guide to Knowledge," or the "Rudiments of Geography" presented to them in an attractive guise. My brother was most successful in the way he conversed with them, provoking me, from pure envy, to compare him with the celebrated Mr. Barlow in "Sandford and Merton."

Although I found these French-speaking Persians rather difficult to get on with, they were a great improvement on their fellow-countrymen of the old school, notwithstanding the Persian proverb regarding Europeanised Orientals: "There was a crow that wanted to walk like the partridges, but in imitating their gait he lost his own and could never copy theirs properly."

My brother started weekly *Gymkhanas* as soon as we had settled down again at Kerman. A racecourse was marked out in the desert, a ground cleared for tent-pegging and lemon-cutting, a butt arranged for rifle-practice, and here the gentry of the neighbourhood were wont to assemble. They liked the friendly gatherings, with their accompaniments of tea and sherbet, but never attained to any great pitch of excellence in our sports, the majority of them being afraid of their horses. The only good performers were nomad chieftains, who, being capital horsemen, very soon mastered the art of tent-pegging, showing us, in return, some of their own sports, one of which was galloping past a handkerchief laid on the ground, and dropping a stick exactly on its centre—by no means such an easy feat as it sounds. The Prince did not altogether appreciate these gatherings, as he could do nothing with the tent-pegs, and his nearest approach to success was when his horse managed to knock over a peg with its hoof. So he persuaded my brother to attend his private sports every Friday, where he loved to fire at a mark, a Persian lamb's-wool *kolah* being frequently used as a target. According to Persian ideas a Prince ought to do everything better than his inferiors, the result of this notion being that no one dares to surpass his royal master in any game or sport; and it was distinctly noticeable how the weekly *Gymkhana* was improved by the absence of the Farman Farma. In fact, many of the competitors frankly told me that they never dared to do their best in an event for which his Highness had entered.

Towards the end of September we had a race-meeting, which was the subject of conversation for weeks beforehand, and which kept me busy for several days preparing refreshments for the hundreds of guests expected.

It was hoped that the gentry of Kerman would ride their own horses, but they were fertile in excuses, some considering that such a proceeding would be exceedingly lowering to their dignity, while others feared that they might fall off; and a proposal for a donkey race was immediately vetoed, as it would be the depth of degradation for a Persian Prince to be present at such a form of entertainment. Numerous were the jealousies as Nasrullah Khan entered the names of competitors on a list, every one appearing to consider that his name should precede every one else's. At last the great day arrived, and when I imagined that the races must be in full swing I ascended the roof of the Consulate to survey the course with my field-glasses, and was astonished at the swarms of spectators present. The Prince and his suite on horseback, the merchants and priests in turbans and on donkeys, the whole poorer population of the city, men and women alike, all had poured forth to see the show, a crowd of some thousands of souls.

I heard afterwards that the Bejat's horse, ridden by his servant, had won the first prize, and the Prince's horse the second. The former was delighted with his victory, and going into one of the tents to have tea, he called a number of the gentry to him, presenting them with handfuls of sweetmeats in the joy of his heart. I fancy, however, that he was not quite so happy that evening, when the Prince visited him in the intimacy of his *anderoon* and admired his horse. The only possible answer to such a remark in the East is, "*Pishkesh*" ("It is at your service"), and the animal was transferred to the Farman Farma's stables the next morning. So universal is this custom that the Persians have a proverb which says: "If you possess a good horse it always becomes a gift;" and I believe it went far in accounting for the small number of entries in the horse-races. Every one talked to us a good deal about the fine horses they possessed, but they were certainly shy about displaying their qualities in public, and confined themselves to trying their luck at shooting at a large mark, the practice being so bad that the winner only succeeded in scoring two hits out of seven shots.

Altogether the Kerman races were most successful, although the Farman Farma gloomily prophesied a bread-riot and other disagreeable consequences from the assemblage of so many people.

The only adverse criticism, however, came from a deputation of priests, who called on his Highness to ask whether he was aware that the Consul, by enclosing part of Kerman Desert for a racecourse, had appropriated it on behalf of the English Government, Persian law ordaining that an enclosure belongs to the person who has made it. They were, however, pacified when the Prince assured them that the work had been performed by his own general and soldiers, and we laughed a good deal over the joke.

The Farman Farma usually spent a few days every month at his beautiful garden of Mahun, some twenty miles from the city, and on these occasions he always sent us a pressing invitation to be his guests, and we would pitch our tents outside his garden, there not being enough accommodation inside his grounds for all of us.

I will give an account of one such visit, which will stand for them all. We started off early one afternoon in August, the servants, tents, &c., having been sent on, and rode through the gap in the hills out on to a great sandy desert, the monotony of which is only broken by a small mud tea-house, erected close to the one solitary spring for miles round. Here we halted for afternoon tea, and, after watering our horses, rode on; while across the desert, columns of sand, dark at their base with swirling dust, rose into fantastic shapes as the light wind drove them in circles upwards. These *jinns*, as the Persians call them, occasionally approached us at such a pace that we were forced to gallop our horses to avoid them.

In the distance we saw the bright blue dome and tall minarets of Mahun's famous shrine, and as we neared the village the setting sun bathed the eastern hills in a rosy glow with long, purple shadows, while the gardens clustering round the dome seemed enveloped in a golden haze.

Shah Niamatullah, to whose memory this beautiful shrine was built, was a notable personage in his day. An Indian dervish, born in the year 730 of the *Hejreh*, he is supposed to have prophesied that the English rule in India would cease in 1857. Mrs. Steel in her book "On the Face of the Waters," renders the prophecy thus into rhyme:—

> "Fire-worship for a hundred years,
> A century of Christ and tears,
> Then the true God shall come again,
> And every infidel be slain."

And the Mutiny has been attributed partly to this jingle which was on the lips of every native at the time. Be that as it may, the fame of the saint was spread far and wide; for on one occasion, being specially warned not to land on a certain island infested with lions, he went there straightway, saying his fate lay in the hands of Allah. Events proved his faith to be well founded. The lions rushed in a body to greet him with many an uncouth *salaam* as he stepped on shore, killed a gazelle to feast their guest, and collected wood wherewith to roast it. As neither Shah Niamatullah nor the lions were provided with matches, the intelligent animals lay huddled up close together on the brushwood, until the heat of their bodies set it on fire, after which process the gazelle was cooked to a turn! Many people, hearing of these marvellous experiences, tried to visit a spot where the lions served man so well, but from that day it was never seen again by mortal eyes.

Some time after this episode the saint made his way to Persia, where he was received with great honour at Court, and consulted on all matters of State. Splendid presents were sent to him from Indian princes on which the Custom House officials of that day tried to levy duty, but were forced to desist, public opinion holding that they were outraging the holy man by such devices.

Hundreds of enthusiastic followers aspired to become his disciples, following his example of dispensing with their clothing, as they affirmed that they were perfectly warm in the coldest weather if in the presence of the Master. And at last, full of years and honours, he ended his days at Mahun, at the ripe age of one hundred and four, the great Shah Abbas erecting a sepulchre above his remains to keep his memory green.

The predecessor of the present Shah[1] built the graceful blue-domed shrine, which is such a prominent feature in the Mahun landscape; and this brings to the mind another of Shah Niamatullah's prophecies, to the effect that the last Shah of Persia would be called Nasr-ed-Deen and that his reign would only last five years, and as the name is an uncommon one, the prophecy is very generally applied to the present Shah. Perhaps the best known of his prognostications, and one which is very frequently quoted in Persia, is that which concerns the fate of three of her principal

---

[1] Now the late Shah.

COURTYARD OF THE MOSQUE OF MAHUN.

cities. It runs thus: "Isfahan will be destroyed by water, Yezd by sand, and Kerman by the hoofs of horses."

When we had left the pretty village behind us, an exceedingly stony three miles took us to the Prince's garden, above which we found our tents pitched by a stream, and in a moment he himself was with us, charming and courteous as usual, insisting on staying to dinner, his servants bringing the dishes to our tent. At Kerman his Highness never cared to come often to the Consulate, fearing the remarks of the *mollahs* and townspeople, but at Mahun he always felt free as air, and his spirits rose in proportion.

Our conversation usually turned on England, which he ardently longed to visit, and on English customs; and he discussed with us the best way of educating his eldest son in that happy land. During one of these conversations he told us that he intended to send to Tabriz for the boy, and if we returned to Europe *viâ* Bombay, he would put us in charge of him. I remarked that it was not usual to send a boy of six to school, but the Prince waived aside all objections by saying that he could live in our family during the three years before his regular school-work commenced!

On the day following our arrival his Highness invited us to accompany him partridge-shooting, and accordingly, at about half-past eight, we all started off across the boulder-strewn plain to the hills. The Prince rode a horse with a gold collar and embroidered saddle-cloth, his English *Terai* hat with its flowing *puggree*, being strikingly out of harmony with the trappings of his mount; and he was followed by some hundreds of wild-looking retainers on horseback, clad in all kinds of flying-skirted coats, and carrying guns and heavy hunting-knives.

We had hardly left the garden when his Highness's favourite servant, a handsome youth in a green silk coat, galloped up, calling out the magic word *shikar*, at which every one stopped, and the Prince, dismounting, cautiously approached the game. I was puzzled at seeing no partridges, and my surprise was not lessened when the Prince fired at a magpie, which flew off unharmed.

Our way led up stony valleys, along dry river-beds, and the Persians galloped their ponies over the rough ground with the greatest dash, men on horseback rushing full tilt up the low hills, riding along their summits and howling vigorously to frighten the partridges into the crowded valleys beneath. The unfortunate birds were flushed by mongrel pointers to be dropped at a few yards' distance by the eager sportsmen, while the falconers loosed their charges to swoop down upon any birds which might try to escape up the hill-sides. The Prince was greatly excited, and shouted orders and encouragement without ceasing. He would gallop half-way up a hill on his wiry horse, would dismount, fire, and remount, and gallop down again, a prominent figure on the steep slopes. It was an animated scene. Scores of horsemen raced helter-skelter in every direction, shouting in a frenzy of excitement, and so reckless was the firing on all sides that I was surprised that no casualties occurred. Soon after midday lunch was served in a garden of peach-trees, beside a running stream, the food being spread on a large carpet around which the Persians sat on their heels, bending forward nearly double as they ate, to the great detriment, I should imagine, of their digestions.

They manipulated the various *pillaus* with much skill, rolling up balls of meat and rice between their fingers, and inserting them in their mouths. I was glad, however, that a few knives and forks, as well as chairs, had been thoughtfully provided for my brother and me, thus enabling us to enjoy the different dishes in comfort. We had a profusion of grapes, melons, figs, and dates for dessert, and I tasted, for the first time, a sweetmeat called *halwa*, from Muscat, a compound of barley-jelly and chopped almonds. There was no wine, but throughout the meal big glasses of water, filled to the brim with masses of snow, were handed round.

I observed that there was a certain amount of etiquette regarding our positions on the carpet. The post of honour next to the Prince was allotted to us, the doctor sat on the outer edge, while the Photographer humbly ate his meal on the grass, and young Beough Khan stood afar off, bowing. When the Prince retired, however, for a siesta to a small summer-house, the whole company came and seated themselves without demur on the carpet, to entertain us until the return of our host.

On the conclusion of the day's sport we accompanied the Farman Farma to his garden, and the view that here met my eyes enabled me dimly to realise the charm and glamour of those earthly Paradises of which I have read in tales of old romance, where the skies are eternally blue, the leaves and flowers never fade, and the musical plash of water wraps every sense in a magic slumber.

Spenser's description of Armida's bower might have been even more alluring had he seen the fairy picture that lay before me. The long slope of the garden, from end to end, was a dazzling, glancing stream of water, broken up into dashing cascades, and adorned with fountains rising high into the air, while the August sun, gleaming on their foam, tinted them with all the colours of the rainbow.

In the far distance appeared a fantastic tiled gateway, against the columns of which the lofty fountains seemed to be dashing themselves, and this exquisite waterway was bordered with weeping willows, beneath whose branches grew a wealth of flowers, casting their reflections into the stream.

We were taken by the Prince to a large bare room, devoid of furniture, save a few cushions and chairs which had been placed for us, and with great windows overlooking the garden. When small glasses of tea, flavoured with an infusion of cinnamon, had been handed round, the Prince gave an audience to the Assad-i-Dowleh, Governer of Baluchistan. I did not then pay much attention to the elderly, black-bearded man in his dark blue military uniform, not thinking how often I should see him a few months later on.

I was interested in watching the Prince's *mirzas*, or scribes, at work, one of whom, on being shown by his Highness an error that he had made in copying a letter, squatted on his heels, holding the paper in one hand, while with a wet finger he rubbed out the offending word. He then held the writing close to his eyes, laboriously etching in the fresh letters, and went on to erase another word with his tongue, making me think that the forging of documents must be an easy matter in Persia. At one end of his long pen-box was a diminutive ink-bottle, near which lay a pair of scissors for cutting his paper, which he kept in a roll, to the sizes required. The habit of writing from right to left causes Persians to hold the pen quite differently to Europeans, and their letters when written are by no means easy to decipher, as scraps of information are jotted at random all over the paper.

Our dinner was served in the pavilion, and from its open windows we could see the many fountains glittering in the moonlight. The Prince asked whether I should like to hear Persian music, and, on my eagerly assenting, a youth appeared with a kind of guitar, on which he played most skilfully, but, as his intervals were entirely different to those to which Europeans are accustomed—Persians, so I am told, having twelve notes to our octave—the performance gave me the impression of the twanging of an orchestra before the overture commences. To his accompaniment an elderly man, who had once been possessed of a fine voice, knelt down on his heels and sang some songs of fighting and love-making with great vigour. He had, however, overstrained his voice by always singing in a falsetto key, and when he wished to give utterance to a queer kind of "tremulo," he swayed himself to and fro in a manner curiously suggestive of great bodily pain, and contorted his features into an agonised expression. Some of his songs were weird and lugubrious in the extreme, and he got hoarser and hoarser as he continued, it never seeming to occur to his audience that to sing without intermission for a couple of hours might be detrimental to the strongest of voices, especially when the performer avails himself throughout of the full force of his lungs.

His Highness was most anxious to know how Persian music would be regarded in Europe, and was disappointed when we said that we should look upon it more as a curiosity than as real music, Orientals considering that the mysteries of harmony have been revealed to them alone, and that Europeans are in the most elementary stages of the art.

During our repast we were entertained by the Prince's buffoon, a tall, white-turbaned Persian in black robes, who went by the name of Mollah Lung. He opened proceedings by insisting on shaking hands with us, sending the Prince into fits of laughter by this very ordinary action, and was then regaled with glasses of cherry-brandy and bits of bread smeared with mustard; but what appeared to cause the greatest amusement was when he was given a plate of *pillau* and told to eat it with a spoon. Habit was too strong for him, however, and we were expected to see something extremely funny in the sight of Mollah Lung devouring rice in the ordinary Persian way. To my mind he was one of the poorest of Court fools, and only became bearable when he displayed a Persian natural history book, profusely illustrated with such grotesque caricatures of whales, sharks, octopuses, and other denizens of the deep, and the letterpress teeming with such astounding exaggerations and inaccuracies that we felt sorry to think this was one of the ordinary text-books of the youth of Persia.

Our pleasant visits to the Prince at Mahun were usually followed by a shooting trip to the hills, where my brother generally succeeded in bagging a few moufflon and ibex; but I must reserve the account of these expeditions for another chapter.

CHAPTER XIV

ARABABAD AND SAGOTCH, PERSIAN LADIES AND SOME PERSIAN CUSTOMS

AFTER each visit paid to the Prince at Mahun we went into the hills in order that my brother might get some big game shooting.

On one of these occasions we wended our way at the beginning of September to Arababad, some fifteen miles from our quarters near the fairy garden, past big stretches of wheat, the second crop of the year, and patches of the castor-oil plant, or willow-fig as the Persians call it, and finally pitched our camp in a valley beside a stream, bordered with sweetbriar bushes, which issued from the neighbouring hills. The place was haunted by a leopard, which a shepherd told us had carried off a dog and two sheep the day before our arrival, and all the servants felt that we had brought them into the very jaws of death. Many jokes were perpetrated at the expense of the Fat Boy, whom they affirmed would be the first victim, and he was in great request as a sleeping companion that night, every one feeling that no leopard of any discrimination would spring on thin mortals while such a substantial meal lay close at hand!

Nasrullah Khan amused me by narrating to us next morning the details of *his* plan of campaign. When he retired to rest he forced his reluctant servant to lie across the door of his tent, and in the event of the leopard rejecting Haji and going for his master instead, the latter intended to envelop the animal in his bedding and turn the bedstead over him, upon which he and Haji would sit until help came!

However, the occasion for these herculean feats never arose, although whenever we camped among the hills the tracks of some leopard, which had been prowling round our tents during the night, were generally visible.

One morning we all went off at sunrise to climb to the crest of a ridge which dominated the camp. As we were ascending a range to the east it was gloomy and cold until we reached the summit, though behind us the valley was being flooded with light, which crept slowly up towards us. The *shikarchis* made us lie down among the boulders before we reached the sky-line, and we then saw a herd of nine or ten mountain sheep quietly feeding, about three-quarters of a mile away. My brother and his huntsmen went off to stalk them, leaving us hidden carefully, when, to our great surprise, some six or eight ibex, headed by one great goat, passed between the *shikarchis* and their quarry, it being most unusual to find sheep and goats on the same ground.

My brother fired at and hit the leader of the little herd, and then ensued a lengthy chase, and we, when they were all out of sight, stretched our cramped limbs and revelled in the view across the plain to Mahun, while Jupa, Kuh-i-Hazar, Kuh-i-Shah, and many another mountain-giant of the Kerman district rose up in their majesty; and the thorny scrub on the hills as we descended reminded Nasrullah Khan of the proverb, " Do not think that that object on the mountain is merely a spotted plant; it may turn out to be a leopard," which is the Persian equivalent of " Don't judge by appearances."

Two rams and an ibex were the result of my brother's *shikar*, while I also had a taste of the hunter's joy, as I captured a large tarantula, with yellow legs, a grey hairy body, and scarlet beak-like mouth, which was lying half-torpid in my bath sheet.

On our homeward way to Kerman we zig-zagged through the narrow lanes of Mahun, enclosed with such high mud walls that we could not get a glimpse of the gardens between which we were riding. Here and there we had to cross streams beside which willow or jube-trees would be growing, and occasionally the low wooden gate in the high mud wall of a garden would be abruptly opened for some one to stare at our party. The shrine was in an open space by the broad, dry river-bed which acts as an approach to the village, and though its blue dome and graceful minarets were charming in the distance, yet, as is the case with most Eastern buildings, much of its beauty disappeared when inspected at close quarters, it being so hemmed in and built on to with mean mud buildings.

My brother, who visited the *mollahs* once or twice, said that there was nothing of interest inside the shrine, everything being covered with white plaster, and a few druggets replacing the carpet which M. de Rakovszky had carried off.

Sagotch was another spot we explored in search of sport. The Consul of Isfahan had told us that the Mahun shrine, or another in its vicinity, possessed a certain black pyramidal stone, with an inscription relating to Darius engraved upon it, which stone had been seen and described by the French *savant* Gobineau. Our interest was greatly aroused by this piece of information, and my brother made every inquiry at Mahun, but with no result. However, we heard that at Sagotch were two sacred stones with writing upon them, and accordingly, armed with camera, sketching materials, and tracing-paper, we made our way thither.

It was about the middle of October when we visited the shrine, embowered in walnut and jube-trees, the small, reddish fruit of the latter being sweetish and woolly to the taste, but, for all that, a great stand-by for the poor.

The entrance to the courtyard was guarded by an iron chain, which signified that here was *bast*, or sanctuary, for any evil-doer who could get past it, this privilege, exercised without check by the *mollahs*, accounting for much of their power among the people.

As we rode up, a thief, in charge of some soldiers, on his way to Mahun to be bastinadoed, was passing by. His guards gazed with all their eyes at the Europeans, and the man, seizing his opportunity, slipped from their grasp, and was under the chain and out of their power before they had taken in the situation.

The shrine was an ordinary-looking mud dome, surrounded with mud rooms in which pilgrims lodged, the interior being whitewashed, with two rows of trellised windows high up in the dome, while common little looking-glasses hung round the walls. The whole place was filled with cotton handkerchiefs and bits of stuff, glass beads, bangles, &c., suspended along ropes stretched over the tomb, most of these offerings being presented by parents, to ensure their children being shielded from harm.

Among these masses of kerchiefs stood the escaped prisoner, his arms tightly bound with a thick cord, while he convulsively grasped two poles with a metal hand at the top of each, symbolic of Abbas, the standard-bearer of Mahomet's army.

The poor fellow stared wildly at us, gasped, and then began to work himself up for a good cry, a somewhat theatrical performance, I fancy, as the snowy-turbaned *mollah* in charge endeavoured to check his emotion by telling him that there was no need for it, since he was safe. The tomb was a great white plaster platform, covered with a white sheet, on which was laid a copy of the Koran, wrapped in a cloth. Both this and the sheet were kissed and patted by each faithful Mussulman who entered, and were decidedly grimy from this method of veneration. Our inquiries elicited nothing about the history of the holy man buried here, and when the sacred stones were produced we were keenly disappointed. They were merely natural curiosities, the white markings on one black boulder looking something like Persian characters, while the other had much the same appearance in shades of grey, and I noticed several of the same kind near our camp, which we pitched some three miles above the village, to be nearer the mountains.

Next day my brother went up a high peak, bedding, provisions and all, so as to have two days' shooting at a stretch, and I explored the long, savage-looking ravine down which rushes the torrent that supplies Sagotch. The defile was so narrow that I had to jump backwards and forwards across the stream to get any foothold, but the walk was well worth the trouble, as the stream, dashing down in waterfalls and cascades, was blocked here and there with huge boulders, beneath which it lay in deep pellucid pools, or was broken by broad rocky steps, fit for water-nymphs to sit on and comb out their golden tresses. On the banks were masses of sweetbriar, barbary (the red fruit of which is used in *pillaus*), the tamarisk, and hill almond, and far up I came across men engaged in burning charcoal, who told my attendant that the torrent comes down in winter with such force that a loaded camel cannot stand against the current. Bright and sunny as the day was in the morning, yet it suddenly turned grey and cold: a dust storm arose, the rain began to pour heavily, and I retired to rest full of nervous forebodings as to how my brother, up aloft, was passing the night. To my great relief he turned up on the morrow shortly after midday, as the rain had rendered shooting impossible, and *Bargi* speeded us on our homeward way by burning a handful of the seeds of a sacred plant, which when squeezed into the eye acted as a most potent charm against witchcraft.

Two Persian ladies announced their intention of calling on me when I returned to Kerman—sisters, and married to *Khans* in the neighbourhood, so my brother betook himself to the Prince for the afternoon, and I made the most elaborate toilette that the circumstances of my wardrobe allowed, and strained every nerve to procure an elegant tea, which *Bargi* was to serve out. At three o'clock my visitors appeared with two daughters, three women slaves, two small boys to guard their slippers, which they left at the door of my sitting-room, and three eunuchs, who brought *kalians* to them at intervals. The older ladies were most chatty and agreeable, but the girls would not say a word, so stringent is Persian etiquette, which literally enforces the rule that young people should be seen and not heard in the presence of their elders and betters. Unmarried sons or daughters are never supposed to turn their backs to their parents, and, in company, address them with almost servile respect. My guests all wore handsome brocaded silk or velvet jackets, but only partly slipped off the black silk sheets which transform every Persian woman into a shapeless bundle, and persisted in keeping on their embroidered cotton gloves, upon which they sported many rings. If I had requested them to remove their black *chaddars* and green silk trousers, they would have imagined that I was inviting them to stay to dinner, and perhaps spend the night!

Poor *Bargi* began to pour out tea, but was promptly checked by the negresses, who informed her that she was *nejus*, or unclean, and that their mistresses could partake of nothing offered to them by her; and, somewhat to my disgust, they took the direction of affairs upon themselves. One even went so far as to seize and put back on the dish a stick of chocolate which one of the girls had taken, telling her that probably she would not like the Feringhee sweetmeat, and must help herself to a smaller piece to try experiments upon. The young lady, who seemed about twenty years of age, submitted meekly, so tyrannical is the sway of slaves in Persia.

These latter probably have a better time than they would in their own country, Persians giving their slaves very light work, as they say they are costly articles and must therefore be well treated. All jewellery and money are as a rule confided to their care, for, as they are cut adrift from their own family ties, they are supposed to attach themselves strongly to their masters and their interests. An Ethiopian is frequently the confidant of his master, knows all his secrets, and is entrusted with the upbringing of his children. In Persia there does not seem to be the slightest slur attaching to slavery; in fact, as far as my experience went, it was just the contrary, and the negroes appeared to command the whole household.

But to return to my ladies. I did my best to amuse them with a dancing nigger wound up by clockwork, which performance nearly sent one of them into a fit, as she gasped out that it was a Feringhee *shaitan*, or devil; a clockwork train was also a great attraction to people who had never left Kerman, and they positively revelled in my photographs. We had a large assortment of portraits of the Prince and his suite, and all these gentlemen were examined with the closest and most flattering attention, and I had to name each likeness two or three times, so anxious were they to impress them on their memories. They all professed to be sorry for my solitary condition, evidently not understanding that my brother and I could be companions in any way, and were incredulous of my assurances that I was perfectly happy—which assurances I reiterated with fervour, as I dreaded offers of a three or four days' visit from my guests. Like all other visitors, they were most eager to have a description of my home and life in England, and amused me by warning me earnestly not to enter into the state of wedlock with a Persian, as their marriage customs were *khaili karab* (very bad).

I was always afraid of allowing my female friends to compare their secluded lives with my free one, as it only made them discontented with their lot, and as I could do nothing to help them I felt it was cruel to stir up vain longings for existences less like those of prisoners.

I wound up the entertainment with a song on my guitar, which probably wounded their musical senses, but caused one to exclaim to the others that Feringhee ladies could do everything, and we parted with much effusion, the black silk sheets and white veils being carefully adjusted before they left the safety of my sitting-room.

Persian ladies, I fear, have rather a dull time as a rule, though they probably get more fun out of life than is apparent to English people. They have numberless parties among themselves, at which they take great pride in displaying their garments and jewellery, and the weekly bath is in reality their day at the club. They stay many hours in the steaming atmosphere, taking their servants and young children with them, and gossiping with the dozens of friends they meet there. As women are admitted half-price, and children and servants free, the bath is a popular institution, and all ladies are most particular about having elegant wraps for their towels and handsome cushions to repose on after their ablutions. They bring lunch with them, which is usually a light repast of lettuces and vinegar, fruit and *scangebee*, and the bath takes the whole day when the lady's hair is dyed with henna and her eyebrows artistically painted. If in mourning, they are not supposed to dye their hair, as henna is a symbol of happiness, whereas the dyeing of the finger and big-toe nails is a religious observance.

Only princes can display scarlet tails to their horses, and even they (speaking of the use of henna) merely in the provinces, for at Tehran the Shah's horses alone are allowed this distinction.

A Persian bath hardly recommends itself to European ideas of cleanliness, as it is composed of two large tanks, one of hot and one of cold water. Every one performs his or her ablutions in the hot tank first, and as it costs a considerable amount of money, expended in firewood and charcoal, to heat such a large expanse of water properly, and as bathing is very cheap, it is necessary to have a great number of bathers to make it pay, and I fear it is cleaned out at very long intervals.

The second, or cold tank, is in an adjoining room, ready for the final plunge. Fastidious Persians, however, do not avail themselves of this, but make their servants bring pitchers of water with them from their homes, seemingly ignoring the fact that it is the hot water-tank that they should chiefly avoid.

* * * * *

When it is time for a Persian youth to get married—which he can legally do at the age of fifteen, and girls at that of twelve, his mother goes to inspect a suitable wife for him. If she does not know of any likely maiden she enlists the services of an old woman, whose office it is to go from house to house and act as an intermediary in matrimonial arrangements, all mothers of marriageable daughters treating her with the greatest respect in order that she may give a good report of their belongings.

The young lady being fixed upon, and such important details as social position and dowry being satisfactory, the gentleman's mother and other female relatives pay a call of ceremony at her home. Every one of course knows for what object they have come, and the girl is told to hand them tea and *kalians*, her manner of doing these little services being severely criticised. It sometimes happens that the damsel is perfectly well acquainted by sight with her would-be betrothed, and if he has not met with favour in her eyes she now makes a point of behaving rudely to his mother, and the negotiations come to an abrupt conclusion.

If, on the other hand, she has approved of him when her slaves have pointed him out to her in her walks abroad, all goes smoothly, and she attends a party in turn at his house, knowing full well that he is doing his best to have a look at her, as he stands hidden away on some balcony, anxiously watching his mother, who will by means of signs show him his future wife.

The suitor is not supposed to see his *fiancée* until the formal betrothal by the *mollah* takes place. If her face displeases him he can draw back by paying to her parents half the sum of money they had agreed to give her for a dowry; but this very seldom happens, as a man behaving in this way is socially disgraced. Moreover, the lady is so rouged and powdered on this occasion, and her eyelids and eyebrows so blackened with antimony, that it is no easy matter to gain a clear idea of what her natural charms may be.

The wedding is a grand affair, the poorest Persian often going deeply into debt, and squandering two or three years' income in feasting his friends, the *mollahs* and beggars, and in entertaining them with hired musicians.

When the couple settle down to a humdrum married existence the Persian theory is that a man has linked himself to a being inferior to him in every way, who must submit to his sovereign will in all things. From his extreme youth he has been taught by the priests to pay no attention to the counsels of his wife, and they have strongly impressed upon him that if a woman advises him to any course of action he had better do the exact contrary.

I remember on one occasion calling on a lady when her husband was present, and the latter at once asked me whether I thought his wife pretty, in much the same way as if she were a horse or dog. He also bade me remark how ill at ease she was in his presence, adding with pride that if they were at table together she would have trembled in every limb from fear of her lord and master. It was impossible to make him understand my indignation at this state of things; but yet, as human nature is much the same all the world over, there are occasionally henpecked husbands even in Persia.

For instance, the wife of one Governor of my acquaintance was a lady of great force of character, and all who considered themselves to be aggrieved at any decision of her husband, would lay their cases before her by means of the servants of her *anderoon*, and it frequently happened that if she thought fit she would insist on her lord and master reversing his decrees.

It is now the fashion in Persia, despite the example set by the Shah, to have only one wife. This is, in a great measure, due to the fact that the Persians of to-day are usually very poor, and naturally the keeping up of two or three entirely different establishments is a very great tax on a man's resources, to say nothing of the trouble involved of superintending the servants and in examining the accounts of each household.

A Persian lady is not really the mistress of her house. All the shopping is done by her *nazir*, or steward, who gives in a monthly account to his master, taking so much percentage for himself, for his trouble. As a rule she is an adept in the making of sweetmeats and sherbets, and these arts, with needlework, fill up most of her time, as she is seldom addicted to intellectual pursuits, few ladies being able to read or write.

She sees very little of her husband, who, if he is an official of any kind, probably leaves her early in the morning not to return till nightfall; and indeed she cannot be a companion to him, as she is entirely precluded from accompanying him on his drives or rides, and so gets to regard him merely as a being to be petitioned for new clothes and jewellery or to be propitiated with *pillaus* or sweetmeats. If her husband met her in the streets and recognised her, all disguised as she would be, he could not speak to or even salute her, so stringent is Persian etiquette on this point.

As a mother, the Persian lady has no great influence in the upbringing of her children, as she hands them over to the charge of servants at an early age. The boys are treated like men from infancy, trained to copy their fathers in every way, checked if they run and romp, as such things are undignified, and made to sit up to the Persian dinner, which never finishes before midnight. I remember one day at Kerman a Persian gentleman and his little son lunched with us, and it was wonderful to see how capitally the latter managed his knife and fork. It was evident that this was his first attempt at handling these awkward articles, but he was not to be daunted, and watched me narrowly, doing as I did, and only using his fingers when baffled by a really unmanageable piece of meat, first glancing round to see whether any one were observing him or not. This custom of never allowing a child to exert himself probably accounts for the fact that the *physique* of the upper classes leaves much to be desired, while the peasant population usually consists of remarkably fine, well-built men.

All travellers in Persia are struck by the way in which the Persians depend on their servants, asking their opinion on all points, and apparently being guided a good deal by their advice; but this is not to be wondered at when it is remembered that as soon as a boy is old enough to leave his mother he is practically brought up by two or three servants, on whom he leans more or less through life ; the patriarchal system being in vogue in Persia, the domestics are a part of the family and seldom change their situations.

Moreover, it is on his retainers that a Persian gentleman depends for a great part of his amusement; these latter on their daily visit to the bazaars, collecting all the gossip of the town, which they retail to their masters, thus helping to while away the idle hours.

No Persian of any standing ever sends his sons to school, but engages a tutor to come to the house daily to teach them to read the Koran, Sadi and Hafiz, and to instruct them in writing, their education commencing at the age of five, the girls occasionally being included in these lessons up to eight years of age, and usually the sons of the servants of the house, as social distinctions are in some ways less regarded in Persia than in Europe.

Besides their teacher proper the boys are in charge of a *lala*, an old man, who performs the functions of the Greek pedagogue, taking his charges out for walks, and keeping a keen eye on all their movements.

If they refuse to learn, two *ferashes*, who are always in attendance at the door of their schoolroom, enter armed with the apparatus for applying the *bastinado* to unruly pupils, which punishment is no disgrace, the sons of the Shah and the highest officials having had perhaps to submit to it. Their education goes on to the age of eighteen, and it is a wonder if they gain much from it, as the meaning of what they read is not insisted upon in the least, a parrot-gabble of the Koran being considered a high achievement. As the *mollahs* are only paid at the rate of 5 *tomans*, or £1, monthly for their services, it is hardly to be expected that they themselves can be profound Arabic scholars, and, as for general knowledge, their ignorance is colossal. Nasrullah Khan has told me how, when the Atlantic Ocean was mentioned in a book he read as a boy, his teacher explained to him that it was a city somewhere in Feringhistan or Europe.

There is no great amount of family affection in Persia, the fathers often disliking their sons, unless sharp and clever, and appearing to treat their daughters with profound indifference.

The "Photographer" had one of his sons with him at Kerman, a good-natured but heavy-witted youth, and actually described him to me in the boy's presence as "*seule-*

ment une bête, rien de plus." The young fellow did not seem to resent this at all, for he remarked one day, apropos of his position at Kerman, " The man who gives me bread, he it is whom I serve. My father feeds me here, therefore I am his servant."

One of my Persian friends described to me the way in which his father treated him on the lad's return from the Military College at Tehran after a successful career there. He was delighted to be at home again, and hastened to greet his parent, who was in a room with all the servants round him, and who hardly deigned to respond to his son's salutations, telling him to retire after a few moments.

The poor fellow rushed from the room cut to the heart, and assured me that he would have taken his life if some of the old family retainers had not followed him and so prevented the rash act.

Suicide in Persia is looked upon as a great sin, because it is considered that a man by killing himself has destroyed unborn generations to which he might have been the ancestor, and the *mollahs* beat his dead body with many stripes, predicting much suffering for the deceased in the next world.

At his death a man leaves double the portion of property to his sons that he does to his daughters, and so far does this division go, that I heard that a most beautiful carpet had been cut into pieces by a family to whom it was willed.

The Persians have a proverb about the disposal of money during a man's lifetime: " Eat it, give it away, and leave some behind you ; " while they have a well-known story about the father who buried his property, which was removed from its hiding-place by his son, and stones put in its stead. When reproached by his father, the young man made reply, " Money is given to be spent. If you wish to hoard, stones and gold are equally good for the purpose."

In the case of a Government official the chances of his heirs are indeed poor, as, in all probability, the ruler of the province will swoop down upon the deceased man's property, on the time-honoured pretext that his accounts are out of order.

Even if it be subsequently proved that everything is correct, yet the survivors will never be able to recover the full amount of which they have been mulcted.

* * * * *

When a Persian lady is advanced in years, she often becomes very devout, frankly telling every one that she is preparing for the next world, and to this end she insists on going on a pilgrimage. If possible Mecca or Kerbelah will be her goal, though, if want of means put these shrines out of the question, she will perforce content herself with Meshed. The journey is a serious affair, as she must travel in the jolting *kajaveh*, or pannier, strapped on to a mule, if she cannot afford the expensive *tachterivan*, and must keep herself veiled the whole time, however hot the weather. Usually when the place of pilgrimage is reached, the lady and her servants will settle down for a year, and she will visit the mosque daily, present offerings of gold or jewellery at the shrine, and pay a *mollah* to recite portions of the Koran to her, if she is unable to read the sacred book herself. Her devotions are not entirely unmixed with pleasure, for a part of the mosque is always screened off for women, and here she will sit and chat with friends from her native city. She does not trouble herself about the husband and house that she has left behind, for, as she has never had the management of either of them, they can easily get on without her, and her children are safe with a faithful slave. The pilgrimage to Meshed confers the title of *Meshtedi;* that to Kerbelah, of *Kerbelai;* while the most coveted is that of *Haji*, given to those who have visited Mecca, and even to boys born in the month of the *Hejreh* (the flight of the Prophet from Mecca), who thus get the title without the trouble of going on the pilgrimage. To go to Mecca requires a long purse, the Arabs levying blackmail on visitors to their holy city, and accordingly the Persians form themselves into big caravans, paying an Arab guard to protect them from being looted by his inhospitable fellow-countrymen.

On the third day of the pilgrimage, when the holocaust of sheep takes place (which commemorates the supposed sacrifice of Ishmael by Abraham), the pilgrims pluck out the eyes of the animals, which they dry, and consider a most effective talisman to avert the evil eye from children, if a turquoise be stuck inside them, stitching them on to the little caps worn by their sons. (Most juvenile Persians carry about a perfect armoury of charms, such as verses from the Koran hung in a bag from the neck, or bound to the forearm, blue beads, and so on. It is most unsafe to admire a child, unless you take the precaution to say "*Mashallah!*" for should it fall ill after your gaze rested upon it, the parents will give you the credit of its indisposition.)

Travellers to the holy places wear a peculiar dress, *ihram*, which they lay for a day and a night on the shrines to sanctify them; and keep them to be used for their shrouds; and they bring back bags of earth from the same spots to be sprinkled on their corpses when about to be buried, and for use during their devotions.

I always thought highly of the courage and endurance of the Persian ladies who undertook these pilgrimages, especially when I remembered how grudgingly they are admitted into Paradise.

From what I could gather, the after life appears to be arranged solely for the convenience of the men. These latter pass an eternity of bliss in exquisite gardens, beside running streams, surrounded by bands of *houris* of surpassing beauty, who lull them to repose with their enchanting music. Nor are the creature comforts of the faithful forgotten. A certain wondrous tree sends its branches into all their dwelling-places, each branch being laden with the favourite dishes of the man to whom it offers itself, and the believers can rest at will beside a broad river of milk.

The poor women can only attain their own Paradise by extraordinary exertions, and there does not appear to be much provided for their entertainment when they do reach the goal of their longings, save angels, to whom probably they pay court as they did in a former state to their earthly lords and masters.

In one part of the Koran it is stated that the Prophet was

permitted a glance into hell, and observed that the great majority of the poor victims writhing there in torment were women!

No well-to-do Persian would care to eat food cooked the day before, as a *jinn* or *deeve* might have looked at it during the night and so rendered it evil; and for the same reason youths are not allowed to sleep alone, as, "Who can tell what may happen during the night?" rich men usually paying a *mollah* to be with them during the hours of darkness. I should not be surprised if the evening meal had something to do with these ghosts. It begins at 9 p.m. with much drinking of wine and arrack, and eating of dried fruits, the dinner proper not making its appearance till 11 p.m. or even midnight.

Before this latter appears, the company adjourn to the tank in the courtyard, to rinse their mouths and wash their hands, as, unless all traces of the forbidden wine be got rid of, every dish and platter will be rendered *nejus*, or unclean, and will have to be subjected to extraordinary cleansing operations on the next day. Although Persians believe that it is a sin to drink wine, and that in the next world they will be forced to partake of a horrible water in expiation for this propensity, yet it is rare to meet any one in the upper classes who is not fond of intoxicating liquors, albeit they indulge in the taste secretly.

The dinner, when at last it arrives on the scene, consists of six or eight dishes of soup, *pillau, chillau, kabobs,* and so on, arranged on a leather tablecloth, which is unrolled and spread on the ground. The food is disposed of with marvellous celerity, and then the whole company throw themselves on their respective divans to sleep.

Persians have a deep-rooted repugnance to killing anything at night, looking upon it, indeed, as a sin to despatch a lamb or fowl after dark, while the greatest criminal is never forced to pay the penalty of his misdeeds until the morning.

Although the dog is an unclean animal, yet Persians make an exception in favour of greyhounds (*tazi*) and all hunting dogs, saying that the heads of every species are clean, as that is the only part of itself that the animal cannot lick.

Cats, however, although clean, are not much in favour, as their hair is so much in the habit of coming off, and may adhere to the garments of the Faithful when they are engaged in prayer.

Throughout my stay at Kerman I was struck with the curiously aimless existence of most of the gentlemen with whom I came in contact.

The Prince and the Bejat, his deputy, were, however, very busy men, as the work of a whole province devolved on them, and a Persian Governor occupies himself with the settlement of a trifling dispute among his servants, as well as with the matters of moment that come under his notice. His sentences are usually very severe. In a case that I was told of, a stable-boy was supposed to have stolen some copper money from another servant, and this latter went to the Governor for redress. He had, however, no proofs to offer, except that the thief had left a footprint, or rather the mark of his cotton shoe, near the rifled hoard. The Governor at once commanded that this impress should be measured with a piece of string, and the length compared with that of the *givas* worn by the whole household of servants. This was done. The unlucky groom's shoe fitted best, and upon this circumstantial evidence, worthy of a Lecoq, he was condemned to lose his right hand—a punishment which would degrade him for the rest of his life to the already overcrowded ranks of the city beggars. Fortunately for him intercession was made, with the happy result that a portion of his ear was cut off instead—a sufficiently stern award, a European would think, when he reflects that very probably the youth was innocent, or the whole thing a plot got up by a malicious fellow-servant to injure one whom he disliked or who stood in his way.

But if a Persian gentleman is not in a position where he acts as judge and ruler, or has not a large property to attend to, he spends his time as a hanger-on of the Governor or of any high official of his town, if there is no royal court at which to make his obeisance. To lounge about the hall in which the ruler is dispensing justice is considered as a sign of respect to the powers that be, and the settlement of the various cases is watched with keen interest, the onlookers debating among themselves how much money it will be necessary for a client to offer the Governor to decide the case in his favour, justice in Persia being entirely ruled by the man who has the longest purse.

As some reward for his "service," as this method of doing honour is termed, the hanger-on may partake of a *pillau* which will be served at noon in the hall of justice, after which the Governor will probably retire for a siesta, and, if keen on getting money, will return later to settle more cases, or, if not, will go for a slow amble, attended by many parasites and servants, all intent on flattering him in somewhat fulsome manner.

But here again I feel that perhaps I am too severe. Most of the gentlemen with whom I was brought in contact never appeared to me to do anything much beyond sleeping, talking, and eating, never reading a book on any pretence whatever, and not even throwing themselves heartily into sport.

Yet, of course, the Oriental point of view is not the European one, and probably they looked upon us as lunatics for our ceaseless energy, our love of exercise, and our habit of filling up every spare moment with some occupation or other.

"*Kismet!*" ("It is fate") is sufficient explanation for an Oriental to give when he is ill, or when things go wrong, even from his own fault; and this fatalism is too alien to my Western mind to permit me, I fear, to be quite fair when writing of my Persian acquaintances.

CHAPTER XV

A PICNIC AT KERMAN

DURING our stay at Kerman we were thrown much upon the society of the gentry of the neighbourhood, and found them easy to get on with, being very sociable, quick-witted, and intelligent, although we speedily discovered them to be somewhat lacking in such qualities as truthfulness, honesty, or honour.

It is, however, unfair to attempt to criticise Orientals by European standards, as one soon perceives that their "point of view" is widely divergent from that of the West.

My brother, after some years in India, where friendly intercourse with the high-class natives seemed an impossibility, was glad to be living with a race who would eat, drink, and smoke with the infidel Feringhees without demur.

For my part, I found them exceedingly courteous and attentive to me—a matter for wonder, considering the low position held by women in Persia, which fact made me stand very much upon my dignity. The most educated among them were weary of their Government and its doings, and again and again I was asked, with that strange lack of patriotism so noticeable in Persia, as to when the English were coming, my interlocutors seeming to imagine that a British army was already disembarking on the coast, and was about to march inland from the Persian Gulf.

One of the most intelligent of our *habitués* once told me that Persia was, as it were, at the last act of the *Tazieh*, or

Passion Play; for when the audience perceives that the play is about to conclude, one man gets his slippers ready, another wraps his cloak around him, while a third hunts for the bag of dried fruits with which he has been regaling himself at intervals. No one attends to the actors in the least; all are thinking of themselves and their belongings, and how best to hurry out of the theatre. And our friend applied the analogy by remarking that thus it was with Persia at the present time, every Persian thinking that the kingdom was nearing its end, and being fully occupied in looking out for his own interests.

On another occasion he interested me by saying that there was a certain bird that travelled from country to country. Rome, Carthage, Spain, and many another land had been blessed by its sojourn among them, and now, he affirmed, it had fixed its abode in England. Upon asking what attracted the " bird " to a country, I was given the answer in earnest tones, " Good laws, justice, an incorruptible Government—everything, in short, that England has, and Persia lacks."

As they got to know me by degrees, some of them spoke bitterly about the need of education for their women, comparing these latter with me, to whom they did the honour of saying that I could understand whatever they said! They complained that their wives could talk nothing but gossip picked up at the weekly bath, and that as their religion forbade the men seeing their womankind, save in the house, they had very few interests in common. I always told them that they alone were to blame, and when I explained to them how I had been educated, my school and college life, and my final months of tuition in Germany, they were quite aghast, and one of them exclaimed indignantly, " It is all the fault of our accursed religion, that binds us in chains as well as our poor women!"

One topic of conversation was of unfailing interest to men and women alike—our Queen. They were never tired of asking questions about her Majesty's age, the years of her reign, and so on, holding her in an extraordinary esteem. One gentleman expressed himself to the effect that if a great nation like the English were ruled by a woman, whom they one and all regarded with an indescribable admiration and reverence, she must indeed be a supernatural being!

They were also curious about the institutions of *Yangi Dunya* (New World), the Persian name for America, and I used to wonder if the term "Yankee Doodle" could possibly be a corruption of it. Speaking of names, our Persian friends insisted that "Kerman" and "German" were one and the same word, and that Germania owed its origin to a colony from distant Carmania, but they could find nothing further in support of this rather startling theory.

An ordinary Persian's idea of light conversation is to ask what you have paid for each of your possessions, from your horses, carpets, furniture, and downwards. He will, moreover, make a series of searching inquiries as to your income, age, position in society, and will not hesitate to question you on your most private affairs.

At first I used to be somewhat taken aback at a habit, equally common among our acquaintances and our servants, of saying "*Chira?*" (Why?) to every proposition. "Will you dine with us to-night?" would be answered by "Why?" when the invited guest had every intention of coming; and frequently an order given to a domestic would be accepted with the inevitable "*Chira?*"

Morier's inimitable "Hajji Baba" was a work in which we greatly rejoiced during our stay in Persia, and I lent it to Nasrullah Khan, thinking that he would enjoy perusing it. The book, however, puzzled instead of amusing him, and he used to say to me that he was reading steadily on in the hope of coming in time to something terrible or romantic or even comic. "The other day I read two or three pages to Meshtedi Mehdi," he told me, "and Meshtedi said it was ridiculous to print things that were done every day in Persia, and conversations just like those which we ourselves hold with one another!"

We frequently entertained our acquaintances with luncheon-parties, dinners, and picnics, and it may interest my readers if I give an account of one of these latter, which took place at the garden of Fathabad, some nine miles from Kerman.

We sent off the servants and the mules, laden with provisions, on the day before, and we ourselves started about half-past eight one fine September morning, old Haji Muhammed Khan arranging to be our guide. Our destination was one of the numerous places in and around Kerman that he affirmed had once belonged to a prehistoric sister of his—a sister whom we could never help regarding as mythical, so extensive and all-embracing did her possessions appear to have been!

Whenever Haji Khan took us a ride, it was always to escort us to some garden, the possession of this lady, and he invariably gave such flowery descriptions of these places beforehand, and we considered them so unworthy of a visit when we reached them, that his pride reminded us of the proverb, " A Persian thinks that a hen's egg, if it belongs to him, has been produced by a swan."

On this occasion we made our way to a point outside the city, where our eight other guests had agreed to meet us, but as Persians have no great regard for punctuality we were not surprised to find no one there, and having despatched a servant to inform them of our movements, we rode on.

Although Haji Khan was conducting us to a well-known spot, yet he seemed curiously uncertain of the direction in which it lay, and I was fast feeling that we had a very erratic guide, when suddenly the " Photographer" galloped up, took the direction of affairs, and steered us safely to the shady poplar avenue of Fathabad. A long tank full of water, and alive with ducks and geese, lay in front of a fairy-like erection, all dainty columns, white stucco-work, and stained glass—a most refreshing sight after the glare and heat of our ride through a barren country. The big garden behind was full of zinnias, dahlias, petunias, asters—in fact all the autumnal flowers that one finds in an English garden; vines were trained over mud-columned *pergolas*, and a pretty kiosk had steps leading down to a round pond, whose water was reputed to be highly beneficial for certain complaints.

We climbed upon the roof of the principal building to enjoy the fine panorama of the desert, and here the serpent of this little Paradise was discovered, as the "Photographer" seized a long snake by the tail, and pretended to chase Suleiman Mirza with it, which proceeding frightened the doughty commander-in-chief half out of his wits.

The rooms were charmingly furnished with green and gold floorcloths, and comfortable silk-covered divans, with a profusion of huge downy cushions, although the artistic effect of the Persian adornments was considerably spoilt by a series of hideous German prints, representing languishing ladies in evening dress, smoking cigarettes; inferior mirrors shared the wall spaces with these pictures, while from the numerous lamps hung blue, yellow, and red glass balls, identical with those used to decorate Christmas-trees. We all sat on a carpet for lunch, as no chairs were forthcoming, and our meal began with tomatoes from the garden. I mention this as, after a *régime* of marrow for two months, with not even a potato or an onion, it was indeed a treat to taste a fresh vegetable. All our guests were accustomed to the use of knives and forks, but some of their habits at table were distinctly odd. If bread were handed round they would turn over every piece with their fingers, until they found one to their taste, and they thought nothing of biting a corner off a sweetmeat or biscuit and then replacing the mutilated fragment back on the dish! After a time I never had cakes when Persians came to tea, as they seemed unable to take a slice in an ordinary way, but would pull the whole thing to pieces, breaking off a bit here and a bit there, until they had messed the entire confection! As a rule they refrained from putting the spoon or fork they had been using into the dishes, and only ate with their fingers when the food was hard to manipulate in a civilised way.

However, to drink from the lip of a water-jug seemed an

irresistible temptation, and apparently their chief idea of a teapot was that it was a vessel the spout of which was specially adapted to sip from.

I always did my best to give my guests a European *menu*, and they frequently told me how much they enjoyed it, as there was so little variety in their own food.

Twice daily a tray containing bowls of soup, *pillau*, *chillau* (plain boiled rice), and *khoroosh* (stewed meat and grease) was sent to each member of the Prince's suite from the royal kitchen, and I fancy that this never-changing diet occasionally palled upon its recipients.

When our lunch was over my brother and I betook ourselves to the garden, so as to leave the Persians free to indulge in their customary midday siesta, after which the Photographer, Beorgh Khan, and myself set up our respective cameras. Tea over, we mounted our steeds for the homeward ride, and by chance got on the wrong side of a stream which must be crossed. Our horses, well accustomed to such work, took their leaps in fine style, but it was curious to see the alarm and hesitation of the others, who would probably have turned back to find an easier course if they had not feared our laughter. Fortunately all struggled across somehow or other, and I devoted most of the rest of the ride to giving the doctor a lesson in English, not considering his instructor to be altogether reliable, as he had impressed on the doctor that the past participle of all English verbs ended in *en*, and had written out for his pupil a list of such words as *hunten, loven, liken*, &c.

The "Photographer" and Beorgh Khan rode with small hawks on their wrists, inciting them to swoop upon any harmless "cockyolly" bird they came across, or, seizing their guns, they would gallop furiously after the numerous crows, which did not appear to be much alarmed when fired at: probably Persians had taken aim at them before. The "Photographer" told me how he used to capture larks in Tabriz in the winter. He would ride out with some friends, one of them having a hawk on his wrist, and as soon as a lark was espied, the falcon was made to fly on to the hand of another member of the party. The lark, seeing the hawk, would crouch closely to the ground, and was then captured by a noose attached to a stick. Partridges are caught in much the same way, as they huddle into the snow at sight of an enemy, giving rise to the saying in the North, "As the partridge hides its head in the snow," which is equivalent to our "ostrich" proverb, and which in other parts of Persia is rendered, "As a man riding on a camel thinks he is not seen if he bends his head down." Our friend highly appreciated the forbidden *gusht-i-bulbul* (literally flesh of nightingales), or pork, and had hit upon an ingenious way by which he could enjoy it when at Tabriz. He told me he was in the habit of making expeditions to Lake Urumieh to shoot wild boar, but of course could not eat the unclean food in the face of the religious scruples of his family and servants; therefore he was accustomed to send the hams to his European acquaintances, who would invite him to their houses in return to partake of these delicacies!

It got dark before we reached the city, where we said goodbye to our friends, and, as there was no moon, we had rather a bad time traversing the couple of miles, outside the walls, to our house, the road being broken away in places, with numerous dangerous holes at intervals. "Charters," however, seemed always possessed of super-equine intelligence on these occasions, keeping his head very low, avoiding all specially black-looking places, or testing them first with his hoof, so that I felt it was wiser to trust to his sagacity rather than to my own.

As our china and glass sent out from England the previous October reached us early in September, we felt that we could now give dinner-parties in style, and the Farman Farma was among our earliest guests.

It was rather an undertaking entertaining a Persian Prince, as besides having to prepare a varied repast for our *invited* guests, I had to arrange for *pillaus*, melons, wine, *kalians*, &c., to be got ready for at least twenty of their followers. It was amusing to see how solicitous our servants were that these latter should fare well, all Persians saying that it does not much matter if the master gets a poor dinner, but that if his servants are ill-fed they will give the inhospitable house a bad name in the Bazaar. "Fill the mouth of a servant" is a Persian proverb to this effect, and I could not impress upon my henchmen that it made not the slightest difference to me whether the Farman Farma's followers approved of my hospitality or not.

His Highness had agreed to be with us half an hour after sunset, *i.e.*, seven o'clock, but with Oriental procrastination he, with the Bejat and doctor, never arrived till past nine o'clock! He was greatly pleased to see me in evening dress, and was much astonished when I told him that we both made a point of changing for dinner, even when alone, the Persian habit of never changing the clothes, whatever work had been done in them during the day, being a particularly unpleasant one to me.

Nasrullah Khan, and a certain stout Persian gentleman, had quite a bad name in Kerman, on account of their attention to the toilette, Persians saying that it is effeminate for a man to be clean, and despising any man who is obtrusively so, while they specially resent any one indulging in more than one shave per week!

At dinner the Prince was delighted with an Indian curry made by our invaluable *syce*, and begged us to send the latter to teach the novel dish to his cook. This Fakir Mahomet was only too pleased to do, and in course of time was presented by his Highness with a robe of honour, consisting of some yards of Kerman shawl.

Our little factotum was extravagantly proud after this dignity had been conferred upon him, and he got into the habit of calling the servants by an uncomplimentary Hindustani word, which of course none of them understood.

When, however, they took to applying this term of abuse to him it was more than he could stand, and he betook himself to Nasrullah Khan to explain that he was, as it were, in a cleft stick, not daring to explain the meaning of this particular expression to the servants, but yet furiously indignant with them for presuming to use it to him!

His Highness ordered our servants about freely, calling for tea and *kalians* at intervals after dinner, and saying to Hashim, "*Shuma, chitor ast?*" ("How are you?")—which mark of favour nearly turned the head of that worthy.

In Persia it is a sign of particular friendship to give orders to the servants of your host, and a Persian only takes this liberty when he is on terms of great intimacy with the household.

The Prince was the only one of our acquaintances who did this, but the others always made a point of inquiring after the health of our head-waiter, when they came to the house, this attention being supposed to be an indirect politeness to ourselves.

After dinner on this occasion we sat and talked, the Farman Farma taking the greatest interest in the details of our system of Government, our Army and Navy. He was wonderfully quick at understanding the gist of any subject under discussion, and, what was perhaps more remarkable, he remembered in its smallest particulars anything that he had once grasped thoroughly.

Catching sight of my guitar, he begged me to give him a song, and I complied with some amusement, knowing that he would consider that I was evoking the most barbarous "cat's music" from the instrument. He professed, however, to admire my performance greatly, and went on to say that he had heard European ladies sing at Tabriz, but that their melodies seemed so terrible to him that he could with difficulty refrain from stopping his ears! On this I could not resist from remarking that most Oriental singing was apt to affect me in much the same way, and then changed the conversation, feeling that a discussion on the respective merits of Eastern and Western music would hardly be a profitable one.

Glad as I was to have my crockery, yet its advent deprived us of the services of Fatullah, a worthy youth, who acted as second waiter. He was unfortunately of a very nervous

A PERSIAN GUITAR PLAYER.

disposition, and when our china was unpacked Hashim came laughing to tell me that the boy wished to leave the Consulate, as he had not courage to stay in face of such a formidable array of plates and dishes. However, he did not go for some time, until one unlucky day he smashed a saucer, and at once fled to his home in the town. We recaptured him, told him that we were not angry, as we felt it was not his fault, and all went well for about a month. Then one evening a howling, sobbing figure made its appearance bearing the fragments of a broken decanter to show me. It was Fatullah, whom I consoled as best I could; but alack, his nerve was gone, and he went off for the second time, firmly declining to have anything further to do with such dangerous goods as glass and china! "*Il n'y-a-pas d'homme nécessaire*" is as true of Persia as of everywhere else, and his place was speedily filled up by a substitute, who suited us better in every way.

Although we did not regret the loss of Fatullah, yet we should have been thankful if our other servants had copied, in even a small degree, his unusual conscientiousness; for about this time an evil spirit seemed to have taken possession of them. From Fakir Mahomet (whose backsliding was a real grief to me) down to the lowest servant they became lazier than ever, forgot the simplest order, went about dirty, and were conspicuous by their absence from the Consulate.

It did not take Nasrullah Khan long to find out the reason of this unpleasant change in their behaviour, and he soon reported that all, save Hashim, had taken to themselves wives, Ali, the fat boy of sixteen, leading the way. Cheap as is the married state in Kerman, yet their wages were not sufficient to keep their wives in the luxury which those ladies evidently demanded, and, as a consequence, they had to steal or run into debt. The cook and the grooms tried the former course, and, after a time, it became obvious to us that our horses were not in the condition that they had been. My brother accused Vali roundly of making away with their barley, and he replied in the plausible Persian way, "Let the *Sahib* beat me if he will, or even kill me, but let him not accuse his servant of such a low crime as theft, for I have never learnt to steal." However, in spite of his protestations we superintended the daily feeds ourselves, and had the satisfaction of seeing our beloved horses improve in condition very soon. Fakir Mahomet had charge of the key of the barley-room, and was supposed to give out the day's supply before he went off to the Bazaar to do my housekeeping. But one day Vali was tracked to his house in the town by a long trail of corn, and it transpired that the *syce* had actually handed over the key of the store-room to him to help himself, as his only idea at this time was to spend the whole day in the society of his wife. Vali was dismissed on the spot, confessed everything, saying that he had stolen all he could since we had returned from the hills, and demanded with marvellous effrontery a character, as he said all grooms stole, and such a trifle should not weigh against him in obtaining a fresh situation.

The other servants came in a body to beg for him to be taken back, and when they found that their pleadings had no effect, clubbed together to give him a sum of money to speed him on his way—all Persian servants being full of sympathy for a comrade who cheats his master.

Our best servant was Hashim who, when blamed, however, used periodically to pack up all his belongings, announcing that he was going to leave us; but these preparations for departure were merely a vent to his feelings, as he, in common with all the others, looked upon himself as *the* necessary man of our establishment, and greatly magnified his office.

If we had been at Tehran he would most probably have left at an early stage of his acquaintance with us, and would then have vainly implored us to take him back again.

He always rode the *abdari* horse on our expeditions, and having let it down twice from careless riding, he was exceedingly upset when found fault with, as he said that on both occasions some passer-by had audibly admired the handsome little animal and thus given it the evil eye.

An *abdari* pony (an animal specially bred for carrying water, as its name signifies) is a great Persian institution. It is like a miniature cart-horse and is loaded with two saddle-bags which contain the porous jars of water, dishes of *pillau*, and dried fruits, to form a Persian lunch. From one side hangs a bucket full of burning charcoal to supply the *kalians* and *samovar*, and from the other depends a thing like a wooden umbrella containing the skewers for roasting the *kabob-i-sikh*. The rider mounts upon a folded felt, and leans his back against a sort of leather box in which various provisions are stowed away, and it is incumbent on him to have a long stick with a metal knob stuck in somewhere in a conspicuous position. All the dishes and bottles have leather cases, so that it is a rare thing for articles to get broken. Persian gentlemen would never think of going out an ordinary afternoon ride unless accompanied by their *abdari*, for which they frequently give large sums. Friday, the Mohammedan Sunday, is the great day for taking exercise (?), and many were the family parties we used to come across ambling along very slowly. A servant would always precede his master, and was closely followed by the father and eldest son on horses, while younger scions of the house and a medley of retainers closed the procession bestriding mules and donkeys, very young boys being held in front of their special servants. The richer the family the more horses they displayed. The animal *par excellence* of Persia is the donkey, which is usually ridden by the *mollahs* and the merchant classes; and at Kerman, at all events, it seemed to be within the reach of the humblest. The Persian donkey proper looks like a small edition of the animal that is to be seen in any costermonger's cart, and ought not to be confounded with the white Bahrein ass, big as a mule.

It is the fashion in Persia for elderly gentlemen to ride Bahrein asses, which they consider equal in speed to horses; but they are always careful to have a horse led by a servant, to show to the world that it is choice, not necessity, that makes them ride a donkey. Writing about donkeys leads one naturally to mention horses, and though Persia is in a certain way the land of these noble animals, their quality bears not the smallest proportion to their quantity.

To walk would be beneath the dignity of any Persian gentleman and also of his chief servants, and so perforce he has several horses, although for the most part they are mere ponies with no particular breeding about them.

The Persian rides his horse with an exceedingly heavy bit, his great object being to pull it up and turn sharply—the mouths of all young horses bleeding till they get hard and callous and their quarters being frequently strained from the same cause. The high-peaked saddle, though comfortable, lifts the rider too far above his horse to control it properly, and instead of a whip he kicks its sides with his big iron shovel-stirrups. Though some of the nomad tribes ride capitally, yet all the city-bred Persians with whom it was my fate to come in contact, were miserable performers on horseback, some of them frankly confessing that they never allowed their horses to go out of the comfortable amble, universal in Persia, as they considered galloping so dangerous!

Towards the end of our stay at Kerman we had a little stud of ten horses, nearly every one of whom required many lessons from my brother to cure them of their tricks of flinging back their heads, "stumping," and taking exceedingly short strides, all attributable to the Persian bit, as were their hard mouths.

Riding was our great pleasure, and it was fortunate for us that we could indulge freely in horseflesh, there not being many countries where five pounds will purchase a respectable mount, and where every one considered that thirty pounds was an enormous sum to pay for my beautiful Arab "Nawab," which was so profusely admired on all sides that it was quite a marvel how he managed to escape the evil eye, said to be so prevalent in Persia.

Usually the horses were wiry little Arabs about fourteen hands high, plucky, enduring, and very easy to manage by their riders. None of them ever took exception to my habit-skirt, looking on it probably as a sort of variation of the flapping Persian coats to which they were accustomed. They also adapted themselves at once to the light bridles with which we always rode them, and never made any objection to my side-saddle.

The post and *Gymkhana* were our weekly dissipations, while we varied our rides with rifle-practice and occasionally long walks, these latter being somewhat tedious, there never being any particular point to make for, and it was disheartening to know that those hills, whose every boulder, seam, and tuft of vegetation we could see, were in reality several miles off.

CHAPTER XVI

LAST MONTHS AT KERMAN

TOWARDS the end of October Kerman was visited by a violent thunderstorm, which considerably lowered the temperature, and covered all the higher mountain-peaks with snow. It became so chilly that we feared winter was beginning to set in, but were assured that a spell of cold weather in October, to be succeeded by warmth in November, was usually the case in Persia.

The unaccustomed floods of rain converted the whole place into a muddy morass, making riding out of the question for some days, and doing a good deal of damage to all the mud-built houses in the place, so that we were glad when November brought us hot sunshine again.

As winter approached it was a constant source of wonder to me as to what the jackals could find to eat. Perhaps my imagination had something to do with it, but certainly it seemed as if their howls had quite altered in character and become more despairing since the summer nights, when they made the round of the well-stocked gardens to devour the fruit.

According to the Persians, whom I quote without looking upon them as especially accurate observers of natural history, the jackals, when they are half-famished during the winter, sit down in a circle, staring at one another. The first animal that dozes is at once torn to pieces and devoured by the others; and thus the theory of the "survival of the fittest" is kept up.

My brother and I wound up our picnic season with an

KALAH-I-DUKTAR.

expedition to the *Kalah-i-Duktar* (maiden fortress), the remains of a savage-looking and almost inaccessible stronghold, some ten miles to the north of Kerman, perched on the summit of a curious hill, cleft from crest to base, the sole mode of access being by climbing up this fissure.

Probably the garrison only resorted to this eyrie in time of need, as the whole foot of the hill on which it was erected was covered with the remains of houses, enclosed with a high, castellated mud wall, with a gateway at its lowest point, and watch-towers at intervals.

The citadel, now deserted and falling into decay, was supposed to have been inhabited by a band of robbers in the days when Kerman was a great commercial centre. From this point the bandits could command the caravan route across the great desert, and could swoop down at their ease upon the long strings of slowly moving camels laden with merchandise.

It was by no means an easy task to penetrate this stronghold, as after scrambling upwards over big boulders a wall of sheer rock had to be scaled. This I did not attempt, as my brother had his work cut out for him in hauling up our Persian guests one after the other over this steep place.

Once on the summit they were disappointed to see little save the remains of water-tanks and fragments of mud walls, nor did a solitary Kufic inscription excite any emotion in their breasts. They were helped down again, and returned to enjoy their lunch, giving me highly coloured accounts of the dangers through which they had passed. I fancy that they allowed their imaginations to run riot when they reached home, for the Farman Farma begged my brother not to have a picnic in such a perilous locality again, as he felt sure that the lives of his suite had been seriously endangered!

That morning, just before starting off on our expedition, Fakir Mahomet came to us in great alarm, saying that a terrible creature was lurking among the boxes in the dark passage which led up to my store-room. As he affirmed that it was as big as a mule, and, moreover, that it had flown at him when he approached the store-room, our curiosity was naturally excited, and we went to see this marvel. In the semi-darkness there lay what looked like a huge dragon-fly on one of the boxes, and I rushed off for my insect-net and lethal bottle, full of excitement at getting a novel "find," imploring every one to keep their distances, as it might fly away if disturbed. My brother took the net and brought it right down on the object, which made an odd rattling noise. The *syce* pulled me back hastily as I tried to inspect it, begging me, in heartrending tones, not to go near. I advanced, however, and to my amusement and astonishment saw a little cardboard-winged dragon, coloured green and yellow. My brother and I laughed heartily, but the *syce* fled in a panic of terror as I picked it up. It had come out from home in one of my boxes, but as I had never set eyes on it during the seven months I had been at Kerman, its appearance at that time and in that place will ever remain a mystery. I took it upstairs to the sitting-room, and in a short time all our servants had assembled on the terrace outside and were peeping nervously in through the open window at the toy as it lay quietly on a table, the *syce* leading the party and giving realistic details of the way in which the "mule hyæna," as he called it, had sprung at him. I laughed at the men, and, to show them how harmless it was, took up my dimunitive dragon, whereupon a regular stampede ensued. A few days after this episode some of our Persian friends came to tea, and we told them the story, producing the little pasteboard creature, so that they might enjoy the joke with us. To our surprise, however, they were all obviously nervous of it, and only after some persuasion the boldest gentleman was induced to touch it, which he did most gingerly, another turning to ask me in what part of the world dragons had their habitation, and not at all convinced when I declined to assign a locality to these fabulous monsters.

At the end of November we went for three or four days' shooting in the hills, and chose a place called Baserjùn, one of the wildest and dreariest camping grounds I have ever seen. We were in a long defile, the ground covered with boulders, and the *débris* from the hills that shut us in, while the pink Kupayeh Range rose like a long jagged plateau, frowning down upon our tents. As my brother was after wild sheep during this trip, and these animals frequent the lower ground, while the ibex choose the most inaccessible parts for their haunts, I was able to accompany him into a world of brilliantly coloured mud hills, with conglomerate cropping out of their sides. Among these a few herds of goats were feeding, and one day, as we were up aloft, far above them, we heard the most blood-curdling yells. Our *shikarchi*, looking keenly down into the valley, announced that a wolf had just carried off a goat, the boy in charge of the herd waking the echoes with his cries to such an extent that it was difficult to believe that he himself was not the victim. It was wonderful to see the agility of these huntsmen. In long, blue cotton blouses, sheepskin jackets, and their legs bound in *puttis*, they ran up and down the hills in search of game, grievously disappointed when nothing was disclosed to their keen eyes. We kept below in the valley for the most part, and one could not but remark on the great silence and lifelessness in these barren mountains. Not an insect was to be seen, save perhaps a beetle or two; occasionally a vulture hovered noiselessly over our heads, and sometimes near the brackish streams, which looked as if icebound, such broad belts of salt lay on their banks, a small covey of partridges would fly up. I came upon bleached tortoise-shells, and here and there the quills of a porcupine, but of wild sheep there seemed to be none, and our *shikarchis* got quite in despair, and gloomily squatted near us for a rest after all their efforts. Suddenly, almost as if they were close to us, instead of being about a quarter of a mile away, so clearly could we see them in the pure atmosphere, a herd of six or eight moufflon sprang one after another down from a hill, and were off and out of sight before we could get to our feet, the chase that ensued being a failure. The nights in tents were now very cold, and as the evenings drew in early I was thankful to be back again at home, the servants more delighted than I, as they found camp life always very tedious, lying about and gossiping all day long, with frequent interludes of a concertina performance by the *syce*, and a topical song composed by Hashim concerning us and our doings, with a good deal of mention of the hard lot of the *Sahib's* servants.

Kerman was notorious even among Persian cities for the number of its beggars, and during the winter we were there the Prince organised a scheme for relieving them, which is worth mentioning, as I have never heard of any other Persian, be he royal or the reverse, doing the like. He issued so many hundreds of lithographed tickets monthly, and each of these entitled the recipient to so many pounds of bread, which was made at a certain bakery in the town. To prevent abuse as far as possible, the Prince sent his officers down to the shop to take bread from it by haphazard daily, and insisted on having this mixture of millet and barley-flour on his own table. He furthermore forced all his suite and the gentry of Kerman to buy tickets from him for distribution, telling each man how many *tomans'* worth he was expected to take. My brother, as Consul, had six hundred tickets to give away monthly, and at first used to bestow them on the few beggars at our gate, as we went out for our afternoon rides. However, the little knot of ten or a dozen soon swelled to one or two hundred, and as we did not wish to dispose of every ticket before the month had half run out, we resorted to the expedient of having a fixed day for giving them, choosing Sundays. When we went out for our weekly walk, the horses, which we rode on all other days, being led in solemn procession after us, we would see outside our garden a ragged, dirty, voluble crowd of beggars, which my brother ordered to squat down in rows while he distributed the tickets. I always stayed inside until the ceremony was over and the crowds had dispersed, leaving a cloud of dust behind them.

On one occasion my brother left them to return to the house for more tickets, as the hundred he had taken with him had all been used up. He put a soldier in charge, but the moment his presence was removed every beggar sprang

BREAD TICKET ISSUED BY THE FARMAN FARMA.

up, and on his return he was surrounded by a howling, yelling mob, the worst members of which were the women, who at the best of times were adepts in the art of changing their places so as to get a second or even a third ticket. They surged round him, pulling his clothes, screaming, whirling up the dust, and trying to snatch the tickets from him, until he was obliged to retreat, further distribution being out of the question, and the soldiers promptly barricaded the garden door against the imperious hordes outside.

I never thought that the destitution among these beggars was at all extreme, as they were always in such capital spirits, not seeming in the least degree depressed by their life and its surroundings. Of course among the crowd there was a percentage of aged people, blind folk, and poor wretches with manifold complaints, who were always provided for first of all; but the large majority were eager and active in their movements, a considerable proportion being young women, apparently well fed, and by no means in rags.

Kerman is, on the whole, a very favourable locality for the poor. The sun saves them from the need of fires and much clothing; very little rain falls; lodgings are to be had without payment, and it is possible to live in comfort on a penny a day.

It is considered most unlucky to turn beggars away from the door unless they are given something, be it only an onion or a scrap of bread. If a child of the house is ailing two or three *krans* in copper money are put under its pillow at night, and in the morning the coins are given to the mendicants making their rounds, the child's complaint having been supposed to have passed into the money; and of course, as is natural, the beggars are not forgotten at the festive seasons of marriage or the birth of a son.

Christmas was now approaching fast, and I found our pretty house a very chilly winter residence. As we expected to leave Kerman after the New Year, and travel, my brother thought it would be wiser to forswear fires altogether, fearing that if we got accustomed to them we should probably get ill when our tent life began. So in the house we wrapped ourselves up in furs and long-lined boots as if equipped for an Arctic expedition, dressing far more lightly when we went out, as it was always warm in the brilliant sunshine. The servants, on the other hand, indulged in fires, and caught bad colds and chills, calling for all our skill in doctoring. *Bargi* went about in the same thin cotton garments that she affected during the summer heats, and of course got ill. I had presented her with some woollen clothes on the occasion of our tour in the hills, but she had actually not donned them in this bitter weather, and when I demanded the reason, she could only reply that she thought they were given her for a journey, and must not be used on any other occasion, and, moreover, the flimsy coverings she wore were the *dastùr*, or custom, of her people.

She developed a "churchyard" cough, and had a great oppression on her chest, which I tried to cure with a mustard poultice. Unluckily it blistered her skin, and she bathed the affected part with cold water to relieve the heat which my remedy had engendered. Either her remedy or *mine* was too drastic a one, for her skin seemed as if burnt, and although she suffered me to dress her chest, yet she was convinced in her own mind that Feringhee doctoring was a disastrous failure, and, taking French leave, went home with all her effects. No message on my part could induce her to return.

On the third day after her departure, she suddenly reappeared in the best of tempers with herself and all the world, bursting into fits of laughter when she approached me. This peculiar conduct was, I suspect, to conceal a considerable nervousness on her part as to what her reception would be; but I was far too thankful to see her looking so well to be able to reprove her, and could not help being further mollified when she assured me that she had never removed my dressings, in spite of the remonstrances of her aged mother. This lady had doctored her daughter with an infallible Parsee cure for burns, which was simple, if not effective, it merely being to drink quantities of pomegranate juice.

Just about this time we received letters from Meshed,

telling us that two Germans, who were making a walking tour round the world, were on their way to Kerman, and would probably reach that city very shortly.

On the morning of Christmas Eve a couple of alert figures, clad in dark green Tyrolese costumes, with big cloaks hanging over their shoulders, walked into our courtyard, and the famous pedestrians were with us.

Herr Kögel and Herr Stupp hoped to accomplish their formidable journey in less than two years, and were spurred on to their efforts by the prospect of winning 10,000 dollars should they be successful. The former had left San Francisco in June, 1894, with a Herr Thorner as his companion, walking with him across America and part of Europe, but had been forced to leave him behind at Bucharest on account of illness. However, while crossing the St. Gothard Pass, the two comrades had encountered Herr Stupp, a mere boy; and this historic meeting was immortalised in a photo, in which the long cloaks, Tyrolese hats, alpenstocks and revolvers of the heroes played a great part.

The visiting-card of Herr Stupp struck me as somewhat original.

EUROPA.   HEINRICH STUPP Jn.   *AFRIKA.*
Fusstourist um die Welt
Start: München 31st July 1895.

1st Dauerwanderer Europa's
Meisterschaftsgeher der Rheinlande
Mitglied des Wander-Club "Fortuna"
Koeln am Rhein.

ASIEN.   *AMERIKA.*

The journals carried by both gentlemen were full of autographs of consuls, police officials, magistrates, hotel-keepers, and so on, most of whom inscribed some laudatory remarks with their names, compatriots usually bursting out into poetry—one, for example, beginning his effusion with " Stupp und Kögel, Wandervögel." The "young heroes," as they were frequently named by their enthusiastic fellow-countrymen, had, according to the terms of their wager, started without a penny in their pockets, trusting to their wits to help them on their way. These latter, or perhaps rather the newspapers, did them good service throughout America and Europe. On their entry into any town they were met by officials, who conducted them in carriages to see all the sights of the place, depositing them finally at a first-class hotel, where they were given the best accommodation without disbursing a sou. Clothes and money appeared to have flowed in in abundance, and, as they were permitted to sell their portraits for fancy prices, apparently they were never short of cash. At Vienna they had given accounts of their journey to crowded audiences, who escorted them back to their hotel in triumphal procession; and they informed me that they had had interviews with princes and even with crowned heads—all of which experiences they had recorded in their diaries, which were to appear as books of travel on their return to their native lands. They had found travelling in Persia very different from being *fêted* in Europe, and had had a trying time from Askabad, *via* Meshed, to Kerman, bread and water being their principal food, and the one thin blanket they carried being quite inadequate to the rigours of a Persian winter. We lodged them with our friend the merchant, Meshtedi Mehdi, in the town, sending down bedding, furniture, and stores to supplement what they could get at his house; and they spent a week at Kerman in seeing the sights and repairing their scanty wardrobes.

My brother and I had been anxious for some time to have a real Christmas dinner, but the beef was the stumbling-block, as none was to be obtained in Kerman. However, we procured a calf as a substitute, and it was fattened up and picketed in a remote corner of the garden, so that we should not be tempted to make a pet of it. From some cause or other it did not do much credit to its feeding, and looked such a meagre little animal that Nasrullah Khan felt it was unworthy to grace our festal board. Ever since we had been at

Kerman we had hired a cow from our gardener, and, as is the custom in Persia, this animal had its calf tied up within hail of it, and about half the milk was always left for the calf to drink after we had been served with our strictly limited supply. Consequently it was a most sturdy, well-nourished creature, and just before Christmas Day Nasrullah Khan cast his eye upon it. He sent the gardener off to the Bazaar on some pretext or other and then gave the order to execute the wrong calf, as if by mistake. He was narrating this to us during lunch with much glee, when the gardener appeared at the open doorway, evidently under the influence of some strong emotion, his weeping wife peeping over his shoulder. "I understand now why you sent me off to the Bazaar," he said reproachfully to Nasrullah Khan, whose well-feigned surprise fell flat, the man clearly seeing that he had been duped ; and he and his helpmate broke out into violent sobbings.

A few questions elicited the fact that this exhibition of sorrow at the loss of his favourite was entirely due to mercenary causes, and when he was offered ample amends he became more than reconciled to our *mirza's* " mistake."

We found this "young beef" most excellent eating when we had our Christmas party. The Prince and some of his suite with the two Germans came to share the turkey, plum-pudding, and mince-pies, and I was pleased at the success of my culinary efforts ; the Persians being unable to disguise their astonishment on the entry of the plum-pudding encircled with flames.

We instructed them in the art of pouring burning brandy over their mince-pies, and they dignified these delicacies with the title of firework puddings.

His Highness was deeply interested in our European guests, and I had to work hard as interpreter, as the latter could only speak German. The Prince wished to ask them all sorts of personal questions—such as the trades of their respective fathers, the incomes of those gentlemen, as to how long they intended to honour Kerman with their presence, and so on—and it required a considerable exercise of tact on my part to satisfy him without wounding their feelings.

He was impressed at their novel methods of travelling, and turning to my brother said he would much like to make such a tour "on the cheap" with him. The Germans took themselves very seriously, and when the time for toasts came round, they clinked their glasses with ours fervently, walking round the table so as to omit no one, and Herr Kögel broke forth into a fine speech. He said that fifty thousand (*sic*) people were thinking of him and his friend on this festive night, and were probably picturing them as wandering forlorn in some pathless desert, whereas—and he then gave us some gracefully turned phrases anent the hospitality of Kerman! After dinner the Prince wrote in Persian characters in their respective autograph-books, and, producing my guitar, we sang some of the well-known German "Folkslieder"; and so ended my second Christmas Day in Persia.

On the day after Christmas we had the pleasure of welcoming Count Magnis to Kerman. He had travelled from Tehran, *viâ* Isfahan and Yezd, and as, until the arrival of Messrs. Stupp and Kögel, we had seen no Europeans for over six months, we greatly appreciated his society.

He was somewhat surprised to find compatriots in this out-of-the-way part of Persia; but these latter left us shortly, to finish in India and Japan the remainder of the 12,700 miles that they had yet to traverse on their feet.

Speeded on their way by the Prince and my brother, they made for the port of Bander Abbas, intending to take steamer from there to Karachi; and some time later on we caught a glimpse of them in an Indian paper, which spoke of their doings as "apostolic"—a singularly ill-chosen word to apply to men who were in quest of money and notoriety. They lost their wager after all, being unable to reach San Francisco by the appointed time, and we could not feel altogether sorry at the failure, as their peculiar mode of travelling would have considerably lowered European prestige in Persia if many had been inspired to follow their example.

Just at the end of December the news that a Boundary Commission was being formed to delimitate the last piece of frontier between the Indian and Persian Empires reached us.

My brother hoped to be put on this Commission, as the boundary line would run between his consular district of Persian Baluchistan and British Baluchistan, but our orders did not come for some time. However, I did my utmost to get ready, in case we were sent off in a hurry, packing many boxes of stores, writing lists of their contents, numbering them, and so on.

But the days passed by, and no tidings of any sort came; and just after the New Year the Persian Commissioner arrived on his way from Tehran to the frontier and came to call. Years ago Mirza Asraf Ali had been with the late Sir Oliver St. John on the Sistan Commission, and he was in consequence quite accustomed to mixing with Europeans. We found him a most pleasant man of about sixty, straight, and well set-up, his clean-shaven face having a curiously ascetic look, somewhat belied, however, by the twinkle in his humorous eyes. Unfortunately he had forgotten all his French, if indeed he had ever known much; but a certain Haji Khan accompanied him as interpreter, a gentleman whose English "as she is spoke" was very amusing. We were both anxious to be "on the march" again. Kerman was cold and somewhat dreary at this season of the year; the Farman Farma and his suite were busied with preparations for an immediate departure to the warmth of Khabis, where palms and orange-trees flourished only thirty miles off, and I felt disappointed when the Persian Commissioner—the *Itisham*, as his title was—left us on his long journey to the frontier to join Colonel Holdich and the other officers of the Boundary Commission.

However, we were not kept long in suspense. A telegram came from the Minister ordering my brother to start for the frontier as soon as possible after the arrival of a *gholam* with instructions and maps from Tehran; and on the afternoon of January 13th the expected messenger galloped into the Consulate, having accomplished the six hundred miles from the capital in record time.

My delight was somewhat tempered by the whirl and turmoil of packing; for we settled to start off early on January 15th, and although I had made most of my preparations in the way of stores beforehand, yet the house had to be dismantled; all our carpets, embroideries and skins done up to be forwarded to England; arrangements made with Mehdi to look after our furniture, as we were giving up our house; and the camp equipment to be supervised. Luckily for me a box of dresses arrived from England at this crisis, as it was impossible to tell into what civilised parts this journey might lead us.

My brother was occupied with the weighty question of transport—a matter made easy in this case by the friendship of the Prince, who generously placed his own camels at the Consul's disposal. We engaged about fifty of these animals, loading them lightly, as they would be obliged to carry forage and water when we reached the desert stages of our journey.

The Farman Farma had left his citadel in the town, and, after the custom of all Persians when about to travel, had taken a pavilion outside, the better to collect his servants and belongings. As his garden adjoined ours, a large breach was speedily made in the mud wall between them, and his Highness gave us a good deal of his society, dining with us without ceremony, and inviting us in return to repasts in one of the prettiest rooms I ever entered in Persia, a large apartment entirely decorated with mirror-work (that is, bits of looking-glass arranged in intricate patterns on stucco-work), and having two rows of elaborately carved niches, in which Persians place quinces, being much addicted to their perfume.

The Prince's band played to us throughout these evenings, some of the airs being very pleasing, especially the Farman Farma's own song, verses of which were sung at intervals by the band with great spirit, his Highness usually joining in the chorus. This song was composed in honour of his father, and to Western ears the opening line is the reverse of complimentary—

"Good Heavens! what a tyrant thou art!"

This being repeated with every chorus *ad infinitum*.

After dinner *kalians* and tea were handed round at intervals, all the Persian guests partaking of three or four cups of the latter beverage, which habit perhaps may account for the nightmares of which they used naïvely to complain.

And so ended, amidst many a warm farewell, our life at Kerman—a time so pleasant, so full of interest for me, that I shall ever look back upon it as one of the happiest of my existence. The charm of novelty had been upon it, and we had enjoyed life to the utmost in a superb climate—a climate which seemed to endow us with such energy that we could well afford to laugh at and make a joke of the hundred and one worries inseparable from trying to force a European establishment on Orientals who refuse to take kindly to the niceties of civilisation. I regretted that this part of my life had now come to an end, and yet we were both glad to be off, for both of us felt strongly the charms of a nomadic existence, and desired nothing better than to be on the march again.

CHAPTER XVII

GOODBYE TO KERMAN

THE morning of January 15th dawned cold and grey, and our last partings with the Prince and the members of his suite took place. The Farman Farma was much affected at saying goodbye to my brother, his feelings for whom he thus described to me: "I love my dear Sykes to such a degree that whenever I see him I long to throw my arms round his neck and embrace him." Seeing my involuntary smile, he added hastily, "But I don't do it because I know that the English do not like being kissed, although it is with difficulty that I refrain." I myself had quite a harrowing scene with a green-trousered lady who was wont to undertake our weekly washing. I had ordered a small *backsheesh*, to be handed over to her as a farewell gift, and was horrified when she presented herself plunged in violent grief, sobbing convulsively, as she seized my hands to cover them with kisses, protesting that her heart was "pierced with many needles" at my departure; that to see me every week had been the great joy of her life, and that she could not live without that entrancing vision! "Send away *Bargi!*" she cried dramatically. "She is not worthy to attend on you. Take me instead, who love you so much more!" All this was most embarrassing to me, as my acquaintance with her had always been of the slightest, and my attempts to calm her unreasoning sorrow brought on fresh accesses of the most despairing and heartrending howls.

I myself felt sad at heart at leaving the place where I had

been so well content; but there were too many last things to arrange for me to dwell much on my own feelings. I had to soothe *Bargi's* mother, who had come up to commend her daughter to me in a series of moving appeals, and I could not help having a nervous fear lest *Bargi* herself might cry off at the last moment, surrounded as she was with weeping relatives and children. However, she stuck to her mistress nobly, and we rode away down the avenue amid the crowds assembled to see us off, while Sultan Sukru distributed coppers for the last time to all the beggars of Kerman, who showered blessings on our heads as we passed along.

Outside the gate many personal friends were in waiting for a last word, and some accompanied us across the hill-encircled plain which would lead us out on to the road to Mahun, where we were to stop for that night. We reined up and halted at the last point from which we could get a glimpse of our late home, of the white-columned house and leafless garden which had become very dear to me; and as we looked a host of pleasant memories came rushing into my mind. The wide desert brought back the remembrance of many a glorious gallop; of many a merry picnic or *Gymkhana* meeting; of many an exciting insect-hunt; of many a photographing expedition; while the mud domes and blue cupolas of the city meant for me the Oriental life in which I was so keenly interested; and the sight of the ruined fortresses recalled the legend and history of Old Kerman. However, the feeling of depression did not last long when once we had fairly started on our journey of six hundred miles to the frontier. And perhaps what distracted my thoughts more than anything else was the fact that I was riding a new horse for the first time—a horse that had never had a lady on its back before, or a side-saddle and English bridle; and to me there are few things more interesting than to get the mastery over a spirited animal, and to establish that delightful sympathy which makes the rider and his steed as one. So hurrah for the road again! hurrah for nomadic existence! and hurrah for the *Wanderlust* that lurks in each man's blood, which drives our English race so far from home and kindred over the face of the globe!

After waiting a couple of days in the fairy garden of Mahun for our caravan of camels to collect, we set off for Hanaka, and although we began our journey during the forty days which constitute the cold weather of Kerman, yet we found the sun almost too hot for comfort in the middle of the day; and I was seldom able to dispense with my veil and blue glasses.

Our servants had professed to be filled with horror at the idea of travelling through the dreaded country of Baluchistan, but when it came to the point they were greatly reassured at the sight of our seventy camels loaded with supplies of rice, sugar, *rogan*, and so on, infinitely preferring the " rough-and-tumble " existence of camp life to the regular work of a settled household.

At Hanaka we had to lodge in a *serai*, which word recalls Omar Khayyam's comparison of this mortal life to such a building when he says—

> "Think, in this battered Caravanserai,
>   Whose doorways are alternate Night and Day,
>   How Sultan after Sultan with his Pomp
>   Abode his Hour or two and went his way."

Our particular "hotel" was fairly good for Persia, though the small brick rooms was doorless and windowless. My vaulted apartment was blackened with the smoke of years; a big heap of mud and straw was swept up into one corner of it, while two large archways opened on to the courtyard; and even when these were curtained off I found my room an exceedingly chilly one, especially when, towards evening, an icy wind began to blow. I consoled myself, however, with the thought that we were travelling with all speed towards a warmer climate, and that the cold, unpleasant though it was, kept the tarantulas and scorpions, which probably abounded here, safe in their winter quarters.

It was certainly a trial to have to turn out before sunrise

in the bitter weather with the thermometer some degrees below freezing-point; but we walked a considerable distance to warm ourselves along the banks of a frozen stream, my brother forcing the reluctant servants to do likewise, as they lay, shapeless bundles of wraps, on their respective mules, their heads bound up in many cloths. No Persian will ever walk a step if he can ride, having no idea of sparing his mount in any way, and they always looked upon my brother and me as lunatics for walking when we possessed plenty of horses.

Rayin, our destination, looked a very different place from the tree-embowered village we had halted at during the summer, and it was pathetic to see the one sign of life, the almond-trees in full bloom, as we could not but feel that the year's crop would in all likelihood be ruined by the premature appearance of the lovely blossoms in such weather. We arranged things from now onwards in a very comfortable way, halting for an hour or two about eleven to eat the lunch which Haslim produced out of his capacious saddle-bags, and when we reached the end of the day's march we found preparations for afternoon tea in full swing, our second waiter having gone on ahead with the caravan of mules.

One of our longest marches was to Khanakhartùn, some four days after we had left Kerman. It was about thirty-five miles from our last halting-place, so we had to start betimes in the chilly darkness that precedes the dawn. Of the scenery during our journey I cannot say much; for the greater part of Persia has a curious monotony about it. A series of plains, great or small, separated from one another by low passes in the hills, seems to be the prevailing characteristic. The plains are usually completely barren, unless there be a rare stream of water which produces grass and willows on its banks, and so relieves the deadly sameness of the landscape; and the mountains only compensate for their sterility by their beautiful colouring and often quaint configuration.

The traveller may have to caravan across one of these plains for days, always riding in the direction of some pass in the encircling chain of hills, and when he has reached and surmounted his goal, lo and behold! another plain is stretching at his feet, probably almost identical with the one he has traversed, and so on *ad infinitum*.

On this particular occasion we had the rare phenomenon of a river to diversify our route; and on leaving it found ourselves in a weird country. Clusters of mud hills rose up, moulded into a hundred fantastic forms. Cathedrals, castles, fairy palaces, coloured in all shades of ochre and green, met our astonished eyes. Here, quaint mud pinnacles threatened to topple over; there, a monstrous excrescence, shaped like an owl's head with enormous hollowed-out eyes, appeared to be glaring at us; while toads and curious prehistoric creatures seemed to be poised everywhere on the sides or summits of these queer hillocks. The whole scene was dominated by a ruined fortress, which so closely resembled many of the rocks around that it took us some time to make up our minds as to whether it was natural or artificial. It was a most uncanny region, fit abode for witches and hobgoblins, and I should have been sorry to have been wandering about alone in the dead silence, only broken by a stream, which rushed along its deeply cut bed with a most disagreeable hollow groaning. The grotesque shapes on the hillsides seemed to grin and gibe at us; and it needed only a slight effort of the imagination to enable me to see the huge saurians writhe and the monstrous toads begin to creep towards us—such a nightmare of a country it was!

Our destination this night was a Persian camp. The Farman Farma had sent on part of his army from Kerman to arrange supplies and forage for him, and our friend, fat Haji Khan, was in command of the detachment. It seemed for a time as if we had quite lost our way among these bewildering hills, and darkness was coming on before we espied the gleam of tents and the ruddy glow of bonfires, and heard Haji Khan's welcome salutations. Tents had been erected in readiness for us; and I was thankful to retire to mine, as it was over twelve hours since we started off that morning.

But a night in a Persian camp is not by any means a restful experience to a novice, owing to the fact that every Persian soldier on the march carries his kit on a donkey, and the hundreds of these animals keep up such an incessant braying that even the seven sleepers of Ephesus would have been hard put to it not to have awakened from their slumbers.

When one further remembers that the groaning of camels, the crackling and replenishing of the wood fires, the chatting of the men bivouacking round them, and the wail of uncouth musical instruments are all items added to the asinine concert, the reader will not wonder that none of our party felt much refreshed on the following day.

On the next morning we were escorted for some distance on our way by our host and a troop of horsemen, and as soon as we emerged on to the inevitable plain we saw in the far distance our goal, the *Kalah-i-sang* of Abarik, a striking looking mud-brick fortress on the crest of a black shale rock rising up abruptly from the ground, and said in local legends to have been built in prehistoric times by Bahman, son of Isfundiah.

The little village of Abarik is almost entirely encircled with range behind range of low hills and snow-crested mountains, and its position has given rise to a Persian saying, "The wind was asked one day where its home might be. It answered, 'I often make expeditions to Tahrùd and Sarvistan, but my abiding resting-place is Abarik.'" Owing to this predilection of the wind the houses here are low and more squalid than most in Persia; and our quarters for the night were practically underground, my room being entered by crawling through a low door. A limited supply of light and air was provided by means of a hole knocked in its roof, and I fancy that I must have ousted a previous occupant from it, for a large dog banged violently at my door during the night, and when he found that his efforts to get in were fruitless he rushed up on to the mud roof, and exhausted himself in barking down at me through my air-hole, scrabbling at it with his paws until the loosened mud fell in showers into the room, making me fear lest my would-be visitor might effect an entrance if he persevered long enough. We were still in the country of legend, for at Deharzin ("the place of the gallows"), our next halt, the story went that the village once belonged to the mighty Rustem, who had killed the son of the King of Persia. Bahman, the then Shah, bent on revenge, descended with an army on Deharzin, but finding Rustem dead took his son Feramouz as a substitute, and hanged him on a lofty gibbet.

It was only a week since we had left Kerman, travelling south-east, and gradually leaving snowy peaks and ice-bound brooks behind us, and now we were at Bam with its famous fortress, second to none in the estimation of the Persians, and, as a rule, jealously guarded. Bam was the frontier town of Persia before the annexation of Baluchistan. It was a new land that we had entered, a land of feathery palm-trees, and many a running stream bordered with lush grass and waving pampas, while numerous mud-domed villages, peeping out of groves of graceful palms, dotted the plain. Bam was embowered in these lovely trees, over which I waxed enthusiastic, to the amusement of my brother, who warned me that I should cease to admire them so much when I understood that their presence meant heat, and was invariably connected with an abnormal degree of dirt and squalor among their inhabitants. However, it appeared to me that I had hardly been in the real East until now, the palms recalling a hundred pictures of Biblical scenes, familiar to me from childhood, and also seeming to bring with them the mystery and glamour of the Orient, the dark passions, secret intrigues and terrible revenges which have ever fascinated the colder imagination of the West. At every moment I expected to see shadowy, gliding figures stealing on their way to carry out some wild vengeance with the dagger or the poison-bowl; and every veiled woman I passed, engaged in the prosaic duty of shopping in the little bazaar, was possibly the heroine of some weird romance to my excited fancy.

Several notables of Bam, among whom was our old friend Asadilla Khan, rode out to meet us and escort us to our quarters by way of the main street of the town, a dried-up watercourse. The ubiquitous palm was used to build the booths where rice and sweetmeats were sold, and its leaves formed a rough thatching for these shelters, or were woven into porches in front of many a doorway. At last we reached a partly built mud house in a small garden of palms, and it was a relief to get indoors, for the sun was oppressively hot, and during the next two or three days we found the heat most trying, although the thermometer only stood at 76°. We had made too sudden a plunge into the warm country, which was being visited just then by an unusually early spell of hot weather, and my brother, who, from his long residence in the East, was very susceptible to the sun, got a violent headache and giddiness, making me feel most anxious, as sunstrokes are of common occurrence in this region. However, next day he was so much better that he and Count Magnis went off to inspect the celebrated fortress, the Governor having specially invited them to visit it, a privilege probably never before accorded to a European.

It was in this stronghold that the gallant Zend Prince Lutf Ali Khan was captured after his flight from Kerman. Betrayed by the Governor in whom he had trusted, he was put to death by the ferocious Agha Muhammed Khan (the founder of the present dynasty), who, it is affirmed, blinded him first with his own hands before sending him to Tehran to be strangled. My brother was allowed to take photos of the interior of the huge mass, which is built on a mountain spur dominating the town, and in its stern strength contrasts strikingly with the feathery palms ever swaying and waving far below it.

Despite its beauty, I was glad to quit Bam, being always kept more or less a prisoner when staying in a town, as my brother considered that the appearance of the first European woman who had ever been in these parts excited too much comment in the streets. Moreover, romantic as was our garden of palms, yet no cool breeze sprang up to soothe us during the hot, airless nights, save now and again a gust of burning wind, which whirled clouds of dust through the paneless windows of our unfurnished mud rooms.

When the town at last lay behind us, we struck across a vast, grey, gravelly plain some forty miles broad, and destitute of vegetation save where it was traversed by a small stream, which bore a wealth of dates, pampas grass, or tamarisk shrubs on its banks; the narrow belt of dense, vividly coloured vegetation forming a strong contrast to the dreary waste stretching away for miles on either side of it.

Camels were browsing here and there, and the sight of the ungainly animals made me realise in what a different part of the country we were now travelling. Hitherto we had journeyed with mules, which were clean and quick-stepping in comparison with the evil smelling, slowly moving "ships of the desert." But now we were on the borders of Baluchistan, in a country for the most part the "abomination of desolation," where a mule could not well survive the intense heats of the summer and autumn, and, above all, would die of starvation on the apparently barren plains, where the camel flourishes on the abundant thorn. Our servants, only accustomed to mules, were most reluctant at first to mount these unknown creatures, the awkward shuffling gait of which made many of them violently sick at the commencement; but in a short time they got quite used to them, guiding them with the nose-rope and a light switch, or falling fast asleep on their backs if they formed one of a long string, and it was curious to see our grooms perched up aloft leading the horses alongside, the latter looking mere pigmies, so dwarfed were they by their tall escorts. There are few things more unpleasant than to get entangled in a crowd of camels during the loading-up process. The groaning and roaring of the animals and their disagreeable odour are bad enough; but one has besides to run the gauntlet of many a bite or kick. A camel's long neck can reach inconveniently far, and the stroke of his springy pad is a thing to be carefully avoided by those who wish to keep their bones whole.

From now onwards oxen were largely used as beasts of burden, men riding them or leading them heavily loaded. In a country where time is no object they are not to be despised as a mode of locomotion; but their sluggish

THE LUNCHEON CAMEL.

pace must, I should fancy, try the patience of even an Oriental.

We reached Burj two days later, and here we were struck with the great size to which the tamarisk-trees attained Up to now we had been accustomed to see scrub, or at the most small shrubs, and these specimens, with their thick trunks, heavy boughs, and masses of plumy needles, were quite a revelation. Their grey-green foliage was much the same tone as that of the olives, and seemed to soften down the blue glare of the sky, which a vivid green would have only intensified. A swampy river, probably abounding in game and wild pig, had to be crossed, and here we bade adieu, with much regret, to Count Magnis, who had arranged with the Prince to await his arrival at this spot, so as to have some wild-ass shooting in his company.

We now proceeded on our way to Regan, the frontier village between the provinces of Kerman and Baluchistan, and could complain of the sultriness no longer, as a heavy shower of rain brought down the temperature by 11°; this sudden and delightful change forcing us to unpack our warm things, which we imagined we had stowed away for good since reaching Bam.

The country here was quite unlike any other part of Persia through which I had travelled, and gave the impression of passing through a wild, deserted park, so abundant were the branching tamarisks, gnarled acacias, and graceful clumps of pampas ; while the *konar*-tree grew to a great size. This latter is a species of wild cherry, from the pounded leaves of which a soap is prepared, used for washing the dead and also for toilet purposes. Both here and in Baluchistan I constantly noticed a plant some three feet high with big, fleshy leaves and masses of velvety mauve flowers, remarkably like auriculas, its dull purple seed-vessel being of the size of an egg. I never could find out the properties of this commonest of plants, some saying it was a dye, others that it was the deadliest of poisons, (of course it could easily have been both), while one man confuted the latter statement by devouring flower and leaf in my presence.

Streams of water abounded, and all around us rose the loud, clear call of the hot-country partridge or *francolin*, while myriads of small birds twittered in the jungle with its background of stately palms. We lunched by a very muddy, swiftly running stream, and to my excessive surprise it had departed on its way and left its bed dry before our repast was completed—such a phenomenon being, however, far from uncommon in Persia whenever heavy rain has fallen.

Our rooms in the caravanserai had a cheerful outlook over a small grove of oranges, and although we were still in the month of January bees, wasps, and a curious sandhopper were actively employed about their various avocations.

At this point we had nearly caught up the Persian Commissioner and his suite, who had had a week's start of us, and who would most certainly have been in no hurry to reach the frontier unless we had been behind them. They had naïvely told the headman of Regan that they hastened on their way because they did not wish the Consul to get up with them and see the meagre equipment of tents and horses with which they were travelling from Kerman. Once arrived at Faraj or Pahra, where they were to join the Governor of Baluchistan and proceed on to Kuhak, the frontier town, in his company, they would be provided with an outfit ample enough to brave the inspection of any eye. The Commissioner always left messages behind him to the effect that we were killing his transport by forcing him to press on at such an unseemly pace; and Suleiman Mirza, our Kerman friend, who had been sent by the Farman Farma to form part of the Commissioner's suite, amused us by leaving a message for my brother at every stage to the effect that he hoped he was bringing along with him a certain gift which he had promised him at Kerman and had ordered from India. To give a glimpse of a disagreeable trait of Persian character, I must mention that when he finally got the much-desired present he never took the trouble to acknowledge it. Gratitude with a Persian is strictly a sense of benefits to come, and over and over again I have been disgusted with the servants, who never spared floods of persuasive rhetoric to gain some favour, for which, when granted, they would hardly deign to mumble the customary "*Iltefath-i-shuma-ziert*"—a phrase which, by the way, is characteristic of the nation, as it means "May your kindness be increased!"

From now onwards we had the vision of the magnificent cone of the extinct volcano Kuh-i-Basman, the Demavend of Baluchistan, standing up superbly from a range about a hundred miles from us. My brother had made the ascent of this mountain during his previous journey in Baluchistan, and had had hard work in struggling through the masses of deep snow near its summit. It is curious how much the traveller gets attached to a grand peak which dominates the landscape through which he passes. Demavend became almost a part of my life when I was at Tehran, the fine mass of Jupa taking its place during my stay at Kerman; while the snowy pyramid of Kuh-i-Hazar was visible nearly as far as Bam; now Basman was to cheer us in the wilds of Baluchistan, to be succeeded in its turn by the remarkable Kuh-i-Taftan. We were obliged to spend a couple of days at Regan to get in supplies of forage for our mules and horses, not to mention food for the camels, which were given cakes of barley-dough at night, in addition to what they picked up for themselves; these preparations were made with a view to the desert marches that now lay before us, as we were about to cross part of the great Sahara, which cuts Persia in half. We provided lambs and a crate of fowls for ourselves, and the servants were warned that they must carry supplies of food to last them for a fortnight.

It seemed strange that Regan, with its swampy river, its luxuriant brushwood and profusion of game, should be on the verge of a terrible desolation. But so it is, and in Persia one realises more clearly than elsewhere the magic power of water. It was the presence of the river that gave Regan its fine crops of barley, its ample jungles of tangled yellow grass where lurked the snipe and wild duck, and its picturesque tamarisk scrub, among which fed the beautiful *doraj*, king among the partridges; while only bare sand lay outside the narrow strip of cultivation.

And it was the presence of a sun more powerful than we had hitherto encountered that made the inhabitants of this country darker and slighter than the usual Persian type, the unveiled women looking withered and dried up, as they peeped out of rudimentary huts made in some cases of bundles of rushes propped against the trunk of a tree, with an aperture on one side to serve as a door.

It was here that we saw our first Baluch—a swarthy young man with greasy, flowing ringlets, clad in a long white cotton shirt and loose white trousers, and wearing a small black cap on his head. The servants were greatly interested in seeing an inhabitant of the country, which they regarded with an almost superstitious dread; and as they considered the new-comer to be of abnormal ugliness, they at once began to chaff the unpopular *ferash* Akbar about him, asking him whether he recognised his brother! Poor Akbar, being the son of the late executioner of Kerman, was considered to have inherited such a perverted nature that all that went amiss was invariably laid to his charge without any one caring to search for proof as to whether he were in fault or not!

Our horses, owing to the extra barley and the regular work, got livelier daily—a great contrast to what they would have been if they had had Persian masters. The Prince himself complained to me that he and his following had lost over fifty horses during one of his journeys, and I could well believe him, as a Persian will set forth on his travels on a horse that probably has not been out of the stable for several days, and is naturally "soft" and unfit for work. My brother's method of walking until the sun was well up, and of giving our steeds a rest and feed at midday, caused them to arrive in first-class condition at the frontier, and so quarrelsome as to be somewhat unpleasant mounts. In fact I had to give up riding "Charters" when there was any question of an *istakbal*, as I could not keep him under control among a troop of strange horses without great vigilance. So I used to resign him to a groom with instructions to lead him away from the throng of horsemen accompanying us. On the first occasion, however, the servant "knew better," as is the way of all Persians, and "Charters" scattered our escort ignominiously. I can still hear the hollow thud of his hoofs as he kicked the chest of the horse behind him, and I can still see him turning this way and that, lashing out furiously with his hoofs on all sides, and thoroughly enjoying himself.

As forges and blacksmiths are unknown in Baluchistan, we had to carry many dozens of native horseshoes with us, which our grooms applied as needed, "Cotmore" having had particularly large sets made for him. A Persian horseshoe covers the whole of the hoof save a small space in the centre, and is well adapted to a stony country, where a horse would soon go lame if fitted with English shoes.

CHAPTER XVIII

THROUGH THE DESERT TO BAMPUR AND PAHRA

WE had talked so much about the Great Persian Desert, which stretches up to Khorassan and forms an almost insuperable barrier between the different parts of the country, that I was prepared to pass the next week toiling through wastes of rolling sands and perhaps suffering the tortures of thirst so eloquently described by Professor Vambéry.

The *Dasht-i-Lut*, a term interpreted by some to mean "naked land," by others the "Land of Lot," is believed to have been a great inland sea, Yezd having been an island on its outskirts. This theory is carried out by the volcanoes of Basman and Kuh-i-Taftan rising up from its supposed shores, as volcanoes are almost invariably found by the sea.

One of the few small villages in the vast area of this desert is called Yunsi, and tradition says it was here that the *Yunsi*, or Jonah, of Bible history was cast up by the whale, lending some plausibility to the derivation of the name from Lot.

Marco Polo traversed this uninviting region from the north to the south, and my brother is probably the first European who has followed the route taken by the great Venetian.

On this occasion we were merely crossing the fringe of the Sahara, but nevertheless my mind had been so stored with reminiscences of Eastern travel that I was considerably surprised to find this portion of the desert at all events not unlike many other parts of Persia, and, owing to the recent heavy rainfall, there was a fair amount of water to be had.

Despite all this, however, our elaborate preparations were

by no means in vain. There was, it is true, water at most of our halting-places, but of such indifferent quality, being bitter, brackish or foul, as to be quite undrinkable, and when I add that we saw no inhabitants, and no flocks or herds in this desolate region, it was just as well that we had laid in supplies of food and forage beforehand. Four horsemen were attached to our party at Regan to act as guides, a necessary precaution, as the tracks were by no means so clearly defined here as is the rule in Persia, the traffic evidently being small.

We started off on our first march about six o'clock on a windy morning, the golden full moon sinking slowly in the purple sky, across which the "dappled dawn" was stealing. Masses of clouds low down on the east lay like couches of rosy foam from which the sun sprang into the turquoise heavens, a great eye of light, rousing the world to a fresh day of existence, and reminding us of Omar Khayyam's lines—

> "Awake, for morning in the bowl of night
> Has flung the stone that put the stars to flight."

Our tents had been pitched among sandhills bound together with the coarsest of grass; but we soon entered upon a dreary region, the ground strewn with grey, black, and reddish stones of volcanic origin, *débris* from the gloomy hills, where the only signs of life were lizards with flat heads, stout bodies, and tails cocked high, coloured so precisely like the boulders among which they lived as to be indistinguishable from them unless in motion.

I picked up one of these "poison-spitters," much to Nasrullah Khan's horror, and found it to be of the purest white underneath, copying as it were the salt efflorescence to be found in patches on the lava-strewn plains.

The wind, which increased in violence as we rode on, raised up a sand-storm after noon, through which we had to make our way in spite of cut faces, smarting eyes, and protesting horses. Fortunately there was some tamarisk scrub where we halted for the night, and as it was impossible to pitch tents in such a wind, we crouched down with our books and writing materials among the bushes, waiting for the gale to abate as evening came on.

I amused myself by watching the camels come in. Three or four linked to one another would be led up to the camp, and by dint of pulling the chain, shouting, and slapping their woolly necks, the tiresome animals would be persuaded to kneel down to be unloaded amid a terrible amount of groaning and grumbling, just as if they were enduring great bodily anguish. The loads were carried in big cord bags slung on each side of the saddle, and had plenty of rope to keep them in position—a great contrast to the miserable equipment of the Baluchi camel, when later on we had to depend on him, and send the Prince's fine animals back to Kerman. The work of unloading was by no means an easy one, as the creatures, eager to go off and feed, did their best to get up before the boxes were unfastened, and the men had often a hard task to keep some unruly camel on its knees during the necessary few moments. Those that were *must* were the most troublesome, uttering awe-inspiring gurglings, a red bladder coming out of their foaming mouths. I always dreaded camels in this state, as they were half mad, and would attack any one without respect of persons, and to be bitten or kicked by one of these infuriated creatures, and possibly to have one's life pressed out by the formidable chest pad on which the animal lies, would not be an agreeable experience. The drivers say that a *must* camel eats scarcely anything, and yet is so strong that it will carry double loads without murmuring; at this time it will probably wreak vengeance on a cruel master, for it is accredited with an exceedingly tenacious memory, and is supposed to store up unmerited beatings against a day of reckoning.

The only way to deal with a camel desirous of attacking you is to face it boldly and threaten it with a stick, the merest switch having a good effect, especially if you can manage to hit it on its neck, the vulnerable part

We used to send on all the stores, luggage, and extra

tents every night about ten o'clock, six animals staying behind to carry the remaining tents and camp equipage on the following morning. This *pishkhana*, as the advance-guard was called, was a good arrangement when travelling with such slow-moving creatures as camels, for it enabled us to have the tents in position and tea ready when we reached camp the next day. It had, however, its drawbacks, for our usual bedtime was at the early hour of eight o'clock, and it was impossible to get to sleep until the cessation of roars and groans announced that the loads were at last adjusted, and that our caravan was on its way. Another disadvantage of this system, so excellent for the most part, was that the camels were brought up close to our tents to be loaded up, and the horrible fetid odour, seemingly inseparable from these creatures, would penetrate to us, reminding us of an ill-kept menagerie.

Our second desert march was to Zahu, still through a dreary volcanic region, where not even a bird was to be seen, while on either side rose up black, forbidding-looking hills, flushed with a dull red.

A most uninviting region, but yet the name Zahu means "springing up," in reference to three or four pools to be found at the camping ground. These were only discoverable by the initiated, and had to be scooped out before water slowly trickled into them, which, when emptied, repeated the slow process over again. I fear that sometimes the precious life-giving fluid concealed its whereabouts too well, for among the rocky ground behind our camp the camel-drivers came upon a human corpse, probably that of some poor wretch who had braved the terrors of the desert alone, starting forth with a packet of damp Persian bread in his waistcloth, from which his small wooden water-bottle would be suspended. He had perhaps been obliged to travel before the rain had filled up the pools, or he may not have succeeded in finding them, and so died miserably in their immediate vicinity.

We ourselves were in no danger of a death from thirst, as the rain clouds were gathering in the sky, and Ali Agha, the Fat Boy, had thoughtfully pitched our tents in the bed of a dry torrent, the very place to avoid in Persia, for if it rains in the hills a roaring flood may be at any time on its road to sweep away tents, men, and animals. Alexander the Great's camp, with his baggage and the women, was overwhelmed in this way during his celebrated march through Baluchistan; and my brother, not wishing to experience a similar catastrophe, got our tents changed to the highest ground available before a perfect deluge descended from the heavens.

Rain was still falling when we marched off early the next morning, leading our horses to keep ourselves warm, as, with a thermometer at 35° and an icy wind and sleet blowing into our faces, we should have been chilled to the bone in our saddles. After walking for some time, however, we were obliged to mount, as we came upon a large expanse of fairly deep flood-water, hurrying on its way to the site of our late camp. During the day we had to cross the watershed separating the north from the south drainage, all the streams and rivers we encountered henceforth draining southward instead of northward as before. There were three difficult stone-strewn passes to be traversed, and we were obliged to walk for the most part, leading our horses in and out among the boulders. To me there was something horrible in this sinister-looking mountain range, so dark and lifeless, full of strange echoes, every now and again weird sounds striking the ear, not to be accounted for in any natural way. It appeared to be an utterly forsaken region, and I can well understand men going mad if they were forced to wander day by day in solitudes such as these, where there is never a sign of animal or bird to break through the awful desolation, the very vultures and crows seeming to avoid the accursèd ground. Though this march was only twenty-seven miles in length, yet, on account of the steepness of the mountain passes, it was one of the hardest we had ever done. We ourselves were nine hours on the road to our camping-place, which was near some pools of water in the usually dried-up river-bed. Everything was wet and damp, and as our *pishkhana* had not started at its proper time the night before—the drivers protesting that they could not find their way in the darkness—we had to wait until ten o'clock that night for our bedding and camp equipage. Dead-tired and soaked through as I was, I had the grace to spare a little pity for the poor animals that had been marching for sixteen hours at a stretch and were by no means such adepts at climbing as their Baluchi relatives, with which I became acquainted later on.

Two days after this hard march we passed through a charming region to which it seemed absurd to give the name of desert. We started from Abi Kishkin, the meeting of three long valleys, bounded by magnificent limestone peaks, above which Basman's snowy cone towered in the sunshine, and our guide led us along the sandy bed of a river amid a jungle of grasses and tamarisks, high concrete cliffs forming the banks of the stream. It was by no means a first-class road, as we had to pick our way in and out among big granite blocks, crossing and recrossing the water every few moments, and it was impossible to remain in our saddles, for we could not let our horses leap from one slippery boulder to another with riders on their backs. So perforce we dismounted, and I made up my mind that the boots I was wearing must be sacrificed, as the agility of a chamois would be needed to keep dryshod in such a place, the sacrifice being by no means a joke in a land where it is impossible to replace such articles. On and on we stumbled, jumping from stone to stone, crossing patches of sand saturated with moisture, in and out of masses of wet yellow grass, until, after some hours, we came to a dead halt, owing to the mouth of the valley being blocked up with boulders piled one above the other in mad confusion, as if Titans had had a game of play and had left their giant missiles all heaped up here. The guide frankly confessed that he had lost the track—there never had been one visible to my uninitiated eye—and he clambered up the concrete cliff and disappeared from view, hoping to fall in with some of our camels, which were, we fervently trusted, progressing under more efficient guidance than was vouchsafed to us.

After a long wait he reappeared, and announced that we

must retrace our steps for at least two miles, and we should then be able to make our way across the steep cliffs into the parallel valley, where was the right road. It is always disagreeable to have to go back on a march, but on this occasion it was something more, as both we and our horses were tired and discouraged, and this made the by no means imaginary dangers of the route far more formidable. My Arab had got quite nervous by this time, hanging back at all the bad places, and requiring much coaxing to persuade him to surmount them; and as for me, I could not help seeing very plainly that a false step might mean a broken limb—and then? I do not think I am a specially nervous person, but throughout my stay in the uncivilised parts of the East I was never quite free from fear lest one of us might be ill or injured far away from any medical aid. On our journey down to Kerman we had had a litter carried by mules, but we had been obliged to leave it behind on this occasion, as it would have been impossible to get it over much of the country we should now have to traverse. Of course we could have improvised some sort of a stretcher, but I felt that our "First Aid to the Injured" certificates were a sadly insufficient equipment for setting broken bones, though I fondly imagined that I could hunt out the symptoms of fever or of any ordinary ailment in our medicine-book and cure them with the tabloids in the medicine-chest.

This time, however, no medicine-books were needed, and we finally emerged on the vast Bampur Plain, my brother pointing out to me Kuh-i-Hamant, Kuh-i-Fanoch, and many another peak well known to him from his former journeys in Baluchistan, and showing me where the Bampur River lay, and Bampur itself, the so-called capital of Baluchistan, supplanted, however, by Pahra, or Faraj, a few miles beyond it, where the Assad-i-Dowleh, Governor of the province, held his court.

The plain was overgrown with poisonous oleander scrub, fatal to unwary camels, and here and there small groves of stately palms made oases in the sandy wastes, honeycombed with rat-holes, the little inhabitants of which sat sunning themselves near the tamarisk scrub, and scuttling into their burrows in a great hurry as we rode past. After some hours we reached a country of low sand-dunes, among which grew three or four kinds of the ubiquitous *gaz*, or tamarisk. There were big-trunked, spreading trees with plumy bundles of needles; others again springing straight up to a great height like a new kind of poplar; a third species having bright green rudimentary leaves like broom, and a fourth, growing in bushes, was breaking out into rosy bloom.

When we had left the *kah*, or chopped straw of Persia, behind us, our horses and mules were not confined merely to the barley carried on our camels, but soon took to the *durrumshuk*, a long, coarse, jointed grass which grows throughout Baluchistan in great masses some three or four feet high.

On the Bampur Plain we passed a dervish carrying a furled white flag with a red fringe at the top of its staff. He was a tall, good-looking fellow, exceedingly dirty, and was tramping the country to solicit alms in the name of Abbas, Hussein's brother, the standard-bearer of the little army of the Faithful, massacred by the Arabs under such moving circumstances. Other *fakirs* carry a water-skin instead of a flag, recalling to the minds of Mohammedans an episode of the *Tazieh*, or Passion Play, in which Abbas dashes for the well which is surrounded by hosts of enemies, and dies in the heroic attempt to get water for the miserable company of men, women, and children, who had been suffering all the agonies of thirst for three days under the scorching rays of the Arabian sun.

Apropos of the *Tazieh*, Nasrullah Khan told me that Persians often send their children to take part in it, believing that a special blessing will descend upon them. Babies of two or three months old are sent to be held in the arms of the Hussein of the play during one of its most tragic incidents, which is as follows:—

When the beleaguered relatives of the Prophet, half-dead from thirst, could resist no longer, Hussein, the grandson of Mohammed, held out his infant to the Arabs, begging them to take pity on it, even though they had none on him and his relatives; but, alas, the only answer to his appeal was an arrow piercing the child's throat.

Nasrullah Khan, when a boy of six, watching the play at Shiraz, and sitting close to the stage, was much surprised to find himself suddenly picked up by the Abbas of the piece. The drama had reached the point when Abbas takes a fond farewell of his two children and hands them over to his sister. On this particular occasion no boy was forthcoming, and what more natural than that the actor should supply the want from among the audience, reproving his victim in whispers for laughing when crying was the order of the day?

This Persian Passion Play is to commemorate the death of the *Imam* Hussein, the second son of Ali, who refused to acknowledge the usurper Yezid as the lawful *Khalif*. The inhabitants of Kufa offered to espouse his cause, and on his way to that city he was overtaken by Yezid's troops on the fatal plain of Kerbelah, where he and nearly all his family were killed in the sixty-first year of the *Hejreh*. The play comprises all the events connected with the martyr's flight from Mecca to his tragic death, and is acted in every city throughout Persia, causing the most intense emotion among the spectators.

Before we reached Bampur I made my first acquaintance with the characteristic camelry of Baluchistan. About three miles from our camp we observed a procession coming towards us between the tamarisk-trees. Wild-looking soldiers armed with *jesails*, or native rifles, were mounted on the usual rat-like steeds, but my glance quickly flew beyond them to a long line of men mounted on camels and "salaaming" vigorously. Two men sat on each animal, one behind the other, and were equipped with round brass-bossed shields, huge curved scimitars, and the usual brass-bound, inefficient rifle of the country. They seemed a warlike crew, and were clad in black woollen tunics, and such wide white cotton trousers that they looked like skirts hanging over the sides of the camels, while long, greasy locks fell from beneath their turbans. A body of men carrying wands and wearing a pretence of a uniform preceded us, and cavalry and camelry fell in behind, escorting us in style to our camp on the game-haunted Bampur River, our tents being pitched near the palm-leaf matting huts which sheltered our would-be protectors. In lands where water is a rare commodity a real river has a charm quite indescribable, and we hastened down to this one, getting lovely peeps of it through the intervening tamarisks, and admiring the many islets of grass and reeds scattered on its surface, these giving it quite the aspect of "ornamental water" such as we see in great parks at home.

I noticed a curious plant here, growing under the tamarisks. It had no leaves, but its pale yellow flowers, reminding me of those of the mullein, clustered in masses on the thick, fleshy stems, which were about a foot high, and which, when pulled up, appeared to have no roots.

Bampur, the now deserted capital of Baluchistan, lay some miles away from the river, and the old fort, perched upon the summit of a great mound of earth, reminded me somewhat of Mont St. Michel, as it loomed in a dusty sky, rising picturesquely from the surrounding wastes of sand. However, the castellated mud towers, seen nearer, dissipated the fancied resemblance, and we pitched our tents under some of the few remaining date-palms for which this fever-stricken place was once famous, near squalid palm-leaf huts, the miserable inhabitants of which were in sad contrast to the cheery, healthy Normans of the Mont. Pottinger records the tradition that a huge army of *Guebres* filled the bags from which they fed their horses with earth, and the amount was so great that it formed the curious mound on which the fort of Bampur stands.

Many of the people here were of distinctly negroid type, descended from the slaves settled in these parts, and probably slaves themselves at the present day, the dress of the women, who did not cover their faces, reminding me much of that of nuns as they glided about in white robes, long black woollen veils being draped over their heads. Pahra, or Faraj, the real capital, was fourteen miles from Bampur, and it was a relief to leave the countless flies which infested our camping ground at the latter place, and push on to meet the Persian Commissioner and his suite.

Our servants were almost as excited as if we had been entering Tehran, smartening themselves up and polishing saddles and bridles for our horses to look their best; for as we were to be met by an *istakbal*, sent by the Governor of Baluchistan, we must muster an imposing array to make an effective entry into the town, the position of a traveller in the East being high or low in proportion to the number of his followers. A cavalry escort in nondescript apparel, but armed with rifles, closed in behind us, and about a *farsakh* from the masses of date-groves hiding the town the *istakbal* appeared, headed by the Governor's nephew, a good-looking young man in a lavender cloth frock-coat adorned with brass buttons. White horses with silver collars and trappings were led before us, and, surrounded by a crew of men in the shabbiest of clothing, mounted on the veriest screws conceivable, we rode forward very slowly in the direction of a huge square castellated enclosure having mud towers at intervals, and much resembling a caravanserai. Outside this fort the Governor's army was drawn up to welcome us, clad in grey cotton coats and trousers, while the strains of our National Anthem burst forth from the band, gorgeous in a parti-coloured blue and red uniform, profusely braided in yellow. Though "God Save the Queen" was played with queer variations, yet we could not but be touched with the compliment to our Sovereign, and passed on to our tents, pitched on a stony plain not far from the large Persian camp.

There were abundant streams of water in the place, and I was charmed with my first view of Faraj, with its cool, shady groves of palms, rippling streams, and picturesque old fortresses, planted in the midst of a howling waste.

The Persian Governor and the Commissioner hastened to call on the Consul, and my brother asked them, with Suleiman Mirza and Haji Khan, to dine with us that evening. Hashim was somewhat depressed, because he greatly disliked using our enamel camp equipage on the occasion of a party, and he warned me moodily that the entertainment would be a failure, as he did not consider that we had enough plates and cutlery to go round. However, the evening went off very well. The Assad-i-Dowleh, rather an imposing-looking, black-bearded Persian with a sad lack of teeth, could not keep his eyes off me, being the first European lady he had ever seen. I complimented him on the beautiful playing of his band, whereupon he hastened to assure me that he would order it to discourse sweet music in front of my tent every day and all day if I desired, and I had some difficulty in declining such a tempting offer! Sport was, as usual, the staple subject of conversation, and the Assad-i-Dowleh got quite excited over narrating to us a leopard story, which we found out afterwards to be his stock anecdote when in company. It appeared that one day, travelling among the hills, he had had his prayer-carpet spread at some distance from his camp, and had retired to absorb himself in devotion, when his prayers were interrupted by a huge leopard that attacked the kneeling Governor. He did not attempt to rise, but picking up his sword cut off with one stroke the head of the animal, and returned to his tents bearing with him one of its paws as a trophy of his heroic deed, which all applauded with many a *bah! bah!* of admiration.

Baluchistan was only conquered by the Persians about thirty to forty years before our visit, the father of the Farman Farma and a certain Ibrahim Khan subjugating the country after a desperate resistance on the part of its chieftains. The latter were persuaded to trust to Persian oaths sworn on the Koran, and coming to Kerman to enter into treaty with its Governor were thrown into chains for the rest of their days; Persian policy in these cases reminding one of Tarquinius Superbus and the story of the poppy-heads. Minus its leaders, the country became a comparatively easy prey, but it has been in an unsettled state ever since its annexation.

It needed a strong and a long arm to keep the land quiet, and, as the Assad-i-Dowleh had much difficulty in quelling numerous petty raids on his frontier, which for about a couple of hundred miles was an exceedingly ill-defined line, the object of the present Boundary Commission was to assign the date-groves, the subject of dispute, to their respective Governments.

Faraj is, in all probability, the same town which was the capital of Baluchistan in Alexander's day. At the time of our visit it was merely a village of miserable huts, the better sort, like huge beehives with a thick palm-leaf thatch, topping their round mud walls; while the great majority were merely shanties made from the palm-leaf matting. The Baluchis, as a race, were much darker and smaller in build than the Persians, the type of features Arab in the better class and frequently negroid in the lower. The men looked picturesque in baggy white trousers, over which they wore a long black or white shirt, while a white cotton shawl was sometimes wound as a turban round their skull-caps, or put over the head in the way that a Lancashire lass wears her shawl. The elder men sported a mass of greasy black hair that had seldom known the discipline of a comb, matted locks hanging over their shoulders, while their long beards and moustaches had all the centre parts plucked out so as to prevent the hair being rendered unclean by drinking wine. The young men were great dandies as regarded their *coiffures*, dragging their curls forward to hang over their ears, and often cultivating a specially long and well-greased one to droop over their chests, much as I have seen the locks of ladies arranged in old-fashioned portraits. All the Baluchis are *Sunnis*, and fervently hate the Persian *Shiahs*, adoring Omar, who is execrated by the Persians; and one of our servants nearly caused a disturbance here by speaking in disrespectful language of that vigorous, all-conquering *Khalif*.

The Baluchi women looked thin and starved, poor things, wearing white or black woollen garments, strongly suggestive of nightgowns, and only making a half-hearted pretence of covering their faces with the veil worn over head and shoulders.

It was most pleasant to wander about the extensive date-groves, watered by three parallel streams winding among the crops of barley and Indian corn springing up under the trees. The whole place was perfumed by patches of beans in full

BALUCHIS.

flower, and we had the unwonted sight of lettuces and young onions, while tiny purple irises gemmed the grass. We had to cross and recross the streams continually, over somewhat insecure bridges formed of hollowed-out palm-trunks through which water poured, and on the edges of which we had to balance ourselves as best we could.

It is wonderful with what a charm palms are able to invest any place, no matter how squalid and mean, and we kept within the dimly lit aisles of the graceful trees, for outside the ground was bare and sandy with salt efflorescence in places, tamarisks with curious grey-looking needles growing in abundance. We made an inspection of the various old forts of Pahra, the oldest being merely a large mound of rubbish, with a fragment of mud wall remaining. In this rainless climate it might have dated from the days when Alexander and his army passed through, and we wished we could excavate it for possible traces of a Greek occupation, and offered money for coins or old pottery; but the villagers did not respond in any way. We were escorted all about the place by a long-haired Indian *fakir* (beggar), clad in white garments, holding what looked like a trident, one arm being decorated with a burnished steel bracelet. He was much pleased at seeing a *Sahib* in this out-of-the-way region, and attached himself to my brother at once, claiming acquaintance with him by boasting proudly that he was a British subject, and insisted in walking before us, to keep off all inquisitive Baluchis with the redoubtable trident, posing himself in the front when we began to take photos. He gave us to understand that game existed here in great quantities, and my brother carried his gun on the chance of a shot at wild duck or partridges. However, the only thing he bagged was a teal, and in that he was assisted by a hawk, which swooped down upon the quarry and transfixed it, but flew off as our servant rushed towards the spot. The teal also rose up, but only exchanged the frying-pan for the fire, as it fell a victim to the gun. That night the Governor of Baluchistan invited us to dine with him, and ordered a large crimson-lined tent, like a gigantic parasol, to be pitched between our respective camps. Nominally it was his party, but I had almost as much to do with it as if it had been my own. Our tables, chairs, plates, knives, forks, and so on, were requisitioned for the entertainment; our cooks were borrowed to manufacture European dishes, and the Assad-i-Dowleh sent a special message begging us to provide a jelly, as he had so much enjoyed the one at our dinner-party! We supplied wine, sweets, and biscuits, so that, as far as I could judge, the Governor's contribution to his own feast was merely a couple of *pillaus*. In fact it would almost have been less trouble to have had the whole affair in our camp, although one great point in having it elsewhere was that we were at liberty to retire when we chose. It was a moonless evening when the fat interpreter appeared to escort us to the big tent, and a great bonfire was blazing up in front of it, illuminating the scarlet and blue-clad band which stood round in readiness to discourse (sweet?) harmonies, their big drum occupying a perilous position close to the flames. Branches of wood flaring in high iron stands served as candles for their scraps of manuscript music, throwing up in silhouette the figures of our host and the others who marched out to meet and welcome us. I was placed next the Assad-i-Dowleh, whom I found hard to understand, his total lack of teeth making his articulation far from distinct, so it was somewhat a relief when the band discoursed Persian and Turkish airs. Some were sadly out of time and tune, giving me sensations as of a slate-pencil dragged across a slate, but I fancied that the defective light must have had something to do with the plentiful discords— a charitable idea of which I was disabused later on. Our servants had been requisitioned to do the waiting, as the Assad-i-Dowleh considered that his own were too uncivilised to understand European requirements, and Hashim was quite in his element on this occasion, treating our host with a benevolent patronage, the two having colloquies about every dish with which the Governor was unfamiliar. He wanted to try everything, but explained to Hashim that he was toothless, asking his opinion as to whether he could eat this

THE PERSIAN FRONTIER COMMISSION.

or that, and much shocked our factotum by insisting on drinking Worcester sauce in a wineglass. Hashim remonstrated with him, but the old gentleman was not to be dissuaded from his purpose. Turning to the table he said frankly that he had so much enjoyed it when poured over his meat at our party, that he wanted to have it in larger quantities, reminding me of the story of the farmer at a tenant's dinner who was so pleased with his thimbleful of liqueur that he asked the footman to supply him with some of the same drink in "a mug"!

When the champagne was opened (we always kept this for Persian dinners, as my brother knew from his former experiences how highly it and the toasts we were in the habit of connecting with it, were appreciated), the Assad-i-Dowleh quite won my heart by sending a message to his band, which struck up our National Anthem, upon which our host rose and proposed the health of our Queen, who, by the way, is regarded with wonderful reverence and admiration throughout Persia. My brother responded by toasting the Shah, and we finally parted with much effusion, it being arranged that we should keep a day ahead of the Persians with their great following, as, if the army went first, all supplies would be eaten up before we arrived. And so on February 9th we set off again on the march, the weather being so hot at this low altitude that we started by sunrise daily in order to reach our camps not later than nine o'clock.

We had frequent opportunities of observing the *mirage* on these great plains, and I have seen phantom lakes and shady trees in striking contrast to the barrenness and desolation of the actual country through which we were passing.

The "refraction" near the mountain ranges in the early morning was also a curious phenomenon, the curling mists magnifying small boulders into colossal and weird shapes, and completely transmogrifying the aspect of the country.

CHAPTER XIX

TO KUHAK AND THE FRONTIER COMMISSION

BALUCHISTAN, viewed as a whole, is one of the most sterile countries imaginable, the greater part of it covered with stones and boulders, the *débris* from the countless ranges of hills which cut up the land. In fact it is an uninhabited desert except where the traveller comes upon the oases of date-palms. The moment the small stream by which he has camped is left behind him he is on a Sahara, which may be sandy or stony, but which is always destitute of vegetation, until the presence of water again brings him to dates and cultivation. Everything here seems to be in extremes. The traveller is either enjoying the grateful shade of the palms, the murmur of running water, and the fresh green of the young barley, or he is in the midst of a barren region, where he cannot understand how his camels support life on the scanty, dried-up scrub, and where the water, if he is lucky enough to get any, is bitter, brackish, and foul.

Even in winter the climate is too hot to be pleasant, but the summer heats are so great that no Persian will venture into the low-lying country during that period. After leaving Kerman, where we were at an altitude of 5,600 ft., it was a great descent to the 2,000 ft. of Baluchistan, and as it was the Farman Farma strongly objected to my accompanying my brother on this journey. He affirmed that even if I survived the sun, I should reappear in civilised life with my skin burnt to the colour of that of a negress; this remonstrance of his being one of our jokes when we met him again at Tehran.

The first place at which we halted after leaving Faraj was Aptar. There was nothing specially remarkable about its date-groves, old fort, and mud beehive-like houses, but I remember the spot well because of the extraordinary reputation for sanctity attaching to the late Governor of the village.

This worthy is interred at Manish, a considerable distance from the scene of his labours, and a huge cairn of stones marks his last resting-place. The tomb is hung with bits of rag, ibex horns, and so on, the only reason given for the unusual veneration accorded to the deceased being that he never robbed the poor! This may seem a somewhat meagre claim to saintship in the eyes of a European, but, looked at from an Oriental point of view, the man who has it in his power to oppress, and to amass money as a result of his oppressions, and who refrains from enriching himself by such means, is worthy of all honour.

Shrines are scattered throughout the length and breadth of Baluchistan, and not only is some holy dervish interred close to every village of any note, but the traveller constantly comes upon a ring of stones hung with fluttering scraps of clothing in the midst of the wildest deserts. The pious passer-by tears a bit off his cotton shirt to add to the collection, believing that by so doing the dead saint will bear him in mind and will intercede for him to Allah.

The ibex horns are a sign of honour, and often very fine ones adorn some village shrine, which is occasionally hung with the woollen tassels taken from the leading camel of a caravan, or with camel-bells, these latter, I suppose, to call the attention of the saint.

From Aptar we made our way along the grey, shingly bed of a river, and observed masses of the dwarf-palm, or *peesh*, spreading out its spiky, fan-like leaves. It is a great stand-by to the Baluchis, as it supplies material for the matting of which they make their houses in this part of the country, also for the brittle ropes which they use to bind the loads on to their camels, and the uselessness of which the traveller soon finds out to his cost. The rudimentary Baluchi shoes are made from this palm, and are merely soles of thickly plaited fibre held on to the foot by means of a bit of rope. As they are invariably too long for the foot they have a queer look, and their owners shuffle about in them to all appearance most uncomfortably, so much so that I was never surprised to see them often carried in the hand while their possessor plodded along barefoot. From Regan onwards we met with these shoes, scattered on either side the track in all stages of decay, some quite new-looking ones being among the number. Besides being used for clothing, the roots of the dwarf-palm are eaten as food, and its woody stems supply firewood. Our caravan route through a *peesh* district was always marked by columns of white smoke, the shrub bursting into a tremendous blaze when set alight, its dry fans catching fire at once. The blackened stems left were rooted up for burning, and our camel-men made huge bonfires of them, round which they lay every night.

As the valley along which we were marching opened out, the great mass of Kuh-i-Hamant rose before us in all its majesty. It has three sharply serrated peaks, and when my brother made the ascent in his journey through Baluchistan in 1893 he found on reaching the summit that it was a perfect knife-edge, on which he was obliged to sit astride and so push himself along. The Baluchis were most unwilling for him to ascend this mountain, believing it to be inhabited by evil spirits. This, however, they imagine to be the case with every lofty and inaccessible peak, and the grand volcano of Kuh-i-Taftan, of which I had a glimpse later on, and which my brother also ascended, is usually called Kuh-i-Cheheltun (Mountain of the Forty Spirits).

As I have mentioned in the previous chapter, the Persian Commissioner and his suite were a day's march behind us, which plan was fraught with inconvenience owing to the habit his *pishkhana* had of arriving about 3.30 a.m. or 4 a.m., passing our camp with a trampling of men and camels, jingling of many bells, and a shouting of drivers and servants to halt. I remember on one or two of these occasions *Bargi*, being roused by the noise, called me a couple of hours before it was necessary, and, as there was never any time to spare in the morning, I sprang up without looking at my watch and nearly completed my toilette before she reappeared to say that she had made a mistake.

Magas, one of our next halting-places, is worthy of mention as being the highest point at which dates are grown. The Baluchis call it *Sarhad*, or Cold Country, and the *Garm-i-sir*, or Hot Country, Baluchis could not well exist here. It is quite a fine place for Baluchistan, the clusters of flat-roofed mud houses being dominated by a great square mud fort; and the entire population swarmed forth to greet the Consul *Sahib*, whom they remembered from his visit to them in 1893. The Governor and his brother headed the procession, tall men with flowing black beards, wearing long goat's-hair coats profusely embroidered in red cotton over their full white trousers, while their ample white turbans were in strong contrast to the small embroidered smoking-caps—an Indian importation—affected by some of their retainers, and which must be a most inadequate protection against the fierce sun of this region. The chieftains of the different villages through which we passed were always better-looking men than any of their subjects, their extra cleanliness in dress probably having something to do with their distinguished appearance. As we halted a day at Magas for supplies, we were overtaken by the Persian party, whom we entertained to lunch, and it may interest my readers to hear how I managed about puddings and so on when on the march.

As milk is scarcely ever to be got in Baluchistan, and eggs are practically unobtainable (the Baluchis considering them unclean, and as such unfit for eating), I took with me a large store of Swiss condensed milk and some tins of egg powder, a combination of the two making capital custard puddings. Dried plums, peaches, apricots, and figs had been laid in at Kerman, and were invaluable in a country almost destitute of fruit and vegetables at the best of times, and of course completely so during the month of February in which we were travelling.

Tins of "Chollet's compressed vegetables" were a great

stand-by for our soup, and when I mention that we carried "jelly packets" with us, my readers will see that we travelled in real luxury!

Naturally we were not without dates in a country where a man's social position is settled by the number of date-palms he possesses. We got a skinful of this fruit at Bam, but soon discarded it for the much superior keg given us by the Assad-i-Dowleh. This contained a sort of jam, the juice of other dates being poured upon the packed ones—the whole mass very luscious and half-crystallised. Dates and a sort of *chupatti* are the staple food of the Baluchis, and they cannot imagine the possibility of dwelling in a country where their much-prized fruit is not grown. The tradition is that when the Arabs overran Baluchistan each man carried his store of dates with him, and from the stones they flung away have arisen the great palm-groves of this country.

Suran was perhaps the most beautiful of our camps in Baluchistan. To reach it we struck across the alluvial plain of Magas, and got into a tangle of low hills and long, narrow desolate valleys. When free of these we emerged on to a plain which gleamed white, being encrusted with a glittering efflorescence of salt. Exquisite groves of palms shot up from the dazzling ground, and beyond them the snowy cone of Kuh-i-Taftan, that great volcano, rose magnificently above the umber and mauve mountain ranges bounding the horizon. Here the tamarisks grew tall and slim as Lombardy poplars, and the young date-palms were planted in pits for purposes of irrigation, and most carefully swathed up in pieces of palm-leaf matting, to protect their tender fronds from the animals.

My brother was far less impressed with the loveliness of the place than with the fear lest our horses might get cracked heels from the salt; but by washing their feet in carbolic, and drying them with the fibre growing at the root of the stalk of each palm-leaf, this danger was fortunately averted.

As we were halting for a couple of days at Suran we set out early the next morning in search of game, and found

A BALUCHI BAND.

that beyond the ramshackle mud villages, surrounded by the winter crops of wheat and barley now a foot high, and beyond the shady groves of palms, lay a region of swamp and river with jungles of rushes and tangled yellow grass. Here we began to splash in and out of pools and shallow streams, now nearly knee-deep in mud and water, and now crunching the crisp, bitter salt, resembling hoarfrost as it encrusted the stalks and leaves of the low scrub. Tortoise-shell butterflies were flitting about in great abundance, beautiful humped cattle were slowly chewing the cud, and swallows skimmed over the water in profusion, looking to my unpractised eye so much like the snipe we were in quest of that I should most certainly have loosed off a gun at them if I had been permitted to try my hand at this sport. After an unsuccessful chase after some wild geese we returned to camp with a small bag of snipe, and during lunch the Baluchi band of the village came to enchant our ears. It was a case of *multum in parvo*, being composed of but two men, who managed, however, to produce noise enough to half deafen us. One man beat a drum with much vigour, and the other performed on a long tube with a bag at its end, bringing piercing yells, screeches, and shrieks out of his insignificant-looking instrument. As the Persian Commissioner and his suite arrived about this time, the parti-coloured band of the Assad-i-Dowleh began to discourse sweet music, quite ignoring the rival band only a hundred yards off; and when this latter redoubled its exertions the strain on sensitive ears may be imagined rather than described.

Sultan Sukru appeared that afternoon, delighted to have caught us up again. He was full of pride at having mapped in a little-known part of the country, and as his way had led him past Isfundika he had taken gifts for the Governor and his three wives. These latter ladies I had had the pleasure of meeting at Rahbur the previous summer, during our tour in the hills from Kerman, when they had presented me with saddle-bags and engraved seals. I questioned Sultan as to whether they had approved of what I had sent them in return, and he amused me by describing how the head eunuch had come to him secretly, saying that the Governor had told his wives that I had sent them no gifts, but that the ladies did not place implicit faith in this assertion of their lord and master. Sultan Sukru accordingly gave the man particulars of the cases of perfumes, cut-glass bottles for rose-water, needle-books, and so on, that he had brought for them; and as the ladies sent me some old pottery and a saddle-bag, I trust that they extracted my presents from their wily husband. This Governor dwelt near an ancient buried city mentioned by Marco Polo, from which he dug up the old china and the curious seals I have spoken of before, and he had given my brother a great account of a certain Kalah-i-Suleiman (Solomon's Fort), which he had affirmed to be built of stone and covered with fine rock-sculptures and inscriptions. Like so much in Persia, however, this was very unlike its imaginary description, and turned out, when inspected by Sultan Sukru, to be a big mud building in three tiers, with no stone-work of any kind about it.

Before leaving Suran some Baluchis arrived at our camp with the news that fifteen ladies had landed at Gwadur with the officers forming the Frontier Commission, and the men asserted that they themselves had seen these *Khanums*. Allowing a large margin for Oriental exaggeration, my brother and I thought that there must be some foundation for such a report; and as nearly a year had elapsed since I had seen a European lady, I felt greatly delighted at the prospect of meeting some of my own sex again, and was proportionately disappointed when I met the Commission a few days later on, and found that the female element was conspicuous by its absence. At the next stage of our journey a fine-looking Baluch came to visit my brother. His snowy turban and full trousers were set off by a magnificent tunic of brilliantly striped silk—a veritable Joseph's coat—and attended by two or three servants he rode up on a horse, which is a sign of unusual wealth in this country.

As soon as my brother set eyes on him he recognised him

as the Governor of a village, who two years ago had begged a belt or a blanket, or even a pair of old boots from him, running after him in the fervour of his entreaties. This time the Baluch demanded a revolver, and on being asked what he had done to merit such a gift, he said, "I have certainly performed no service, but generosity is noble, O *Sahib*, and we Baluchis all expect presents from Europeans!"

As many of the marches we were making lay through a practically desert region I became perforce acquainted with all kinds of water, and after a time did not dislike the brackish variety, which was about the best of the many brands we sampled. Having always been practically a teetotaler, I am rather a connoisseur in *ab*, as the Persians term water, and all the bad kinds we encountered made me thoroughly appreciate the occasional clear streams rippling beneath stately palm-groves.

Our camels had often to go without a drink, but they kept very well on the whole, as they were fed every evening, and were not obliged to pick up their own livelihood, as the Baluchi camels have to do. At sunset they were driven into camp with much shouting and yelling, two men and a boy being in charge of every seven camels. The animals then knelt down in circles, each set keeping to its own mess, and the men driving off any outsiders who attempted to force themselves in. A big bundle of *ard-i-jo*, *i.e.*, a dough made of coarse barley-flour, was placed in the middle of each party, and the creatures would sniff at it, trying to extract bits from it before the time to serve it out arrived. When all were in their places, the men and boys made up balls of dough, thrusting them into yawning mouths, which opened out to a surprising extent, and always reminded me of mediæval pictures of dragons. All the camels behaved in the most orderly way during this process, swallowing their portions in turn, the favoured ones taking the hands of their drivers into their capacious jaws, and sucking them clean from the dough adhering to them.

On one occasion a huge animal was *must*, foaming at its mouth, and the men tried to make it fight with another camel, and brought the two great creatures close together. The *must* one was eager for the fray, and advanced with a gurgling roar, whereupon the other retreated in hot haste, considerably to my relief.

This custom of feeding the camels was an excellent one, as it kept them from going afield in search of food during the night. Baluchi camels do this very frequently, and thus often delay the start of a caravan for some hours, the drivers, perched upon *mahri*, or riding-animals, having to scour the country in all directions for their missing charges.

The Baluchi camel-driver is dirty, good-humoured, and lazy, an exceeding trial to the patience of the modern traveller, who has to make superhuman efforts to get his caravan off in good time in the morning, and who will find his drivers desert him in a body if he is not careful to temper his energy with much tact. Luckily for us, we had no trouble in this way, as the camels lent us by the Farman Farma were all under the authority of a certain Ibrahim Khan, who was responsible to the Prince for them and their drivers.

To talk of roads in Baluchistan is a complete misnomer. The traveller finds his way from place to place along narrow tracks beaten down by the feet of camels. If separated from his caravan, as we invariably were, he often loses all traces of the path, if it passes over a boulder-strewn ground or over hard, gravelly soil, and has to hunt in all directions before he recovers it again. Moreover, there are all sorts of secondary tracks running seemingly in the right direction, but which, if followed, will assuredly lead the wayfarer astray.

At several of our halting-places all the inhabitants had fled into the hills at the approach of the Assad-i-Dowleh's army, taking their sheep and movable property with them, but leaving perforce their crops of barley and lucerne, their mud houses, and tiny mosques at the mercy of the soldiery.

The places of worship in these villages are mean in the extreme, small, square mud edifices, the palm-beam roofs so low that the hand can reach them. Creeping inside through the hole serving as a door, there is not much to be seen save

KUHAK, WHERE THE FRONTIER COMMISSION MET.

palm-leaf matting on the ground, an old copy of the Koran in a hole in the wall, and near it a *mihrab*, or recess, indicating the direction of the *Kiblah* at Mecca, to which all the faithful turn when they pray. And yet, poor as are the few mosques in the country, the despised *Sunni* Baluchis are most strict in the performance of what religious duties they have been taught, keeping, for example, the Fast of *Ramazan* with far greater strictness than the civilised Persians who laugh at them.

The big cairns of stones by the wayside, adorned with sticks hung with fluttering rags, are all a proof of their desire to venerate and to pray; although they themselves are not very clear as to the supposed dervishes or other saintly personages buried beneath them. Mr. Floyer, in his book on Baluchistan, says that he sometimes started a *zierat*, or shrine, himself, by collecting together a small heap of stones, as he walked on ahead of his caravan, and then waiting to watch his camel-drivers, who invariably added their quota of boulders to the cairn.

We reached Kuhak on February 24th, having accomplished the distance of six hundred miles from Kerman in forty days, almost a record journey with camels, when it is remembered that a great part of our way had lain through desert, and that we had had to carry supplies of every sort.

The servants were greatly excited at the prospect of joining the Feringhee camp, and we noticed that they one and all became titled, evidently with the idea of impressing the Hindustani domestics whom they were about to meet. They no longer called one another by their plain, unvarnished names as formerly, but added such terms of honour as *Beg*, *Meshtedi*, or *Sultan*, never reflecting that in all probability the Indians would not be able to understand the significance of their dignities.

We ourselves were hardly less excited at the thought of congenial English society, after having been so many months away from civilisation; and it was with much delight that we saw the gleam of white tents on the plateau above the wide bed of the Mashkid River, and were hospitably welcomed by Colonel (now Sir Thomas) Holdich and his staff.

Kuhak itself is a prettily situated village among palm-groves and running streams, with a mud fort on the spur of the hillside. The houses are either square mud hovels with holes for door and windows and thatched with palm-leaves, or *koutuks*, *i.e.*, dwellings composed entirely of palm-leaf thatch on a framework of boughs.

It was from here that the work of the Frontier Commission was to begin, as the little district of Kuhak was one of the disputed points between Persian and British Baluchistan left unsettled during the Goldsmid Mission, as was also a stretch of some three hundred miles of frontier stretching up to the river Helmund.

On the day following our arrival the Persian Commission rode in in great state, with the band playing, and entered their camp, which was pitched on the opposite side of the Mashkid River to that of the English. The first question to be settled was which party was to call on the other. Europeans may think that it mattered very little, but any one versed in Oriental etiquette will understand that on such a point would probably hang the entire future relations of the two parties. The Persians naturally wanted the English to call on them first, but as the Itisham had paid the first visit to my brother as Consul of Kerman, he could not do less by Colonel Holdich the Commissioner. The old Assad-i-Dowleh tried hard to make a fuss about the business, but the Farman Farma, who proved himself an invaluable ally of the English, warned him by every post that he would be called to account should he obstruct the Commission in any way. After this matters went on smoothly, and the boundary pillars began to be erected, these being huge cairns of boulders, built up by a sepoy work-party on several of the most conspicuous hills along the line of demarcation. One day we climbed to the top of one of these low shale ranges, and I took a photograph of the pillar and the English party while we waited for the Persians to join us. These latter made much ado about ascending the hill; and really it was a comic sight to watch the Assad-i-Dowleh being pulled up in front by his bandmaster, and pushed from behind by a servant, until he arrived at the summit and sank down in a heap. He confided to Nasrullah Khan that nothing would have induced him to attempt this feat, but the fear that I, sitting up aloft, would laugh at him if he declined.

From this point of vantage the country lay spread out before us, and the old Governor could show the direction in which lay the valuable date-groves, the quarrelling about which was the reason for a demarcation of one of the barrenest, most desolate and stony regions imaginable.

It was fortunate that my brother was good at talking Persian; for the English interpreter, an Afghan, was not readily understood by the Persians, and their interpreter's (fat Haji Khan) English was of the most elementary description.

It was at this point that one of the difficulties of the delimitation began, the Assad-i-Dowleh trying to make trouble by proposing a ten days' delay, a reference to the authorities at Tehran, and so on; but during the next day Nasrullah Khan and Haji Khan went continually backwards and forwards between the two camps, and the result of their unusual amount of exercise was the removal of all friction for the time being.

Although Orientals have a love of procrastination, yet on this occasion, owing to a variety of causes, the Persians despatched their business with commendable rapidity. One reason that urged them was their horror of any great heat. The climate of Baluchistan is well-nigh unendurable during the summer months, and even now, at the beginning of March, we were always in shelter by nine o'clock at latest, as the sun was getting fiercer daily; and we noticed that the Persians, stout, and little addicted to taking exercise, were much less able to bear the heat than we were.

At the close of our week at Kuhak the English Commissioner invited the Persians to a formal dinner-party, which did much to promote friendly relations. The arrangement of the guests was a matter of some consideration, as there was a lack of languages in common; but somehow every one understood his neighbour more or less, and when Colonel Holdich proposed the health of the Shah the toast was received with enthusiasm, and followed by those of our Queen and the members of the two Commissions.

Personally I was glad when we left our camp at Kuhak, for it was by no means an attractive spot. We were perched on a hard, gravelly plateau above the broad, boulder-strewn bed of the Mashkid River, and behind us lay range after range of barren, arid hills, where scarcely even a sand-partridge was to be seen.

The so-called river was dry at the point we touched it, with the exception of some few pools at intervals, and it was difficult to realise the Baluchi proverb that says, "He is a dead man who stops to fasten his shoe in the bed of the Mashkid;" but of course this refers to later on in the year, when the melting snows from distant mountains send swirling torrents along these usually empty channels. When we were at Kuhak the river-bed was overgrown with tamarisk and oleander scrub, and from beneath its great boulders peeped out a dainty little plant like a miniature bougainvillia. Kuhak, and indeed the whole of Persian Baluchistan, is a "most distressful country" for horses. The ground is so thickly strewn with boulders and stones that it is hardly ever possible to go out of a foot's pace, which my brother and I found so monotonous that we got into the habit of walking all the short marches when they were only about twelve to fifteen miles.

We were really in the country of the camel, and although I was prejudiced against that slow-moving, evil-smelling animal, yet its supreme usefulness grew on me by degrees.

The Baluchi camels were for the most part small and underfed, each one being led by a cord fastened through its nostrils—a most cruel arrangement—and having a driver apiece, who had an interest in the animal, owning one of its legs in lieu of pay or rations; and, in consequence, grumbling if it had to carry any save the smallest of loads. As these burdens are fastened on in most careless fashion frequent halts have to be made to readjust them, and this process appears to be extremely repugnant to the camel mind. The creatures groan and roar as if possessed during the operation, opening their long jaws wide, and grumbling and gurgling somewhat like a very naughty boy in a tremendous passion, and even when they are up on their springy padded feet again they utter more remonstrances, and twist up their absurdly inadequate tails. The Baluchis ride one behind another on their camels, and the man who has the front seat climbs with his bare feet up the shoulder and neck of the lofty beast, which only kneels to receive one of its riders; the creatures are driven by a rope halter, and guided and punished by being struck on the neck with a light stick. The human voice comes much into play in this part of the world. Noises somewhat resembling such sounds as "*M-m-m*" and "*Dru-u*" urge the camels on; while a sort of "*Hah*" induces them to quench their thirst, when there is enough water; they would probably stand by the pool or stream, wrapt in a reverie, for an hour at a time if this form of persuasion were not resorted to. "The life of a camel is but forty days" is a Baluchi proverb, referring to the little hold these primeval sort of creatures appear to have of existence, a camel lying down and giving up the ghost on the merest pretext. On the other hand, they are wonderfully good climbers, carrying their loads up and down the steepest passes; and we noticed that whenever they were unloaded and let loose they invariably made their way to the summit of the low hills and would stand there silhouetted against the sky-line.

CHAPTER XX

WITH THE PERSO-BALUCH BOUNDARY COMMISSION

WE left our first camp at Kuhak on March 3rd, and it may be as well to give some account here of our mode of progression.

The English Commission had a small detachment of Bombay Cavalry and a company of sepoys, both under the command of Lieutenant Price, of the Baluchi Rifles, the cavalry always escorting Colonel Holdich, and the foot-soldiers starting off at an early hour daily to march the entire distance between the halting-places. These latter were well-set-up men, and wore a most serviceable *khaki* uniform—tunics, turbans, baggy trousers and *puttis* being of the same dust colour—their ammunition and water-bottles slung from broad belts, while they carried their rifles over their shoulders. Their departure from camp between 3 a.m. and 4 a.m. was attended with a ringing cheer—a signal to us that it was high time to be bestirring ourselves for the day's march.

The *pishkhana*, or advance-guard of camels, always left camp during the afternoon of the preceding day, carrying on an extra set of tents and the stores to the next halting-place; but notwithstanding this diminution in its numbers, the Commission was a most imposing procession, or series of processions. Hundreds of loaded camels plodded along, each camel's nose bored with a small wooden nut to which was fastened a cord attached to the tail of the animal in front of it, and some of the creatures were furnished, instead of the usual loads, with great, shallow baskets, one on each side, in which reposed sick sepoys or disabled camp-followers.

The leading camels were often hung with much betasselled woollen ropes studded with small white cowries and tinkling with bells, while a kind of worsted garter was worn by a favoured few, and the young ones trotted along by the side of their loaded mothers, and were never fastened in any way.

After passing the camels we would come upon the one *dhoolie*, or litter, or the flocks of sheep and goats, slowly driven along by a tall Baluch with wild cries, these creatures supplying the camp with milk and meat, and diminishing greatly in numbers as the Commission drew to its close. Then we would get up with the detachment of brisk, sturdy mules laden with the ammunition, or perhaps overtake the sepoys, who always made a halt on the way.

These latter had picked up some pets since coming into the country. A baby moufflon kept close to one man, and a fat-tailed sheep faithfully followed another, not to speak of a *tazi*, or greyhound, which always wore a coat on the hottest marches.

A contingent of wild-looking Baluchis, armed with rifles and long, curved knives, and carrying shields, were a frequent sight, looking picturesque mounted in pairs on their running camels, their white garments fluttering as they rolled along; or perhaps a Baluchi Governor, anxious to pay his respects to the Assad-i-Dowleh, would gallop his little horse ruthlessly over the stony plain, he and his followers clad in gay silk tunics, and their mounts covered with the most gorgeous saddle-cloths.

From Kuhak to Jalk we travelled with the Persian Commission and the Governors of Baluchistan, whose horses, mules, and camels moved along in a great mass, mixed up with the army and its donkeys. My brother and I used to walk in the chilly hours before dawn, but had, however, to mount almost as soon as the sun rose, as it sprang up suddenly into the sky and seemed to flood the country with an intense light and heat, making us thankful for pith hats even at this early hour. We were generally in camp by 8.30 a.m. at latest, very ready for the breakfast spread in the big *pishkhana* tent, after which we amused ourselves as best we could until our caravan turned up with our camp equipage, and we could indulge in the luxury of baths, and have a siesta during the heat of the afternoon to make up for our short nights. It was impossible to go out until after 5 p.m.; but I occupied myself with writing this book, and luckily we were by no means badly provided with literature, exchanging books with the officers of the other camp, which was usually pitched at a short distance from ours.

Nearly every afternoon, about four o'clock, we were visited by a sand-storm—by no means an agreeable experience if it happened to be a violent one. Nothing heralded the approach of these *shaitans* (devils) as the servants called them; but suddenly the tent might be blown down upon us, as happened twice, by a sort of miniature tornado, and oh, the dust! Everything was thickly coated with sand, our faces, books, and writing materials covered, hair and ink-pots full of it in a second; and when it had passed away and the tents were swept out, it was almost impossible to write, so gritty were pens and paper, and so sore were our eyes from the sharp particles of sand.

Our worst experience of this kind was a never-to-be-forgotten night that we spent at Lajji during the beginning of March. This place was one of the prettiest we had ever camped in, being a broad, stony valley, intersected by a stream, which divided into half a dozen branches fringed with rushes, coarse yellow grass, and graceful palms, while bees, butterflies, grasshoppers, and dragon-flies were in abundance.

Several queer old mud forts were dotted about, on one of which a formidable stuffed dummy was erected to scare away simple-minded besiegers, the story being that it was manufactured by a dervish, who promised that, as long as it stood there, the fortress would never be taken. The whole scene was so charming that Colonel Holdich made a beautiful sketch of it, allowing me, as usual, to try my prentice hand at daubing under his skilful eye.

The English camp on this occasion was pitched on a

barren plateau, surrounded by low hills, and far above the deliciously cool and rippling river; but as it was a windy day my brother ordered our tents to be pitched on a small oasis below the aforesaid plateau, where it seemed much quieter, and we retired to rest as usual.

At 11 p.m., I was aroused from my soundest sleep by feeling the tent flapping my face violently, while clouds of dust and grit were swirling in, and before I quite realised what was happening, my table, chair, and washing apparatus were on the ground, and all my clothes and small movable articles were whirled out of the tent and into the darkness. The wind was roaring and shrieking with a terrific violence, and I clung desperately to my wavering tent-pole, calling *Bargi*, who slept in the back part of my tent, to come and assist me. I had a vague idea of going to my brother, but found the gusts of wind so formidable, and the torrents of rain descending so drenching, that I had perforce to desist.

After holding on for a considerable time to my rocking, swaying pole, very cold and almost overpowered with sleep, I heard the welcome voice of Ali Agha, who had come to hammer in my pegs, and who called to me to retire, saying that he would make things all right, and that the *Sahib* was superintending the covering of the luggage with tarpaulins. As the wind had considerably abated in force I crept back to bed, thankful to feel that the worst was over; but was shortly undeceived, for the hurricane soon recommenced with fresh vigour. The wind seemed racing and galloping overhead with a sound as of thunder or rolling artillery, flashes of lightning gleamed at intervals, and, of course, every peg was torn up again in an instant, leaving the guy-ropes hanging.

The first part of the night was as nothing to this, and my brother sacrificed his own tent to come and hold one of my poles, while *Bargi* and I clung frantically to the other, both of them creaking and groaning till we felt that they must crack with the great strain upon them. At every gust clouds of sand poured in, half choking us, and it was with great relief that we heard the rain descend, and at about 2 a.m., the wind went down enough to permit us to resume our interrupted slumbers. I woke up to a scene of veritable chaos, and my dripping, muddy clothes, sponge, and other belongings were brought to me at intervals, as the servants rescued them from the patch of green barley, which had checked them in their wild career, and held them fast. The English camp had fared far worse than we had, being in a more exposed position, and the Persian Commissioner sent a pathetic message to the effect that he could do no Boundary work that day, as the whole of the Persian tents had collapsed during the night, and he and his followers were all ill from the effects of their drenching during the hours that they had been without shelter.

At Aibi, a place a little further on, I noticed that the crowds of women surrounding my tent with cries of "*Salaam Bibi*," and offerings of dates and bread, were remarkable for their bad teeth, such a contrast to the gleaming, pearly rows usually possessed by Orientals. They wore the usual long black or white garments embroidered in yellow or red cotton, and had red or black shawls over their heads, many of them having nose-rings, usually big turquoises set in metal. All the women and children, save the poorest, were lavishly ornamented with bead bracelets, necklaces and earrings, mostly of blue glass, as this colour is considered to avert the evil eye.

It was in this valley that one of our great excitements took place. The doctor was taking a stroll in the hills close to the camp about sunset when a grey bear, about the size of a small donkey, came from its haunts to have its evening drink in the stream running through the valley. Directly it saw the European it made towards him, and the latter, being armed only with a hunting-crop, judged discretion the better part of valour, and returned in haste to camp for his rifle.

The other officers joined in the chase which ensued, but the bears (for this one turned out to have a mate) had got too good a start, and the pursuers only got glimpses of them, making off in a clumsy gallop, which covered the ground very quickly. This was a great subject of conversation, and the Baluchis promised endless bear-hunts to the Commission, but when it came to the point and their statements were severely scrutinised, it was discovered that they had indulged in the usual Oriental exaggeration and that, in reality, bears were few and far between in that part of Baluchistan at all events.

We did not, however, lack for snakes, although we never came across many of them. As a rule two or three were discovered on each camping ground, and speedily despatched, one being found in Colonel Holdich's tent. For aught we knew these long, slim creatures with speckled backs and white bellies might have been perfectly harmless, but naturally we could not be sure.

I remember one afternoon how, when writing in my tent, I looked up by chance and saw a long snake glide in under the curtain right up to me. I seized my riding-whip to despatch it, but it was out of my premises like a flash, and although I pursued it into the broiling sunshine, yet to my regret it escaped me.

The barren land through which we were passing was inhabited by legions of lizards, making me sorry that I was no naturalist, as the great variety of species would have made an interesting study. Mr. Turnbull collected them for the Curator of the Bombay Museum, so we all tried to capture specimens for him to bottle. Some were large, waddling creatures, much like miniature crocodiles, and I always feared lest Tim, the doctor's fascinating fox-terrier, might get bitten by these saurians, which he pursued with great zest. We heard that an officer travelling in Baluchistan had lost two of his dogs from this cause. They caught and worried a great lizard and returned foaming at the mouth to their master, dying in much pain shortly afterwards.

The work of the Commission went on steadily from day to day, although it received checks at intervals from the Assad-i-Dowleh's desire to give trouble, and the Itisham felt that he must object to every point as a matter of form "to save," as he expressed it, "his honour in the eyes of the Persians."

A coldness, however, soon sprang up between the Persian Commissioner and the Assad-i-Dowleh, owing to the overweening pride of the latter gentleman; and this circumstance decidedly conduced to the speedy settlement of the line of demarcation which had practically been arranged at Tehran, as did also the frequent letters of admonition from the Farman Farma, carried on riding camels from his camp in the district near Regan. We were all amused by a small incident about this time. Colonel Wahab, R.E., who was undertaking the surveying and mapping, had put up some trigonometrical marks on a hill. The Persian party made up their minds that these were a new boundary pillar erected unknown to the Shah's representative and sent over their interpreter (save the mark!) to ask for explanations, while the Itisham himself visited my brother later in the day to apologise for the mistake and to assure him that it was only the Assad-i-Dowleh who had made the blunder!

On that same evening we nearly had a quarrel with the latter gentleman. He had, on one occasion, given us some of the white palm-tree pith, which tastes much like celery, and is esteemed a great delicacy; it is quite a royal gift, as the palm has to be felled to procure it.

Having understood that we appreciated his present, the Governor sent us over a plate of "pith sweetmeat," probably to make amends for his mistake about the boundary pillar; but this stuff was indescribably nasty, and even Master Tim turned away his nose when some one offered him a morsel. Evidently Hashim, who was waiting at table that night, reported this incident to the Assad-i-Dowleh, for the latter visited Nasrullah Khan in high wrath the following day saying, "Not only did the Feringhees despise my gift, but they offered it to the accursèd dog, which did likewise!" Our *mirza*, with a truly Oriental disregard of stern facts, airily replied that he was at table on the occasion referred to by the Governor of Baluchistan and could assure him that his sweetmeat had been much enjoyed by all present. He took great credit to himself for so adroitly preventing the coolness which would certainly have arisen, but which, as certainly, would have speedily passed away, for Persians allow a wide latitude to the eccentric European.

From Lajji we made our way to Jalk, where we were to have a standing camp, sending a survey and party of men to Kuh-i-Malik-i-Siah (the extreme point of the frontier) there to erect the last boundary pillar as, since it was a waterless region, it was impossible for the whole Commission to go there.

As we approached Jalk the inhabitants were lining the hilly path in dense, dirty white masses to see the *tomasha*. A great pool of blood marked the spot where a goat had been slain in honour of the Assad-i-Dowleh, and further on we passed a body of his soldiers dividing the animal. We made our way by mules, camels, sowars, infantry with all their accompaniments of bells, cries, and trampling, and came in sight of an old brick-domed tomb to the right of the road, while ahead of us the usual picturesque grey fort reared itself from among a grove of date-palms, in strong contrast to the barren route along which we had come. The braying of the trumpet of the Assad-i-Dowleh's army resounded near at hand, and in another moment we were upon the shabby soldiers in their dirty grey cotton coats and red trousers, marshalled by common *ferashes* armed with sticks with which to keep the defenders of their country in line!

As we were a fortnight at Jalk I must try to give some account of the place and its special points of interest, of most of which we took photos.

On the day following our arrival we rode out with the Persian Commission and a great following of Baluchis to have a sort of international ride to explore the neighbourhood. Jalk consisted of about three miles of date-groves, watered by running streams, and was rich in crops of barley and wheat, millet, and beans, its gardens being crammed with fig, pomegranate, and orange-trees and vines. Here and there were strong forts built of large stones embedded in mud and seemingly most durable, and in them the people lived, emerging in veritable swarms to gaze at us as our cavalcade passed.

The most interesting feature in the place were the tombs of

the Kaianian Maliks, this dynasty reigning as late as the eighteenth century until conquered by Nadir Shah.

These mausoleums were mostly square enclosures varying from twenty to sixty feet in height, built of sun-dried mud bricks, and roofed in with pointed mud domes. The tombs lay on the ground, flat mud slabs, two or three placed one above another, and there was usually a hole in the roofs by which to admit light. Other mausoleums had an antechamber, in one of which we perceived traces of blue and red frescoed patterns, and the remnants of the blue and white tiles which had been embedded as a frieze under the line of the dome, while a third sort had an upper chamber, evidently reserved for the head of the house, servants and inferior members perhaps being interred on the lower floor.

The mausoleum we passed when riding into Jalk had greater attempts at ornamentation than any of the others that we visited.

Round its walls were a series of low, recessed arches in which were rough plaster bas-reliefs of horses, camels, and elephants, much like the early attempts of a child, so *unlike* were they to any of the animals in their normal state. Above these quaint figures were rude frescoed patterns in blue and magenta, entirely lacking in form and symmetry, and so unfinished that they gave us the idea that they must be the tentative efforts of some amateur artist who was perpetually leaving off one crude design after another in disgust. Inside this particular mausoleum a big mass of pebble and mud concrete roofed in the vault of the king or chieftain once buried here, and two or three holes gave access to the rifled tombs inside, which, to judge from the quills strewn about, were now tenanted by porcupines.

From the bare hills surrounding Jalk we got extensive panoramas of the country. Below us lay the villages peeping out with their grey fortresses and ochre-coloured mausoleums from among the lovely palm-trees, the date-groves ending abruptly in *kavir*, or salt marsh, and on all sides of them stretched low hills and desert, save for a line of palms showing where Ladgusht, rich in tombs, lay some fifteen miles off.

KAIANIAN MALIK TOMB.

The fertilising of the date-trees was going on, men climbing up the female trees and introducing a little of the pollen from the male tree into their flowers, which looked much like bundles of wheat ears. The male trees do not bear fruit, and the Baluchis eat their masses of flowers, which travellers affirm are not unpalatable. During our visit to Jalk the inhabitants were suffering from influenza, which carried off several of the poor people daily, as they were less able than usual to combat illness, the Fast of *Ramazan* drawing to its close, leaving the population in an exhausted condition.

None of us, fortunately, were attacked by the scourge, but some were visited by a mad dog, which might have been worse. This creature came into my brother's tent one night and growled and snarled for a considerable time before it could be ejected. It then rushed into the tent of the Persian Commissioner and attacked him as he lay in bed, tearing his clothes; but fortunately he drove it off, one of his guards coming in and wounding it with a sabre. On this the animal fled, but bit one of the sentries badly before it finally disappeared.

I confess to feeling very uneasy the next night, as tents have so many entrances for an animal determined to push its way in; but numerous precautions were needless, our nocturnal visitor not making its appearance. On the following day, however, I saw the poor creature dragging itself painfully along near our tents, and, as my brother was over at the English camp, I called Ali Agha, the bravest of our servants, and, loading my brother's gun, told him to put the dog out of its misery. Unluckily it had reached the low hills surrounding our camp before the boy could overtake it, and he returned saying that he could not find it. As I had noticed two or three crows hovering close at hand it is probable that its end was very near, for we never caught sight of it again.

While at Jalk my brother and I went out every morning at seven o'clock to take photos and to exercise the horses at a foot's pace among the date-groves in the fresh morning air, crossing stream after stream, which reflected in their deep pools the palm fans, passing the young crops, among which was grown a peculiar double-eared wheat, and coming here and there upon a picturesque fort with perhaps a mass of reddish, waving reeds for a foreground, among which the small, humped cattle might be feeding.

Palms and running water were everywhere; but yet only a step away from the little oasis lay a sterile, shelterless region of stony desert and low, barren hills on which the sun shone with a pitiless glare.

On one of our morning rides we had the grief of losing "Prince," my brother's favourite horse, a beautiful grey Arab, renowned for its speed in pursuing gazelle, and the gift of the Farman Farma. We were passing at the time along a narrow path composed of palm trunks, which edged a steep bank, at the foot of which lay a big pool of water. My brother rode on ahead, and to my horror I saw one of the palm trunks give way, and "Prince" and his rider half over the bank. The brave horse made great efforts to recover his footing, and actually managed to scramble back to the path again, trembling with fright. He seemed none the worse for the adventure until some hours afterwards, when he appeared to have a bad attack of colic. Everything that could be done was done, my brother superintending relays of servants who looked after the poor creature during the night. But all was in vain, and at two o'clock he passed away, both of us feeling that we had lost a real friend, so much attached had we always been to this gentle and affectionate creature.

Nasrullah Khan tried to console me for his loss by saying that a Persian would consider that some evil had been lying in wait for my brother, but that it had fallen on his horse instead, the animal thus becoming a sacrifice for the man; but this view of the case did not comfort me as much as he expected.

On the night of March 16th the Fast of *Ramazan* came to an end, and the firing of guns announced the *eed*, or holiday, which terminated it, and the next morning we had to wait a considerable time for our breakfast, as all the servants were at a big prayer-meeting near the English camp, one of the sepoys acting as *mollah*, and the Baluchi *Sunnis* prostrating themselves with fervour and muttering responses.

The majority of the population of Jalk was squatting on the rocky bluffs overlooking the camp, their dirty white garments in striking contrast to the snowy attire of the Indians, among whom I noticed Sultan Sukru leading the prayers with a whole-hearted enthusiasm pleasant to see.

On the day after *Noruz*, on which occasion visits of ceremony were exchanged between the English and Persians, the International *Gymkhana* took place on a bit of desert, partially cleared of stones to make a course. Colonel Holdich ordered a tent to be put up, in which tea was served, and the various revolvers, knives, &c. (the prizes for the winners), were laid out. All the Persian party arrived punctually, the Assad-i-Dowleh looking very smart in a vivid blue cloth coat and cream-coloured trousers, and keeping an eye on his cotton-coated army, while hundreds of Baluchis assembled to see the novel sight. The first event was tent-pegging, done by the Indian troopers, then followed horse-races, donkey-races, foot-races, and camel-races. These latter were a revelation to me, and seemed as if taken from the "Prehistoric Peeps" in *Punch*. The unwieldy animals tore along at a surprising pace with outstretched necks, their riders seemingly mere bundles of dirty garments, which floated wildly in all directions.

After these diversions a piece of the ground was smoothed for the wrestling, and the big Persian *pahlavan* strutted about defiantly, confident that he would easily beat his opponent, a Scinde man, chosen from among the sepoys. At this point of the entertainment I retired to the tent, and a great crowd closed in round the performers. After waiting about ten minutes I heard a mighty shout of "Ali!" arising, and the masses of onlookers began to surge backwards and forwards, while, to my surprise, the Indian *sowars* appeared to be galloping into Persians and Baluchis alike. The Itisham and Haji Khan rushed to the tent, and the Assad-i-Dowleh galloped off to his own camp, surrounded by a swarm of his soldiers, who were with hearty goodwill actually belabouring their General! A few stones began to fly, and as the plain was thickly strewn with these handy missiles, I thought we were in for something unpleasant. My brother's promptitude, however, saved the situation. As he had been starting the races, he was the only Englishman on horseback, so he hastened after the Assad-i-Dowleh and constrained him to return and finish the sports and assist at the giving away of the prizes. The cause of this row was that the wrestling aroused all parties to a state of wild excitement, as each side believed that to be beaten in wrestling was to be defeated in the race of life. The Persians, imagining that their champion was getting the worst of it, began to belabour his Indian opponent, and Mr. Price saw a man on horseback lash at him with his whip. The English officer seized the fellow's bridle to send him to the Assad-i-Dowleh for punishment, when the man drew his sword upon him. The sepoys, seeing their officer threatened, made a rush at once upon the Persian soldiery in general, and so the fight began. As Mr. Price and my brother were in the thick of the fray, they intercepted many stones, and felt their bruises for some days, as also did the Assad-i-Dowleh. The whole mass of Baluchis, who had been looking on at the sports, rushed in a body to the English camp to offer their services in exterminating the hated Persians, feeling that the moment had come for them to avenge themselves on their conquerors.

The Assad-i-Dowleh was naturally much upset at such an ending to the *Gymkhana,* and when the whole thing was over announced that he should have every one of his soldiers bastinadoed; whereupon my brother and I had the amusement of seeing the entire Persian army taking refuge among our horses, as in Persia a stable is always *bast,* or sanctuary! Soldiers were squatted about everywhere under the palms to which our steeds were tethered, and there they stayed until the next day, when the Assad-i-Dowleh, finding the situation embarrassing, came, attended by a single servant, and harangued them, promising to let bygones be bygones if they would return to their allegiance forthwith.

After this eventful afternoon we all dined with the Persian

party in a huge red umbrella tent, pitched on the bank of the stream, on the other side of which a large space was fenced in with palm leaves. We had an excellent Persian dinner, our servants doing the waiting as usual, and the Itisham made a fine speech about the Queen, calling her the "ruler who dwelt in the shadow of Allah," the band playing our National Anthem in style. After dinner we sat by the stream, dammed up to form a cascade, watching the fish which were attracted to the lights, and listening to the discords of the band, chiefly composed of small boys, whose great idea was to blow with all their might, the continuous *fortissimo* being deafening at such close quarters. One of our party said he would like to annihilate a youth who clashed a pair of broken cymbals with much zeal, but I felt that if it came to that three parts of the band, which numbered some thirty performers, would have to be doomed, as nearly every instrument was out of tune! Every one, moreover, performed on his own instrument without the slightest relation to the others, time and tune being disregarded with a fine recklessness, the bandmaster, who sat at table with us, never turning a hair at the pandemonium.

We also had "fireworks" at this banquet, one of the Persians striking a peculiar sort of match, which had a rose-coloured flame, and flinging them, one after another, up into the air.

On March 24th the whole Frontier Commission was satisfactorily finished, the treaty and maps signed, and we all were packing up for a start on the morrow, the Persians to return to Kerman, Nasrullah Khan accompanying them to act as agent there during my brother's absence, and we ourselves to march to Quetta with the English party.

Colonel Holdich gave a farewell dinner that night, which went off with much spirit, and was a good termination to the Frontier Commission. Fat Haji Khan came to the front that evening, and sang a Persian song with zest, electrifying us when he suddenly struck up the "Highland Laddie," which had been taught him, so he told us, by an English lady, to whom he became tenderly attached during his stay in London. Haji had further composed a Persian poem on the doings of the Commission, with moon, stars, rose-gardens, nightingales, and London experiences all thrown in, and had sent it to Nasrullah Khan to translate it for him into English ; but the latter declined the task, saying the whole effusion was utter nonsense, which perhaps deprived us of a great intellectual treat !

Our goodbyes were most effusive, every one hoping to meet every one else again, and numerous and fervent were the handshakings and pretty speeches as we said adieu to our Persian friends.

Next day we made our way back to Lajji, my brother and I being very sorry to part with Nasrullah Khan, who had been with Europeans for so long that he did not at all appreciate returning to undiluted Persian society, and so we began our 430-mile march to Quetta.

CHAPTER XXI

TO QUETTA WITH THE ENGLISH COMMISSION

WE were now making our way towards the Highlands of British Baluchistan, but still suffered a good deal from the heat, which had often been 94° in our tents, making the midday siesta, with its accompaniment of buzzing flies, almost an impossibility. From Lajji we retraced our steps to our old camp at Isfandak (my third visit to that village) by a peculiarly narrow winding gorge, our path being along the dry river-bed at its bottom. A violent storm of rain and hail, with an accompaniment of thunder and lightning, came on during the afternoon while we were encamped in this aforesaid gorge, and we feared lest there might be a flood during the night, which would infallibly have swept us all away, as there was no foothold on the steep cliffs on either side of us; but fortunately we were spared such a disaster. The days passed quickly as we marched across interminable stone-covered plains or got in among the hills, clambering up and down the steep tracks with some difficulty. At first I imagined that the whole country was one dull yellowish-grey, but Colonel Holdich's sketching lessons showed me what an infinite variety of tints and tones there were in reality, although the utter desolation and neutral-toned sterility were not attractive, even to the most enthusiastic traveller. This latter, as a rule, chooses the rare oases for the subjects of his paintings, and when he displays stately palms, running streams, picturesque forts, and domed houses embowered in lime and orange-trees to his friends at home, they naturally think that this is Baluchistan. We returned to Kuhak, here found a Kaianian Malik tomb resembling those at Jalk, and in a ruinous condition. It had four tiers of big square mud tiles on its outside walls with crudely executed geometrical patterns and images of primitive animals and quaint figures of men. One tile had an inscription to the effect that the mausoleum was erected in honour of Malik Shumsidin 1027 of the *Hejreh* 1617–1618 A.D.

On April 1st we left the Mashkid Valley, crossing the river and some low hills, and so got into the Rakshan Valley, saying goodbye to Persian soil for a considerable period. It was the first time for weeks that we had been able to canter our horses, and the soft, gravelly soil was a delightful change after the region of perpetual boulders through which we had passed. It was still hot, and we breakfasted by moonlight at four or five o'clock, when it was quite chilly, starting off in the dim twilight before the dawn, the hour called by Persians "between the wolf and the lamb," and arriving at camp about 8 a.m., in broiling sunshine which scorched me considerably in spite of my huge pith hat, two gossamer veils, and a cosmetic for my face. At night again it was quite cold, and the great changes of temperature made it very hard to avoid chills.

Pleasant as the sand and solidified mud were to canter over, the water of the Rakshan Valley left much to be desired, and it was at times so salt that I felt as if I were bathing in sea-water. I well remember one occasion when the couple of pools of water at our halting-place were surrounded with a white efflorescence of brine, and consequently quite undrinkable. It was a particularly hot day, not a cloud in the deep blue sky, and we reached camp very ready for breakfast, but found both the tea and coffee provided in the mess-tent too nasty to swallow. There was a supply of claret, which was produced for the evening meal, but as I am a water-drinker from choice, and this beverage, undiluted, was most unpalatable to me, I preferred to go thirsty to bed.

It was a comfort to know that Panjgur, rich in water and palms, was our next halting-place, and we started for that village about half-past four the next morning, the chilly air before the dawn preventing us from feeling over-thirsty from the lack of our customary morning cup of tea.

Some seven miles before we reached the village we passed through the big date-groves of Kalag, and then came a long stretch of desert before we arrived at the palms which dispute with Kej the claim of producing the best dates in the world.

During Captain Kemball's tour of the previous year Mr. Parker, of the Bombay Artillery, returning from a parade of his troops, was nearly killed by a Panjguri, who rushed upon him with a knife and severely wounded him. The man, being a *ghazi*, or fanatic, believed that the meritorious deed of killing a Feringhee would transport him straight to the Mohammedan Paradise; but Captain Kemball, Political Agent of Baluchistan at the time, ordered the would-be assassin to be hanged and his body burnt, thus, according to Mohammedan ideas, preventing his entrance into the heaven he was so desirous of reaching.

As is customary in such a case in the East the relatives of the culprit were fined, and it was considered probable that they would try to wipe out their blood feud by an attempt on the life of Captain Kemball.

My brother and I had forgotten this incident, which, however, was brought forcibly to my mind that morning as we got near Panjgur. We were riding alone and unarmed far ahead of our caravan, and passed groups of Baluchis who salaamed politely, when I noticed that one wild-looking man began to follow us in the most persistent manner, running when our horses quickened their pace, and keeping close to us. I put him down at once as a *ghazi* or one of the relatives of the deceased fanatic of the previous year, and fearing lest he might have sinister designs on my brother, who looked remarkably like Captain Kemball in his pith helmet, insisted on riding between them, keeping a watchful eye on the object of my suspicion until we came in sight of our tents, when to my great relief he disappeared.

Panjgur is said to have been inhabited by a lawless tribe, who extended their depredations to the Arabian coast, and thus forced Omar to send an expedition to exterminate them. Five of the chieftains were slain, and the name of the place was altered from Khurmabad to Panjgur (Five Graves).

The inhabitants looked both clean and prosperous, and the streams were of crystal clearness, but nevertheless we were not sorry when our two days' halt was over, as Colonel Holdich took unusual precautions in the way of guards, and ordered none of us to go near the villages unless accompanied by armed sepoys, which considerably hindered my photography.

The houses were chiefly composed of palm leaves, the long leaf-stalks being stuck into the ground in a circle and interlaced with palm fibre rope fastened at the top so as to form a sort of cage. Palm-leaf mats were placed over this foundation, or the interstices were merely filled up with palm leaves thrust between them, and I noticed some huts most neatly thatched all over with palm fans, tightly packed together. These dwellings seemed very small for human habitation, but in a land where our thermometers stood at 94° during our visit at the beginning of April, the inhabitants practically passed their lives in the open air.

We left Panjgur on Easter Monday, passing the ruined barracks and mud houses where the English troops were quartered until the garrison was withdrawn, and we noted two of the distinctive Kaianian Malik tombs in a ruinous condition, and very inferior to those at Jalk.

To me it was a great relief that we were now in a country where we could trot and canter at intervals, as the weariness of sitting hour after hour on a lady's saddle and walking at a foot's pace was great. I used to vary my position by taking my cramped knees from the pommels and letting my feet hang down; but the more I rode the more I saw the disadvantages of the saddle to which I was condemned. The side-saddle is by no means an ideal invention in my eyes. It is difficult to mount into it from the ground; it is dangerous in riding among hills to be unable to spring off on either side in case of accident; the habit is very apt to be caught on the pommels if the rider falls, and the position in which she sits cramps her much if persisted in for many hours at a slow walk, which is the usual thing in hilly and stony countries. Looking at it from the horse's point of view, it is much heavier than a man's saddle; is very apt to give the animal a sore back; the weight being on one side tires the horse, and it is more difficult to adjust. Some of my lady friends at Tehran always rode on a man's saddle when they went among the hills, modifying their habits to the altered position, which they all assured me was preferable in every way to that which custom obliged them to conform to.

The first week in April we had a long march to Nagar Kalat, starting in the darkness, there being no moon, at three o'clock, and with some difficulty finding the track across the black, gravelly plain. However, Colonel Holdich, who had the start of us with his Baluchi guides, kindly got them to light bonfires on the path wherever they could find palmetto bushes to set in a blaze. It was about four o'clock when the small remnant of moon came to the aid of the dim glimmer of the stars, and then the "false dawn," called by Persians "the tail of the wolf"—a phenomenon very common in the East—made its appearance, and heralded the true dawn and the sun.

The horses were wonderfully clever about keeping to the track, and seldom stumbled over the scrub which often grew on the winding path, too narrow for us to ride abreast. Before reaching our camping-place we passed the *pishkhana* camels, which had been fifteen hours accomplishing the thirty miles, which we had done in a third of the time. They looked quite worn out, and one poor creature had been cut adrift a couple of miles back and lay on the road, looking with appealing eyes at those who passed it by. A camel is always given a chance to recover; for if it revives it can pick up a livelihood in any district, however barren, and will rejoin its own caravan, or perhaps be found and annexed by another one.

It was somewhat comfortless to find no tents pitched on our arrival; but there was nothing for it but to water our plucky horses at two weed-covered pools, and, after tethering them, to rest in the blazing sunshine until some shelter was erected, and then to wait in patience for an hour, which seemed interminable, until a hastily improvised breakfast made its appearance.

We had to make a two days' halt here to give the camels time to recoup after their unusually long march, and our party shot sand-grouse up the stream, bagging several of these pretty, mottled, brown birds, with yellow patches on either side of their heads, a most welcome addition to our limited bill of fare.

All about this part of the country were traces of a once widespread cultivation, and the ruins of many apparently large towns. Colonel Holdich picked up specimens of pottery and glass beads in these mounds of *débris* which pointed to a higher state of civilisation than that possessed by the few and dirty inhabitants who dwell here at the present time.

The whole of the valleys through which we were now passing were terraced, tier above tier of low slate walls often reaching some way up the sides of the hills, and these remains, which point to a much greater rainfall than at present, are called by the Baluchis *Ghor* (or *Gabr*) *bastas* (buildings of the infidel). Colonel Holdich was inclined to put them down to the Arab occupation of the country, in the eighth century, but he could not explain whence came the water to irrigate the vast areas once plainly under cultivation and to fill the great storage tanks, indications of which we frequently came across.

One theory is that deforestation, both here and throughout Persia, was the cause of the present dryness and barrenness of both countries; and probably it is so, as the rainfall of Tehran has become considerably greater in the memory of man, since Persians and Europeans have vied with one another in planting its environs.

Shrines of holy men were frequently to be met by the roadside, and we noticed one walled in with tall, upright stakes on which were scratched animals and figures—a

A DERVISH WHO ACCOMPANIED THE FRONTIER COMMISSION.

proceeding quite contrary to Mohammedan law. In other *zierats* the head and feet of the dervish were marked by slate monoliths, and in this country holiness, when interred, seemed to run to length, as many of these saints apparently measured several yards from head to foot.

Very often near the track we observed large, round spaces, swept clear of the black, shingly gravel, and formed into a circle with low, upright slates, a small pile of stones being left in the centre. These are to commemorate Brahui weddings, the musician standing in the centre and the dancers posturing round him. Dr. Bellew, in his work "From the Indus to the Tigris," speaks of these *chaps*, as they are called, and explains that the name means "clapping of hands," the dancers thus beating time to the music.

We were now in the country of the Brahuis, and noticed that the members of this tribe were more compact and shorter than the Baluchis, rounder faced and of manlier appearance, these differences to be accounted for in great part from the fact that they dwell among the cold hills and feed almost entirely on meat.

Pottinger, who lived among them for a considerable time when he went his adventurous journey through Baluchistan disguised as an Indian horse-dealer, preferred their character to that of the Baluchis, praising their honesty, industry, and hospitality.

Spring had come, and even in these wastes flowers were appearing. Low, spiky-leaved bushes were covered with what looked like masses of small white convolvuli, others had countless whorls of white flowers clustered down their long stems, while prettiest of all was a plant growing in tufts like sea-pink, sprinkled with a wealth of minute crimson buds which opened out into pink, starry blossoms. A few days later near Kalat I noticed rich, purple lilies, campions, dandelions, small St. John's wort, yellow broom, and tiny scarlet anemones, quite an astonishing variety of flowers, while one plain was covered with pale lilac hyacinths in full bloom, and another with the mauve umbels of the wild garlic. The high spring winds were in force and we had not as yet left our daily sand-storm behind us, for which Colonel Holdich considered we should have been grateful, as in all probability it tempered what might have been an almost unbearable heat. Throughout our journey in Baluchistan the temperature was never what we expected it to be. At Razé, for example, I find in my diary that on April 16th I was sitting wrapped up in a thick cloak during the afternoon, while Captain Kemball, who was in the same place during the year before, had found his thermometer at 95° on this particular date.

We were steadily climbing up day by day, and at Gidr had reached an elevation of 5,300 feet, necessitating the opening of our boxes of warm clothing, and at night the temperature was below freezing-point. The plains about here were overgrown with strongly smelling wormwood or absinth, on which the flocks feed, and it is used as fodder for horses when dried. At Gidr we saw the last Kaianian Malik tomb that we met with on our travels, and in this neighbourhood noticed a new kind of cairn to commemorate the dead, *i.e.*, a neatly built pile of stones surmounted by a large white boulder, which in the distance looked for all the world like a turbaned head.

Gidr was a very pleasant halting-place with its fields of green barley, blossoming fruit trees, and profusion of scented willows in full flower. A river added considerably to these attractions, although it was but a marshy stream flowing between high sandstone banks. We looked down from them on to crowds of camels feeding on the tamarisk scrub growing close to the water's edge, and enjoyed the unusual sight of plenty of bird life.

Scores of brown-backed snippets were paddling in the water, uttering their wild cries, and mostly too absorbed in fighting spasmodically with one another to mind our presence; while the tame, yellow-breasted water-wagtails hunted for insects on the water plants.

Flocks of small dun-coloured birds flew about, and the whole place resounded with their calling and chattering—a delightful contrast to the lack of life so observable in Baluchistan. I noticed one very pretty bird. Its head, wing and tail feathers were black, and all the rest of its body a delicate salmon pink, the bill being of the same shade.

The Brahuis here were a handsome, lively race. The good-looking young chieftain of the village surmounted his snowy raiment with a gorgeous red and gold turban, and when my brother and I appeared armed with our camera, he came up and offered himself as a suitable subject for a photograph. His younger brother emerged from a *koutouk* near at hand, and the two striplings fell into one another's arms, embracing with as much effusion as if they had been parted for years, and then threw themselves into picturesque attitudes to be handed down to posterity.

On April 22nd we reached Kalat, the capital of Baluchistan, which is at a height of some 7,000 feet, too high up for rice to grow, and where wheat and barley ripen later than in England.

We rode through a low pass in the hills, and at once came in sight of the picturesquely placed fort and palace built on a ridge of rock above the town, which is an assemblage of flat-roofed mud houses.

The name *Kalat* signifies "the City" in Baluchi dialect, and the wild tribes regard their *Khan*, or ruler, with a considerable amount of reverence. The brother of the latter, with part of the army carrying lances, came out to escort Colonel Holdich to his quarters; and we found our tents pitched near the rows of low mud barracks in which Goorkhas and Pathans were quartered, and not far from the mud bungalow of the Resident. The valley, some eight miles in length, was well cultivated, and there were young crops in plenty, the whole place looking green and springlike, and having water in abundance. We had spinach, lettuces, onions, and cauliflowers from the Residency garden, and it was a pleasure to see apple, pear, and apricot-trees in blossom, not to speak of the reappearance of the familiar sparrow, which had been invisible throughout all the low-lying parts of Baluchistan.

The telegraph line with its black poles seemed linking us to civilisation again, and it was hardly possible to imagine the condition of Kalat in the days of Pottinger, when it was a centre for Baluchi raiders. These latter were wont to ride their camels some eighty or ninety miles a day, and led crowds of Persians into captivity. Besides camels they used to ride mares on their *chapars*, as these animals do not neigh, and so highly were they valued for their speed and endurance that male foals were accounted but of little value and were usually destroyed. There is a local song about the feats performed by a Baluchi mare, which I was informed is frequently sung in the country.

As, unlike the Turcomans, the Baluchis had not the markets of Bokhara and Samarcand in which to dispose of their captives, they were in the habit of ruthlessly killing men, women, and children alike if they had a sufficiency of slaves, being inveterate *Sunnis*, and, as such, savagely hating the Persian *Shiahs*.

In spite of this characteristic Pottinger speaks of them as being most humane to their slaves, treating them as part of the family, in striking contrast to the methods of the Turcomans. At Munshur Chur, our next halt, the women were most picturesque in long red gowns embroidered richly in yellow with a criss-cross stitch much like the work of the Russian peasants. Three lines of open *kanats* separated us from our camping ground, and we had to cross these by narrow bridges of boughs and mud, and were glad when we had left them behind us, as it would not have been a pleasant prospect if our horses had shied and dashed themselves and us into the depths below. When the English passed through to storm Kalat fort, they halted here, and we saw the remains of a small fort, the low mud enclosures for tents, and the mud feeding-troughs for their horses, the traces of their occupation. The crops round here were *damin*, *i.e.*, dependent on the rainfall and not on artificial irrigation, and were usually of the scantiest. Their owners sow the ground and leave the corn to take its chance, coming at the right season to gather it in.

After a couple of days we got into the rich Mustong Valley with great stretches of barley forming in the ear, and looking northwards we saw the peaks of Kuh-i-Cheltun (the Forty Beings) and Tukatu rising up, the former mountain having a quaint legend attached to it, recording how forty children wandering among its spirit-haunted rocks were turned to goats, which eternally hurl stones down upon any hunter rash enough to seek game in the mountain.

The chains of villages reminded us of those we had left behind in Persia, as we zig-zagged in and out of their narrow lanes, between high mud walls over which fruit trees, scented willows, and trailing vines were peeping, the mulberries growing beside the frequent streams of water. It was now the end of April, and huge dung-beetles were flying about in all directions, occasionally coming into collision with us or our horses. They were, as a rule, busily engaged in rolling along balls of dung three or four times their own size with their back legs. It was interesting to see the speed with which they made off with these treasures, burying them in the sandy soil and retiring with them for the purpose of laying their eggs in them. Sometimes two would contend for the possession of a ball, one rolling the other over and over as it clung to it, or a couple would chivy an intrusive beetle away from their special possession.

There were some peculiarly friendly little birds about here. Dun and grey-coloured, with white tails tipped with black, they went about in pairs, and seemed full of insatiable curiosity, as sometimes a couple would follow me quivering in the air just above my head, and uttering a note resembling the watchman's rattle of the robin ; and one night we heard the wild cries of the demoiselle cranes flying northwards.

It was at Mustong that I had the pleasure of meeting Mrs. O'Hara, the first European lady I had seen for over a year. I had hardly realised how much I had missed the intercourse with my own sex until I began to talk with her, and I felt quite excited to think of all the female society I should enjoy at Quetta and Simla. We sold three of our horses to her husband in the P.W.D., disposing of the others at Quetta and Simla later on.

The Baluchis in this Happy Valley looked prosperous and fairly clean, and I noticed many men wearing old scarlet military tunics, buttons, braiding and all.

There was a low pass to be crossed before we could emerge into the Quetta Plain, and just before reaching it we got upon the new road which Mr. O'Hara was making from Quetta down to Kalat—a strange contrast to the ill-defined tracks along which we had proceeded hitherto. The road was cut on the side of a hill and was by no means broad, and at the narrowest point we met a great drove of female camels and their young, which were being driven by some nomad tribe into Baluchistan.

The creatures were much alarmed, and seemed to have no clear idea as to where they were going, scurrying from side to side of the road, and groaning and roaring. Luckily we were on the inside, and wedged our frightened horses closely to the rock wall, as otherwise we should have run considerable risk of being pushed over the cliff in all the thronging and pressing. But with patience, the two parties passed one another in safety, and we congratulated ourselves, somewhat prematurely, however, as when we had reached the top of the pass we perceived some hundreds more of camels ascending from the plain in front of us and blocking up the road entirely. My brother rode on ahead slashing his hunting-lash like a stock-driver, and to my surprise the great drove was apparently seized with panic, for the animals all turned tail and raced to the bottom of the pass, going along at a tremendous pace. One small child, perched on a big camel, did not seem to mind all the hurly-burly in the least, and I quite envied him his coolness in the midst of the wild excitement around him.

At our last camp at Sariab we were close to the railway line at the entrance to the Bholan Pass. Hashim and Ali Agha evidently thought that I had never seen such a work of civilisation before, and took the trouble to explain its use to me, as both were acquainted with the little line at Tehran!

It was exciting to feel that we should be at Quetta and in the midst of civilisation on the morrow, and I busied myself in unpacking the clothes sent to me from home the previous autumn, and which had travelled in boxes stitched up in oilcloth. On April 30th we rode along a metalled road into the cantonment, having a lively time with our unsophisticated Persian horses, which persisted in shying at every wall, regarding with especial suspicion the *ticca gharries* as they rattled by, and almost refusing to pass the perambulators which we encountered along the shady roads planted with trees, before we turned down a drive and were in front of the fine columned portico of the Residency, where Sir James Browne welcomed us with genial hospitality. The luxuries of civilisation were indeed a treat after our lengthy sojourn in the wilds, which had, however, agreed so well with me that I had ridden from the Caspian Sea to India without half an hour's illness at any time of my journey.

That afternoon Sir James drove us round Quetta and showed us all the sights. The *Gymkhana* ground was the scene of the investiture of the present Khan of Kalat by the Viceroy of India, and we were told how the Grand Stand was converted into a big Durbar Tent for the occasion, while soldiers lined the ground and cannon roared out salutes, much impressing the wild Baluchi chiefs who were assembled, with many hundreds of their followers, to witness the ceremony; and at night the great peaks of Tukatu, Cheheltun, and Murdan were lit up with huge bonfires which could be seen at a distance of many miles by Baluchi and Brahui; thus showing forth the power of the British *raj* to the remote nomad tribes.

We were shown the handsome church, the long line of barracks, the club, the *miri*, or old fort—an unimposing mud erection, the centre of what was once the little mud village of Shàlcot—and, most interesting of all, the new Parliament House for Baluchistan, a memorial to Sir Robert Sandeman, who had done so much to bring in the chiefs to allegiance to British rule.

This building was an Oriental-looking structure, with small

domes at each of the four corners, and a huge dome in the centre. Inside was a large assembly-room, out of which opened all sorts of small rooms, where Baluchis could meet in committee; and Sir James had thoughtfully provided for the women, giving them places behind marble-work latticed screens, from which they could see and hear all the proceedings.

On May 2nd we left Quetta for Simla, and as our friends saw us off at the station and we said goodbye to our kindly host, we little thought that in a few weeks' time he, a man whom India and British prestige could ill afford to lose, would have passed away.

It had been arranged that Sultan Sukru, Hashim, and *Bargi* were to accompany us to Simla, while the rest of our servants would proceed to Karachi, the *syce* going to visit his relatives at Gujerat. *Bargi*, however, intimated to me the day before that she preferred to stay with Ali the muleteer, her husband, to coming with me. I asked her whose servant she was, and who gave her her wages, and thought that the matter was settled. But on my arrival at the station *Bargi* was nowhere to be found, having hidden herself in the Residency gardens, and no searching could discover her.

She had served me so faithfully for a year, and had invariably appeared so devoted to me and my interests, that I was hurt at this desertion at the last moment, and although I forgave her, yet I felt, as a Persian would say, "A cut string may be joined again, but the knot remains." However, there was nothing for it but to get into our comfortable carriage, with its broad seats, its smoked-glass windows to keep out the glare of the sun, and its arrangement of wet *kus-kus tatties* to cool the hot air, and, accompanied by an ice-box full of fruit and soda-water, we started off in high spirits for our three-and-a-half days' journey to Kalka.

We had only been a few hours on our way when a station official handed my brother a telegram forwarded from Quetta with the terrible news of the assassination of the Shah on May Day by a fanatic, in the Mosque of Shah Abdul Azim, just outside Tehran.

We feared that all Persia would be in an uproar, and that probably a general massacre of Europeans might take place, so my brother at once wired to Tehran for orders, expecting to be recalled to Kerman, and, as in that case he intended to send me home by sea from India, we pursued our journey in a very unsettled frame of mind.

The Shah was to have celebrated his Jubilee on May 6th; and whatever may have been the defects of his administration it was generally conceded that he was probably the most capable man in his kingdom, and that during his long reign he had been indefatigable in suppressing disorder in Persia, which had become, under his sway, one of the safest Eastern countries in which the traveller can wander. It was supposed that the crime, that cut short the life of Persia's king, originated with the *Babis*, those followers of the *Bab* (Gate of Truth), as Mirza Ali Mohammed, the *Mollah* from Shiraz, designated himself, who was shot at Tabriz and his adherents cruelly suppressed some fifty years ago. It is said that *Babi-ism* would have infused life and spirit into the set ceremonial of Mohammedanism, although no true believer could well have yielded to the pretensions of the *Bab*, who claimed to be divine. Throughout Persia many men of the highest rank are credited with being *Babis*, but the sect keeps very quiet, and is seldom heard of.

As so much has been written about India I will refrain from giving any account of the pleasant three weeks we spent at Simla with the Holdiches and other friends, and only say that while there my brother received orders to go to the Karun Valley and inquire into several matters connected with British commerce and recent outrages on Europeans in that part of the world. We said goodbye to our friends at the Queen's Birthday Ball, on May 28th, and the night of June 1st saw us on board the British India steamer *Kapurthala*, on our way to the Persian Gulf.

CHAPTER XXII

UP THE PERSIAN GULF TO BUSREH

THE *Kapurthala* had the reputation on the Persian Gulf of pitching and tossing more than most vessels, and for a couple of days and a night she did not belie her character, and I bore the worst horrors of seasickness in the suffocating atmosphere of my cabin, the portholes of which were perforce closed. On the evening of the second day my brother came and dragged me up on deck, and told me that he, all the servants, and even some of the officers, had succumbed to seasickness; but that we should be off Jask on the morrow, and well out of the region of the *monsoon*. I was indeed thankful for the good news, as these seasons of enforced starvation on the ocean always pulled down my strength considerably. Poor *Bargi* had suffered in company with the others, and was, moreover, ashamed of herself for having left me in the lurch at Quetta. I tried to meet her apologies and her attempts at embracing my hands and feet with becoming sternness; but I felt that the devotion she had shown for me during a year ought to outweigh the one misdeed I could record against her, and we parted with mutual regret at Bunder Abbas, she weeping bitterly although she was returning to her home at Kerman in company with her husband the muleteer and some of the servants, and would soon meet her mother and children again, and I trusted be none the worse for her experiences while in the service of the Feringhee *Khanum*. Jask, with its picturesque old fort and its lofty telegraph buildings with their background of palms and greenery, looked a pleasant enough place of abode as seen from the ship; but the Europeans living there have a very different opinion, the heat and fever telling on the strongest. Bunder Abbas, on the contrary, was most unattractive, its long line of mud houses being backed with the barrenest of hills; but to me it was naturally interesting as being the port of Kerman and a place of great wealth in the days when the entire overland trade of Europe with India poured into it by way of the city twice visited in its prime by Marco Polo.

We had but few first-class passengers on board, one European, a Turkish officer, a Persian merchant, and a party of ceaselessly chattering, white-clothed Hindoos who were bound for the pearl-fisheries. The British India steamers, however, take large numbers of deck-passengers, from whom they often have great difficulty in extracting their fares.

It is practically useless to search these wily Orientals, who will hide their money in most unlikely places—between the soles of their shoes, for example—and the only efficacious plan is to threaten to put all defaulters ashore. Even then the required money is very often withheld, and the man allows himself to be landed, waits for the next steamer to stop at the port where he is left, gets on board and plays the same game, with the satisfactory result of being taken yet a further stage on his journey.

As it is impossible to collect the fares until the vessel has started, and as time is of absolutely no account to these dwellers in the East, the latter often get decidedly the best of it with the British India line.

The officers occasionally carry their lives in their hands when great mobs of deck-passengers are on board, as, if a fight arises, the English have to do their best to separate the opponents, and are very likely to be set upon by one and all. It has also happened that attempts have been made to loot the steamers by some gang who have come on board for that purpose; so altogether it may be seen that the carrying of deck-passengers (who are often fanatical pilgrims) on the Persian Gulf is a service not devoid of incident.

It was so hot in our cabins that we had our mattresses brought up on deck every night, and as I was afflicted with prickly heat the greater coolness was agreeable. Moreover, huge cockroaches—insects to which I have an unbounded antipathy—prowled in numbers down below, rustling about the saloon floor at night in search of food. One of my friends always affirmed that the British India line boasted a breed which grew to an abnormal size, and that when Nature forbade them to increase in length they made up for the prohibition by broadening out until a tablespoon could scarcely contain them! These formidable-looking creatures glided about my cabin freely, and I was sometimes under the delusion that they deliberately charged at me if by any evil chance they happened to be driven to bay, and I could never summon up courage enough to despatch them, disagreeably conscious of their proximity as I often was, the odour of a cockroach being unmistakable. They were not content to be merely seen and smelt, but we frequently had to taste them, as food overrun and nibbled by these enterprising insects acquires a peculiar *cachet* of its own never to be forgotten.

As the British India line is a cargo line, we lay-to all day at the different ports on the Gulf, and native boatmen surrounded our vessel in their *buggelows*, chanting weird songs and uttering guttural cries as they handled their awkward-looking craft, bringing merchandise on board or taking it ashore from the *Kapurthala*. The weather was by no means disagreeably hot, at all events for those who had no need to exert themselves; the vessel was most comfortably fitted up, the food excellent; and with a pleasant captain and officers to help pass the time I quite enjoyed the voyage as long as we had calm seas. Mrs. Bishop, the well-known lady-traveller, had come out to Persia some five years before with the same captain, and I was never tired of questioning him about the lady for whose pluck and talent I have such an admiration. Lingah, celebrated for its pearl-fisheries, was certainly the prettiest place on the Gulf, its houses and minarets backed with feathery palms, while the mountains behind it were tinted in delicate greys and pinks. I was assured, however, that this vision of beauty would not stand a close inspection, so I did not land anywhere until we were off Bahrein.

The principal island of this group is some twenty-seven miles long and ten broad, a sandy desert with oases of water and palm-trees. It was once held by the Portuguese, who were masters of the Persian Gulf for over a century, and the ruins of their forts may be seen here as well as at Hormuz and Muscat.

But, to go further back in history, Sir Edward Durand's excavations, and those made quite recently by the late Mr. Thedore Bent, have led both travellers to the conclusion that Bahrein was the cradle of the famous Phœnician race, who were such remarkable seafarers, traders, and colonisers. In the interior of the island is a huge necropolis, and when Sir Edward Durand and Mr. Bent opened some of the double-chambered tombs (one room built above the other), they found fragments of carved and inscribed ivory, besides other relics, most certainly of Phœnician workmanship.

Nearchus (the admiral of Alexander the Great's fleet) mentions that he saw the tomb of Erythras, the Red King, when he anchored off Bahrein; and it is interesting to think that somewhere in this City of the Dead, the monarch, who gave his name to what is now called the Persian Gulf, lies buried.

At the present day the island is chiefly known for its pearl-fisheries, and when we approached it, early in June, a flotilla of pearl-boats, with full sail set, were making their way to the more distant reefs, from which they would gradually work in homewards. About four hundred vessels are engaged in this industry, carrying some eight to twenty men in each boat. Each diver is supposed to have an attendant, who lets him down by means of a rope weighted with a huge stone. This takes the man right down to the bottom, and he collects the oysters in a small-mouthed wicker receptacle, being drawn up every few seconds to take in fresh air before he repeats the operation. As Matthew Arnold so beautifully puts it:—

> "And dear as the wet diver to the eyes
> Of his pale wife, who waits and weeps on shore,
> By sands of Bahrein in the Persian Gulf,
> Plunging all day in the blue waves, at night,
> Having made up his tale of precious pearls,
> Rejoins her in their hut upon the shore."

The profits are divided among the owners of the boat, the crew, and the divers, the Sultan of Bahrein taking his share as a matter of course.

The whole industry is in the hands of a ring of Hindoo dealers, and they buy in all the smaller pearls by weight, only the larger ones being sold separately, and their price being fixed by the demand in the market for big pearls. I was informed that thousands of imitation pearls are yearly sent from Paris to Bahrein and Lingah, and these the wily Hindoos skilfully mix with the real article, making it almost impossible for an amateur to detect the fraud.

Some of these dealers were on board our vessel, clad in white muslin draperies, wearing "reach-me-down" European coats, and much-betinselled velvet smoking-caps. Several had a gold earring, with two or three fine pearls hanging from it, stuck in the upper part of the right ear. Two dandies had bandages fastened round their faces and under their chins, just as if they had the toothache, but this arrangement was merely to force their moustaches to grow in a specially *wildcat* manner. They were brisk, bustling, chattering fellows, and would wait at Bahrein for the return steamers, giving their pearls, stitched up in white linen bags, to the captain, to be stowed away in the specie-room. A captain will often give a receipt for 117,000 rupees' worth of pearls, and probably this sum does not nearly cover their real value.

The *Kapurthala* had to anchor at some distance from Bahrein, as the sea is exceedingly shallow near the islands, and we were soon surrounded by heavy native boats, the bronzed Arab rowers sitting with their backs to the sides of the craft, and propelling them in most unscientific manner with oars shaped like great spoons, others being merely long poles with a square, thin bit of board fastened crossways at their ends. A kind of native yawl carried our party to within a short distance of the shore, and from the straggling, picturesque town a troop of the famous Bahrein asses, with their lightly clad Arab drivers, came splashing through the water towards us.

These fine creatures, called white by courtesy on this occasion, were decorated with henna—tails, manes, forelegs, and chests in many cases reddened—others being spotted all over with the pigment until they resembled Noah's Ark animals. Their saddles were formed of two narrow pieces of bent wood lying flat on the back and curving over the neck, and as stirrups and bridles were entirely lacking I confess I felt somewhat nervous as to how I should stick on. However, there was nothing for it but to select a steed from the crowd, which the yelling, screaming Arabs were pushing one against another, and as soon as I perched myself gingerly on its back it made straight for the shore without any hint on my part. The British agent, a Persian living in a showy-looking mansion, on which the Union Jack was flying, came out to receive us, and then we settled ourselves down to ride to the Bahrein wells. I would have given much to have dispensed with ceremony and sat astride, which I should most certainly have done had I been alone with my brother, but was obliged to cling on to the curved front of my insecure perch, having near escapes of falling off when my donkey stumbled in the middle of its rough gallop on one occasion, and one of the riders collided with me on another.

We passed through the town, which looked much like a Baluchi village, most of the dwellings being composed of palm-leaf matting, and fenced in with stout palm-branch palisades. The Sultan's palace was a flimsy-looking, castellated construction, and in the space kept clear in front of it were several rusty old cannon, once belonging to a couple of antique fighting-dhows which lay close to the shore.

A stretch of bare, sandy road brought us to big date-groves and streams of wonderfully clear blue-green water, and near at hand were the ruins of a large mosque with two minarets, built after the Persian manner. Not far from here were the springs, the object of our visit, and we descended from our asses to see a great tank of aquamarine-coloured water, its roof supported by one huge column of masonry; and beyond it, through the well-known Arab arch, lay a second tank of delicious water, the springs that feed it bubbling up strongly. On our return from this short expedition, bumped, chafed, and jolted as I was, I was thankful to slip off my uneasy mount into the boat waiting for us, which the rowers poled for some distance through the shallow sea before hoisting the sail. Much of the fresh water to supply the town is procured from springs gushing up beneath the sea, and we watched men and women wading out with skin *mushks* or earthenware jars, which they pushed, mouth downwards, through the salt water to the fresh liquid below; these springs gushing up with such force that they do not get brackish from their contact with the sea. The next morning we were still off Bahrein, and my brother went ashore again and visited the Sultan, who received him in gorgeous raiment, and gave him coffee out of a gold pot, so quaint that we bought a brass edition of it in the town, the pattern being a speciality of Bahrein. These pots were incised all over in concentric rings, and the spouts shaped like a bird's beak, perhaps copied from that of the ibis, at least so one of my friends thought.

Although we were out of the region of the *monsoon*, yet a strong *shamàl*, or north-east wind, arose, and when we lay off Bushire during a whole day I was unable to accept Colonel and Mrs. Wilson's invitation to lunch at the Residency, as the four miles of much-disturbed ocean lying between the ship and the shore would have been too much for so bad a sailor. The Persian navy, in the shape of one big white vessel, the *Persepolis* by name, was lying off Bushire, and was decorated with flags in honour of the enthronement of the present Shah; while the *Sphinx* and *Lawrence* gunboats both lay in the harbour.

Next day we were in smooth water again, steaming between low, palm-covered shores, from one point of which the little telegraph station of Fao arose. Beyond here the flat banks narrowed in, and we crossed the Fao bar with much caution, and reached Mohammerah, at the mouth of the Shat-el-Arab, the splendid river formed by the confluence of the Tigris and Euphrates at Kurnah, the legendary site of the Garden of Eden, and which has its outlet in the Persian Gulf.

From here, leading into the Karun River, up which lay our destination, is a great canal connecting the two streams, supposed by some to have been made by Alexander the Great, but in all probability of much earlier origin. We stopped at Mohammerah, expecting to change over into the *Malamir*, the boat belonging to Messrs. Lynch and Co., which runs up to Ahwaz every fortnight, and which was lying off the Vice-Consulate. However, on inquiry we found that she would not be making her trip for another week, so we decided to take our passage in her to Busreh on the following day.

Mr. Butcher, the acting Vice-Consul, an old acquaintance of my brother's, came out in his *bellum*, or native boat, to receive us, and hospitably insisted that we should be his guests for the night, and should leave most of our baggage and servants at Mohammerah, picking them up in a week's time. So we dined upon the roof of our host's house, which looked very pretty from the water surrounded by a vegetation which, however, brought creatures enough and to spare into my bedroom. Bats flitted about, lizards crawled on the beams of the ceiling, locusts plopped down on the floor at intervals, a scorpion hurried into a dark corner, and the song of the mosquitoes was so loud that I was thankful to feel I was secure from their attentions, with my head and shoulders muffled up in a net made much like a meat-safe.

Next morning in selecting our baggage for our trip to Busreh I made a most unpleasant discovery. Neither my new saddle nor the box of photographic plates, which our agent at Karachi had been instructed to put on board the *Kapurthala*, were to be found.

The saddle I had taken out to Persia had been worn out with constant and often rough usage, and this new one had been sent out to me from London, arriving in Persia last December, when our agents had lost sight of it as it wandered up and down the Gulf; and now for the second time it was lost, and my horizon was overcast with the blackest of clouds, my old saddle being quite unfit for use, and my hopes of taking numerous photos in the little-known region of the Karun being rudely dashed to the ground, nor, to anticipate matters, did I catch sight of the photographic plates and my saddle again until September.

On the shores of the Persian Gulf, as well as in the country of Turkish Arabia, whither we were bound, and also along the banks of the Karun, dwell Arab tribes, and their *Sheikhs* are fine-looking fellows, wearing long white, gold-embroidered shirts, quaint slippers, and the great *burnoos*, or *abba*, often of some bright colour embroidered with gold at the neck, while the checked handkerchief, or *kafia*, is held in its place on the head by a black camel's-hair rope twisted with gold. Mr. Zwemer, the American missionary at Busreh, told me that this camel-rope was the origin of the aureole always depicted round the heads of saints, being drawn of unusual proportions in the case of specially holy personages.

On June 11th we started off on the *Malamir* for the pretty five hours' journey to Busreh, steaming up the fine river, on the banks of which grow the millions of palms which supply the greater part of the world with dates. About a mile from the dirty village of Mohammerah we passed Feilieh, the residence of Sheikh Mizal, one of the last of the old chieftains who bear rule over the wild Arab tribes. (Since our visit he has been murdered by one of his followers.) Every British India steamer passing up the Shat-el-Arab fires a salute when it reaches this house, in memory of the day when Sheikh Mizal's father went to the assistance of a British India vessel which was being attacked by a band of Arab pirates, and in sore straits. A cannon is placed in front of the chief's house, who always returns the English salute with punctilious care.

Much further up the river was another mansion belonging to some Arab Sheikh, who had painted the greater part of its façade a brilliant blue, to keep off the evil eye; but I was told that ill-luck had haunted him and his family in spite of this precaution. Our crew were mostly Chaldeans from near Bagdad, Christians of the ancient and well-nigh extinct Nestorian Church, and fine, well-built fellows. Genial Captain Adey of the *Malamir*, however, told us that he never employed them in steering, as they had no pluck and nerve should any difficulty arise, the Mohammedan Arabs being far more dependable in an emergency. As we got nearer Busreh, houses became more frequent, and we passed well-built, airy residences belonging to the different European firms engaged in the date trade here; but alas, the whole place was flooded, as, owing to the melting of the snows in the spring, the river had risen some five feet. All the date-groves were standing in water about a foot deep, the bunches of fruit looking withered, making it a serious question as to whether the crop for the year might not be a failure. It is an Arab saying that the palm ought to have its roots in water and its head in the fire; but on this occasion it was considered that the water had outstepped its due bounds, and was no longer a beneficent agent. Every garden was a swamp, the roses and flowers all dead, and the trees dying; while the fruit and vegetables were practically destroyed, and, what was even worse, whole families of Arabs had been washed out of their palm-leaf matting houses and were camping on the few dry spots to be found, having in many cases to bewail the loss of cows, sheep, and poultry, the bodies of which could be seen cast upon the banks of the great river.

The British Consulate was one of the best buildings in the place, and Captain Whyte, an old Indian friend of my brother's, came out to us in his *bellum*, and carried us off to enjoy a generous hospitality, to which, later on, we were to owe more than we could ever repay.

Busreh has been called the "Venice of the East," and the title is not a misnomer, as the broad Shat-el-Arab might pass as a much-magnified Grand Canal, and branches on either side into dozens of fairy creeks stretching far inland, and fringed with palms, willows, broad-leaved bananas, and shady vines, which might be considered a counterfeit of the narrow canals of the Bride of the Ocean. To complete this somewhat fanciful resemblance, the river is always alive with *bellums* not so unlike gondolas in appearance, painted white picked out with blue or green, and poled along when near the shore by their Arab crews. The passengers sit on cushions at the bottom of the boat, and with an awning to keep off the glare of the sun the *bellum* is as much conducive to *dolce far niente* as the gondola itself. All luggage, merchandise, and cargo are carried out in these boats to the British India steamers or to Lynch's vessels running between Busreh and Bagdad, and I have even seen horses conveyed in them from one bank of the stream to the other.

The only way to get about from house to house is by means of these native boats, as the creeks branching off from the main river separate many of the houses from one another, and during this time of flood the *bellum* was needed to be in closer attendance than usual, although, as is the case in Venice, it is possible to reach most places by dry land, if one knows the way.

The city of Balsora, or Busreh, was founded by the *Khalif* Omar, and was famous as a great port before the rise of its rival, Bagdad, under the dynasty of the Abbasides.

It was a celebrated seat of learning in the Middle Ages, and its colleges and professors were renowned throughout entire Asia, while it was from Balsora that Sindbad commenced his voyages in some picturesquely painted *dhow* or *mehalah*, that has hardly altered since his days; and it is the opinion of many savants that the romance of which the intrepid sailor is the hero was in reality compiled from the accounts of Arab travellers voyaging during the Middle Ages.

After the taking of Busreh by Suleiman the Great, and its annexation to Turkey, the famous town fell by slow degrees, until at the present day it is hard to find even a trace of the exquisite architecture of which the old chroniclers tell us; while its Bazaars, once great marts of all the merchandise of the Orient, were spoken of by our disgusted servants as being far inferior to those of Kerman. Mr. Buchanan, the *doyen* of Busreh society, which is composed of some fifteen merchants engaged in the date trade or in the export of wheat and wool from Ahwaz, and the traffic with Bagdad, took us several pleasant rows in his Thames boat up the lovely creeks in the evenings, and we could then appreciate the devastation caused by the floods in this land of the "Arabian Nights." A watery expanse marked the site of the golf-links and cricket-ground of the Europeans, the gardens and tennis-courts were small lakes, and further afield we came upon swamped palm-leaf huts, and saw the few cattle left slowly dying of starvation, as their grazing grounds were all under water. After the heat of day the evenings and nights were generally cool, as the blessed *shamàl* was blowing at this season, and we got through the hottest hours between mid-day and four o'clock by taking siestas under the punkahs, which seldom ceased working at the Consulate, and reading Madame Dieulafoy's superbly illustrated book on Persia. Busreh in the early part of June was decidedly a warm place of residence, but neither of us felt exhausted by the heat, and it was not until our enforced stay in August that we properly realised the capabilities of its climate.

Personally, I enjoyed everything, even to my taste of hot weather, which I hoped to escape from before long, as we expected to travel from Shuster among the high hills of the Baktiari country. Owing to Mr. Buchanan's kindness, I was able to replace my saddle; but riding, even at six o'clock in the evening, was a hot pastime, and we had to make our way by narrow paths, along creeks, or between date-groves standing in water, looking out for the holes and broken places in the road with which our residence in the East had made us familiar. Occasionally we could get a five minutes' canter between mud walls or past the neglected graves of the horribly ill-kept cemetery; but there was no real riding possible, unless we could get free from the town and into the desert, and this the lateness of our start precluded.

The prettiest "bit" of Busreh was its one bridge, spanning the creek with a high central arch to permit vessels to pass beneath it. On either side of it rose tall houses with projecting windows filled with stained glass in elaborately carved and fretted frameworks. Crowds of natives flocked at this point, and on the water lay great laden *buggelows* with gaudily painted prows. Everything else had fallen into ruin; most of the encaustic tiles which had once adorned the domes and minarets of the squat mosques having long ago dropped off, never to be replaced.

At the end of our stay the *shamàl* ceased, and the atmosphere became oppressively close, although we seldom had the thermometer above 95°. As the sun sank the whole place appeared to steam and the air to be filled with a hundred evil odours, many rising from the decaying vegetation in the swamps around the palm-trees. I wondered sometimes how it would be possible to survive when the water sank at last, leaving only green slime behind it, and my query was amply answered later on. If we sat upon the roof after dinner, as our custom was, our clothes would be soaked through by the heavy dew falling, and we understood the object of the palmleaf shelters erected on every house to keep this feverish moisture from those sleeping at night in the open air.

I did not feel the loss of *Bargi* nearly as much as I expected, for Fakir Mahomet took upon him to supply her place. I remember coming into my room one morning with the fixed determination to overhaul my wardrobe, when to my surprise I saw the *syce* seated on the floor of my apartment with an array of undarned stockings around him, which he was busily patching up in a quaint manner with the aid of my work materials. On seeing me he grinned from ear to ear, much delighted with himself, and remarked proudly, "*Khanum*, I am your *Bargi* now!" and he further signified that he had taken me under his wing by appropriating one of the shelves in my room on which to stow away various purchases that he had made in India! Ali Agha, the Fat Boy, who had behaved with conspicuous virtue during our tour in India, here succumbed to temptation and made off to the Bazaar with a bag of coins which he got hold of through the unaccountable stupidity of Sultan Sukru. Being captured at a coffee-shop, where he was gambling freely, he had the effrontery to affirm that he had carried the *Sahib's* money to the Bazaar in order that it should be in safe keeping. Sharp and severe punishment was meted out to the culprit, and my brother dismissed him as soon as he got him back into Persia again. He had been with us so long that we quite regretted parting with him, and was, moreover, such a cheery, plucky lad, so ready to turn his hand to anything, that he would have been invaluable as a servant, if he could only have mastered the difference between his property and that of others.

If we had only had time we should have greatly enjoyed going up in one of Messrs. Lynch's steamers to Bagdad, although for my part I should most certainly have been haunted with the fear of returning with the celebrated Bagdad boil, which, if it makes its appearance on the face, disfigures the sufferer for the rest of his or her life. It is much the same thing as the Persian *salic*, so called from lasting a whole year; and, what makes the matter worse, no doctor can explain what causes the boils, so that none can guard against them, nor is there any reliable cure for them.

There are various theories as to their origin. Some say they are caused by the water; others, that the flies carry the microbes from the pariah dogs, the noses of which are generally afflicted with this complaint; but the usual opinion is that the germs are contained in the soil of the city. Old houses built of the sun-dried mud bricks have an evil reputation on this account, and children almost invariably fall victims.

The Goanese, besides being employed as servants in some parts of India, are to be met with all down the Persian Gulf, and at Busreh and Bagdad. These little dark men make excellent cooks, waiters, and stewards, always looking spotlessly clean in their European white clothing, and being, as a rule, alert and most intelligent.

They are very proud of their European origin, and rejoice in high-sounding Portuguese names, and even in such titles as Duke or Count!

I was told that they are greatly attached to their tiny fatherland, to which they pay visits at intervals, reading its newspapers assiduously, and they are devout Roman Catholics, never forgetting that Goa has the distinction of possessing the remains of the heroic missionary St. Francis Xavier.

As the Arabs make far worse servants than even the Persians, it will be understood how highly appreciated the Goanese are, and I heard their praises sung on all sides.

On June 19th we bade goodbye to Busreh and its hospitable English colony, steaming down between the low flooded palm-covered shores of the broad Shat-el-Arab in the launch of the *Lawrence*, lent us by the kindness of Captain Piffard. We were again leaving civilisation behind us, and my thoughts were now bent on the Baktiari country and its lofty passes where we should not feel the summer heats. At Mohammerah we removed our luggage from the steam-launch to the *Malamir*, and with many goodbyes to our kind hosts and reiterated hopes of meeting in the future, we turned our faces north, and were soon on the snow-fed waters of the Karun, the one navigable river of which Persia can boast.

CHAPTER XXIII

THE KARUN RIVER AND AHWAZ

THE whole climate appeared to change as soon as we had left the palms of the Shat-el-Arab behind, and were surrounded by a sandy desert stretching on either side of us to the line of the horizon. The enervating damp heat of Busreh had given place to a very different kind of warmth, so dry that it seemed almost bracing by comparison.

A high, hot wind blew clouds of burning sand from the desert wastes, and the disturbed waters of the Karun reflected the glare of the sun with a million facets, very speedily making us have recourse to our blue glasses; and we felt vitality and energy returning to us, and slept that night as we had never done under the waving of the punkahs at Busreh, where the great question of life seemed to be how to keep fairly cool.

The scenery on the river was highly monotonous. The Sahara was partially flooded, and grass, with occasional willows and banks of reeds, grew close to the water, while flocks of pelicans and small white gulls gave a touch of life to the picture. It would have been delightful to have seen a lion stalk along the banks, a sight vouchsafed to travellers in the days before deforestation took place, and when the Karun, as described in Layard's delightful "Early Adventures," was thickly wooded; but not even a gazelle, much less a hyæna, met my eye. Every now and again the *Malamir* stuck on one of the sandbanks of which the river abounds, and had to plough its way through; later on in the season, when the Karun is low, this being a matter of considerable difficulty. The water, fed from the snows of the Baktiari hills, is renowned for its coolness and excellence, Bushire being supplied with it, as the tanks of that town are infested with the guinea-worm, and it tasted as nectar and ambrosia in comparison to the boiled and filtered liquid drawn from the Shat-el-Arab. Further up the river the banks were of high sandstone, and nomad tribes in palm-leaf matting huts were encamped here and there, their mares picketed near at hand with manes and tails flowing wildly in the wind. Men and women alike were clad in long, black garments, made from the wool of their goats, and crowded to the banks to see the *Malamir* go by. Not far from our destination was Sheikh Mizal's summer residence, almost a village of matting huts, where the chief exercised patriarchal sway, surrounded by his tribe with their flocks and herds and much-beloved mares, in a district where the pasturage seemed to be good.

On the afternoon of the second day we neared Ahwaz, or Bunder Nasseri, to speak more correctly, as the former town is further up the river, and has decreased in importance in proportion as its rival has grown in prosperity. When Mr. Curzon was here in 1892 he wrote of a dirty village composed of a few mat huts, but now it is almost a town with an imposing erection doing duty as the Governor's palace; and two large houses, which at the time of our visit were inhabited by Messrs. Hotz's agent and the captain of the s.s. *Shusan*, rose above the mud-built bazaar.

We anchored at the wharf belonging to Messrs. Lynch, in front of a well-built, comfortable-looking house, and were surprised to hear Mr. Parry (Messrs. Lynch's agent) asking in anxious tones whether the doctor were on board. There was no doctor with us, owing, as we afterwards found, to the not infrequent occurrence of the Persian telegraph wire which connected Bunderi Nasseri with Mohammerah, and so with Busreh, being broken; and sorry indeed we were when we learnt the cause of these inquiries. Mr. Tanfield (Messrs. Lynch's agent at Shuster) had been brought down that day from that fanatical city in a terribly mutilated condition.

One of his servants, a man Saduk by name, had stolen his master's watch and also some money, and when Mr. Tanfield paid him his wages he deducted part of them to punish the man, whom he could not well dismiss as no other servant was to be had at Shuster. Upon this Saduk vowed vengeance on his employer, and even went so far as to tell his fellow-servants that he would have his life.

On the night when he made his criminal attempt he came up some three or four times to the roof where his master and the Armenian clerk were in the habit of sleeping before he found Mr. Tanfield really asleep. He then set upon him with a sword, and when his master woke and parried the blow he cut off his left hand, mutilated his face terribly, and leaving him for dead went to rouse up the town, affirming that his employer had been attacked and killed by Persian thieves. This story was, however, not credited, as Dromio, the Goanese cook, had met Saduk on his descent from the roof, and had fled in fear of his life from the ruffian, who had done his best to murder this witness to the deed. Moreover, the Armenian clerk on the roof had seen everything, but had buried himself in his bedding, not daring to interfere, unarmed as he was, and Mr. Tanfield, having recovered from his swoon, gave evidence to the authorities of Shuster against the wretch, who was arrested by the Governor and thrown into prison.

Mr. Parry was telegraphed for, and at once went up the fifty-six miles on the steamer *Shusan* to Shuster, and brought Mr. Tanfield down with him, the fanatical mob stoning the wounded Feringhee as he was carried from the town to the boat. My brother and I felt that we had arrived at Bunder Nasseri at a singularly inopportune time; but as there was no caravanserai in the place, and as the *Malamir* was to return almost immediately to Busreh to take Mr. Tanfield down to the doctor, there was no help for it, and the next morning we were installed in Messrs. Lynch's mansion, where we were treated by Mr. and Mrs. Parry with a kindness and hospitality for which both of us will ever feel the liveliest gratitude; especially as circumstances forced us to linger many weeks, instead of days, at Bunder Nasseri.

Sunday was a long, sad day for us all, with the wounded man lying bandaged up under his mosquito curtains in the entrance hall, the coolest spot in the house. I would have given much to have been of use to him in any way, but my brother and Mr. Parry did all that could be done, changing the dressing of his terrible wounds, and trying to keep him cool by means of the freezing mixture, a parting gift to us from Captain Piffard of the *Lawrence*.

His heroism and pluck were something wonderful, and made us prouder than ever of the name of Englishman! Knowing that he was maimed for life—that perhaps his health was ruined, and his means of livelihood taken from him—he never uttered a complaint, and scarcely a cry or groan passed his lips, even during the torture of having his bandages changed by amateur hands.

All our servants helped in the unloading of the *Malamir* so as to get her off the sooner, but as, unfortunately, it was the season of *Moharrum*, no one could be got for love or money to reload the vessel with the customary bales of wool from Messrs. Lynch's and Hotz's warehouses, and it was not until midnight that, half-loaded up, she steamed away, and we all felt a weight lifted from us, as we trusted that in fifteen hours she would reach Doctor Scott at Busreh.

Unfortunately, however, the *Malamir* stuck for twenty-three hours on a sandbank on her course down-stream, and on Mr. Tanfield's arrival at Busreh the immediate amputation of the whole arm was imperatively necessary. By dint of his never-failing courage and a good constitution he finally recovered, and on my second visit to Busreh in August I found him convalescent and about to embark for England; and I was glad to hear that since then he has again returned to his work in the East. That June was the month of *Moharrum*, during which the Mohammedans celebrate the sufferings and martyrdom of the revered Hussein and his followers; and on the 22nd, the great day, after sunset, the long, low brick building with its pillared verandah, constituting the seat of government in Bunder Nasseri and Ahwaz, was crowded with all the notables and *seyids* in the place. Drums were beaten vigorously, and a kind of small, four-columned shrine, with a green silk canopy, was carried about, and behind this came a coffin (representing Hussein's) draped all in black, with a vivid green turban at its head. Fantastically attired horsemen, clad in pieces of armour, gave a sort of sketchy representation of the Persian Passion Play, and a great crowd of onlookers beat their breasts as they gave vent to a wild lament. The rhythmic chant, with the thud as they struck their bosoms to the measure, had an indescribably weird effect, heightened by the glare of torches lighting up the scene, illuminating scores of grim faces, their owners wrestling with the steps of a dance which appeared to be a series of leaps. I should have been sorry for any European in the midst of the fanatical throng, working itself up to wilder and wilder excesses of religous fury, for the rash intruder would probably have paid for his temerity with his life.

Our life at Bunder Nasseri at once fell into a well-defined groove, settled for us by the climate. We slept on the roof, where a cool breeze usually blew all night long, and at 4 a.m. we all rose so as to get a ride in the fresh morning air and be safely indoors by seven o'clock at latest, as after that hour the sun became dangerously powerful. We could not leave the house again until after sunset, when the wind, which all day long had blown hot as the blast of a furnace, dropped for a few hours. We took over three of Mr. Tanfield's horses, so were provided with mounts from the first, horse-dealing being a somewhat difficult matter at Ahwaz, as just then all the horses were required for gathering in and threshing the harvest. Mares alone were considered of value here, the horses being usually so starved and stunted in growth as hardly to be worth buying. The Arab tribes will deprive themselves of food to nourish their cherished mares, and an Arab would be of no account were he to ride a horse. The colts trot along beside their mothers, and should the rider urge his steed too fast for the little ones these latter utter plaintive cries of distress, at which their respective mothers pull up so sharply as almost to unseat their riders.

Mares being such valuable property are bought and sold in a peculiar way. The whole animal is seldom purchased by one man, but three or four buyers have each an interest in one or more of her *legs*. The man to whom the *fore*legs belong has the task of stabling, feeding, and exercising the creature, and he will, if possible, buy out the possessors of the hind legs by degrees. One of Mr. Tanfield's steeds was a very fine mare, and we were told that he had her for a considerable time in his possession before he could come to terms with the owners of her hind legs!

As a rule the best mares, being brought up in the Arab family circle, are wonderfully docile and intelligent, and their owners are usually reluctant to sell them unless pressed for money. The horses about here were only fed once a day, in the evening, and then merely with the finely chopped straw, or *tibbin*, this meagre diet, as well as the Arab custom of beginning to ride a horse at two years of age, accounting for the half-starved appearance of these animals. Every Arab apparently possessed a steed, which he usually rode at an easy amble; but occasionally, when he wished to show it off, forced into a short rush, pulling it up sharply on its haunches when in full career, and turning it round so suddenly as to strain its quarters, scarcely a horse in Ahwaz being free from this defect.

The cruel Arab bit made the animals fling their heads into the air to avoid its pressure, and it took a good deal of handling with our light English bridles to induce our mounts to look where they were going.

The Arabs near Ahwaz were tall, straight, slightly built men, holding themselves well, dressed in long, white, or light-coloured cotton robes, with the flowing *abba* of black or brown woollen material draped round them, the better class having this cloak made of such thin texture as to be almost transparent. With the characteristic blue and white checked *kafia* streaming from their heads, and the inevitable rifle slung at their backs, they made imposing-looking figures.

The Arab women by no means equalled the men in looks, although it must be remembered that I never saw any of the upper class. Those I came across were very squalid and dirty-looking, often wearing huge nose-rings, only a few of the young ones appearing to think about keeping their persons tidy. Their dress was usually a shabby, black, loose garment, with a shawl of the same material draped over the head, an unsuitable colour and style for such a climate, some of them, however, having crimson skirts, which looked very picturesque. Perhaps, as they did the greater part of the work, they had perforce to leave fine clothes to their lords and masters.

They made their butter in a curious way, hanging a goat-skin full of milk from a tripod of sticks and knocking it backwards and forwards with their hands; while they baked their bread Persian fashion, in a brick oven, flattening out the dough with their hands into big, round cakes, and then sticking it up against the sides and roofs of the oven to bake, the process only taking about a moment.

But I feel that I ought to give some idea of what Bunder Nasseri and Ahwaz are like, since I hope both are destined to become great commercial centres from the opening up of the trade of the Karun.

The former place was not much to look at, but the stir of commercial life was in the air. Building was busily going on. Messrs. Hotz's agent was building himself a large house, a big caravanserai was in course of construction, and private houses without end. To supply the quantities of bricks required for these works a couple of kilns just outside the scattered village were eternally belching forth volumes of black smoke, and as fuel was hard to procure, the whole Karun district being deforested, the kilns were fed with the golden *tibbin* piled up in heaps beside them—a sight which caused the little European colony to lay in their winter stock of fodder quickly, as later on it might be impossible to procure it. About a mile further up the river lay Ahwaz, a considerable mud village, boasting a big fort, a white-domed mosque, and the only two palms in the neighbourhood. The town was rich in sugar-cane plantations in the days of the Abbasside dynasty, at which period it reached the climax of its prosperity; but, unluckily for itself, it revolted from the Kalifs and engaged in a long war in which it was finally defeated, and gradually descended to its present state of decay. It once belonged to the widely spread Nestorian Church; while to go back to far earlier ages, it formed part of the kingdom of Elam often mentioned in the Bible. All about the ancient site of the city old mill-stones, broken pottery, and parts of old columns are scattered in profusion, while donkeys visited the *débris* daily to be loaded up with the stones of former buildings. A long sandstone ridge rises abruptly from the flat, sandy desert, stretching for miles behind Bunder Nasseri, and its continuation makes the reefs in the Karun below Ahwaz. In the time of the Sassanians a great dam had been built across the river, making it possible to ascend nearly to Shuster; but as this was broken away, only traces of the old masonry being left, it was impossible for the *Malamir* to ascend higher than Bunder Nasseri. Therefore all goods intended for Shuster had to be carried along a tramway up to Ahwaz, where they were reloaded on board the *Shushan*, a steamer bought from Messrs. Cook and Sons, who had had it made for the Nile expedition, and which ran to within seven miles of Shuster.

In the sandstone ridge, to which I have before alluded, were a series of caves, looking at a short distance like natural perforations of the rock. However, closer inspection revealed a small platform cut out before each chamber and a little flight of steps leading up to the summit of the bluff. Probably these chambers were made by fire-worshippers to expose their dead; but we always fancied that perhaps they might have been inhabited by long-since departed monks in the days when Ahwaz was a Christian city: they certainly would have been retreats well away from the world and its vanities.

There are also caves in the ridge which terminates in the river and causes the rapids which impede the navigation of the Karun above Bunder Nasseri. Besides caves there are passages cut right through the friable sandstone to allow for the revolving of the wheels of the old Ahwaz water-mills. These latter rotated with great speed, a cog-wheel turning a spindle, which moved the millstones on the rock above and ground the wheat very fast.

Sharks come up the cool water of the Karun from the Persian Gulf during the summer, and are often to be seen playing about this dam, attacking every now and again some unlucky inhabitant of the place, constant casualties occurring near Shuster from this cause.

I was disappointed at not seeing a single shark during my visit, and had to be content with the sight of a huge water-snake which we surprised one evening coiled up on the dam, and which swam away holding its head high out of the river. There was a rumour one day that a lion, killed by Baktiaris further up the stream, had floated down, and that its corpse was stranded on the dam ; but when we went to inspect the defunct king of beasts it was nowhere to be found.

There was more life on the broad expanse of desert round us than we had ever seen in other parts of Persia. Small herds of *ahu* were often espied, and we used to come upon the holes dug by the Arabs, who lie in wait to shoot these pretty gazelles ; and one morning we beat through the only bit of jungle near at hand to put up some wild pig. Flocks of sand-grouse and hill-partridges were not uncommon, and now and again a pair of silver-grey foxes or a belated jackal would give us a good gallop after them, not to speak of solitary wolves or hyænas, while the dog of the party would frantically hunt the little jerboas or the big ungainly lizards which waddled along like miniature crocodiles. The lovely iridescent bee-birds hovered about, somewhat resembling kingfishers when perched on bushes, in readiness to dart down on the grass-hoppers which form their food. They uttered a sweet ringing note, and were most exquisite and not unfriendly creatures, while in a back-water of the Karun the pretty white cranes with crested heads, much like the egrets of commerce, were wont to disport themselves.

The whole of this district along the banks of the Karun is a great corn-growing country, and stretches of stubble lay on either side of the broad, sandy roads, as at the time of our visit, towards the end of June, the harvest had all been gathered in and threshing was in full swing. The Arabs look upon the *shamàl* which blows at this season of the year as a providential arrangement to assist them in the winnowing of their wheat and barley. They grow the two cereals together on the same plots of ground, and when Mr. Parry tried to persuade them to sow them separately they answered that as Allah made wheat and barley to spring together, it would be a sin to try and do otherwise. So Messrs. Lynch must perforce have recourse to an ingenious separating machine. Outside Ahwaz the corn was piled up into many huge circular stacks, and round each heap a drove of six or eight donkeys or a bevy of oxen, mules, or horses was driven in an endless circle, treading out the corn, as a little at a time was thrown on the ground from the central heap, until the whole of the straw was reduced to fine flakes of *tibbin*.

When the work of treading out the corn was completed, the men and boys winnowed it with wooden forks, made of sticks neatly fastened on to long poles, and tossed the chaff into the air, separating it again and again until the barley and wheat lay in long ridges free of straw and dust and ready to be loaded in bulk on board the *mehalahs* waiting off Bunder Nasseri.

Mr. Parry told me that the Arabs were most honourable in all commercial transactions. He frequently advanced money to them, which they paid off to him at this season in wheat or barley ; and he said that a case was hardly known where a man refused to honour his bond or promissory note. If, however, such an unlikely contingency were to occur, the creditor would merely have to mention the matter to the Sheikh of the debtor's tribe, and if the defaulter himself could not pay his debt the tribe would make up the deficit to save its honour.

Wool is the other great staple industry here, and Messrs. Lynch employ many hands in their great warehouse to sort and pick this commodity, dividing it into heaps according to the shades. White was the most highly esteemed, then came brown, fawn, grey, parti-coloured, and so on, Messrs. Hotz having an apparatus to compress the wool into bales for export.

We had only been some two or three days at Bunder Nasseri when my brother and Mr. Parry went off in the *Shushan* to Shuster, at which town was the Governor from whom my brother was commissioned to extract an indemnity for an outrage committed by his soldiers on three Europeans at Bunder Nasseri, and also to inquire into the attempted murder of Mr. Tanfield and other matters.

I was left behind with Mrs. Parry and a lady visitor from Busreh, as my brother feared the terrible climate of Shuster for me, and thought, moreover, that his party might probably be attacked by the fanatical Shusteris. We were put in charge of the one European in the place, a somewhat hot-tempered Dutchman, who came to tell me on the day after my brother's departure that he had had a quarrel, which appeared to have ended in a regular fight, with some Arabs at his office, and that the Persian Governor, hearing of it, had written to offer us ladies a guard, as he affirmed that we were all in danger of our lives. This offer the Dutchman had promptly rejected; but we, however, resolved never to go near the villages during our morning rides; and I felt the wisdom of this, as two or three days earlier I had been smartly struck between the shoulders with a stone while riding with my Dutch friend. Knowing his hasty temper, I had not mentioned the occurrence to him, but the others thought that it was probably intended as an insult to my unpopular escort, rather than to me, a complete stranger. Mr. Parry's Arab clerk and Fakir Mahomet came to me full of excitement, both imagining from what they had gathered in the Bazaar that the Arabs were greatly enraged against our little European colony.

Very probably the whole thing was much exaggerated; but if anything had been intended against us we were in a singularly defenceless position, as nearly all the servants and weapons were with the gentlemen at Shuster. The *syce* insisted that I should sleep with my loaded rook-rifle (the only fire-arm in the place) by my bedside, and he himself was not far off with a huge dagger, though what the two of us could have done to defend the house against a well-armed crowd I do not know. However, there never arose any need for our prowess, for, to our great surprise, on the fifth day after my brother's departure the *Malamir* was sighted, a week before its time, and Captain Whyte and Mr. Taylor (Messrs. Lynch's agent at Busreh) appeared, giving us at once a delightful sense of security. The gentlemen had heard a report of the quarrel with the Arabs, to which I have before alluded, and considering that we were in an unsafe position they had most kindly come up to look after us, and I think that we realised, now that all cause for alarm was over, that our nerves had been rather on the stretch during the past few days, and we were proportionately grateful to the new arrivals.

The heat at Bunder Nasseri grew more severe as the days went on, and we suffered considerable extremes of temperature. For example, the nights were always cool with a fresh breeze and the thermometer at 75°, making one glad of warm wraps; but only a short time after the sun had risen it was 95°, and in our coolest sitting-room varied from 100° to 105°. By ten o'clock in the morning 112° was no uncommon temperature, and our maximum indoors was 118°. The *shamàl* kept pace with the heat, being merely a pleasant breeze during the morning, and rising to a veritable burning gale during the afternoon and evening, gradually dropping down between eight and ten o'clock to a soft wind soothing us during the night.

What the temperature rose to in my peculiarly stuffy bedroom I never cared to inquire, as I spent the smallest possible fraction of my time in what was a veritable Turkish bath. It was a haunt of mosquitoes and sandflies of the most virulent and persistent order, not to speak of cockroaches, crickets, and the friendly little house-lizards, which both here and at Busreh lived in all the rooms, performing the useful offices allotted to spiders in England, although these latter were not lacking at Bunder Nasseri. We had not very many scorpions, luckily, but I occasionally saw small yellow or black ones running about like miniature lobsters, and the big buff tarantulas lurked in obscure corners of the rooms. The most alarming insects in this part of the world were huge centipedes, some six inches long. They were not unlike gigantic earwigs, having forked tails and glistening scales, while the short, thick legs on either side their bodies were furnished with minute suckers. It is dangerous to try and knock off a centipede (the Persian name is *Pa-i-hazàr*—Thousand-footed One) if it is crawling over the naked skin, for these poisonous suckers will immediately cling to the flesh and inflict a series of small, festering wounds. We caught some of these creatures while at Ahwaz, and it was always a comfort to feel that I was fairly secure from them at night on the roof, for they would have added a real horror to life had they pursued their peregrinations to my eyrie!

Even in this comparatively healthy part of the world fever was not wanting. Mrs. Parry's visitor and the latter's baby-boy had attacks every other day; and, although the baby Parry fortunately escaped, yet his negress nurse, a Bagdadi Christian, who wore long plaits of false hair tied on to her woolly locks, was constantly ill.

The *Malamir* stayed during a week up at Bunder Nasseri, and then had to return, leaving everything quite quiet, and on July 11th our servants came rushing in to say that the *Shushan* was sighted, and that my brother and Mr. Parry would be with us in a couple of hours; so we sent horses to meet them, and awaited their arrival in a state of high expectancy.

At last they appeared, hardly able to stagger into the house, both so wasted away from the effects of the malignant Shusteri fever that I should hardly have known them for the same men who had left us in such health and spirits only a fortnight before. They had been obliged to live in the midst of what Layard describes as "the most pestilent town in Persia," and had been forced to retire to the *sardabs*, or underground chambers, vault-like and ill-ventilated places, in order

to escape the intense heat, which rose inside the house to 118°
at 8 a.m., and to 120° and even 128° during the course of
the day.

They had had a narrow escape of being attacked by Arabs
when coming down-stream on the *Shushan* the little vessel
having laid up for the night at Shillalia, near several great
mehalahs loaded with grain. A band of Arabs, returning
with the spoil of a village that they had just sacked, fired
several shots at the vessels from the steep river-bank, but
they were not suffered to pass unchallenged, for the deck-
passengers of the *Shushan* all turned out to be well armed,
and it was an affair of moments to barricade the decks
of the steamer with bales of wool. Nor were the white-
robed Arabs in charge of the *mehalahs* behindhand. They
screwed up their courage by chanting a wild song of battle,
and, breaking into a weird dance, brandished their weapons
to such good effect that the Arabs on the warpath took their
departure, evidently considering discretion the better part
of valour.

And now we hoped that orders would come for us to start
on our longed-for journey through the Baktiari hills to
Isfahan and then Tehran. My brother had been entirely
successful in obtaining the indemnity from the Persian
Governor of Shuster, and Mr. Taylor, Captain Adey, and
another Englishmen were to receive compensation for their
wounds ; while Saduk, the would-be murderer, had been sent
in chains to Tehran for justice, and the wheat embargo had
not been levied that season. I had packed all our boxes of
stores, and got our camp equipage into apple-pie order, so
that, if transport were forthcoming, we could be off at an
hour's notice.

But no instructions came, and after some days a telegram
arrived to say that we must prepare to stay on at Bunder
Nasseri for several weeks longer. This would not have
mattered if my brother could have regained his health ; but as
the hot days dragged wearily by both the men appeared to
get worse instead of better, and Mrs. Parry and I were at our
wits' end how to provide food that they could eat. Ahwaz

was even worse off than Kerman in the way of supplies. There was the usual diet of mutton and fowl; but it was varied with no vegetables save rice and onions. Not a potato, not even a marrow or an egg-plant were to be procured in Ahwaz, and, as there was no fruit of any kind, it was impossible to cater for invalids.

We had some tins of bovril in our stores, which by no means abounded in luxuries, and fortunately had plenty of condensed Swiss milk, as that and eggs were both hard to obtain; and though the Karun River flowed only a few yards from our doors and was swarming with fish, no money could induce the lazy Arabs to catch what would have been most appetising food.

At first the men tried to take short rides in the cool of the morning; and I remember how longingly I used to gaze at the far-away snowy peaks of the Baktiari hills, and wonder when orders would come for us to leave what was a sort of purgatory. Fortunately, I myself was in the best of health, as indeed I had been throughout my entire journeys, never having had any illness since the day I left England, and I was assured that the prickly heat, which often made me feel as if I were wearing garments woven of nettles, was really a blessing in disguise, as any one having it badly was seldom visited with fever.

By the beginning of August over three weeks had elapsed since the return of my brother and Mr. Parry from Shuster, and it really seemed as if both of them might possibly die of starvation. They refused all food save an occasional cup of bovril or an egg-flip, and it was most distressing to see the state of weakness to which they had been reduced. Naturally I became terribly anxious, and at last persuaded my brother to go down to Busreh to see the doctor, both of us feeling that in all probability the change would completely set him up again. A native boat was leaving early in August, and as he expected to be back again at his post in a few days' time it was arranged that I should stay on with the Parrys during his absence; and I was inexpressibly relieved to get a telegram from him on the next day saying that he had had a successful voyage and was already somewhat stronger. My spirits went up with a rush, and it really seemed as if things were going to take a turn, as Mr. Parry appeared to be a trifle better, and the negress nurse, who was in a perpetual state of collapse, again resumed her duties. But a couple of days later I received a telegram telling me to come down to Busreh in the *Malamir*, and that particulars would be sent by that vessel, which was due in twenty-four hours' time.

Of course I feared the worst at once, and the Parrys, kind as they were, could give me no real hope in the face of such a telegram. I hardly know how I got through the time before the *Malamir* arrived, and with it the coveted letters, which took an almost overwhelming weight off my mind, as they and Captain Adey's report convinced me that my brother was, if anything, better than when he left Bunder Nasseri.

The steamer had brought back a party of Arabs, who had made the pilgrimage to Mecca, but had returned leaving the bones of one of their number behind them in the sacred city. A body of their fellow-countrymen dashed up to welcome the new-comers, their *burnooses* flying in the wind as they pulled their steeds sharply back on their haunches, and among them were the brother and other relatives of the deceased. As soon as they heard the sad news they all dismounted, and broke into wild lamentations, calling on the dead man by name. "Taki Abu!" they cried in despairing accents, throwing dust on their heads and flinging their long *abbas* over their faces to cover them. "*Ya*, Taki Abu! *Ya*, Taki Abu!" they yelled between heartrending sobs, waving their long sticks in the air in a despairing way. It was a scene of wild, uncontrolled grief, the brother appearing quite inconsolable, and I could indeed feel for these poor men to whom the *Malamir* had brought such evil tidings. At last the whole party remounted and went off slowly, in a very different manner to that of their arrival, and later on the women appeared on the landing-place in front of the Parrys' house and gave way to bitter lamentations.

Before daybreak the next morning I went on board the *Malamir*, which was to carry me away from Bunder Nasseri. Although still expecting that my brother and I would return there before long, I could not leave the Parrys without much regret, as they had shown us a true friendship, which had but grown the stronger during the trying weeks of illness and depression that we had spent together. In spite of her anxiety about her husband, in spite of many a household worry and occasional attacks of fever, Mrs. Parry had never failed in an unceasing kindness to me, and our common trouble had drawn us so closely together that we parted like old and tried friends.

It was with very different feelings that I approached Busreh for the second time. All the hope and expectancy of my first visit were now succeeded by an anxiety and a despondency against which I had to struggle until the longed-for day arrived when we could quit that enervating city of Turkish Arabia.

CHAPTER XXIV

FROM BUSREH TO TEHRAN AGAIN

IT seemed to me throughout our stay in the East that we met with more real kindness and more genuine hospitality than we had experienced during the whole course of our lives up to that date, and at Busreh there was no exception to the rule, for it was mainly owing to Captain Whyte's unceasing care and forethought that my brother's life was spared. He had been attacked with pleurisy—no uncommon sequel to the Shusteri fever—and his case was a serious one, requiring great care. In spite of the comforts of the Consulate, in spite of punkahs by day and night, iced drinks and appetising food, it seemed impossible for him to regain his strength in a climate resembling nothing so much as a Turkish bath, and in his condition he could not have borne the journey down the Gulf to the comparative coolness of Karachi.

Of course it was entirely owing to my state of mind, but all the glamour and beauty of Busreh seemed turned to a sinister and hateful loveliness, and the sunshine I had always loved so well hitherto seemed a baleful, death-dealing influence. Our days dragged by slowly in a wearisome routine. We slept at night on the roof, under matting shelters to keep off the deadly dew, and with the punkahs creaking backwards and forwards; and had to descend to our suffocatingly hot rooms below at 5.30 a.m. at latest, the sun being too powerful by then to render it safe to remain longer in the comparatively fresh air above. So perforce we must leave the graceful palms, ever waving their fans against a turquoise sky, and reflecting their carved trunks on the broad bosom of the mighty Shat-el-Arab, and begin a long day indoors, the lazy hours of "sweet do nothing," which is a state of existence by no means sweet to me, beguiled by a little reading, a little writing, and a great deal of sleeping, all done under punkahs.

After lunch we invariably lay on couches in a dark room partly underground, and it was not until 6 p.m. that we could venture out of the house to watch the more energetic of the English play a game of tennis in the short time before sunset, or to be rowed about in the inevitable *bellum*, lying on the cushions at the bottom, and watching the sun as it set, flooding the sky with gold and lending wonderful tints of green to the palms, which they threw back in turn against their soft blue background; while not a ripple would disturb the calm of the amethyst-coloured water.

The entire lack of exercise told on me a good deal, although it was not possible to take much in a place where one was never cool for a moment, save immediately under a punkah, and where three baths a day seemed to exhaust rather than refresh one. As, however, I never succumbed to the effects of the climate, I feel that I have no legitimate cause of complaint against it.

I have alluded in a previous chapter to the many miles of palm-groves on the banks of the Shat-el-Arab, which practically supply dates to the world. The fruit was nearly ready for gathering, and hung on the long stalks in all shades of gold and red. It was too luscious at this stage to be eaten in any quantity, reminding me of nothing so much as of masses of compressed honey, and melting into a sweet syrup in the mouth; but a spell of hot weather in September, called the *khorma puz* (cooking of the date), would ripen it completely.

Date-boxes were coming up to Busreh by every vessel, unwieldy "ditchers" and "tanks" bringing big cargoes from Norway, the tops, bottoms, and sides done up in uniform-sized bundles, to be nailed together on arrival. A knocking and hammering resounded from the wharves in front of the houses belonging to the different firms, and everything was being made ready for the date harvest, which would be picked and packed about the middle of September. There are many different varieties and qualities of fruit; but the crop of one of the best trees is worth about twelve rupees.

The merchants ply up and down the Shat-el-Arab, or encamp in the date-gardens, as they are called, to superintend the harvesting of the fruit. The long stalks are broken off the trees by their Arab proprietors, and the dates shaken into big receptacles, which are carried into matting shelters to be properly packed in neat wooden boxes. The Arab children are the best and quickest packers, and the women come next. Some of the old folk are very slow and stupid, but it would not do to turn them off, for they would most certainly take their whole clan with them if their feelings were ruffled by dismissal.

Some of the dates are pressed in a mass into bags of palm-leaf matting, and all are sent in steamers direct to England and America, where they are used for making sweetmeats or vinegar, and for purposes of distilling, while vast quantities are consumed in the mining districts of England.

August 31st was the anniversary of the Sultan's accession, and the whole of the river front of Busreh was charmingly illuminated with hundreds of tiny oil-lamps in honour of the event. The Turkish Hospital across the water was one mass of lights, the dwellings of the Governor and the Admiral were very gay, while the Turkish men-of-war seemed all flags and lamps, and the National Anthem sounded at intervals. As the Consulate and the houses of the British merchants were likewise decorated, the effect from the river was exceedingly pretty.

At last kind Doctor Scott gave us leave to attempt the voyage down the Gulf to Karachi, and we decided to make our way back to Tehran, *viâ* Bombay, Alexandria, and the Black and Caspian Seas, instead of the delightful journey across the Baktiari country to which we had both looked forward so much. I had plenty to do in packing and arranging, for Sultan Sukru was to take our horses and the greater part of our baggage overland from Ahwaz to Tehran, and we were to travel by this long sea route, as lightly burdened as possible.

On September 4th we left Busreh in the British India steamer *Assyria*, and turned our backs joyfully on a part of the world where we had passed some of the worst months of our existence, although the great kindness we had experienced had done so much to mitigate our troubles.

It is all very well for travellers passing through a country to praise its climate, when they have probably timed their stay during the best season of the year.

Busreh is a most pleasant place in the winter, the air being fresh and almost cold, forcing the residents to don their tweeds, and giving them energy for golf, cricket, shooting, and long rides across the desert. But, as I have tried to show, it is very different during the summer months, and the exhausting nature of the climate is such that, in case of illness, it is most difficult to regain strength.

It seemed, however, at first as if we had exchanged Scylla for Charybdis, for on our steamer punkahs were conspicuous by their absence, and we were much less sheltered from the heat in the vessel than on shore; and as there was no ice, all our drinks were quite warm, although the bottles were kept in a huge porous jar filled with water, which continually oozed from its sides.

During the whole day we lay at anchor in the sweltering heat, which penetrated through the deck awnings, and it was only at night that we went on, and felt an occasional breeze as we slept on deck.

To my great relief, my brother began to mend the moment we had passed the bar at Fao, and were out on the real sea again, and, in spite of the lack of fruit or vegetables, he got better daily.

A little Arab boy, with his tutor and servants, was about the only first-class passenger beside ourselves, all of them dressed in the thinnest of white cotton shirts, drawers, and caps. The boy was the son of a rich Arab chief living near

Busreh, who was sending his child to be educated in an English school at Bombay. The would-be pupil had two very small boxes and a roll of carpets and bedding for all his luggage, and spent his days in sleeping, eating, and chattering. The servants brought a huge *pillau* of fowls, rice, and saffron on a large metal tray twice daily, and round the mat on which the food was laid the small chieftain, his tutor and servants would gather happily, and all feed together, using their fingers most skilfully, while they ate quantities of hard, unripe dates and pomegranates with much relish in between meal-times.

When we lay off Bahrein a number of tall, well-dressed Arabs came on board, holding amber rosaries in their hands, to pay their respects to the young chief, who was stuck upon a small camp-stool by his tutor, this latter squatting humbly behind his charge, and fanning him assiduously. The handsome visitors salaamed the small boy with much ceremony, some of them kissing him on the shoulder, and it certainly was a case of "uneasy lies the head that wears a crown," for the poor child soon grew excessively tired of his novel position, and his back was bent almost double as he curled himself up on the perch, from which he longed, but did not dare, to descend.

A couple of days after this episode I was amused at seeing the chieflet follow my example of tramping the deck. He began to shuffle up and down, escorted by a minute and dirty Arab servant, who kept at a respectful distance behind him, and my example proved so contagious that even the old tutor took to promenading two or three times a day, a marvellous sight in the East, where to take exercise for its own sake is looked upon as a species of lunacy.

We lived on deck all day long, and slept on it at night, our cabins being almost unbearable on account of the terrible heat, the sea-water bath being perfectly hot, and therefore by no means as refreshing as we had shoped. We had about a hundred horses on board being taken to Bombay for sale, and when we lay at anchor their movements caused a most unpleasant rolling of the vessel, something like the heaving of a ground swell. I felt much for the poor animals, which were only watered twice daily, and suffered greatly from the heat, two or three of them succumbing to the hardships of a voyage lasting fourteen days. We passed Bushire, where cargoes of opium were put on board, and had a suffocatingly hot two days off Bahrein, our captain having lively discussions with various occupants of the heavy native boats, as he refused to take any more passengers on board, having barely sufficient water for the horses as it was. There was not a great deal of life on the water. An occasional flotilla of medusæ; numerous large jelly-fish; a shoal of minnow-like fry; the beautiful guard-fish, with bright blue tails and long, orange mouths; a hawk hovering round the rigging, and perching on the bulwarks; a huge serpent swimming high on the sapphire sea; and the crowd of native boats bringing cargoes of the inevitable dates, unsavoury loads of sharks' fins (*chow chow*), assafœtida, skins, dried fish, and masses of rosebuds, these latter to be converted at Bombay into the celebrated attar of roses so characteristic of the East.

The copper-skinned Arab rowers chanted weird refrains as they bent to their curious oars, long poles terminating in oblong pieces of board or round discs of wood, while they shouted "*alàn!*" as the signal to pull off to shore, and indulged in a never-ceasing quarrelling and yelling while round our vessel.

On September 10th we made our way along the coast of Oman, the sea of that name being immortalised by Moore as the scene of his poem, the "Fire-worshippers." A long line of dreary hills rising sheer from the shore, and only broken here and there by small inlets, did not give a very cheerful impression of that "Araby" so sung by poets who have never visited the country. However, it is a mistake to expect too much in the East, and I was quite charmed when at midday we entered the picturesque harbour of Muscat.

The small bay is almost landlocked, high cliffs rising to right and left of it, on one of which is painted the names of the different vessels that have anchored in front of the town. Prominent among them was the *Sphinx*, and the white gunboat herself was lying close at hand.

We had travelled from Bunder Abbas, the last port at which we had stopped, with Captain Bevill, H.B.M's. Consul at Muscat, but the heat was too great to allow us to accept his kind offer to pass the day on shore at the Consulate, and we had to content ourselves with gazing at the little town, crowded in a very limited space at the foot of barren hills, on the spurs of which stand two mouldering old Portuguese forts overlooking the barrack-like, whitewashed palace of the Sultan and the well-built Consulate. A gap in the hills gives a glimpse of more mountains, and there is nowhere a tree or a blade of grass to be seen.

In spite of this, Muscat exports quantities of dates from the interior, and as soon as the *Assyria* steamed into the harbour and fired off her gun, which echoed and reverberated from the cliffs again and again, a crowd of lighters laden with boxes and bags of dates pushed off from the shore, and we were surrounded by a screaming, wrangling swarm of bronzed Arabs. Small boys made their appearance in the roughest of "dug-outs," and prepared to dive for coppers, which, however, they did not appear particularly expert at retrieving, probably from lack of practice. Captain Bevill told us that during the summer Muscat was never cool either by night or day, for the rocks rising close behind the town absorbed the heat during the hours of sunshine, only to give it out again after sunset, making the place almost unfit for Europeans to live in. He said that a certain amount of pearl-fishing went on on this coast, and as the oyster-shells here were all "mother of pearl," they were valuable in themselves, and were exported in great quantities for making buttons.

I was especially interested in this little Arabian town as being the scene of the last labours of Bishop French, of Lahore. After between thirty and forty years of missionary labour this man of marvellous energy left his bishopric at the age of sixty-six to offer Christianity to fanatical Muscat

He denied himself every comfort, and gaining the respect of the Arabs, partly by his asceticism, was permitted to preach in their mosques; but the terrible fever of the country seized upon him before long, and when he persisted, contrary to advice, in making a journey into the interior, he succumbed to it, and was carried back to Muscat to die in May, 1891, after only a few months spent in this stronghold of Moslemism.

When we left the calm waters of the harbour we found ourselves in the swell of the *monsoon* outside; but although I am one of the worst of sailors, and my brother by no means at home on a rough sea, yet after dosing ourselves with *Yanatas*, a cure for seasickness which has spared me many hours of suffering, we got through the two days of tossing and reached Karachi again, where we found it, comparatively speaking, quite cold after the intense heat we had experienced, and drove to our hotel along sandy wastes, with a dust-storm in full swing. A visit to the Karachi Zoo in its lovely gardens, and dinner with the hospitable head of the Persian Telegraph Department, Mr. Sealey, and his charming wife, helped us to pass the day pleasantly, and we returned to our vessel to undergo a stiff gale for two days before we finally anchored in the beautiful harbour of Bombay, and felt that our troubles were practically over.

After a sad parting with our faithful *syce*, Fakir Mahomet, we embarked on the P. and O. *Peninsular* to Ismailia, intending to make our way thence *viâ* Alexandria to Constantinople, and so back again to Tehran. However, we heard at Aden that cholera had broken out in Egypt, and being by no means desirous of spending weeks in quarantine, we decided to go on to Brindisi, reaching it on October 1st. It seemed hard to be so near home, and yet to be turning Eastward Ho! again. However, so it was, and we traversed the Mediterranean, Black and Caspian Seas, and I landed for the second time at Enzeli. So much had happened since I left England some two years before, full of the joy of travel, that I could hardly realise that so short a time had elapsed, feeling that at least a decade had passed over my head.

The Persian sun shone out magnificently, and did not seem to me to be the same sinister luminary that we had dreaded at Ahwaz and Busreh, but a beneficent and life-giving power. I rejoiced in its genial warmth, and realised with satisfaction that I was once more in my beloved land of the "Lion and the Sun."

It was delightful to be on horseback again when we left Resht, even the sorry *chapar* steeds being a pleasure to mount after our long imprisonment on board ship. Our journey up to the capital was one charming picnic. The weather was perfect, and we left all the commissariat arrangements entirely in the hands of that phœnix among Persians, a good and honest servant.

At Enzeli we had met our friend Mrs. Rabino, of the Imperial Bank of Persia, on her way to England, and as our own servants had not yet arrived at Tehran from Ahwaz, she most kindly offered us the services of her two men with some of her camp equipment. I feel that I have said a good deal in disparagement of Persian servants in this book, and Haji would indeed go far to redeem the evil character I have assigned to them, if he had not taken the trouble of assuring us at an early opportunity that he was a Turk, and did not wish us to confound him with the lazy Persians, for whom he had the most profound contempt!

Our eight days' journey up to Tehran in the loveliest of weather was too devoid of incident to merit description, and it was hard to believe that the road could present the difficulties that we experienced two or three months later on.

We reached the British Legation at the end of October, to be treated again by the Durands with a kindness that made us look upon the capital of Persia as a second home, and which probably had far more to do with my rose-coloured impressions of the East, than I at all realised at the time.

CHAPTER XXV

TEHRAN REVISITED, AND THE JOURNEY HOME TO ENGLAND

DURING the first weeks of November the capital of Persia looked perhaps at its best, for the numerous gardens on its outskirts were brilliant with autumn tints, while the Elburz Range looked inexpressibly lovely with its newly fallen snowy covering. Our first act was to pay a round of calls and look up all our old friends again, who were much interested in hearing of our doings since our departure, Baluchistan seeming almost as inaccessible a land to dwellers in Tehran as it is to us in England. My afternoons were spent in riding out to the different gardens; coursing an occasional hare on the barren plains outside Tehran; looking on at the tent-pegging and the polo, which latter sport my brother introduced, or in joining in the paper-chases, a form of amusement which appealed strongly to me.

One afternoon we rode in a party to the ruins of the ancient city of Rhé, or Rhages, the old Parthian capital, close to the town of Abdul Azim, in the blue-domed shrine of which the late Shah was assassinated.

Rhages is supposed by some to be identical with the place visited by Tobit, who placed the talents in the care of Gabael, one of its citizens, and later on sent his son Tobias, in company with the angel Raphael, to reclaim this money. Its ruined fortress crowned a picturesque spur of the range of low hills, beneath which a confused mass of mounds marked the site of the former city, where we found fragments of dark red terra-cotta painted in black designs, bearing a strong resemblance to Greek or Etruscan vases.

Near at hand the warm spring of "Chesm-i-Ali" gushed, out at the foot of a wall of rock on which was a sculpture of Fath Ali Shah and his sons, tradition reporting that the monarch had ordered this glorification of himself and his offspring to be chiselled upon a bas-relief of great antiquity.

Beyond the ruins, and further in among the hills, lay the *dakmé* of the Parsees, a large, low, unimposing-looking tower, and a bare, gravelly desert separated us from the gardens round Tehran.

On another occasion we made an expedition to Karizek, the Belgian minister having invited us to come over to inspect the beetroot sugar factory, which was being started there with a view to underselling the Russian article. It was a bleak, dusty ride of some twelve miles, and our horses were put up at the blue-plastered *Mehman Khana*, where I well remember the cold night we spent on our departure from Tehran nearly two years before, when there were no signs of the factory or of the house to which Baron Bayens presently conducted us, to thaw ourselves.

After lunch we were conducted round the factory, and were astonished to see such machinery in Persia, and to observe that the whole place was lit with electric light.

As the buildings were not yet completed operations would not commence for another month, but in the yards outside there were mounds and hills of yellow beetroot (it being far sweeter than the red variety), and we were told that 20,000,000 kilos of sugar could be made in three months, but that the country did not as yet produce enough of the necessary vegetable to keep the machinery fully employed.

Heaps of chalk were a conspicuous feature of the establishment, and it was explained to us that this substance was used to precipitate the sugar, which it was hoped would be both sweeter and cheaper than the Russian article, which never melts in the tea.

    •   •   •   •   •

THE CHILDREN OF H.H. THE FARMAN FARMA.

The Farman Farma had come to Tehran on the accession of the present Shah, to whom, as I have mentioned before, he stood in the relationship of both son-in-law and brother-in-law. It was very pleasant to meet him again, and I also made the acquaintance of the Nasir-ul-Mulk, who was sent later on by his sovereign to England in the capacity of Special Envoy, when he renewed his friendship with us.

The Farman Farma sent his sons two or three times to call at the Legation, and they made a quaint little party on the occasion of their first visit when I came across them in the garden. Their elderly French governess appeared in the midst of a troop of five small boys, all dressed like little men in long, full-skirted uniforms and black astrachan *kolahs*, while two dirty servants walked behind. When they saw us the domestics pushed forward Firuz, the eldest princelet, to shake hands, volubly running off all his titles with those of his two brothers and the two cousins accompanying them.

Lady Durand asked the party into the drawing-room, and Firuz, bold and intelligent, wandered about, his eyes glittering as he pounced upon various weapons lying on the tables, while Madame made the others recite pieces of French poetry, during which we heard Abbas, the second boy, making inquiries as to when tea and cakes were coming!

Lady Durand took me to call one afternoon on the Farman Farma's wife, who is the daughter of the present Shah.

She was young and good-looking, but very stout, attired in a gorgeous red plush robe with deep gold embroidery, and wearing a quantity of diamonds, pearls, and emeralds, the latter stones being of great size, but uncut. She understood a little French, but was evidently ill at ease, and the French governess did the honours, displaying the accomplishments of the four sons, all of whom were most intelligent.

After we had partaken of tea, cakes, fruits and sweetmeats, the Farman Farma made his appearance, inquired if we admired his wife, and then proposed that he should show us his own apartments, sending a woman-servant on in front to tell all the men-servants to get out of the way, as the Princess was coming.

The rooms were quite European, crowded with rich furniture, the walls hung with carpets and many dozens of china plates, and the Princess wandered about much interested, as this was her first visit to her husband's rooms. When I got her alone and began to talk to her in Persian she became a different being, opening out at once, and telling me how often the Prince had spoken of me and my doings at Kerman, and from what she said he had evidently given her a very highly coloured account of my powers of riding, walking, and shooting.

On November 20th the Sadr Azem, the Prime Minister, who had practically been the ruler of the kingdom during the reign of the late Shah, gave a great banquet to all the European gentlemen of Tehran at his garden-house, very near the British Legation, and only four days later the news came that he had fallen from power. In the East when a man loses his post, as a rule all his possessions are confiscated, and if he escapes with his life he may consider himself fortunate. The Sadr Azem, however, was treated with unusual consideration, owing mainly to strong British and Russian influence, but he was forced to retreat to the sacred city of Koom, where he had a house in *bast*, the quarter which is sanctuary.

He had brought his misfortunes on himself by his arrogance and overweening pride. Instead of conciliating the party of the new Shah, he concentrated all power and office in his own person, although he had been warned of the danger of this course, the fate of Bismarck having been pointed out to him as a lesson that no man is really necessary to a kingdom. But nevertheless the Sadr Azem went to his fate, sulking in his *anderoon* if anything were not to his taste, so that all business came to a complete standstill until he was pacified.

When at last the blow fell the ill-fated Minister was told that he might stay in the capital until the morrow, but that his Majesty would be better pleased were he to leave on the day of his downfall. The deposed Vizier wrote a dignified reply to his monarch, in which he professed thankfulness at being relieved of the cares of office, and begged the Shah to grant him his life and the lives of those belonging to him, adding that he would be satisfied if his Majesty would treat him with as much forbearance as he had shown to the enemies of the State.

The Sadr Azem, with all his faults as an obstructionist, which barred any prospect of reform or good Government in his country, was good to the poor, and the lower classes generally had a high opinion of his capacity. As one of the Legation servants put it, "Now there will be an end of Persia and the Persians, for the members of the new Government will quarrel among themselves, and we cannot tell what will happen."

The present Shah, moreover, owed something to his Vizier for his clever management of events on the death of the late Shah.

When Nasr-ed-Deen fell mortally wounded in the mosque at Shah Abdul Azim, his Prime Minister ordered him to be carried to the carriage in waiting, propped up the corpse and drove beside it into Tehran, the guards surrounding the carriage as usual. As soon as he got the Shah into the palace he gave out that he was merely wounded, sent in haste for the European doctors as a blind to the populace, and for the European ministers, who telegraphed to the Vali Ahd (Crown Prince) at Tabriz, directing the Consuls representing the different nations there to enthrone the new Shah without delay. The Imperial Bank of Persia advanced large sums of money to the Sadr Azem with which to pay various regiments, and the army once in his power the Vizier did not fear the Naib-es-Sultaneh, the Commander-in-Chief (the third son of the late Shah), who, had he been a strong man, would most assuredly have taken advantage of his position and made a bid for the crown.

It is pleasant to know that before the Sadr Azem left Tehran he expressed much gratitude to the representatives of the European Governments who stood by him in his misfortunes, when his own countrymen, many of whom had received great benefits from him, had completely deserted him.

Contrary to public expectation, his fall occasioned no stir of any kind, and he reached Koom in safety, where he awaits the next turn of the wheel of Fortune.

Towards the end of November the rainy season began, and we had a good deal (for Persia) of wet weather, the roads being terribly muddy in consequence. The winter gaieties were commencing, and it was somewhat risky work going out to dinners and dances in bad weather, as, even if the carriage came when ordered, it often happened that the driver had disobeyed the regulations in the Koran relating to the use of alcohol, and I recollect that on one occasion we were upset twice before our Jehu had even left the garden of the French Legation, and not wishing to risk a third mishap, we all walked home in the mire.

As most of the Legations were in the so-called Rue des Ambassadeurs, we used often to walk in our goloshes to and from parties when the frosty weather began, and were always preceded by servants carrying big lanterns made of waxed linen, with elaborately engraved iron or steel tops and bottoms.

The size of these *fanuses* was fixed by inexorable laws of etiquette. For example, if the Minister went out on foot after dark he would be preceded by two enormous lanterns, the *chargé d'affaires* having only one, considerably smaller; while the second and third secretaries had quite diminutive ones, the former gentleman being permitted a lantern slightly larger than that carried in front of his colleague. As the servants do all the buying in Persia it is they who arrange such matters.

During our visit to Tehran the late Shah was still unburied, and lay in state in the *takieh*, or theatre, where the Persian Passion Play is performed during the month of *Moharrum*, as a religious ceremony.

His son had ordered an enormous sarcophagus of marble to be made at Yezd for the remains of the deceased monarch, and Mr. Williams, a gentleman travelling through Persia, who arrived at Tehran early in December on his way home, told us that he had seen the great block of marble in the neighbourhood of Kashan, and that it was being dragged along laboriously by a numerous company of men. As these latter were paid by the day, and not by the job, their rate of progression was exceedingly slow, and Mr. Williams thought that there was not much likelihood of his Majesty being laid to rest until the spring, in which supposition he was correct, as the interment did not take place until the middle of the following April.

Just before Christmas I made an expedition to the Bazaars to buy various presents, as it was arranged that my brother and I were not to leave Tehran until the end of January. Dr. Rosen, of the German Legation, who was kind enough to act as guide to our party on this occasion, took us first to a small booth in which an old Jew sat like a spider among carpets and silks, and displayed to us his treasures of coins, signets, and cylinders, many of the seals being exactly like those which my brother had obtained at the old city of Camadé. Their owner would not come to terms on any account, and at the least hint of a haggle he packed his wares up promptly, being such a rich man that perhaps he asked exorbitant prices in order to keep his treasures in his own possession!

Persians of the lower class use their Bazaars as clubs and general meeting-places. Here all the news of the town is circulated, and every event of importance well discussed, no servant caring for a situation which is at any distance from his favourite haunt.

A Persian coming to London would look upon Regent Street and Piccadilly as our Bazaars, although after a time the radical difference in the way the business is done in the East and the West would dawn upon him. At Tehran there was plenty of life in the long, dimly lighted, vaulted passages, which gave occasional peeps of the outer world—glimpses of courtyards with tanks of water gleaming in the brilliant sunshine, the blue dome of a mosque, or the brightly coloured tilework of minarets and gateways, and behind all the snowy hills, superb in their winter covering.

After awhile we found ourselves near the dungeon, an underground room in the midst of all the traffic of the Bazaar, its low door opening on to the space between the booths. From the entrance leaned a haggard-looking man in rags, with a heavy chain round his neck, the other end of which was fastened to a table standing outside, near which an officer and a couple of soldiers were lounging. Dr. Rosen explained to us that it was his habit to free a prisoner each time that he visited the Bazaar, and he flung a two-*kran* piece to the inmate of the dungeon, and asked the good-looking officer to unlock the chain. That gentleman laughed pleasantly, and sent off an underling for the key, explaining that the prisoner had really committed no crime, but had been put under arrest for being found inside a house in which he had no possible business!

We walked on at this point of the proceedings, as it would have been contrary to etiquette to watch the transfer of the two *krans* from the hand of the prisoner to that of the officer, the former being released so cheaply as he was known to be exceedingly poor.

On our return Dr. Rosen's *protégé*, now freed from "durance vile," loaded his deliverer with expressions of gratitude, and wound up by begging him for more coin of the realm! As a soldier was keeping close behind him, Dr. Rosen feared that the poor fellow might be chained up again as soon as we had taken our departure, but a word to the officer settled matters satisfactorily. That personage waved the prisoner away with a grand gesture, commanding him to "lose himself" as soon as possible, and he vanished in a second down the labyrinthine passages of the Bazaar. Imprisonment, like most things in this ill-governed land, is merely a question of money. If the relatives of a prisoner are rich, they buy him off, but should they refuse to do their duty in this way, the gaolers feed their captive, running up long bills for his nourishment, as they hope to extort a large sum from him on his release. If the man happens to be poor he has indeed

a bad time of it, as he is forced to subsist on the precarious donations of the charitable.

Dr. Rosen, who has an intimate acquaintance with Persians and their ways, told us that he once asked a Persian gentleman how it was that he was able to keep his servants for years without paying them. The Persian acknowledged frankly that he never expended any of his ready money in wages, but explained that he buoyed up his retainers with "lying hopes"!

The weather at this season was as warm and sunny as the early part of an English summer, and I remember that Madame de Balloy, the French Minister's wife, gave a picnic at Kasr Firouzé, a shooting pavilion belonging to the Shah, some four miles north of Tehran, on December 21st, and we ate our lunch in the open air.

Our way to this garden led past the palace of "Doshan Tepe," to which place the Shah often retires for a few days' sport, and we noticed porters carrying up doors, which were evidently borrowed from the palace in the town for the occasion, and would be returned when the monarch wended his way back again to his capital. Other men were dragging along some fine moufflon, which we suspected might very possibly be posted at suitable spots in the hills for his Majesty to fire at; and we were told that a leopard had been caught, and was awaiting the royal *coup de grâce* in its trap!

On Christmas Eve I had quite a busy time helping to decorate the church belonging to the American missionaries, who gave us a service every Sunday, and practising up an anthem and various elaborate chants for the morrow with the musical members of the congregation. Christmas Day was so filled with friendliness and good wishes as to make us forget how far we were from home, and in the afternoon the English played polo on the big Meidan, or parade-ground, of Tehran, and thus the ancient Persian sport of *chogan* was revived, and mighty Demavend again beheld the game once played by the Achæmenian sovereigns. The day wound up with a dinner and dance given by Lady Durand to all the English and Americans in Tehran, at which appeared two journalists in *kharki* suits and flannel shirts, who were actually traversing Persia from north to south on bicycles.

Many of us rode in a big paper-chase on Boxing Day, and on our way home from the "come in" at the Kasvin Gate we encountered the Shah's elephants, one being a huge creature, that had been presented to him by Lord Dufferin. We were told that on one occasion this animal had run amuck during some festivity in the palace, and the terrified Persian nobility had taken refuge in the tanks of water in the garden.

As the great beasts came lumbering on, uttering curious sounds much as if an amateur were blowing on a tin trumpet, they threw all the horses into a wild state of alarm, and as we were outside the city, with the deep moat of the ramparts on our right and a ditch on our left, it was somewhat surprising that no casualties occurred among such a crowd of shying horses, many bolting from the unaccustomed sight.

Riding about the broad streets of Tehran with their frequent holes, one is struck by the number of dead dogs, which no one takes the trouble to remove.

As "dog does not eat dog," the pariah scavengers never touch their deceased relatives, although a dead mule or horse will at once attract a hungry crowd round it. By the way, it is impossible for a lady to ride or walk anywhere alone and be secure from hustling and insult; and the Persians have a pleasing habit of trying to ride Feringhees down, or at all events to push past them rudely.

Horses stand loose all about the streets, their riders paying calls, and leaving their steeds unfastened at the doors. Occasionally, however, a runaway comes galloping along, making straight for its stable, threading its way cleverly among the incessant caravans of mules and donkeys laden with brushwood, charcoal, and *kah*, and not causing the least commotion.

Some horses appear to have a great dislike to the harmless

donkeys, and one of our acquaintances had a steed which astonished me by charging at the patient asses and literally rolling them over, loads and all. On muddy days the flowing tails of all the horses are tied up in bunches to keep them out of the mire, giving the animals a curiously "undress" appearance.

The Shah's race-horses are exercised on a course round the walls of the *Aspidiwani* (race-horse garden). During January they were taken at a slow walk every morning, muffled up to the ears and ridden by small boys singing weird songs, who work their charges up to a frantic gallop during the afternoon. The races take place at *Noruz*, and occasion much excitement. The Persians, having no idea of fair play, press the Europeans to enter for the prizes for which the latter subscribe; but if a Feringhee is seen to be winning, riders will dash out from among the spectators and come into collision with him, so that he may lose the race.

A horse is prepared for a race by being given neither food nor drink for some twelve hours before its trial, the object being to make it lighter, and therefore able to gallop, as its master imagines, faster; and the jockeys are always boys of twelve to fourteen.

The *Aspidiwani* garden is remarkable, not for its long avenues of poplars, with rickety, blue-painted lamp-posts at intervals, or its gaudy palace, but for the bronze equestrian statue of the late Shah, placed on a small islet in the midst of a large tank of water. The monarch is sitting erect on a curvetting steed, and in the dry, pure air the bronze looks almost as if it were freshly cast. The statue is interesting as being the first work of the kind ever made in Persia, and its erection caused considerable comment among the Faithful, as it is entirely contrary to the precepts of the Koran to make an image or painting of anything living.

The snow began after the first week in January, but lasted a very short time, and we got no skating, although we used to inspect the ponds and *yakjals* anxiously. These latter are long canals of shallow water, always facing north and protected by a high mud wall from the rays of the sun. As soon as ice is formed on them it is cut up and stored away in houses resembling gigantic mud beehives, and the canal is reflooded. By means of this arrangement ice is one of the commonest of luxuries, and there is never any lack of it during the hot summer months.

Persia is indeed rightly called the "Land of the Sun," and Tehran would be an ugly and depressing place of residence were it not for that luminary. It is the flood of sunshine lighting up the snowy peaks, bringing out mellow tints on the mud buildings, and making the tilework of cupolas, gateways, and minarets to glitter, which lends a beauty not its own to a Persian town. The long, stony roads, the yellow gravelly desert scattered with bones, relics of the meals of the pariah dogs, and the sallow-faced, dingy-garmented Persians themselves, do not look amiss under the glorious radiance. But take away the god Baal, and in the twinkling of an eye everything is transformed. The magnificent white mountains become stern and forbidding, the chill and desolation of the whole landscape penetrate to the very heart, while the town, now mean and squalid, presents a dead monotony of the most uninspired mud architecture.

But what is more important is the fact that the sun supplements the clothing of a large proportion of the populace, and on a grey winter day it is sad to see so many shivering, ill-clad folk and so many half-starved pariah dogs whose sole refuge is the street. During the first winter we spent at Tehran people were frozen to death nightly, and the beggars became naturally more insistent than ever.

Some of these latter, however, are men of property, as was proved one day when we were walking with the Durands. A dervish loaded our party with such polite salutations that Sir Mortimer said so cheery a fellow ought to be rewarded, and ordered the *gholam* in attendance to give him a *kran*. As the man had only a two-*kran* piece, he asked for change, and we were amused to see the dervish produce a well-filled purse and promptly tender the required coin!

Sir Mortimer quoted to me the motto of a beggar at Koom, who was perpetually chanting this refrain:—

> "Khoda guft, 'bidde'
> Shaitan guft, 'nidde.'"
>
> ("God says, 'Give';
> Satan says, 'Don't give.'")

On February 1, 1897, we said goodbye to Tehran for the second time; but now we were going home instead of turning our faces to the wilds as before, and the Durands, whose wonderful kindness to us it would be impossible ever to forget, were coming to England a fortnight later. So we galloped with some of our friends a couple of miles beyond the Kasvin Gate, and then got into a rickety little hooded carriage to begin our ninety-mile drive to Kasvin. One or two people said they thought the sky looked uncommonly as if it were working up for snow, but the day, though cold and windy, was bright, and we laughed at their fears, saying that all the snow for this winter had certainly descended, and that the early Persian spring was at hand.

We spent the first night at Yungi Imaum, and it was a lovely morning when we set out for Kasvin the next day across a bare, steppe-like country, reaching away on either side the very bad road, which resembled a ploughed field, to snow-covered ranges of hills. There was scarcely a village to be seen, but we stopped and changed our underfed and overworked horses at mud rest-houses at intervals, and I was not surprised to hear that many of the poor animals succumbed to the hardships of the road, the Carriage Company losing a hundred and fifty during one year. The sky was dull and grey as we made our way into Kasvin, the best laid-out town in Persia, as the saying is; but its broad, tree-bordered roads and grand mosque and minars hardly compensate for the ruinous condition of a large proportion of the houses, nor for the general look of decay and stagnation in the whole place.

We had taken our faithful Sultan Sukru and Gul Mahomet ("Flower of the Prophet"), our groom, to escort us to Resht, my brother airily remarking that as every Oriental could cook they would do all that we could want.

When I sounded Sultan Sukru on his accomplishments as regarded the saucepan, he said smilingly that he supposed he could cook if I would do everything first to show him, and Gul Mahomet was even less encouraging! So, not wishing to depend on broken reeds, I took enough bread, tins of soup, cooked partridges, and so on, with us from Tehran to last for some days, packing them up carefully in bags, and at Kasvin we concocted such a satisfactory grill for dinner that we resolved to be our own cooks in future as far as possible, and retired well content to rest. My brother, however, was disagreeably surprised by finding a black scorpion running about in his bedding (which had not been used while he was at Tehran), and hunt as we would we could not capture it, so he had perforce to go to sleep with ammonia and a knife by his side, ready for possible emergencies.

We were told that the route to Agha Baba was impassable for carriages on account of the snow, so we mounted sorry post-horses at Kasvin, and soon came to a region of deep slush, the melting snow on either side draining down into the road. My steed had an unpleasant tendency to topple over on its head, and was so worn out that it needed the most energetic urgings on my part to force it along the twelve miles to the castellated mud village, where we halted and lunched before attempting the seven miles on to Masrah.

The whole country was now covered with thick snow, which had only partially thawed in this high region, and we were obliged to ride at a foot's pace in single file, along a narrow track which abounded with holes filled with muddy water. Our poor horses tripped and stumbled in a pitiable way, every now and then breaking through a thin crust of frozen snow, and plunging down into deep holes, making their riders feel far from comfortable. A few caravans of heavily laden mules met us lumbering along towards Kasvin, and there was then much danger of a collision, as one party or the other was obliged to leave the track and plunge into the deep snow at the side. We noticed, with some anxiety, that the sky was covered with grey clouds and had a steely blue line on the horizon; but our muleteer reassured us by saying that we had had the full amount of snow for the year: nevertheless, fine flakes began to descend as we picked our way to the *chaparkhana* of Masrah, dirty and tumbled-down, with its *balakhana* in ruins.

We knew that a fall of snow would probably block the Kharzàn Pass over the Elburz Range, which was the *crux* of our journey, and we by no means relished a lengthy sojourn in two small rooms with filthy chintz nailed to the walls and grimy turkey-twill ceiling-cloths, put up in honour of General Kourapatkin's visit two years before, most likely harbourage for the poisonous bugs for which Masrah is notorious. However, the snow was falling fast when we woke next morning, and a heavy white pall rested low on the hills, making it impossible to see many feet ahead; while the track was completely obliterated by six inches of snow.

In spite of this we hoped to start, but our *charvadar* and the other muleteers declared it would be as much as their lives were worth to make the attempt, and even refused to try and get to the little village of Kharzàn, only six miles off and at the top of the pass. So we spent our day in reading, writing, and cooking, amusing ourselves by attempting to make savoury dishes out of the materials at our disposal, but not achieving much variety as they all tasted alike.

We were thankful that we had allowed a spare day for our journey, as otherwise we should have missed the steamer at Enzeli, and were yet more thankful when the morrow dawned clear and bright, and we left our dirty, stuffy refuge and started off at 7.30 a.m to do the worst part of our ride. Our horses stepped off briskly in single file along a narrow track, beaten down on the crisp, frozen snow, and we felt that at this rate the ride to Kharzàn, where we intended to lunch, would be a mere bagatelle.

Ahead of us were some fifty or sixty mules and donkeys toiling laboriously along, making the path, and when we came up with them we naturally wished to pass, the wind being so cold that it pierced our wraps as if they had been made merely of paper. However, it was easier to talk about getting in front of these caravans than to do it.

We tried to force our way past a line of humble donkeys, which swerved off the track into the deep snow lying on either side, and straightway fell over, loads and all. So we attempted to struggle through the snow ourselves, and in a moment our horses were floundering helplessly, their legs slipping from under them and we slipping off their backs. However, there was nothing for it but to persevere, and we remounted our steeds, which plunged a second time up to their shoulders, while we again fell off. So we resolved to lead them, and managed to walk in tolerable comfort on the fairly hard snow past the caravans, our ponies floundering after us as best they could.

We now found that we were, in a way, the pioneers of the road, the snow lying smooth and untrodden ahead of us, covering a series of low hills, rising one above the other to the crest of the pass. There was, of course, no track of any kind; but we mounted and went straight upwards, the snow getting apparently deeper as we proceeded, and our unfortunate horses rolling us and themselves over more frequently.

At last we were obliged to take to our legs again, and the next two or three hours will be for ever engraved on my memory. The sun was rapidly melting the snow, so that we could not walk on its upper crust, as we were able to do at first, but sank at each step up to our knees, and occasionally much further if we were unlucky enough to get into a drift. What with the labour of such walking, the rarefied atmosphere, and the intense cold, I frankly confess that I could have sat down and wept from sheer exhaustion. I did my best to follow in my brother's footprints, as did King Wenceslas' page in the Christmas carol; but it was weary work pulling oneself up from hole after hole, and our progress was painfully slow and fatiguing.

Everything, however, has an end sooner or later, and when we had achieved our fifth undulation it dawned upon us that the snow was less deep, so we took heart and remounted, seeing some way off the village of Kharzàn and a great caravan approaching us. We crawled carefully down the next hill, Sultan Sukru and his horse turning a complete somersault on the way; and then came the problem of how we were to pass the slowly moving *karfila*, as there was only room for one animal on the track at a time.

My brother, who was leading, struck out into the deep snow, and his horse and a mule from the caravan rolled over together, so that he had some difficulty in getting clear of their hoofs, and hardly had he recovered himself than my steed sat down with me, and I judged it wiser to slide off.

With many a tumble and struggle we managed to pass the long string of mules and reach the beaten track again, after which we proceeded merrily to Kharzàn, having taken five hours to do a distance not much over six miles, but being too thankful to have accomplished it to complain of the difficulties of the route. After a halt and some lunch we set off for the nine miles down hill to Paichenar, finding no snow, but streams of mud which made the track very slippery in places. Our mules came in that evening, after having been fourteen hours on the road, and we were glad to think that to-morrow's march was only some twelve miles, over a good track for Persia, as both men and beasts were worn out.

The next day we made a late start about 8.30 a.m., and as the rain was falling we decided to ride our four *farsakhs* straight on end, instead of making a midday halt for lunch.

It was a good thing we did not tarry, for half-way we encountered a mild form of blizzard, the rain coming down like a waterspout, while hailstones were driven into our faces by such violent gusts of wind that our horses swerved from them again and again. My waterproof cape was soaked through, and nearly torn from my back by the fury of the tempest, I was almost blinded with the hail, and if my brother had not lashed at my steed with his hunting-whip I scarcely know how I should have got the reluctant creature along the road, which now seemed interminable. It was indeed a relief to reach the *chaparkhana* at Menjil and find a fire by which to warm ourselves, for we were literally wet through, and had to wait two or three hours before our caravan arrived with dry clothing.

I had had an idea that the difficulties of the Resht road were somewhat exaggerated, but these two days had shown me what it could be like in winter, and I have no wish to repeat the experiences of this my third visit.

Two or three days later we had to make our way to Rustemabad, over a dangerous track, resembling staircases and even "shoots" of rock in parts; but the *chapar* horses are sagacious little animals, sliding down these places from point to point, and very seldom coming to grief. However, on this occasion the road was very slippery with yesterday's sleet, and we had to hold our ponies up most carefully. My brother got annoyed with Sultan Sukru for staying so far behind us, but was mollified when that faithful factotum, who was not much of a horseman, explained that he and his steed had already been down three times and the post-boy twice!

Next day we had to negotiate a long thirty miles to Resht in order to catch our steamer which left Enzeli on the following midday, and as it had frozen during the night we found the roads in a terrible condition, it being a wonder that we did not follow the post-boy's example, who fell in a heap with his steed at such short intervals that he quite exhausted my sympathy, which had been active at first.

After awhile we came to the forest, and here the Russian Road Company was at work, pulling up the old cobbled causeway, which, with all its deficiencies, was certainly preferable to the sea of liquid mud left in its stead. Through this our unfortunate ponies waded, nearly toppling on their heads, and my heart was often in my mouth as we escaped again and again by a hair's-breadth from being rolled over in the foot-deep mire. The caravans of small donkeys were coated with mud from head to foot, and in one place a camel, left by its owner, was placidly lying down in a mud bath, evidently considering death a lesser evil than further struggles through such rivers of slush. I do not fancy that it was possible to do much to the road with caravans passing to and fro at short intervals, and the crowds of Persians armed with shovels and pickaxes did not appear to be bestirring themselves at all, though I noticed a spasmodic activity among their ranks when the dapper Russian engineer made his appearance, looking, in his smart uniform, very much out of place amidst the dirt and disorder around him. Primroses, violets, and cyclamens were in full bloom on the mossy fern-clad banks that bordered the leafless forest, and there was a feeling of spring in the air, so superb is the Persian climate, where winter is but a name, and green crops rise up amid the snow and frost.

We reached Kuddum about midday, but no carriages were in waiting to drive us into Resht, owing to the state of the roads, and after a halt for lunch we strapped the baggage we intended to take with us to England on the backs of three horses, and set off at a rough jog-trot, riding behind the loaded animals to keep them up to the mark. The roads were truly execrable, the mud often reaching to our horses' knees as we hurried painfully along; and once or twice our boxes came unloosened, and rolling off ignominiously into the mire, had to be fished out and fastened on afresh.

We reached the outskirts of Resht at sunset, and found the Bazaars all open and lit up as it was the month of the Fast of *Ramazan*. A gun sounded as we entered the town to signify that the Faithful might now begin to feed, and as we passed along every one was drinking glasses of tea, and the savoury smell of cooking reminded us that we were very hungry.

It was quite dark by this time, and our baggage horses were most tiresome, as they persisted in bolting off up side-streets, and had to be headed and driven back in the right direction. It seemed as if we should never reach the Consulate through the labyrinth of narrow alleys, and when we arrived it was to find the house locked up and the servants away, notwithstanding that we had telegraphed

www.ingramcontent.com/pod-product-compliance
Lightning Source LLC
Chambersburg PA
CBHW030543300426
44111CB00009B/839